THE NEW LAW OF STATE AID AND SUBSIDIES

This book presents a positive account of State aid and subsidy control law at the EU, UK, and global levels. It provides the keys to understanding how it is adjusting to emerging realities.

Industrial policy, decarbonisation, de-risking of supply chains: the regulation of subsidies is at the forefront of the transformations that the world economy is undergoing. The book provides an overview of the foundations of EU State aid law, one of the most dynamic areas of EU law. An up-to-date and accessible framework explains the core conditions underpinning the notion of State aid – including advantage and selectivity. The book also looks at how the EU model has changed over the past decade. It helps navigate the complex case law on the application of EU State aid law to tax rulings concluded with large multinationals (such as the *Apple* saga) as well as the perma-crisis of the regime up until the adoption of the Clean Industrial Deal Framework.

The ways in which the EU model extends its reach beyond its borders – convergence and unilateral expansion – are also addressed. The UK Subsidy Control Act 2022 and the EU Foreign Subsidies Regulation are discussed and put in context.

Conceived as a 'modular' book, it can be used both as a tool to navigate the fundamentals of the discipline and as a map to reflect upon its uncertain future.

Online resources to accompany this book are available at www.bloomsburyonlineresources.com/the-new-law-of-state-aid-and-subsidies. If you experience any problems, please contact Bloomsbury at: onlineresources @bloomsbury.com

The New Law of State Aid
and Subsidies

Pablo Ibáñez Colomo

·HART·
OXFORD · LONDON · NEW YORK · NEW DELHI · SYDNEY

HART PUBLISHING

Bloomsbury Publishing Plc

Kemp House, Chawley Park, Cumnor Hill, Oxford, OX2 9PH, UK

1385 Broadway, New York, NY 10018, USA

Bloomsbury Publishing Ireland Limited, 29 Earlsfort Terrace, Dublin 2, D02 AY28, Ireland

HART PUBLISHING, the Hart/Stag logo, BLOOMSBURY and the Diana logo are
trademarks of Bloomsbury Publishing Plc

First published in Great Britain 2026

1

A catalogue record for this book is available from the British Library.

A catalogue record for this book is available from the Library of Congress.

Library of Congress Control Number: 2025949151

ISBN: PB: 978-1-50999-029-0
       ePDF: 978-1-50999-027-6
       ePub: 978-1-50999-028-3

Typeset by Compuscript Ltd, Shannon
Printed and bound in Great Britain by TJ Books, Padstow, Cornwall

For product safety related questions contact productsafety@bloomsbury.com

To find out more about our authors and books visit www.hartpublishing.co.uk.
Here you will find extracts, author information, details of forthcoming events
and the option to sign up for our newsletters.

ACKNOWLEDGEMENTS

When I published *The New EU Competition Law* two years ago with Hart, I wrote that 'publishers make a big difference'. If that (under)statement was true then, it is even more true now. In one way or the other, this project has been a long time in the making. However, it only took its final shape following conversations with Roberta Bassi. The book you hold in your hands is the second part of 'The New' trilogy, which, I hope, will soon be followed by a third volume devoted to merger control. But it was not conceived or thought of this way. It was only thanks to Roberta that I understood the (obvious in retrospect) continuity between this project and the preceding one. For that (and for much more, including, her patience, responsiveness, vision and flexibility), I am grateful. Scholars who have interacted with me for more than five minutes will know that I invariably recommend Hart as the ideal academic home for their project. Those who have not now understand why.

The origins of this book date back to my days as an academic assistant at the College of Europe in Bruges. I was fortunate to start my career there at an exciting time. When I joined the staff of the Department of European Legal Studies, the module devoted (mostly) to EU State aid law (*droit de la concurrence : secteur public*) had just been turned into a semi-compulsory subject. Even though I had not taken it as a student, this novelty gave me the chance to work closely with Massimo Merola, the professor in charge of the course, and craft, virtually from scratch, a new syllabus. I found it fascinating, not least because it was very much in its infancy as a discipline. Back then (the mid-2000s) many doctrines had not been developed and the ones that existed were not fully fleshed out, let alone entirely understood. It really felt like venturing into a world that was in the making.

Since those early days, I kept telling myself that there was a book to be written on the topic, one that would try and conceptualise the core aspects of the discipline and that would look beyond a dry exposition of the law. It might have taken me literal decades to find the resolve to complete the project, but I never lost interest in the discipline (even when my scholarly ventures took me elsewhere). In fact, this book has benefitted enormously from the experience gained while teaching a module on EU State aid law (now called State Aid and Subsidies Regulation) that I set up at the London School of Economics and have been delivering with some interruptions since 2011. In many ways, it was my favourite London course. Groups were small, and students were invariably bright and motivated. More importantly, they happily embraced the tensions, gaps and outright contradictions that are inherent in a discipline in flux.

I have also been immensely fortunate to supervise, and learn from, the doctoral work of Jarleth Burke and Morris Schonberg, whose dissertations addressed EU State aid matters.

The dedicated module I run at LSE has given me the chance to meet and interact with the community of scholars and practitioners that deal with State aid and subsidy-related matters in their daily work. Their contribution was invaluable, as some aspects of the discipline only come to life by practising the law. After so many years teaching, the list of guest teachers is long, but they all have to be gratefully acknowledged: Christian Ahlborn, Filomena Chirico, Natura Gracia, Werner Haslehner, William Leslie, Aymeric de Moncuit, Conor Quigley, Isabel Taylor and Vincent Verouden. I should also acknowledge other people who, even though they have not taught in the module, have always been an inspiration (and some of them have provided really valuable comments on my drafts). These include Andrea Amelio, José Luis Buendía Sierra, Jacques Derenne, Leigh Hancher, Lena Hornkohl, Juan Jorge Piernas López, Nicolas Rey, Nicole Robins and Denis Waelbroeck.

The first time I heard about tax rulings and asked myself whether they might be a vehicle for the award of State aid, it was not from a specialist in the field. In fact, the European Commission had not even announced its investigations at the time. My colleague Eduardo Baistrocchi, a leading expert in tax law, was the one to mention them during one of our runs. All of my research owes much to my conversations with him, and State aid and subsidies more than any other, as it overlaps with his. It is thanks to this overlap that we now co-supervise Ioanna Kladi's doctoral work. I acknowledged Ioanna in *The New EU Competition Law* for her superb support as a research assistant. I am delighted that I now get to thank her for her input as an emerging scholar.

It has become customary for me to mention that Alfonso Lamadrid de Pablo never gets to read any of my books. In keeping with the tradition, I am delighted to do so again. He may not have opened the files I sent him for comments, but he has been a constant (and helpful) presence in the project. He acted as counsel before the EU courts in some of the leading cases discussed in this book, which means I was frequently reminded of the role he plays in shaping this area of EU law. Now that he has become the busiest person in Brussels, moreover, he also reminded me that I had no excuse not to get the project over the line. He also made me think that it is now the two of us neglecting the blog in tandem. But that is a different story.

Finally, I have to thank my partner, who has now endured the writing of another book (my mum, to whom this one is dedicated, asked why I would inflict this ordeal upon myself as soon as I shared my plans with her). Much to Alicia's dismay, State aid and subsidies law have infiltrated the household over the past year. So much so, in fact, that she has now become particularly adept at detecting when I am thinking about the project (or mentally drafting some bits thereof), as opposed to, say, enjoying our hike or dinner together. Alicia's support makes everything easier, and better.

CONTENTS

PART II
TRANSFORMATION AND EXPANSION

Tables

TABLE OF CASES

Judgments of the Court of Justice (EU)

Judgments of the General Court (EU)

Opinions of Advocates General (CJEU)

Case law from other courts and tribunals

Decisions of the European Commission

Introduction

1. The Rise and Rise of EU State Aid Law

One would be forgiven for underestimating the relevance of State aid law and policy in the EU legal order. Some indicators could be reasonably interpreted as meaning that it is indeed a relatively niche or minor discipline, at least so when compared to competition law. There are virtually countless journals, textbooks and monographs devoted to the latter, not to mention courses and entire academic programmes. Undergraduate and postgraduate degrees specialising in EU and/or competition law focus, by and large, on antitrust and merger control, to the virtual exclusion of EU State aid issues. Dedicated teaching modules examining the public dimension of EU economic law – that is, those addressing how, and to what extent, the EU legal order constrains its Member States' ability to intervene in markets and thus distort competition by means of, inter alia, subsidies and exclusive rights – are relatively few and far between.

The picture changes – and the significance of EU State aid law becomes apparent – the moment one takes into consideration the rate of activity at the level of the European Commission (hereinafter, the 'Commission') and before the EU courts. This data suggests that EU State aid law is very much on a par with competition policy. Consider, first, Figures 0.1 and 0.2. They provide the number of new cases in the areas of competition law and State aid brought before, respectively, the Court of Justice[1] (hereinafter, the 'Court' or the 'ECJ') and the General Court[2] (hereinafter, the 'GC' or the 'first-instance court') in the course of the past decade. As can be seen, in any given year there are typically more new cases involving the application of Articles 107 and 108 TFEU than in the area of competition. The difference is particularly marked before the first-instance court. In 2019 and 2022, for instance, there were several times more State aid cases than there were competition ones. While the difference is less stark at the level of the ECJ, it is more likely than not that the former will exceed the latter (on the basis of figures for the past 10 years).

[1] The data is drawn from CJEU, *Annual Report 2024: Statistics concerning the judicial activity of the Court of Justice*, available at http://curia.europa.eu.

[2] The data is drawn from CJEU, *Annual Report 2024: Statistics concerning the judicial activity of the General Court*, available at http://curia.europa.eu.

Figure 0.1 New cases before the ECJ (2015–2024)

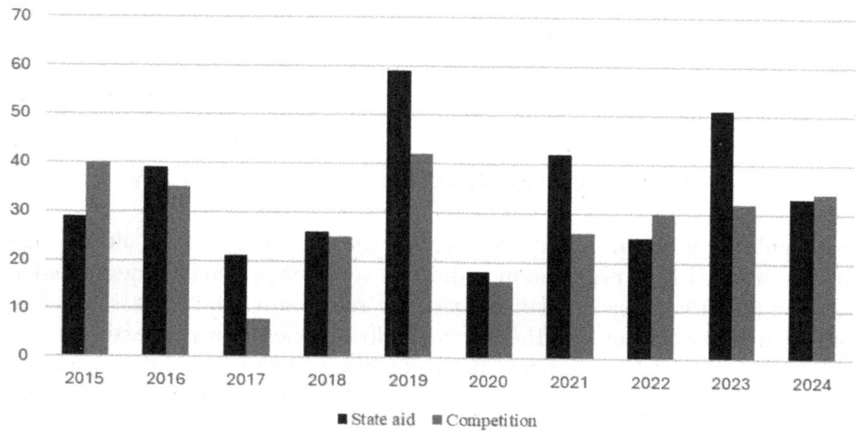

Figure 0.2 New cases before the GC (2015–2024)

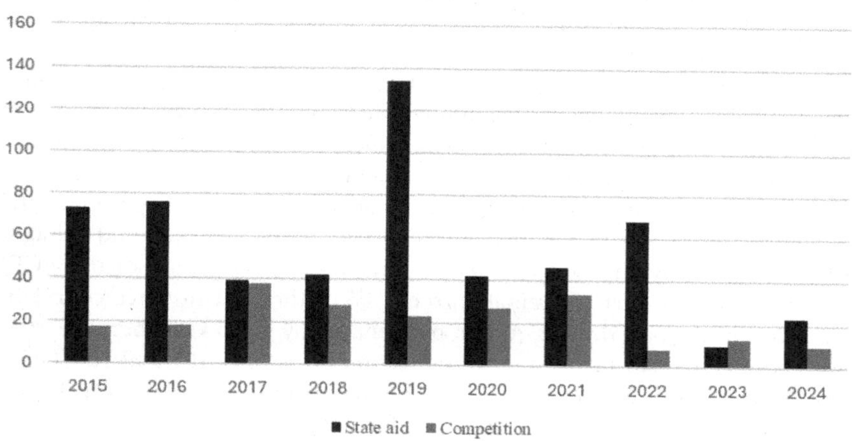

It is less straightforward to compare like with like at the level of the Commission, but the analysis, however imperfect, paints a similar picture. The data available in the Report on competition policy[3] and captured in Figure 0.3 shows that there are more State aid decisions adopted following the opening of the formal procedure

---

[3] The data is drawn from the Commission Staff Working Document accompanying the Report from the Commission to the European Parliament, the Council, the European Economic and Social Committee and the Committee of the Regions SWD(2025) 102 final.

(excluding non-aid decisions and all aid cleared following a preliminary examination) in a typical year than there are formal antitrust (including non-cartel)
decisions. State aid enforcement – at least when measured against this criterion –
seems to be on a par with administrative action in the area of merger control, which
sees roughly the same amount of phase II decisions adopted on an annual basis.
The trend in both instances is similar. The organisation charts of the Commission's
Directorate General for Competition[4] and of its Legal Service[5] (which has an ad
hoc Directorate dealing with State aid) are good proxies for the importance of
enforcement in the area.

Figure 0.3 Commission antitrust decisions and phase II merger and State aid decisions
(2015–2024)

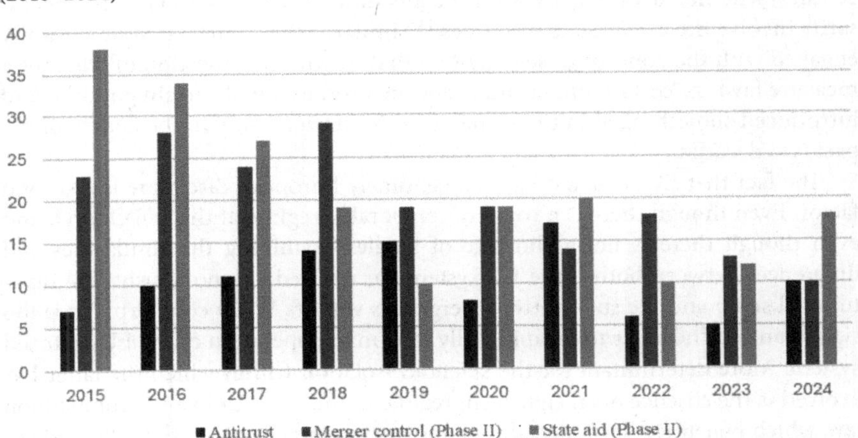

This reality may not be reflected in the more traditional academic settings
described above, but it informs and is captured by the relatively large volume of
regularly updated treatises[6] and a specialised journal[7] that follow and anticipate
developments in the field. These publications are primarily intended for practitioners.
They speak of a discipline that is constantly evolving and, more importantly for
the purposes of the present project, has not been fully conceptualised. It remains,

---

[4] The organisation chart of the Directorate General for Competition can be accessed via: https://
competition-policy.ec.europa.eu/index_en.

[5] The organisation chart of the Commission's Legal Service can be accessed via: https://commission.
europa.eu/about/departments-and-executive-agencies/legal-service_en.

[6] See in particular (and in chronological order) Leigh Hancher, Tom Ottervanger and Pieter J Slot
(eds), *EU State Aids* (4th edn, Sweet & Maxwell 2012); Herwig CH Hofmann and Claire Micheau (eds),
State Aid Law of the European Union (Oxford University Press 2016); Kelyn Bacon (ed), *European
Union Law of State Aid* (3rd edn, Oxford University Press 2017); and Conor Quigley, *European State
Aid Law and Policy (and UK Subsidy Control)* (4th edn, Hart Publishing 2022).

[7] European State Aid Law Quarterly, available at https://estal.lexxion.eu/.

in this regard, very much in its infancy. There is nothing like the methodological apparatus that assists courts and authorities when enforcing competition law, including (just to mention some examples) tools such as the definition of the relevant market,[8] the so-called 'as efficient-competitor test',[9] and the framework for the assessment of non-horizontal effects in merger control.[10]

Several factors explain why EU State aid law remains at the early stages of its full conceptualisation. One of them is the sheer novelty of the field. Even though provisions limiting EU Member States' ability to grant aid existed from the outset in the EU legal order, enforcement took off slowly and progressively. As a result, some fundamental points of law were addressed relatively late. It is explained in Chapter 2 that it was not entirely clear, as late as the turn of the century, whether advantages within the meaning of Article 107(1) TFEU necessarily involve the use of State resources.[11] Similarly, the Court has systematically engaged with the concept of selectivity – that is, with the question of whether a measure favours 'certain undertakings or the production of certain goods' – and introduced something akin to an analytical framework only in the course of the past two decades.

The fact that EU State aid law is a genuinely European discipline is a second factor. Even though there is a roughly comparable regime at the WTO level, and even though there is not a shortage of studies examining the similarities and differences between both,[12] the EU system has evolved autonomously. The institutional setup and the substantive divergences with its WTO counterpart are too significant for the latter to meaningfully inform the operation of the EU State aid system. More determinant for the splendid isolation within which the latter has evolved is the absence of an equivalent regime in the US.[13] Unlike EU competition law, which benefitted from decades of antitrust enforcement on the other side of the Atlantic at the time of its introduction,[14] the Commission and the Court were presented with a blank slate when they were confronted with the interpretation of (what would become) Articles 107 and 108 TFEU.

---

[8] Commission Notice on the definition of the relevant market for the purposes of Union competition law [2024] OJ C 1645.

[9] Case T-286/09 RENV *Intel Corporation, Inc. v European Commission*, EU:T:2022:19, paras 152–159.

[10] Guidelines on the assessment of non-horizontal mergers under the Council Regulation on the control of concentrations between undertakings [2008] OJ C265/6.

[11] Case C-379/98 *PreussenElektra AG v Schhleswag AG*, EU:C:2001:160; and Case C-482/99 *France v Commission*, EU:C:2002:294.

[12] See in particular Luca Rubini, *The Definition of Subsidy and State Aid: WTO and EC Law in Comparative Perspective* (Oxford University Press 2009).

[13] Deborah H Schenk, 'The Cuno Case: A Comparison of US Subsidies and European State Aid' (2006) 5 European State Aid Law Quarterly 3; and Ruth Mason, 'Identifying illegal subsidies' (2019) 69 American University Law Review 479.

[14] From the very early days, there were efforts aimed at considering how the US literature and case law could contribute to shaping EU competition law. See in this sense René Joliet, *The Rule of Reason in Antitrust Law: American, German and Common Market Laws in Comparative Perspective* (Martinus Nijhoff 1967); René Joliet, *Monopolization and Abuse of Dominant Position* (Martinus Nijhoff 1970).

The point of this book, against this background, is twofold. First, it seeks to add to the existing literature[15] by focusing on what scholarly research typically strives to do, namely provide an analytical framework explaining the logic and operation of a legal discipline (and, similarly, any tensions underpinning it). In this sense, the project goes beyond a detailed exposition of the law, where practitioner-oriented work excels. It does so by placing an emphasis instead on big-picture issues, thereby allowing the reader to make sense of, and navigate, the legal landscape. Second, the book engages with the transformations that the discipline is undergoing. In some respects, the regulation of State aid (and, more generally, subsidies) is changing beyond recognition, both from a substantive, institutional and even territorial perspective. This dynamic dimension completes the static mapping of the field.

2. Nature and Scope of the Project

2.1. The Book That Never Was

The relative neglect of EU State aid law by European legal academics is exemplified by the absence of a dedicated textbook in English.[16] To some extent, the point of this monograph is to remedy – even if partially – this gap in the literature. Part I (Chapters 1–4) provides an overview of the notion of State aid within the meaning of Article 107(1) TFEU. It discusses the fundamental concepts that make up the notion (State resources, imputability, advantage and selectivity) in the same way textbooks typically do. Thus, the analysis places the discussion in the relevant institutional and doctrinal context, presents the various substantive choices that the Court can make when construing Article 107(1) TFEU and takes stock of the case law. It outlines, where necessary, any potential frictions and inconsistencies and identifies the ways in which they could be streamlined. By and large, Chapters 7 and 8, which deal, respectively, with the UK subsidies regime[17] and the EU Foreign Subsidies Regulation,[18] cover two nascent areas of the law in the same way a textbook would.

---

[15] In spite of its relative paucity, there is a growing body of academic research contributing to these conceptualisation efforts. See in particular Francesco De Cecco, *State Aid and the European Economic Constitution* (Hart Publishing 2012); Claire Micheau, *Droit des aides d'État et des subventions en fiscalité directe* (Larcier 2013); Juan Jorge Piernas López, *The Concept of State Aid Under EU Law: From internal market to competition and beyond* (Oxford University Press 2015); and Fernando Pastor Merchante, *The Role of Competitors in the Enforcement of State Aid Law* (Hart Publishing 2017).

[16] Alison Jones and Brenda Sufrin used to publish an excellent online supplement to their popular textbook. Some textbooks are published in French. See Olivier Peiffert and Sébastien Thomas, *Droit matériel des aides d'Etat* (Bruylant 2019); Juan Ignacio Signes de Mesa and Aymeric de Moncuit, *Droit procédural des aides d'Etat* (Bruylant 2019); and Michaël Karpenschif, *Manuel de droit européen des aides d'État* (4th edn, Bruylant 2021).

[17] Subsidy Control Act 2022.

[18] Regulation (EU) 2022/2560 of the European Parliament and of the Council of 14 December 2022 on foreign subsidies distorting the internal market [2022] OJ L330/1.

However, this monograph is not a textbook in the traditional sense. It is both more and less ambitious. One can say it is less ambitious in the sense that it does not come close to covering every aspect of the discipline. Some of the constituent elements of Article 107(1) TFEU (namely the distortion of competition and effect on trade conditions) are not covered in detail but in passing where they add to the analysis (in particular in Chapters 1 and 8). More importantly, the compatibility assessment is not examined in the same way the constituent elements of the notion of aid are. There is therefore no chapter devoted to the application of Article 107(3) TFEU to, say, regional aid or energy and environmental aid. The hard and soft law instruments around which compatibility assessment revolves only come to life in the world of practice. Therefore, there was little (other than the matters addressed in Chapter 6) that an academic book could contribute to the existing literature.

In another sense, this monograph is more ambitious than a traditional textbook. It does not simply aim at providing a framework for the understanding of the law as it stands. There are common themes that cut across the whole volume and that inform the analysis of every chapter. Insofar as there are, this project is closer to a research monograph that has the ambition of telling a coherent, unifying story. The simultaneous processes of expansion and contraction of the EU model of State aid control make up the backbone of the book and underpin each chapter. These phenomena are considered at the internal (by ascertaining how ambitious and far-reaching enforcement is within the EU) and the external levels (by considering how the EU model has progressively ventured beyond the borders of the Union via substantive convergence and unilateral expansion). As explained in detail below, this analysis tells a story of retreat within the EU, which is counterbalanced by the flourishing of its substantive and institutional approach beyond its borders.

The focus of the monograph is also different from that found in the typical textbook. A consequence of the abovementioned processes of expansion and contraction is that State aid has sparked interest beyond the relatively small community of practitioners and scholars that traditionally followed developments in the field. The investigations opened by the Commission into the tax rulings issued by some EU Member States, for instance, have attracted the attention of leading tax lawyers and generated a whole new stream of research.[19] Similarly, the changing geopolitical realities have led to a revival of discussions around industrial policy and the EU's strategic autonomy.[20] In this new context, the traditional function and shape of EU State aid policy have come under critical scrutiny. These

---

[19] See in particular the various State aid-related contributions in Christiana HJI Panayi, Werner Haslehner and Edoardo Traversa (eds), *Research Handbook on European Union Taxation Law* (Elgar 2020); as well as Ruth Mason, 'Tax competition and state aid' (2023) 42 Yearbook of European Law 262; and Stephen Daly, '*Fiat v Commission*: a misconceived approach' (2023) 86 Modern Law Review 1489.

[20] Armin Steinbach, 'The EU's Turn to "Strategic Autonomy": Leeway for Policy Action and Points of Conflict' (2023) 34 European Journal of International Law 973; and Leigh Hancher and Adrien de Hauteclocque, 'Strategic Autonomy, REPowerEU And The Internal Energy Market: Untying The Gordian Knot' (2024) 61 Common Market Law Review 55.

developments are not diluted in general discussions about the law (as they would in a traditional textbook). Instead, they are addressed in their own right.

2.2. Concept

The hybrid nature of the book is also reflected in the way in which it is conceived and structured. It is designed as a modular project, so that the two parts of the book – and every chapter within each part – can be read and studied independently of one another. Part I (Foundations and Evolution) is self-contained insofar as it provides an overview of the discipline and of the fundamental elements of the notion of State aid. Chapter 4, for instance, offers a stand-alone account of the concept of selectivity as interpreted by the Court. Part II (Chapters 5–8) on the other hand, focuses on the transformation and expansion of the discipline over the past decade and includes a chapter addressing the issue of tax rulings and another on the EU Foreign Subsidies Regulation. It is hoped that this concept will make the book useful to different types of readers – from the scholar who is interested in the process of change to the student who approaches the discipline for the first time.

3. What is New in the New Law of State Aid and Subsidies

3.1. The Three Meanings of New

The title of this monograph implies that a new incarnation of the discipline is emerging. This idea is true in at least three ways. To begin with, the substantive interpretation of the notion of State aid has been evolving, and in unprecedented contexts and factual scenarios. The most obvious example in this sense is the application of Article 107(1) TFEU to tax planning strategies by multinationals. In addition, the compatibility assessment under Article 107(3) TFEU has greatly evolved in the course of the past decade. The Covid-19 pandemic and the invasion of Ukraine have contributed to the perpetuation of a state of emergency that might have transformed, for good, how the Commission goes about formulating and applying State aid policy. Finally, the law is new in a more literal sense: a novel generation of instruments addressing the award of subsidies has been adopted in recent years.

3.2. The New Law of Fiscal State Aid

It has never been seriously questioned that EU State aid law can interfere with EU Member States' tax regimes. The friction that might emerge in this sense is a function of the primacy of EU law and of the transversal nature of TFEU provisions, including Article 107(1) TFEU. In spite of this fact, the Commission was initially cautious about the reach and scope of the notion of State aid in this context. *British Aggregates* (where the Commission argued, in essence, that EU Member States have the leeway to decide which activities to tax absent harmonisation at the EU level) is an example of this tentative period.[21] Over time, however, the Commission asserted its powers more confidently. *Gibraltar* – where the Commission challenged the core aspects of the corporate tax regime adopted by the British Overseas Territory, and insofar as they favoured, de facto, offshore entities – epitomises this evolution.[22]

However ambitious the preceding administrative practice, the interaction between national tax regimes and EU State aid law entered a different era – and was taken to a whole new level – when the Commission opened a series of investigations into the tax rulings concluded by several EU Member States. The context of these investigations is not a secret. In the aftermath of the financial crisis, tax planning strategies by multinationals gave rise to widespread concern, if not indignation, of the general public. In such circumstances, the Commission explored whether, and to what extent, EU State aid law could be relied upon to tackle some of the arrangements between large corporate groups and tax authorities. Its approach sought to extend the standards and principles applying at the OECD level to the EU legal order via Article 107(1) TFEU.[23]

3.3. The Permacrisis of the EU Model

The formulation of EU State aid policy makes it necessary to strike a delicate balance between the promotion of public interest objectives, on the one hand, and the prevention of distortions within the internal market, on the other. While subsidies and measures having an equivalent effect typically affect – at least to some extent – trade and competition, they may benefit society, whether by increasing efficiency or by redistributing resources among its members. Drawing the precise line between compatible and incompatible subsidies is all the more complex within the EU, considering that the EU Member States' spending power varies widely. If the Commission's policy is too strict, it might hinder governments' ability to improve their economies. If it is too lax, it might exacerbate tensions within the internal market, which would be tilted in favour of the EU Member States with the largest economies and the deepest pockets.

If finding this balance and translating it into a system of rules that can be anticipated and applied by EU Member States was already challenging in normal times,

---

[21] Case C-487/06 P *British Aggregates Association v Commission*, EU:C:2008:757.

[22] Joined Cases C-106/09 P and C-107/09 P *Commission v Government of Gibraltar and United Kingdom*, EU:C:2011:732.

[23] Richard Lyal, 'Transfer Pricing Rules and State Aid' (2015) 38 Fordham International Law Journal 1017.

doing so when confronted with exceptional occurrences – such as a pandemic or a war significantly affecting energy prices – inevitably compounds the complexity of the task. It is therefore not surprising that the Commission changed its policy at the beginning of the 2020s, first in response to Covid-19, then to the invasion of Ukraine. The relaxation of the conditions for the award of State aid in reaction to these unusual circumstances was subsequently extended. The inclination to turn the exceptional into the new normal was favoured by the uncertainty brought about by the changing geopolitical circumstances and, in particular, the rise of protectionism. The question that emerges, against this background, is whether the EU State aid system has permanently changed or whether it will revert to the previous balance.

3.4. The Expansion of the EU Model

The EU model has become the gold standard of subsidy control across the European continent. This reality is obvious where one considers the regimes adopted in the context of the EEA Agreement and by the countries that aspire to join the EU. The EU-UK Trade and Cooperation Agreement[24] is a new milestone in the process. In compliance with the subsidy control requirements enshrined in the deal, the UK has adopted a domestic regime. This regime is unusual in the European landscape in two major respects. Unlike the preceding ones, first, it is not designed to prepare the ground for EU accession. Second, the regime, while adopting the essential features of the EU model (and largely codifying its substantive elements), also departs from it in a number of respects, in particular from an institutional standpoint. It remains to be seen how it evolves and how much it deviates from, and interacts with, the EU State aid regime.

The process of legal convergence around the EU model within the continent is now complemented with a process of unilateral expansion of the essential features of EU State aid law beyond Europe. In a context of rising protectionism and decline in the effectiveness of the rules-based legal order, the Union legislature, by virtue of the EU Foreign Subsidies Regulation,[25] has empowered the Commission to control the award of subsidies by third countries and to impose, where necessary, redressive measures effectively addressing any distortions resulting from them. With this legal development, the EU model enters a new era. It is no longer a tool merely aimed at building and developing the internal market. In a changing geopolitical landscape, it has emerged as an instrument aimed at ensuring that European firms operate on a level playing field.

---

[24] Trade and Cooperation Agreement between the European Union and the European Atomic Energy Community, of the one part, and the United Kingdom of Great Britain and Northern Ireland, of the other part [2021] OJ L149/10.

[25] EU Foreign Subsidies Regulation (n 18).

PART I

Foundations and Evolution

1

State Aid and Subsidy Control in Context

1. The Pervasiveness of Subsidies (and Similar Measures)

Subsidies are a pervasive and prominent tool of policy-making at all levels of government. Public authorities provide financial support to firms for a variety of reasons. In some instances, the point of intervention is to prevent the collapse of a company and ensure its return to long-term viability.[1] In other instances, public authorities rely on subsidies to attract new investments,[2] reshore manufacturing activities,[3] shift production methods to less polluting alternatives[4] or nurture the development of innovation-intensive industries.[5] Financial support is also an effective means to attain solidarity and redistribution objectives. Subsidies, among other things, can guarantee that all citizens have access to services deemed essential for meaningful participation in society, such as utilities.[6] Similarly, they may be relied upon to promote the development of certain regions and rebalance the economy.[7]

These forms of State intervention have come under the spotlight at different points in time in the course of the past decades. The support received by the banking industry at the peak of the financial crisis[8] or that provided by the US

---

[1] See for instance the regime that applies at the EU level. Guidelines on State aid for rescuing and restructuring non-financial undertakings in difficulty [2014] OJ C249/1.

[2] An emblematic example is that of the subsidies granted by various local and regional authorities to attract investment by Amazon; Shannon Bond, Joshua Chaffin and Kiran Stacey, 'Amazon reaps more than \$3bn from New York, Virginia and Tennessee' *Financial Times* (London, 14 November 2018).

[3] Alicia García-Herrero, Heather Grabbe and Axel Kaellenius, 'De-risking and decarbonising: a green tech partnership to reduce reliance on China' (2023) Bruegel Policy Brief 19/2023; and Chul-Woo Kwon and Uk Hwang, 'The Effect of Reshoring Policy on the Host and Home Countries' (2023) 37 International Economic Journal 555.

[4] Guidelines on State aid for climate, environmental protection and energy 2022 [2022] OJ C80/1. For an analysis, see Klaus Conrad, 'Taxes and subsidies for pollution-intensive industries as trade policy' (1993) 25 Journal of Environmental Economics and Management 121.

[5] Framework for State aid for research and development and innovation [2022] OJ C414/1.

[6] European Union framework for State aid in the form of public service compensation [2012] OJ C8/1.

[7] Guidelines on regional State aid [2021] OJ C153/1.

[8] Christian Ahlborn and Daniel Piccinin, 'The application of the principles of restructuring aid to banks during the financial crisis' (2010) 9 European State Aid Law Quarterly 47.

federal government to its automobile manufacturers[9] at roughly the same time are examples that come to mind immediately. Subsidies were back at the forefront of legal and policy discussions in the 2020s. As a result of the combined effects of a global pandemic,[10] rising protectionism[11] and the concomitant revival of industrial policy,[12] the level and intensity of State intervention in the economy reached levels that are not normally seen during peacetime.[13] For instance, financial incentives to reshore economic activity and promote the decarbonisation of energy production were the centrepiece of the US Inflation Reduction Act adopted during the Biden administration.[14] The EU and its Member States implemented similar initiatives.[15]

The comeback of subsidies in policy discussions was accompanied, in the 2020s, with major developments reshaping this area of the law. In an effervescent and rapidly changing landscape, some regimes were conspicuous for their absence. WTO law (and, more precisely, the Agreement on Subsidies and Countervailing Measures or 'SCM Agreement'[16]) had been designed to constrain countries' ability to distort trade and competition by means of financial contributions. It prohibits the award of subsidies conditional upon, inter alia, the use of domestic content,[17] such as those provided for in the US Inflation Reduction Act.[18] The permanent crisis within the WTO system,[19] however, meant that its built-in tools did not and could not act as an effective deterrent on unquestionably unlawful conduct and could not provide an effective remedy addressing the impact of such conduct on trade and competition.[20]

In part as a result of the gap left by WTO law, the 2020s have seen the emergence of new dedicated regimes. These legal developments reveal above all the important role subsidies play in the regulation of trade and competition. The UK Subsidy Control Act 2022 is a prominent example in this sense. Its adoption is explained by the UK-EU Trade and Cooperation Agreement[21] concluded in the

---

[9] Frank H Pearl, 'Too Big To Fail, Too Big To Bail: A Plan to Save the U.S. Auto Industry' (Brookings, 5 December 2008).

[10] José Luis Buendía Sierra and Angela Dovalo Martín, 'State aid versus COVID-19: The Commission adopts a temporary framework' (2020) 19 European State Aid Law Quarterly 3.

[11] Uri Dadush, 'Deglobalisation and Protectionism' (2022) Bruegel Working Paper 18.

[12] Réka Juhász, Nathan Lane and Dani Rodrik, 'The new economics of industrial policy' (2023) 16 Annual Review of Economics 213.

[13] For an analysis in perspective of the evolution of expenditures, see European Commission, *State aid Scoreboard 2024* (April 2025).

[14] Giulia Claudia Leonelli and Francesco Clora, 'Retooling the regulation of net-zero subsidies: lessons from the US Inflation Reduction Act' (2024) 27 Journal of International Economic Law 441.

[15] Commission, 'The Green Deal Industrial Plan: Securing Europe's Net-Zero Industry Leadership' IP/23/510 (Brussels, 31 January 2023).

[16] Agreement on Subsidies and Countervailing Measures [1994] UNTS 1869/14.

[17] ibid, Article 3.

[18] Leonelli and Clora (n 14).

[19] Petros C Mavroidis, *Industrial Policy, National Security, and the Perilous Plight of the WTO* (Oxford University Press 2025).

[20] Alan Beattie, 'A crumbling system of trade rules awaits Trump's wrecking ball' *Financial Times* (14 November 2024).

[21] Trade and Cooperation Agreement between the European Union and the European Atomic Energy Community, of the one part, and the United Kingdom of Great Britain and Northern Ireland, of the other part [2021] OJ L149/10.

wake of Brexit. It became apparent, during the negotiations between the two partners, that a substantive and institutional framework constraining the UK's ability
to award subsidies (and going beyond the requirements not just of the WTO regime
but also of the typical free trade arrangement) was an indispensable condition
for reaching a deal.[22] The UK Subsidy Control Act 2022 added to the universe of
regimes inspired by the EU model across Europe.

The EU model itself has not been immune to the ripple effects caused by deglobalisation and the crisis in the WTO system. On the one hand, EU State aid law has
mutated to adjust to the new legal and economic reality. The European Commission
(hereinafter, the 'Commission') has progressively relaxed its approach vis-à-vis the
legal status of certain measures in response, among others, to the active industrial policies pursued in non-EU countries (including the US and China). From
a regime aimed at regulating intra-EU trade and competition, EU State aid law is
now mutating into one that accounts for the competitiveness of the trade bloc as a
whole and its ability to counter strategies deployed by third countries. For instance,
a measure may be deemed compatible with the internal market if it ensures that
productive capacity remains within the EU, even at the expense of competition
and trade distortions therein.[23]

The legal development that symbolically marks the change in the economic
landscape and the consequences of the vacuum left by the WTO regime is arguably the adoption of the EU Foreign Subsidies Regulation.[24] This instrument seeks,
in essence, to export the logic and operation of the EU State aid model to non-EU
countries. Accordingly, it empowers the Commission not just to oversee and evaluate whether subsidies awarded by third countries distort the internal market, but
also to balance the positive and negative effects they may have therein and adopt,
where deemed necessary, any redressive measures (including the repayment of the
subsidy). In response to the failures of the multilateral regime, in other words, the
EU has chosen to level the playing field by unilaterally applying its own substantive
and institutional standards to the recipients of advantages granted by third countries.

These legal responses reveal, above all, that – pervasive as it may be – the award
of subsidies is rarely ever unfettered (and if it is, it may not be sustainable over
the long run given the long-term consequences it is likely to have). Regulation
constraining the ability of public authorities to provide financial support for firms
tends to emerge, organically, in the context of any trade relationship (and, in some
instances, even at the domestic level). The pages that follow examine the various
rationales for the adoption of subsidy control regimes and describe the institutional
apparatus by means of which they are implemented. One can distinguish, in this
sense, between two broad models: the EU model (which revolves around a centralised authority that allows for the balancing of the positive and negative effects of

---

[22] 'Brexit: Trade talks "have reached critical stage"' *BBC News* (7 December 2020).

[23] Commission, '€902 million German State aid measure to support Northvolt' IP/23/6823 (Brussels,
7 January 2024). See also the discussion in Chapter 6.

[24] Regulation (EU) 2022/2560 of the European Parliament and of the Council of 14 December 2022
on foreign subsidies distorting the internal market [2022] OJ L330/1.

subsidies) and the WTO model (which revolves around inter-State disputes). Each model may result in different varieties of subsidy control in practice.

2. The Rationale Behind Subsidy Control

2.1. Trade-related Justifications for Subsidy Control

A subsidy control regime is an indispensable aspect of any (bilateral or multilateral) trade arrangement worthy of the name. It is therefore not a coincidence that an ad hoc framework featured, from the outset, in the legal orders of the (then EEC) EU (Articles 107 to 109 TFEU; originally Articles 92 to 94 EEC)[25] and the WTO.[26] A close look at the legal landscape shows, in fact, that provisions dealing with subsidies tend to become more stringent, and the enforcement regime more centralised, as the trade relationship grows closer. At one end of the spectrum, the provisions on subsidies in a plain-vanilla free trade agreement will barely move beyond the requirements of the WTO regime. At the other end of the spectrum, arrangements aiming at creating or expanding the geographic reach of an internal market (such as the Agreement on the European Economic Area[27]) will mimic, in effect, the EU model.

The fundamental reason why subsidy control regimes are ubiquitous in trade deals has to do with the fact that subsidies may have, if not the object, at least analogous effects to the sort of barriers to trade that these agreements are designed to bring down.[28] A State that seeks to prevent or limit imports may do so by means of a tariff, a quota (or a measure having an equivalent effect) and also a subsidy. The first of these obstacles negatively affects cross-border trade by raising the price of foreign goods on the domestic market. The latter, by contrast, restricts the flow of goods by lowering the price of domestic products vis-à-vis imported ones. The consequences, from the perspective of the trade relationship between two or more

---

[25] The provision remains virtually unchanged since the Treaty of Rome. Pursuant to Article 107(1) TFEU, '1. Save as otherwise provided in the Treaties, any aid granted by a Member State or through State resources in any form whatsoever which distorts or threatens to distort competition by favouring certain undertakings or the production of certain goods shall, in so far as it affects trade between Member States, be incompatible with the internal market'. Article 107(2) TFEU identifies the instances where State aid falling within the scope of the first paragraph 'shall be compatible' with the internal market, whereas Article 107(3) TFEU deals with instances where aid 'may' be declared to be compatible with it. Article 108 TFEU provides the kernel of a procedural regime (including an obligation on EU Member States to inform the Commission of any plans to grant new aid). Article 109 TFEU, finally, empowers the Council of the EU to adopt legislation implementing Articles 107 and 108 TFEU. For a historical overview, see Juan Jorge Piernas López, *The Concept of State Aid Under EU Law: From internal market to competition and beyond* (Oxford University Press 2015).

[26] SCM Agreement (n 16).

[27] Agreement on the European Economic Area [1994] OJ L1/3.

[28] See, for a discussion, Pablo Ibáñez Colomo and Damien J Neven, 'State aid control beyond the EU: legal convergence and unilateral expansion' in Philipp Werner and Vincent Verouden (eds), *EU State Aid Control: Law and Economics* (2nd edn, Kluwer 2025).

countries, are essentially the same. For the same reason, eliminating some, but not all, of these barriers is likely to frustrate the liberalisation ambitions of the parties. This idea is illustrated with a simple example in Figure 1.1.

Figure 1.1 Impact of subsidies on trade

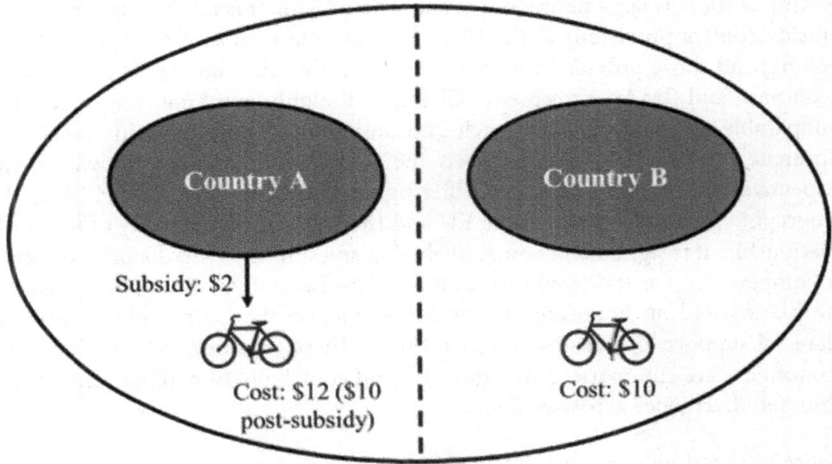

If an agreement that is otherwise aimed at liberalising cross-border trade fails to provide for constraints on partners' ability to award subsidies, the expected economic benefits of the deal may fail to materialise. The removal of barriers to trade is expected to lead to productive efficiency gains, insofar as firms expand their capacity and increase their output.[29] In addition, it can be presumed to be a source of allocative efficiency gains. This is so for two reasons. First, increased competitive pressure within each domestic market is likely to bring prices down and increase the choice of products available to consumers. Second, trade liberalisation creates the conditions where each trading partner can specialise in the activities where they have a comparative advantage, thereby improving the allocation of resources within the area covered by the agreement.[30] It is not difficult to see how the unfettered award of subsidies can negatively impact these expected benefits.

The need for substantive and institutional coordination in relation to subsidies increases with the depth and breadth of the trade relationship. It is not by chance that the EU State aid regime is more detailed, centralised and sophisticated than its WTO counterpart. The features of the former are a function of the fact that EU Member States have reached such a degree of legal integration that they cannot resort to traditional trade remedies to counteract the distortions on competition and/or trade resulting from the award of subsidies. This is so, first, because the project of European economic integration rests, above all, on the elimination of

---

[29] ibid.

[30] Elhanan Helpman and Paul Krugman, *Market Structure and Foreign Trade* (MIT Press 1985).

tariff and non-tariff trade barriers and the creation of a customs union.[31] One should bear in mind, second, that the usual trade retaliation tools are unavailable for the simple reason that EU law precludes its Member States from circumventing the Union's institutional framework by taking unilateral action.[32]

The adoption of stringent subsidy control rules is also a necessity where the volume of trade is large between two countries. Again, it is not by chance that the subsidy control provisions in the EU-UK Trade and Cooperation Agreement go well beyond those provided for in, for instance, the EU-Canada Comprehensive Economic and Trade Agreement (CETA).[33] Roughly speaking, both deals are comparable in terms of their reach and ambitions – they seek, in essence, to eliminate tariffs and quotas between the two trading partners. However, the respective subsidy control chapters differ significantly from one another. Given the geographic proximity between the EU and the UK and the intensity of the trade relationship, it is significantly more likely that any subsidies will distort trade and/or competition. For the same reason, it is unsurprising that, as mentioned above, the EU insisted on imposing greater constraints on the UK's ability to provide financial support to industry and investment. These two dimensions – legal and economic – are summarised in Figure 1.2 and contribute to making sense of the observed divergence across systems.

Figure 1.2 Legal and economic determinants of subsidy control regimes

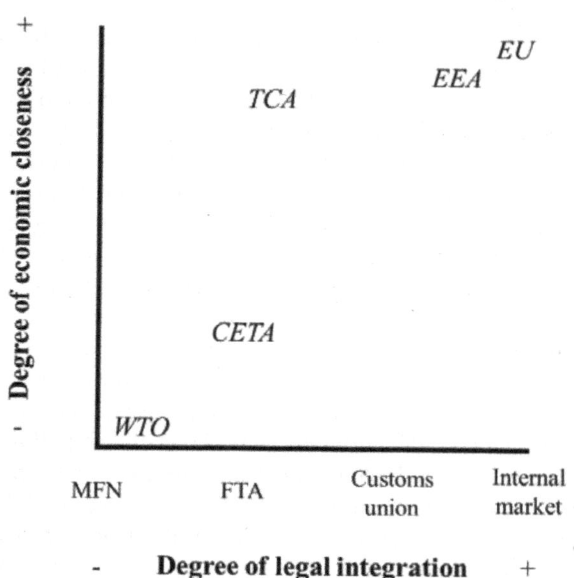

---

[31] See Article 3(3) TEU and Articles 26–66 TFEU. See also Catherine Barnard, *The Substantive Law of the EU: The Four Freedoms* (4th edn, Oxford University Press 2022).
[32] Articles 258 and 259 TFEU.
[33] Comprehensive Economic and Trade Agreement (CETA) between Canada, of the one part, and the European Union and its Member States, of the other part [2017] OJ L11/23.

2.2. Competition-related Justifications for Subsidy Control

There would be compelling reasons to introduce subsidy control mechanisms even if one were to leave aside trade-related considerations. The first and most obvious one is that subsidies distort the competitive process. Competition is widely accepted as desirable insofar as it incentivises firms to improve their processes and develop new and better products. It is assumed to benefit consumers and society as a whole. An inevitable (and no less desirable) side effect of competition is the departure of firms that are less attractive in terms of, inter alia, price, quality and innovation. Where the award of subsidies is unconstrained by law, these dynamics may be affected in several ways. To begin with, the standing of firms in the relevant market would not (or not necessarily) reflect their ability to offer new and better products and/or to improve their processes, but on their ability to lobby for financial support from public authorities. By the same token, firms would not be penalised for their inability to withstand competitive pressure.

The distortions of the competitive process resulting from the award of subsidies are more insidious and harmful over the long run. One of the effects of subsidies is that they divert the attention of firms away from the very efforts that the competitive process rewards. As a result of these financial incentives, in other words, firms may find themselves competing not so much in the marketplace to attract the favour of consumers as competing before public authorities to secure support. Their ability to remain in business would no longer be a function of their products and processes, but of their ability to persuade governments to allow them to stay afloat. Over time, firms may find themselves fully dependent on subsidies. It is not difficult to think of examples of firms that were repeatedly rescued and restructured by public authorities due to their chronic inability to adjust their products and processes to the prevailing conditions.[34]

The long-term distortions of the competitive process are likely to be all the more acute – and their consequences all the more undesirable – if one considers that not all firms have the same ability to secure financial support. Typically, larger firms and industry incumbents are more effective at influencing public authorities. A well-publicised example is that of Amazon, which (exploiting the absence of a subsidy control system in the US) pitched local and regional authorities against one another to secure incentives for its second North American headquarters.[35] It is unlikely that a smaller (and potentially more innovative) rival would have been able to attract the same degree of support from public authorities. This example suggests that, over the long run, the unfettered award of subsidies is likely to have the perverse effect of strengthening incumbents, disadvantaging rivals and favouring existing activities and business models (as opposed to novel, innovative and disruptive ones).

---

[34] An emblematic example of a firm that has received repeated support from the State is that of Alitalia. For an overview, see Marco Di Giulio, 'Alitalia, or the inability to align regulation with industrial policies' (2018) 10 Contemporary Italian Politics 377.

[35] Bond, Chaffin and Stacey (n 2).

Some commentators have occasionally objected to the idea that subsidies necessarily affect the competitive process in a negative manner. It has been argued, for instance, that financial support from the State is desirable insofar as it is capable of bringing prices down. This is so, the argument goes, at least if one accepts (as is frequently argued[36]) that consumer welfare should guide the interpretation and enforcement of legal provisions aimed at protecting competition.[37] Such a position, however, ignores two crucial considerations. The first and arguably most obvious one is that consumers are simultaneously customers and taxpayers. Thus, it would be difficult to argue that subsidies improve their welfare (if anything, the opposite is likely to be true[38]). The second point to note is that lower prices are valuable not in and of themselves, but insofar as they are the outcome of the competitive process.

A second, potentially more compelling, argument is that – contrary to what has been suggested above – subsidies may inject competition, not reduce it. Suppose, for instance, that a firm enjoys a monopoly in a given market. In such circumstances, subsidies may contribute to the emergence of a rival capable of exercising effective competitive pressure on the incumbent. An example that is frequently cited to make this point is that of Airbus, which became a rival to Boeing thanks to the support of a number of European countries.[39] This argument suggests two potential justifications for the award of subsidies: one that sees them as beneficial insofar as they are capable of addressing a market failure (market power) and another one that relates to the implementation of an active industrial policy. These two potential justifications are examined below.

2.3. Preventing Subsidy Races

If competition among private firms is widely accepted as desirable and in the interest of consumers and society, competition among States through the award of subsidies is likely to be destructive and welfare reducing.[40] Intervention by public authorities to attract or keep investments within their territory may have several undesirable consequences. First, resources may be diverted away from more productive uses. Instead of investing in, say, education, research and infrastructure, which may be in the long-term interest of the community, governments

---

[36] Nicolas Petit and Lazar Radic, 'The Superiority of the Consumer Welfare Standard' (2024) EUI LAW Working Paper 2024/20.

[37] The idea that consumer welfare should guide the assessment of State aid was advanced by Thibaut Kleiner and Alain Alexis, 'Politique des aides d'Etat : une analyse économique plus fine au service de l'intérêt commun' (2005) 2 Concurrences 45.

[38] For an analysis, see Vincent Verouden and Philipp Werner, 'Introduction: The Law and Economics of EU State Aid Control' in Werner and Verouden (n 28).

[39] Timothy Besley and Paul Seabright, 'The effects and policy implications of state aids to industry: an economic analysis' (1999) 14 Economic Policy 14.

[40] Hans Friederiszick, Lars-Hendrik Röller and Vincent Verouden, 'European State Aid Control: An Economic Framework' in Paolo Buccirossi (ed), *Handbook of Antitrust Economics* (MIT Press 2008).

may choose to focus on short-term goals and subsidise firms instead. The amounts awarded may reach a level that wipes out, in effect, any expected benefits. Several examples from the US – including the abovementioned one involving Amazon – suggest that, in the absence of a subsidy control regime, every job created may come at a very substantial cost.[41]

These undesirable effects – diversion of resources, cost to the community – will be exacerbated where there is intense rivalry among public authorities to attract the favour of private firms. An additional consequence of unfettered subsidy races (or, put differently, an additional reason why a subsidy control regime may be desirable) is that they tend to favour larger and wealthier jurisdictions at the expense of smaller and/or less developed ones. The latter may not be able to exploit their comparative advantages to catch up with the former, and economic inequality may become entrenched as a result. It is not by chance that, when the Commission chose to relax EU State aid rules in the context of the Covid-19 pandemic, commentators expressed concern about the fact that it might distort competition within the internal market and favour larger EU Member States with deeper pockets.[42]

2.4. Subsidy Control as a Pre-commitment Device

As mentioned above, subsidies may sacrifice productive long-term investments to prioritise short-term gains instead (such as attracting flagship investments or rescuing failing firms). If a public authority favours the latter over the former, this is not necessarily the consequence of opportunistic conduct, ignorance or, more generally, of its inability to adequately weigh what is in the best interest of the community. It may simply be the case that public authorities, when subject to real-world constraints, find themselves unable to yield to pressure. For instance, a government may be aware that providing aid to support an ailing business will not achieve anything to ensure its return to long-term viability. In practice, however, it may be unrealistic for it to refuse support due to the clout enjoyed by the potential beneficiary or to the political consequences of business closure.

Against this background, a system for the control of subsidies may introduce a substantive and institutional framework allowing a government to justify its refusal to support private actors. A subsidy control regime can act, in other words, as a pre-commitment device[43] giving public authorities the necessary cover to stick to their preferred course of action (that is, devoting resources to productive long-run

---

[41] Alessandro Ferrari and Ralph Ossa, 'A quantitative analysis of subsidy competition in the U.S.' (2023) 224 Journal of Public Economics 104919.

[42] Alfonso Lamadrid de Pablo and José Luis Buendía Sierra, 'A Moment of Truth for the EU: A Proposal for a State Aid Solidarity Fund' (2020) 11 Journal of European Competition Law & Practice 1.

[43] David Spector, 'State Aids: Economic Analysis and Practice in the European Union' in Xavier Vives (ed), *Competition Policy in the EU Fifty Years on from the Treaty of Rome* (Oxford University Press 2009).

investments) and avoid yielding to short-term pressures. From a substantive standpoint, the control system may provide that subsidies are only acceptable where it can be shown that they make a substantial contribution to a public interest objective and are on balance positive for society. From an institutional standpoint, the government may be legally bound by the analysis carried out by an independent authority offering expert advice. The pre-commitment device may be more effective where the authority is a supranational one that is less subject to pressures at the national level – as is true of the Commission in the EU legal order.

3. Justifications for the Award of Subsidies

3.1. Context

The effective regulation of subsidies is complicated by the fact that they are a potential source of positive effects for citizens and society at large. Due to the ambivalence of their impact, any regime will have to design legal avenues to ensure that subsidies are only prohibited where any distortions of trade and/or competition outweigh the alleged or expected benefits. One can think of three public interest objectives that may justify financial support for certain firms or activities. It is accepted, to begin with, that the award of subsidies may be an appropriate response to a market failure[44] (that is, to an instance where the market does not deliver on its promise of efficient outcomes). Second, State intervention along the same lines is an effective means to attain solidarity and redistribution objectives. Finally, it is frequently (and increasingly) discussed whether, and if so in what circumstances, industrial policy (of which subsidies may be a part) may be justified and work effectively.

3.2. Market Failures

There are a number of reasons why markets fail to deliver efficient outcomes. Some of them are frequently put forward as justifications for the award of subsidies and similar measures. Externalities – whether positive or negative – are among these reasons. This concept can be defined as a benefit or cost that is inflicted on an agent other than the one responsible for it. Where externalities are positive, third parties derive a benefit from the activity of another agent. If the latter is unable to internalise this benefit, it will underinvest (relative to the social optimum) in the activity generating the externalities. This idea is best illustrated in light of a specific example. If a firm trains its employees, for instance, other firms will derive an advantage from a more skilled workforce. To the extent that the firm investing in the activity is unable to internalise the externality (that is, it is unable to prevent

---

[44] Verouden and Werner (n 38).

its employees from leaving), it may choose not to do so (or reduce its efforts in this sense). For the same reason, State support incentivising employee training may be socially desirable.[45]

Externalities can also be negative. The activity of an economic agent, more precisely, may inflict, without bearing it, a cost on third parties. As a result, the former will have no incentive to reduce the activity generating it. The traditional example of a negative externality is that of pollution, the cost of which, absent public intervention (for instance, through the introduction of the 'polluter pays principle'[46]), is not supported in full by the firm generating it. In some circumstances, subsidies may be an appropriate mechanism to ensure that economic agents internalise the cost inflicted upon society. In the 2022 iteration of its Guidelines on State aid for climate, environmental protection and energy,[47] for instance, the Commission identifies a number of scenarios where financial support from public authorities may be warranted. One of them relates to the adoption of measures aimed at improving the energy and environmental performance of buildings.[48]

Similar dynamics arise where public goods are involved.[49] A public good is characterised, inter alia, by the fact that it is non-rival in use.[50] In other words, consumption by one agent does not prevent consumption by another one. The fact that one person listens to the performance of a song does not affect others' ability to enjoy it at the same time. Where public goods cannot be appropriated by the agent producing them, the rate at which they are offered is likely to fall below the social optimum. A number of interventions can be designed to incentivise their production. The award of intellectual property rights is the most prominent of these.[51] Subsidies may also play a role. In its Framework for State aid for research and development and innovation, the Commission explains that, unlike applied knowledge, it may be difficult for economic agents to appropriate the results of fundamental research, which is the same reason why subsidies and similar measures may be an appropriate tool to increase its rate.[52]

---

[45] Criteria for the analysis of the compatibility of State aid for training subject to individual notification [2009] OJ C188/1, para 6 ('Undertakings may refrain from training their workforce at the level that would be optimal for society as a whole. This is due to the market failure linked with the positive externalities of training and to difficulties in appropriating the rents if employees are free to change employers').

[46] Stefan Ambec and Lars Ehlers, 'Regulation via the Polluter-pays Principle' (2016) 126 The Economic Journal 884.

[47] Environment and Energy Guidelines (n 4).

[48] ibid, para 135: 'Measures aimed at improving the energy and environmental performance of buildings target negative externalities by creating individual incentives to attain targets for energy savings and for the reduction of greenhouse gas and air pollutant emissions'.

[49] Public goods are, in fact, often presented and analysed as an extreme externality.

[50] William H Oakland, 'Theory of public goods' in Alan J Auerbach and Martin S Feldstein (eds), Handbook of Public Economics Vol 2 (North-Holland 1987) 485–535.

[51] Richard A Posner, 'Intellectual property: The law and economics approach' (2005) 19 Journal of Economic Perspectives 57.

[52] Framework for State aid for research and development and innovation [2022] OJ C414/1, para 61 ('as is often argued for fundamental research, it may be difficult to exclude others from gaining access to the results of some activities, which might therefore have a public good character. On the other

Markets may fail, third, where there is an asymmetry of information. Such a reality arises where there is a disparity in the quality of the information available to two economic agents. As a consequence of this asymmetry, socially desirable transactions may not materialise. This idea is often illustrated by reference to the insurance and financial sectors. A bank, for instance, may not have the ability to evaluate the quality and chances of success of a project presented by a start-up, in particular where the latter does not have a track record.[53] The bank may therefore be reluctant to finance it, even if doing so would have been in the interest of both parties. Some of the most transformative and disruptive ventures may never take off where asymmetries of information are pervasive.[54] This reality may be addressed if public authorities provide support in various forms, such as venture capital investment.

It makes sense to mention, finally, two additional market failures. One can think, first, of coordination problems, which may arise when the different actors across an industry lack the incentives to coordinate their activities. Lack of coordination leads to inefficient outcomes.[55] An example that is often given is that of electric vehicles and charging stations. The value of the former depends on the availability of the latter, and vice versa. As a result, State intervention to deploy charging stations may be desirable to ensure that the sector takes off.[56] Second, market power is also a source of inefficient outcomes. A monopoly, in particular, will make consumers worse off (that is, it leads to allocative inefficiency) and can be expected to become less productive absent competitive pressure. One can therefore argue, at least in theory, that subsidies promoting the emergence of a rival could be justified.

3.3. Redistribution and Solidarity

Public intervention is not necessarily a response to a market failure. There may be instances where market outcomes, even assuming that they are beyond reproach from an economic perspective, are not acceptable from a societal one. To begin with, subsidies may be used to address regional disparities within a country. Such disparities may simply reflect economic dynamics that lead to shifts in terms of population and economic activity. However, governments may deem it necessary

---

hand, more specific knowledge related to production can often be well protected, for example through patents, allowing the inventor to reap a higher return on the invention').

[53] Guidelines on State aid to promote risk finance investments [2021] OJ C508/1, para 3.

[54] ibid: 'As a result of that asymmetric information, business finance markets may fail to provide the necessary equity or debt finance to newly-created and potentially innovative and high-growth start-ups and SMEs, resulting in a persistent capital market failure preventing supply from meeting demand at a price acceptable to both sides, which negatively affects SMEs' growth prospects and undermines the Single Market's productivity growth and overall resilience of the Union's economy'.

[55] Verouden and Werner (n 38) 45–47.

[56] Luis Garicano, 'Why tariffs won't save our car industry' (*Silicon Continent*, 9 October 2024), available at www.siliconcontinent.com.

to rebalance the situation by providing incentives to firms to relocate their investments towards relatively less developed and/or more isolated regions. Article 107(3) TFEU, which identifies the instances where State aid may be declared compatible with the internal market, makes an express reference to regional aid in two of its sub-paragraphs – (a)[57] and (c).[58]

A second area where intervention in the name of redistribution and solidarity is frequent relates to the provision of public services. As mentioned in the introduction, some services are deemed essential for meaningful participation in society. It is therefore relatively commonplace for public authorities to step in to guarantee that citizens have universal access to them reliably, continuously and affordably.[59] For instance, a government may require that the airline service between a remote island and the mainland is provided on a year-round, daily basis, even when it would not otherwise have been profitable. Similarly, it may provide that all households within its territory must be within no more than a kilometre from an office providing basic postal and banking services, or that they have access to the Internet at guaranteed speeds and levels of quality.

Public services have a special status in many legal orders. EU law, for instance, refers to 'services of general economic interest' and provides that the rules on competition enshrined in the TFEU may even be disapplied where they are an obstacle to the performance of firms entrusted with their operation.[60] A number of mechanisms allow governments to attain the objectives underpinning public service obligations. The award of exclusive rights, for instance, makes it possible for the firm subject to the obligations to cross-subsidise the loss-making activities with the profits generated in the rest of the territory. Where the market is liberalised, thereby allowing for competition in profitable areas, subsidies compensating the firm for the costs involved in discharging its public service duties may be an effective mechanism to reconcile competition and solidarity goals.

3.4. Industrial Policy

Industrial policy has made a comeback in policy discussions.[61] Some of the contemporary challenges, including the decarbonisation of the economy and the growing geopolitical tensions, have created the environment where an active role by the State in shaping and directing the economy is widely seen as desirable.

---

[57] Article 107(3)(a) TFEU refers to 'aid to promote the economic development of areas where the standard of living is abnormally low or where there is serious underemployment, and of the regions referred to in Article 349, in view of their structural, economic and social situation'.

[58] Article 107(3)(c) TFEU, in turn, refers to 'aid to facilitate the development of certain economic activities or of certain economic areas, where such aid does not adversely affect trading conditions to an extent contrary to the common interest'.

[59] See for instance Framework for State aid in the form of public service compensation (n 6).

[60] See Articles 14 and 106(2) TFEU and the extensive discussion in Chapter 3.

[61] See in this sense the so-called Draghi Report, *The future of European competitiveness: Part A | A competitiveness strategy for Europe* (September 2024).

Intervention in this sense may be aimed, inter alia, at reshoring economic activity, improving the resilience of supply chains, adjusting sectors and activities to changing conditions and avoiding (or minimising) reliance on certain suppliers. In some instances, it may simply be a response to industrial policies pursued elsewhere. It is not difficult to see the central role that subsidies would play in pursuing these objectives. For instance, financial support from the State may allow a firm or sector (an infant industry[62]) to become competitive vis-à-vis its rivals. Alternatively, subsidies may seek to compensate for the costs involved in relocating a firm's activities, or to make up for the cost differences relative to other jurisdictions.

The question of whether the State should pursue an active industrial policy, including by means of subsidies, is not wholly uncontroversial.[63] The desirability of intervention along these lines depends, to a significant extent, on its nature, aims and scope.[64] Some of the measures that could reasonably come under the umbrella of industrial policy could be rationalised as a means to tackle a market failure, or on equity grounds.[65] For instance, subsidies aimed at allowing for the emergence of an alternative source of supply may be justified by the market power exercised by a monopolistic provider. In other instances, intervention by the State may be a necessary response to the inability of the private sector to evaluate the profitability of some ventures (that is, an information asymmetry), to invest in fundamental research or to effectively coordinate supply chains.

The real controversy arises in instances where efficiency or equity are not the drivers of industrial policy. The question, therefore, is whether the promotion of economic activity within a territory can, in and of itself, justify the award of subsidies. It is not disputed that intervention in this sense can sometimes prove successful and has indeed proved successful (as the examples of Airbus, mentioned above, and South Korean steel producer Posco[66] show). On the other hand, the limits of governments' ability to conduct successful industrial policy are well understood. Commentators often point out, in this sense, that governments are not necessarily in a position to select successful projects ('picking winners'[67]) and that the promotion of economic activity can easily lend itself to cronyism and rent-seeking.[68] Against this background, the consensus view appears to be that the

---

[62] Marc J Melitz, 'When and how should infant industries be protected?' (2005) 66 Journal of International Economics 177.

[63] See, for a discussion, Spector (n 43).

[64] The definition of what amounts to industrial policy is itself somewhat contentious. See in this sense Juhász, Lane and Rodrik (n 12), who define it broadly as encompassing 'government policies that explicitly target the transformation of the structure of economic activity in pursuit of some public goal' and therefore beyond the subsidisation of manufacturing activities.

[65] Joanna Piechucka, Lluís Saurí-Romero and Ben Smulders, 'Industrial Policies, Competition, and Efficiency: The Need for State Aid Control' (2023) 19 Journal of Competition Law & Economics 503.

[66] Larry E Westphal, 'Industrial policy in an export-propelled economy: lessons from South Korea's experience' (1990) 4 Journal of Economic Perspectives 41.

[67] See Juhász, Lane and Rodrik (n 12) for an evaluation of this critique of industrial policy.

[68] Spector (n 43).

success of industrial policy is contingent on several ingredients that may or may not be present.[69] For the same reason, the award of subsidies on these grounds alone remains contentious.[70]

4. Institutional Models

4.1. Institutions and the Challenge of Balancing

The main conclusion to draw from the preceding section is that, even though subsidies can lead to distortions of competition and trade, their blanket prohibition would deprive governments of an effective tool to achieve public interest objectives. The challenge, from a legal perspective, is to design a substantive and institutional framework that is capable of distinguishing between interventions that have a net positive effect on citizens and society and those that are on balance negative. It is possible to differentiate between two broad approaches to this legal challenge: the EU model, which provides for the explicit balancing between the positive and negative aspects of State intervention and revolves around a supranational authority with the power to oversee the award of subsidies, and the WTO model, which is decentralised and thus relies on State-to-State disputes.

4.2. The EU Model for the Control of State Aid

4.2.1. *The EU Model* Stricto Sensu

The central role that the Commission plays in the State aid regime is the key peculiarity, from an institutional standpoint, of the EU model. In the areas where it enjoys discretion to shape policy (which are, as discussed at below, by far the most relevant in practice), it is for the Commission to define the conditions under which intervention falling within the scope of Article 107(1) TFEU is compatible with the internal market. It does so acting in the interest of the EU as a whole,[71] and on the basis of an analytical framework that allows it to weigh the contributions (if any) to a public interest objective against any distortions of competition

---

[69] Juhász, Lane and Rodrik (n 12) undertake a literature review to conclude that 'a balanced reading of the emerging literature suggests that it is no longer possible to dismiss industrial policy as ineffective or counter-productive'. For a discussion of these ingredients in the specific context of the EU, see the Draghi Report (n 61).

[70] See in this sense the reservations expressed by Piechucka, Saurí-Romero and Smulders (n 65).

[71] Case 730/79 *Philip Morris Holland BV v Commission*, EU:C:1980:209.

and trade.[72] It implements this framework by means of individual decisions,[73] and also secondary legislation[74] and soft law instruments[75] (which are essential to the operation of the regime).

The exercise by the Commission of its discretion comes with broad enforcement powers to shape policy. In addition to the competence to decide on the compatibility of aid with the internal market,[76] it has jurisdiction to interpret Article 107(1) TFEU and, by the same token, to take remedial action against EU Member States that fail to notify a measure falling within the scope of the regime and/or implement it before a decision on its compatibility is adopted (the so-called 'standstill clause').[77] The Commission can, inter alia, adopt interim measures, such as the suspension of the award.[78] When the unlawfully granted aid is found to be incompatible with the internal market, the Commission can, moreover, order its recovery.[79] These decision-making powers are assorted with the ability to conduct investigations, receive complaints and gather information from 'whatever source'.[80]

From a substantive standpoint, the EU model has two main features that stand out, in particular when compared with the WTO regime. One of them stems from the very choices made by the drafters of the Treaty of Rome, which remain unaltered in the TFEU. The other substantive feature is a consequence of the interpretative choices made by the Court of Justice (hereinafter, the 'Court' or the 'ECJ'). Starting with the letter of the Treaty, Article 107 TFEU does not provide for the prohibition of every measure affecting trade and/or distorting competition. Instead, the EU model provides for a system of rule and exception, which is common in EU law.[81] Accordingly, State aid is deemed incompatible with the internal market insofar

---

[72] See in this sense the wording of Article 107(3)(c), which expressly provides for 'aid to facilitate the development of certain economic activities or of certain economic areas, where such aid does not adversely affect trading conditions to an extent contrary to the common interest'.

[73] These decisions are adopted in accordance with Articles 4 and 9 of Council Regulation (EU) 2015/1589 of 13 July 2015 laying down detailed rules for the application of Article 108 of the Treaty on the Functioning of the European Union (codification) [2015] OJ L248/9.

[74] See in particular the so-called General Block Exemption Regulation: Commission Regulation (EU) No 651/2014 of 17 June 2014 declaring certain categories of aid compatible with the internal market in application of Articles 107 and 108 of the Treaty [2014] OJ L187/1.

[75] Some of the most prominent examples have been provided in this chapter, including the Environment and Energy Guidelines (n 4), Framework for State aid in the form of public service compensation (n 6) and the Guidelines on regional aid (n 7).

[76] This said, one should bear in mind the role that Article 108(2) TFEU reserves for the Council of the EU, acting unanimously, when it is justified in 'exceptional circumstances'.

[77] The standstill clause is enshrined in Article 108(3) TFEU, pursuant to which 'The Commission shall be informed, in sufficient time to enable it to submit its comments, of any plans to grant or alter aid'.

[78] Article 13 of the Procedural Regulation (n 73).

[79] ibid, Article 16.

[80] ibid, Article 12(1).

[81] See for instance the relationship between Articles 34 (which provides for the prohibition on quantitative restrictions on imports) and 36 TFEU (which provides for a justification); and, similarly, between Article 101(1) (which provides for the prohibition of agreements restricting competition) and 101(3) TFEU (which introduces an exemption mechanism for agreements that bring about positive effects).

as it affects trade between EU Member States, 'save as otherwise provided in the Treaties'.

Article 107 TFEU identifies a number of instances where State aid is, or may be declared to be, compatible with the internal market.[82] Article 107(2) TFEU relates to the circumstances that leave no scope for discretion to the Commission. Where the conditions set out in the provision are met, therefore, the measure is deemed to be a net benefit. These are, generally speaking, instances where the aid is not aimed at favouring a firm or a group thereof, but rather at supporting individual consumers, as well as measures aimed at addressing the consequences of 'natural disasters or exceptional occurrences'.[83] Article 107(3) TFEU, in turn, gives the Commission ample leeway to formulate and implement its policy choices.[84] This is, by some distance, the legal basis most frequently relied upon in practice. It encompasses both equity (for instance, regional aid[85]) and efficiency (for instance, research and development aid[86]) considerations.

The second substantive feature to note about the EU model is that the scope of the regime is broad, in particular when compared with its WTO counterpart. Where the other conditions set out in Article 107(1) TFEU are met (that is, where a measure imputable to the State and involving the use of State resources[87] is found to grant a selective advantage to a firm or a group thereof[88]), it is virtually always the case that the measure will be found to distort or threaten to distort competition and to affect trade between EU Member States. The requisite threshold of effects, in other words, is very low. The Court suggested in *Philip Morris* that the mere fact that financial assistance displaces productive activity within the EU is sufficient, in and of itself, to show that these distortion of competition and effect on trade conditions are met.[89] One should note, in addition, that such effects may be actual or potential.[90]

The fundamental consequence of the substantive choice made by the Court in *Philip Morris* (unchallenged since) is that the balancing exercise between the effects on trade and competition, on the one hand, and the contribution to a public interest objective, on the other, only occurs once the measure is characterised as State

---

[82] One should note, in addition, that the compatibility of State aid with the internal market may be declared pursuant to provisions other than Article 107 TFEU. A prominent provision in this sense is Article 106(2) TFEU, which is considered at length in Chapter 3.

[83] Article 107(2)(b) TFEU.

[84] The Court acknowledged that the provision gives the Commission the requisite discretion to formulate policy in the area in *Philip Morris* (n 71).

[85] The legal bases being, as mentioned above, Articles 107(3)(a) and (c) TFEU. Guidelines on regional aid (n 7).

[86] The default legal basis for such initiatives is Article 107(3)(c) TFEU. See Framework for State aid for research and development and innovation (n 5).

[87] See Chapter 2.

[88] See Chapters 3 (advantage) and 4 (selectivity).

[89] *Philip Morris* (n 71).

[90] The letter of the TFEU refers to a measure that 'distorts or threatens to distort competition'.

aid. Thus, and with the relatively minor exception of de minimis interventions,[91] the negative consequences of State intervention only play a meaningful role when evaluating whether it is compatible with the internal market. This feature of the EU model has important consequences in practice. It means that balancing occurs once the Commission has discharged its burden of proof and – arguably more importantly – in accordance with the terms of a provision that gives it the discretion to formulate and shape its policy in the field.

4.2.2. Variations on the EU Model

The EU model has been followed, to a greater or lesser degree, in most other European jurisdictions.[92] Given the constraints that Articles 107 and 108 TFEU impose upon its Member States, it is unsurprising that the EU, in its negotiations with neighbouring countries, requires the adoption of an equivalent system as a *conditio sine qua non* for the conclusion of a trade agreement. The degree of legal convergence with the EU model depends on the depth of the relationship with the EU. At one end of the spectrum, one can think of the European Economic Area (hereinafter, 'EEA'), which has the effect of exporting all the features of the EU model to the participating EFTA Member States. One can identify, at the other end of the spectrum, the UK subsidy control regime, which embraces the spirit of EU State aid law but departs from it in significant ways.

The EEA Agreement, in essence, allows Iceland, Norway and Liechtenstein to participate in the EU internal market.[93] It extends to them the fundamental economic freedoms currently enshrined in the TFEU as well as the provisions on, inter alia, EU State aid law. The convergence with the EU model is therefore complete, both from a substantive and an institutional standpoint. From a substantive perspective, the wording of the provisions in the EEA is virtually identical to that of the TFEU and therefore revolves around the explicit balancing of the positive and negative effects of awards.[94] Moreover, the core substantive choices made by the Court inform the interpretation of the EEA Agreement.[95] From an institutional standpoint, EEA State aid law requires the EFTA Member States to set up a supranational authority with equivalent powers to those enjoyed by the Commission.[96]

---

[91] Commission Regulation (EU) 2023/2832 of 13 December 2023 on the application of Articles 107 and 108 of the Treaty on the Functioning of the European Union to de minimis aid granted to undertakings providing services of general economic interest [2023] OJ L 2023/2832.

[92] See in this sense Ibáñez Colomo and Neven (n 28), and Luca Rubini, 'Transcending territoriality: Expanding EU State aid control through consensus and coercion' in Juan Jorge Piernas López, Leigh Hancher and Luca Rubini (eds), *The Future of EU State Aid Law: Consolidation and Expansion* (EU Law Live Press 2023).

[93] EEA Agreement (n 27).

[94] Article 61 EEA.

[95] Article 6 EEA.

[96] Article 62 EEA.

The UK Subsidy Control Act 2022,[97] which incorporates into domestic law the relevant provisions of the EU-UK Trade and Cooperation Agreement (hereinafter, the 'TCA'),[98] does not depart from the core institutional and substantive aspects of the EU model. As far as the former is concerned, the UK regime has entrusted an independent body, the Competition and Markets Authority (hereinafter, the 'CMA'), with the duty to oversee the implementation of the regime. Its powers, however, are more limited than those of the Commission. The CMA's role is merely advisory.[99] From a substantive standpoint, the UK regime – as much as the TCA itself – codifies large swathes of the EU case law and administrative practice.[100] It incorporates into the UK legal order the analytical framework consistently applied by the Commission to balance the positive and negative aspects of subsidies.

As summarised in Table 1.1, the agreements concluded with third countries that aspire to join the EU are in between these two ends of the spectrum. Because the trade relationship in these cases is deeper and more ambitious than that between the EU and the UK, there is a greater degree of substantive and institutional convergence. Thus, the legal concepts of the domestic systems of aspiring countries are identical and are, moreover, to be interpreted in line with the Court's case law.[101] The main difference, as depicted in Table 1.1, lies with the fact that the authority, with powers that are otherwise equivalent to those enjoyed by the Commission, is not a supranational one. This factor is not necessarily decisive where the third country's hope is to join the EU. However, a national authority – as opposed to a supranational one – may be less able to withstand the sort of short-term pressures identified in Section 2.

Table 1.1 Variations on the EU model

System	Substantive aspects	Administrative authority	Powers of the authority
EU	Article 107(1) TFEU	Supranational	Interpretation Remedies Compatibility analysis
EEA	Virtually identical to Article 107(1) TFEU	Supranational	Same as European Commission
Accession countries	Virtually identical to Article 107(1) TFEU	National	Same as European Commission
UK	Formally WTO concepts	National	Advisory powers

---

[97] Subsidy Control Act 2022.

[98] EU-UK Trade and Cooperation Agreement (n 21).

[99] See ss 52–69 of the Subsidy Control Act (n 97).

[100] For an extensive analysis, see Chapter 7.

[101] See for instance Article 264 of the Association Agreement between the European Union and its Member States, of the one part, and Ukraine, of the other part [2014] OJ L161/3.

4.3. The WTO Model

4.3.1. *The WTO Model* Stricto Sensu

The main institutional difference between the WTO and the EU models is the absence of a centralised authority in charge of policy-making (and, indeed, the balancing of the positive and negative aspects of subsidies). The WTO regime relies instead on State-to-State disputes to achieve its goals. What is more, it does not preclude its members from taking unilateral action against one another. Accordingly, a member that believes the relevant provisions on subsidies have been breached can seek relief either by means of the multilateral dispute settlement mechanisms enshrined in the SCM Agreement or, in the alternative, by means of countervailing measures.[102] The multilateral route will lead either to the adoption of a Panel Report by a Dispute Settlement Body or a decision by the Appellate Body.

From a substantive standpoint, one difference between the two models is the limited scope of the SCM Agreement, which applies to trade in goods alone.[103] The second point of divergence relates to the way the WTO regime handles the ambivalent nature of subsidies. Instead of balancing, it relies on an alternative technique. As the law stands,[104] the SCM Agreement identifies two categories of subsidies: prohibited and actionable. The former encompasses measures that have, as their object, the distortion of trade. These are instances where financial support is made contingent on export performance or upon the use of domestic goods.[105] Actionable subsidies, in turn, are those that do not have the object of distorting trade and/or competition but have 'adverse effects', as defined in Articles 5 and 6 of the SCM Agreement. Such adverse effects cannot simply be inferred from the fact that the measure qualifies as a 'subsidy'. The threshold for intervention, accordingly, is significantly higher than it is under the EU model.[106]

4.3.2. *The WTO Model as a Template*

The typical trade agreement has provisions dealing with the award of subsidies by the parties. These provisions, generally speaking, do not depart from the principles and spirit underpinning the SCM Agreement. In fact, the obligations imposed upon the parties will barely, if at all, move beyond the duties stemming from the WTO regime. It makes sense to mention an example to illustrate what a plain-vanilla trade deal provides in this sphere. For instance, the agreement between

---

[102] For an analysis of the process, see Peter Van den Bossche and Werner Zdouc, *The Law and Policy of the World Trade Organization: Text, Cases, and Materials* (5th edn, Cambridge University Press 2021).

[103] See in this sense Recital 5 of the Foreign Subsidies Regulation (n 24).

[104] As originally adopted, the SCM Agreement (n 16) introduced an additional category of subsidy, the non-actionable subsidy. This category encompassed a number of efficiency and equity objectives, but ceased to apply pursuant to Article 31 in the absence of an agreement to extend its application beyond the initial five years.

[105] ibid, Article 3.

[106] For a comparative analysis, see Luca Rubini, *The Definition of Subsidy and State Aid: WTO and EC Law in Comparative Perspective* (Oxford University Press 2009).

Canada and the EU (CETA), mentioned above, shares its substantive features with the SCM Agreement.[107] From an institutional standpoint, the requirements do not go beyond consultation and transparency. In fact, CETA expressly excludes subsidies from the ad hoc disputes settlement mechanisms enshrined therein.[108] Even when agreements make timid attempts to formally acknowledge that subsidies may have positive effects, they barely depart from the WTO framework.[109]

5. Varieties of State Aid and Subsidy Control

5.1. Introducing the Varieties

The substantive and institutional features of a legal system necessarily have an impact on the way it is shaped and evolves. Thus, and even though the core definitions of subsidy (in the SCM Agreement) and that of State aid (under Article 107 TFEU) are similar, other differences between the WTO and EU models mean that they will take divergent paths over time. Divergence will be reflected in the nature of the cases that are considered and in the material scope of the regime. Substantive and institutional factors, in other words, will lead to the adoption of one or other variety of enforcement. These varieties are presented systematically in Figure 1.3. As the figure shows, it is helpful to think of varieties of subsidy control as concentric circles: the inner circles represent the inescapable core of any regime worthy of the name, whereas the outer layers capture the more ambitious (and, as such, more controversial) approaches to enforcement.

Figure 1.3 Varieties of subsidy control

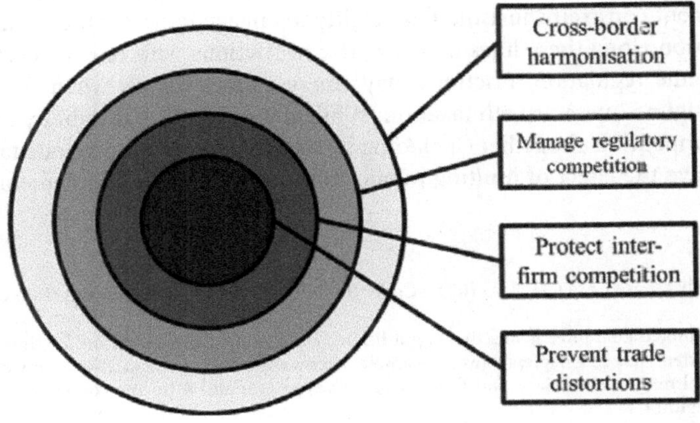

---

[107] In fact, Article 7.1 of CETA (n 33) provides that 'a subsidy means a measure related to trade in goods, which fulfils the conditions set out in Article 1.1 of the SCM Agreement'.

[108] ibid, Article 7.9.

[109] The degree to which they embrace features of the EU model varies from one agreement to another. For a complete mapping, see Rubini (n 92).

The first variety in Figure 1.3 seeks to capture the original – and arguably fundamental – aim of a subsidy control regime, namely the prevention of cross-border trade distortions. Prohibited subsidies within the meaning of the SCM Agreement are the most obvious examples in this sense. A measure that is contingent on the use of domestic content and one that is contingent on export performance have, as their very object, the alteration of trade patterns. To the extent that they do, they can be seen as the functional equivalent of a tariff or a quota and can be treated as such from a legal standpoint (that is, they can be subject to an unqualified prohibition). One can think of other measures having, as their object, the restriction of trade. These include the award of subsidies aimed at compensating domestic firms for the additional costs that they bear (whether relative to foreign rivals or other sectors of the economy).[110]

The second concentric circle is made up of what can be seen as the second central mission of any regime aimed at regulating the award of subsidies, namely the protection of inter-firm competition. It is not difficult to think of instances where the point of intervention is the preservation of firms' ability and incentive to lower their costs, improve their products and develop new ones. Rescue and restructuring aid are interventions that have been mentioned above and that can significantly affect competition. Other frequently cited measures include unlimited guarantees, which give recipients a substantial advantage that rivals cannot aspire to obtain under normal market conditions.[111] Operating subsidies, the point of which is to cover the current expenditures of a firm (such as the energy consumed, employee costs or the rent of premises[112]), and therefore keep a firm artificially afloat, also come to mind as an example.

The third circle depicts a more ambitious iteration of the discipline, that is, one that seeks to manage competition among States (as opposed to firms).[113] Even though it does not prevent regulatory rivalry across borders, this variety of enforcement constrains jurisdictions' ability to engage in it. For the same reason, intervention along these lines may give rise to frictions with one or several areas of economic regulation. Frictions may emerge, for instance, when the subsidy control regime interacts with taxation. While not preventing the ability to engage in tax competition altogether (including by setting, inter alia, corporate tax rates), it may have the effect of limiting public authorities' ability to implement certain

---

[110] See in this sense Case C-173/73 *Italy v Commission*, EU:C:1974:71 and the analysis in Chapters 3 and 4.

[111] An unlimited guarantee is one that is not limited in terms of the amount and/or time. They are discussed extensively in Chapters 3 (as an example of a measure that can be safely presumed to depart from normal market conditions and thus award an advantage) and 8 (in the context of the foreign subsidies regime).

[112] Generally speaking, the EU State aid regime sees with reluctance so-called 'operating aid', that is, 'aid aimed to reduce an undertaking's current expenditure' – as defined in para 19 of the Guidelines on regional aid (n 7).

[113] This term is used in Christopher McMahon, 'Selectivity as discrimination: lessons from the case law on fiscal measures for identifying State aid' (2024) 43 Yearbook of European Law 261.

measures deemed harmful.[114] Utilities regulation – to mention a second example – may also come into conflict with this variety of enforcement. Friction may emerge, for instance, where the subsidy control regime limits the extent to which public authorities can subsidise fibre-based telecommunications infrastructure.[115]

The fourth circle captures an approach to law and policy-making that results in (de facto) harmonisation of regulation across jurisdictions, that is, in States sharing a common set of rules in a particular area of the law. The application of subsidy control provisions in such a way may be a consequence of intervention aimed at addressing a risk of fragmentation that could come from unfettered regulatory competition. For example, the introduction of different electricity capacity mechanisms to ensure the security of energy supplies may be found to have such potential for distortions that the adoption of a uniform response via the subsidy control regime is deemed necessary.[116] In other instances, regulatory harmonisation may play a gap-filling role, thereby complementing a pre-existing regime (or correcting and/or refining the latter).

5.2. Factors Influencing the Reach and Scope of the Regime

As already pointed out above, a subsidy control regime will be more or less far-reaching (that is, it will encompass more or fewer of the varieties identified in Figure 1.3) based on the substantive and institutional choices made. As far as substance is concerned, the broader the range of measures potentially caught by the regime, the more likely it is that it will be relied upon to manage regulatory competition and/or for harmonisation purposes. The scope and ambition of intervention, in other words, depends in part on how the notion of subsidy (or State aid) is defined. If only clear-cut measures (that is, positive transfers of State resources attributable to a public authority and expressly aimed at a distinct firm or group thereof) are subject to the regime, it is more likely that intervention will remain confined to the two inner circles depicted in Figure 1.3. If, conversely, the notion of subsidy or State aid were construed more expansively, the potential for the regime to constrain regulation or, indeed, harmonise it would be greater.

This point is arguably best illustrated by reference to two specific examples. Suppose that the scope of action under the subsidy control regime is broad enough to encompass not just clear-cut subsidies but also regulatory advantages having an equivalent effect to a subsidy. Consider, more precisely, the example of a municipality that seeks to favour taxis (or cabs) by allowing them to use bus lanes, to

---

[114] See for instance Joined Cases C-51/19 P and C-64/19 P *World Duty Free Group SA and Spain v Commission*, EU:C:2021:793.

[115] See for instance Guidelines on State aid for broadband networks [2023] OJ C36/1.

[116] Commission, 'State aid: Sector Inquiry report gives guidance on capacity mechanisms' IP/16/4021 (Brussels, 30 November 2016).

the detriment of other private hire services.[117] Consider, also, an instance where legislation limits the opening hours of grocery stores exceeding a certain size (or, similarly, chains exceeding a certain number of stores) with a view to giving smaller ventures a competitive advantage.[118] If such measures (and comparable ones) were deemed to fall within the scope of the regime, intervention in the name of subsidy control would have significant potential to write or rewrite economic regulation in many areas.

The role of institutional factors in shaping the reach and scope of a regime is, if anything, more apparent. An entity like the Commission, which is empowered to interpret the relevant legal concepts and which is, in addition, in charge of policy-making, can influence the evolution of the system (and move it towards its outer boundaries as defined in Figure 1.3) in two main ways. To the extent that its ability to shape policy is determined, at least in part, by the scope of the notion of subsidy (or State aid), an administrative authority would have an incentive to favour a relatively expansive interpretation of the regime. One can therefore expect it to seek to expand the reach of the relevant concepts so as to capture a wider range of measures. An adjudicating body (such as those around which the WTO model revolves), by contrast, has less of an incentive to construe provisions broadly.

Similarly, an administrative authority's ability to engage in policy-making provides it with significant leeway to venture into the outer limits of the regime. One must bear in mind, in this regard, that both the management of regulatory competition and the harmonisation of national legislation require the imposition of positive duties on public authorities (that is, an obligation to behave in specific ways or to adopt certain measures). Intervention along these lines, moreover, may only be effective where positive obligations are applicable across the board, as opposed to implemented on a case-by-case basis in relation of a specific award. Thus, the adjudication of disputes by independent decision-making bodies (such as the ones created by virtue of WTO law) may not be particularly conducive to the more ambitious styles of enforcement. Under the EU model, by contrast, the Commission can rely on a variety of instruments, from individual decisions to soft law instruments, which allow it to engage in effective policy-making.

6. Conclusions

The main conclusion to draw from this chapter is that a subsidy control regime is an indispensable feature of any trade agreement. Failing to address the distortions resulting from the unfettered support of firms and industries would frustrate the very economic gains that one can expect from the removal of

---

[117] Case C-518/13 *Eventech Ltd v The Parking Adjudicator*, EU:C:2015:9.
[118] See for instance the restrictions introduced, by virtue of the Sunday Trading Act 1994, which constrain the ability of large shops to open for more than six consecutive hours on Sundays.

barriers to cross-border exchanges. If anything, the need for a legal framework constraining the ability to award subsidies is all the more pressing where the trade agreement is ambitious and far-reaching. This economic context helps to explain why the EU regime is more sophisticated and developed than any other. Instead of relying on decentralised enforcement like its WTO counterpart, the TFEU entrusts the Commission with the power to interpret the notion of State aid and with the necessary means and discretion to develop a comprehensive policy in the area.

A second conclusion is that the legal regulation of subsidies requires careful balancing. While the potential negative effects of State support are well understood, the task is complicated by the fact that public intervention does not necessarily have the object of restricting competition and/or trade. Subsidies and similar measures may be implemented for unrelated reasons, such as the need to address market failures. The challenge, from a legal standpoint, is to design a system that makes it possible to filter out interventions that are a net source of benefits (in the sense that the contribution to a public interest objective outweighs any distortions of trade and competition). Unlike the WTO model, the EU State aid system – as much as every regime inspired by it – expressly provides for such balancing. The Commission has the task of defining the instances where State aid is in the EU interest.

There is a third lesson to draw from the chapter. The substantive and institutional choices made when designing a subsidy control regime tend to have a self-reinforcing effect. In other words, a system that is conceived to ensure that subsidies are subject to tight control will naturally evolve to become more ambitious and far-reaching than those designed, from the outset, to be more modest and less intrusive (such as the SCM Agreement and the provisions in most trade deals). The EU model had all the ingredients to emerge as a relatively expansive regime. The status of the Commission as a supranational authority means that it is better insulated from the short-term political pressures that might curtail the ambition and/or effectiveness of enforcement. The very fact that its policy-making powers are tied to the substantive scope of the notion of State aid also means that the Commission has a natural incentive to construe Article 107(1) TFEU relatively broadly.

Coming back to the categories identified in Figure 1.3, a subsidy control regime that has been designed to be relatively expansive – such as the EU State aid system – will naturally venture into the varieties of enforcement that make up the outer boundaries of the discipline. The regime, in other words, may be relied upon as a tool to manage regulatory competition among jurisdictions. These varieties of enforcement are necessarily more controversial insofar as they come into conflict with other legal disciplines. The management of regulatory competition constrains, by definition, States' ability to exercise their powers in certain areas overlapping with subsidy control, such as taxation or utilities regulation. In some instances, enforcement may go as far as to mandate a common set of rules across all jurisdictions (that is, regulatory harmonisation).

The self-reinforcing tendency towards expansion of a subsidy control regime is manifested, in particular, in the way its substantive scope is construed. An aspect of this phenomenon has already been mentioned above. In the EU legal order, State intervention falls within the scope of Article 107(1) TFEU where a measure 'distorts or threatens to distort competition' and, in addition, 'affects trade between Member States'. As EU law stands, however, the threshold of effects is deemed met in virtually every instance. The mere fact that the award of a selective advantage is established is in essence sufficient, in practice, for the regime to come into play. As a result, the impact of public interventions on trade and competition plays no meaningful role when drawing the boundaries of Article 107(1) TFEU. By and large, they are only considered once an advantage has been characterised as State aid and the Commission has discharged its burden of proof.

There are other building blocks that make up the substantive scope of the regime and where the tendency of the regime to venture into its outer boundaries can be observed. These building blocks are explored in detail in Chapters 2 to 4, which are based on the EU model. One fundamental question, addressed in Chapter 2, relates to whether the notion of subsidy (or State aid) is confined to measures that involve financial support from a public authority or whether, instead, it comprises any regulatory advantage – irrespective of whether it is awarded by means of State resources. The latter interpretation would result in a significant expansion of the scope of the regime; it would capture every means by which public authorities favour some firms over others. Another set of questions, considered in Chapters 3 and 4, relates to what it means to favour certain firms or economic activity. There is not a uniform approach to, inter alia, the meaning of concepts such as 'selectivity' (in EU law) or 'specificity' (in the WTO regime). Crucially, the scope and ambition of the regime are highly sensitive to the interpretation that is embraced.

There is a common theme that cuts across the three chapters that follow. As one would expect, the Commission, as the entity in charge of formulating EU State aid policy, consistently favours a relatively expansive understanding of the scope of Article 107(1) TFEU, which allows significant leeway to manage regulatory competition and, on occasion, to engage in regulatory harmonisation. Inevitably, this tendency comes into conflict with EU Member States' ability to formulate and implement economic policies in a variety of key industries, such as energy. In some instances, frictions arise between the EU State aid system and some core EU Member States' competences, and in particular in the field of taxation (arguably the very manifestation of sovereignty). Against this background, the analysis focuses on the interpretative choices made by the Court when presented with this tension.

2

The Boundaries of the Notion of Aid

1. Between Subsidies and Regulation

The letter of Article 107(1) TFEU is both vague and potentially far-reaching. It is vague in the sense that it declares that 'any aid' is, unless otherwise provided in the Treaty, incompatible with the internal market. It is potentially far-reaching insofar as it clarifies that an aid within the meaning of the provision may be granted 'in any form whatsoever'. One does not need a great deal of imagination to realise that this wording can be construed as potentially capturing a vast array of economic policy measures. Governments and legislatures favour specific firms and economic activities in myriad ways. It is not infrequent for regulation to alleviate the burden it imposes on small and medium-sized enterprises.[1] More generally, legislation can be tweaked to privilege some economic actors over others.[2] For instance, it may seek to redistribute wealth across the private sector. Regulation introducing a price floor, for instance, transfers resources from consumers to domestic producers to the extent that it reduces the intensity of competition to which the latter are subject.[3]

Early on, the Court clarified that aid within the meaning of (what is now) Article 107(1) TFEU is more than a mere subsidy in the narrow sense – that is, a positive transfer of resources from a public authority (such as a grant).[4] It has never been in doubt that the provision applies to negative transfers, whereby the public authority foregoes monies that would otherwise be due. An aid within the meaning of the provision may exist, therefore, where a public authority sells goods or services below the market price,[5] or, similarly, where it grants a loan at a

---

[1] For instance, labour legislation sometimes becomes more stringent as the number of employees exceeds a certain figure. See in this sense Luis Garicano, Claire Lelarge and John Van Reenen, 'Firm Size Distortions and the Productivity Distribution: Evidence from France' (2016) 106 American Economic Review 3439.

[2] For instance, regulation may be tweaked to favour entry in a recently liberalised industry. The mechanisms by which entry may be favoured may include access obligations and the setting of wholesale and/or retail prices. For an overview, see Christopher Decker, *Modern Economic Regulation: An Introduction to Theory and Practice* (Cambridge University Press 2023).

[3] See, for a discussion, Carlos Eduardo Hernández and Santiago Cantillo-Cleves, 'A toolkit for setting and evaluating price floors' (2024) 232 Journal of Public Economics 105084.

[4] Case 30/59 *De Gezamenlijke Steenkolenmijnen in Limburg v High Authority*, EU:C:1961:2, 19.

[5] Commission Notice on the notion of State aid as referred to in Article 107(1) of the Treaty on the Functioning of the European Union [2016] OJ C262/1, para 52.

preferential interest rate.[6] It has also been clear that the transfer of resources may be implicit, that is, concealed in another measure. For instance, the purchase of goods by a public authority above the market price may also qualify as aid.[7] What matters, the Court clarified in *Steenkolenmijnen*, is that the measure 'mitigate[s] the charges which are normally included in the budget of an undertaking'.[8]

Subsequent case law had to define the boundaries of the notion of aid, and more precisely what the drafters of the TFEU meant when they referred to 'any aid' granted 'in any form whatsoever'. The question that the Court of Justice (hereinafter, the 'Court' or the 'ECJ') had to address was whether, and to what extent, Article 107 TFEU (and/or its predecessors) could become an instrument for the monitoring and re-regulation of EU Member States' economic policies. There was no doubt after *Steenkolenmijnen* that aid is more than a positive and explicit transfer of State resources. It was unclear, on the other hand, whether the provision entrusted the Commission with the power to control and shape any measure distorting competition and trade by favouring certain firms or certain activities. It was unclear, in other words, how much and how often Article 107(1) TFEU could interfere with regulatory choices made by EU Member States. This question has significant substantive and institutional consequences.

There are, prima facie, compelling arguments in support of an expansive understanding of the notion of aid. The first of these relates to the effectiveness of Article 107(1) TFEU. If the regime is to fulfil its function, it must apply to all regulatory measures favouring certain firms or activities. One could also advance an argument based on substantive consistency. It would only be logical to give the same legal treatment to all measures having the same object and effect, irrespective of the regulatory technique on which the public authority relies to attain its aims. For instance, whether a sector is favoured by means of direct grants or, alternatively, by means of an alleviation of some of their legal obligations is likely to be inconsequential from an economic perspective. Introducing legal distinctions between essentially equivalent practices, therefore, would not only be arbitrary but would pave the way for opportunistic behaviour by public authorities. Escaping the application of Article 107(1) TFEU would be as simple as choosing a particular regulatory technique.

Arguments in favour of a relatively narrow understanding of the notion of aid are no less compelling. When drawing the boundaries of Article 107(1) TFEU, one must bear in mind that the – then – European Economic Community was never designed to exercise the functions of a fully-fledged State. Any competences given to the new organisation would have been by definition limited and expressly conferred to it by the founding Member States.[9] It would therefore be difficult

---

[6] ibid, paras 108–114.

[7] ibid, para 84.

[8] *Steenkolenmijnen* (n 4), 19.

[9] For a general overview of the issue, see Vlad Constantinesco, *Compétences et pouvoirs dans les communautés européennes: contribution à l'étude de la nature juridique des communautés* (LGDJ 1974) and Joseph Weiler, 'The Community System: the Dual Character of Supranationalism' (1981) 1 Yearbook of European Law 267; and Pierre Pescatore, *Le droit de l'intégration* (Bruylant 2005).

to claim, against this background, that Article 107(1) TFEU had been intended to entrust the Commission with a general power to evaluate – and, if necessary, correct – every regulatory advantage distorting competition and trade. The assumption, from this perspective, is that any conferral of competences to the EU institutions is by definition narrow and has finite boundaries.[10]

A second argument in support of a narrow interpretation of Article 107(1) TFEU is a procedural one. The State aid regime comes with a number of procedural obligations for EU Member States, the kernel of which is enshrined in Article 108 TFEU. As a matter of principle (that is, in the absence of secondary legislation providing for an exemption), any plans to award new aid are to be notified to the Commission. In addition, existing aid is to be kept under supervision. One could convincingly argue that this institutional apparatus was not designed to oversee EU Member States' exercise of regulatory powers at large. The demands that it would place on the latter would be significant, not to mention the legal uncertainty that a system with a wide scope of application is likely to have. In addition, it would require the Commission to devote substantial resources to ensure the appropriate exercise of its competences.

Figure 2.1 Approaches to the notion of aid

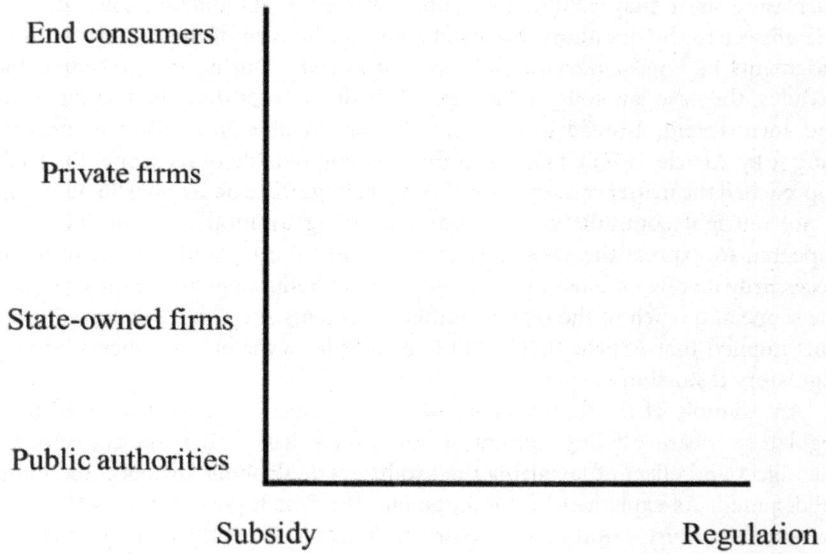

The essence of the debate about the scope of the notion of aid is captured in Figure 2.1. As a starting point, it is helpful to think of the potential approaches to the definition of the notion of aid as a range of options along two variables. The

---

[10] See, for a discussion, Robert Schütze, 'On "Federal" Ground: The European Union as an (Inter)national Phenomenon' (2009) 46 Common Market Law Review 1069.

horizontal axis in the figure presents the spectrum ranging between the notion of subsidy in the narrow sense (defined as an explicit and positive transfer of public resources) and that of regulation. As far as this variable is concerned, the question relates to how far the scope of Article 107(1) TFEU moves away from subsidies in the strict sense of the term and how close it gets to encompassing regulatory advantages granted by EU Member States. The vertical axis, in turn, addresses the spectrum of bodies potentially awarding the measures. At the lower end of the axis, one can identify the central government, which is unquestionably subject to the regime (and this insofar as the letter of the provision refers to the State). At the upper end, there are private firms and individuals. The question, as far as this dimension is concerned, relates to which actors are subject to the provision.

2. The Formative Case Law: An Ad Hoc Approach to the Notion of Aid

2.1. From *Van Tiggele* to *Sloman Neptun*

Surprising as it may sound, the Court only gave an unambiguous, discernible answer to the questions discussed above at the turn of the century, with the judgments in *PreussenElektra* and *Stardust Marine*. During the preceding four decades, the case law followed an approach that is best described as piecemeal and inconsistent. Instead of drawing a clear dividing line between measures caught by Article 107(1) TFEU and those falling outside of its scope, the Court approached the matter case-by-case, thereby giving rise to occasional fluctuations – if not outright contradictions – from one ruling to another. Some judgments appeared to express the view that an aid within the meaning of the provision necessarily involves the use of State resources; thereby suggesting a major limit to the scope and reach of the regime. Other judgments suggested the opposite, and thus implied that Article 107(1) TFEU could play a major role when managing regulatory distortions.

An example of the first category of cases is *Van Tiggele*, which concerned a regulatory measure fixing minimum prices for spirits.[11] That the measure had the object and effect of favouring the producers of alcoholic drinks could hardly be disputed. As explained in the judgment, the Dutch government intended to protect the industry and help it return to 'normal competitive conditions'.[12] By transferring wealth from consumers to producers, the measure worked in practice as an industry-wide crisis cartel.[13] In spite of this fact, the Court concluded that the selective advantage granted to the sector was not caught by Article 107(1) TFEU. This was so, the judgment explained, insofar as the said benefit was 'not

---

[11] Case C-82/77 *Openbaar Ministerie v Jacobus Philippus van Tiggele*, EU:C:1978:10.
[12] ibid, para 9.
[13] ibid, para 18.

granted, directly or indirectly, through State resources'.[14] The Court presented this condition as axiomatic. It did so again 15 years later, in *Sloman Neptun*, where it held that Article 107(1) TFEU only applies to measures 'that impose an additional burden for the State'[15] or for the 'public or private bodies designated or established by the State'.[16] Several subsequent judgments hinted at a similar understanding of the provision.[17]

In between *Van Tiggele* and *Sloman Neptun*, however, the Court delivered judgments relying on a different interpretation of the scope of Article 107(1) TFEU. Some of them went as far as to expressly declare that 'aid need not necessarily be financed from State resources to be classified as State aid'.[18] In *Crédit Agricole*, the Commission took issue with the fact that the French government had encouraged the adoption of measures in support of the country's poorest farmers. The peculiarity of the initiative was that the selective advantages at issue were funded with the surplus accumulated over the years by the *Caisse nationale de crédit agricole*.[19] One could argue, accordingly, that the measures were not funded by State resources, as *Van Tiggele* unambiguously required. In fact, the Commission acknowledged that the encouragement by the French government did not amount to State aid strictly speaking, but should be given the same legal treatment as a measure having an equivalent effect.[20] It argued, in other words, that the scope of the regime should not depend on the regulatory technique on which the EU Member State relies, and that the application of the rules should adapt to prevent their circumvention.

The Court rejected the Commission's approach, concluding that, under EU law, there is no such thing as a measure having an equivalent effect to State aid. On the other hand, it agreed that the measures at issue in the case were caught by (what would become) Article 107(1) TFEU. The ECJ argued, in this sense, that the legal innovation introduced by the Commission was not necessary to reach this conclusion. The wording of the provision, it held, was broad enough to encompass 'any' measure aimed at favouring certain activities or certain firms, without the need to show that it involves, always and everywhere, the use of State resources. According to this interpretation, the notion of aid encompasses not just measures adopted by governments, but also those implemented by public or private bodies in charge of awarding and/or administering them.[21]

---

[14] ibid, para 25.

[15] Joined Cases C-72/91 and C-73/91 *Firma Sloman Neptun Schiffahrts AG v Seebetriebsrat Bodo Ziesemer der Sloman Neptun Schiffahrts AG*, EU:C:1993:97, para 21.

[16] ibid, para 19.

[17] See in particular Case C-189/91 *Petra Kirsammer-Hack v Nurhan Sidal*, EU:C:1993:907; and Joined Cases C-52/97, C-53/97 and C-54/97 *Epifanio Viscido and others v Ente Poste Italiane*, EU:C:1998:209.

[18] Case 290/83 *Commission v French Republic*, EU:C:1985:37, para 14.

[19] ibid, para 2.

[20] ibid, para 9: 'In those circumstances the Commission considers that the grant in question is a measure having an effect equivalent to State aid, which is incompatible with the common market [...]. By its action the French Government created a situation equivalent to that resulting from the grant of State aid and, in so doing, has not abstained from causing measures to be taken which are liable to jeopardize the attainment of the objectives of the Treaty [...]'.

[21] ibid, para 14.

Crédit Agricole could be read as suggesting that the crucial consideration when qualifying a measure as aid is not so much whether it involves the use of State resources (which is what the Court held unambiguously in *Van Tiggele*) but rather whether the intervention is imputable to the State. The subsequent judgment in *Van der Kooy*[22] confirmed this impression. The case concerned the legal characterisation of a preferential tariff given by a gas supplier to glasshouse growers of agricultural products.[23] The Court's approach departed from that adopted in *Van Tiggele* in that it did not revolve around whether the measure involved the use of State resources, but rather around whether the preferential tariff was attributable to the Dutch government. When applying this criterion to the facts of the case, the ECJ noted, first, that the EU Member State owned 50% of the shares in the gas supplier and that it could appoint half the members of its supervisory board.[24] It held that this veto power meant that the energy company acted 'under the control and on the instructions of the public authorities'.[25]

2.2. Two Conflicting Approaches to the Limits of the Notion of Aid

Figure 2.2 Two conflicting approaches to the notion of aid

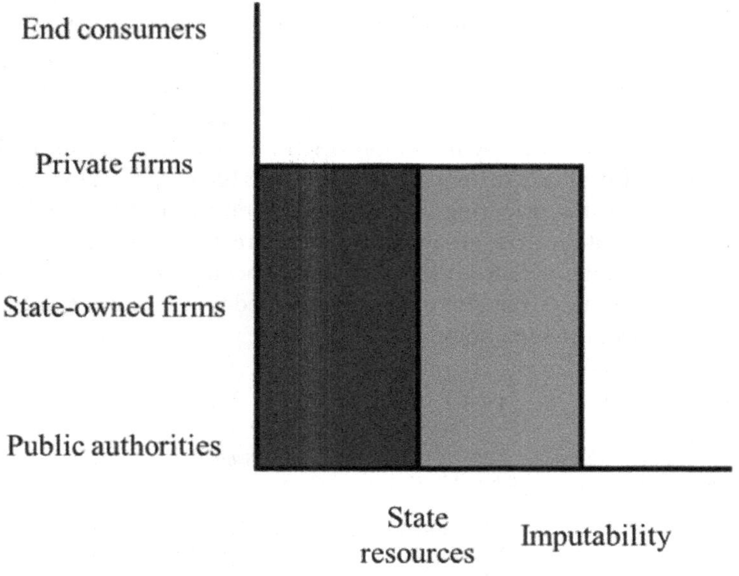

---

[22] Joined Cases C-67/85, C-68/85 and C-70/85 *Kwekerij Gebroeders van der Kooy BV and others v Commission*, EU:C:1988:38.

[23] ibid, para 3.

[24] ibid, para 36.

[25] ibid, para 37.

The two lines of case law (respectively, the *Van Tiggele–Sloman Neptun* line and the *Crédit Agricole–Van der Kooy* line) reflect two conflicting approaches to the limits of the notion of aid. These conflicting approaches are captured in Figure 2.2. The *Van Tiggele–Sloman Neptun* line favoured a narrower Article 107(1) TFEU. The limit of the notion of aid along the horizontal axis would be the use of 'State resources'. Selective advantages that do not involve the use of State resources, but amount to a mere regulatory privilege (as in *Sloman Neptun*) or the redistribution of private resources (as in *Van Tiggele*), would fall outside the scope of Article 107(1) TFEU. The *Crédit Agricole–Van der Kooy* line of case law drew a different boundary. The crucial consideration, according to these two judgments, is whether the measure is imputable to the State, and more precisely whether the transfer of resources (whether public or private) is mandated by the government. This second approach implies that the scope of Article 107(1) TFEU is broader.

There seems to be little divergence between the two approaches, on the other hand, as far as the vertical axis is concerned. Both seemed to be premised on the idea that a transfer of resources from consumers to producers, such as the one at stake in *Van Tiggele*, falls outside the scope of Article 107(1) TFEU, even though it necessarily amounts to a selective advantage. Similarly, both lines of case law did not disagree on another key point: a measure need not be formally awarded by a public authority for it to qualify as aid. Both accept that, in certain circumstances, a measure caught by Article 107(1) TFEU may be administered by a private body. This point is, arguably, uncontroversial considering that the letter of the Treaty appears to have foreseen such a factual scenario. The provision refers to aid granted 'by the State' or 'through State resources' and is thus expressly aimed at capturing it.

3. The Rationalisation of the Case Law: *PreussenElektra* and *Stardust Marine*

3.1. Aid must Involve State Resources

3.1.1. PreussenElektra: *Background*

PreussenElektra[26] provided the Court with an opportunity to address the tension between the two lines of case law presented in the preceding section. The factual scenario was particularly suited for settling the issue on a lasting basis. There was no doubt that the measure at the heart of the dispute had been expressly designed to provide a selective advantage to some firms. With a view to promoting the sector, the relevant legislation required suppliers – whether privately- or publicly-owned – to purchase electricity generated from renewable sources within their

---

[26] Case C-379/98 *PreussenElektra AG v Schhleswag AG*, EU:C:2001:160.

region, and at a fixed minimum price.[27] Accordingly, the measure – by necessity imputable to the German State – involved a transfer of resources from suppliers to producers. The question, against this background, was whether it could be characterised as aid within the meaning of Article 107(1) TFEU.

The answer to this question would be positive if one were to follow the *Crédit Agricole–Van der Kooy* line of case law. To the extent that the measure is imputable to the State, one could argue (as the Court held in *Van der Kooy*) that the electricity supplier was acting 'on the instructions of the public authorities'. In its submission, the Commission relied on these precedents to argue that the measure fell within the scope of Article 107(1) TFEU.[28] It noted, in addition, that requiring the use of State resources would open the door to the circumvention of the State aid regime. As suggested above, the applicability of Articles 107 and 108 TFEU would not depend on the substantive issues raised by the measure, but on the regulatory technique chosen by the government to attain its aims.[29] The *Van Tiggele–Sloman Neptun* line of case law, by contrast, would suggest a negative answer to the same question. One should note, in this regard, that the electricity supplier in the case – Schleswag AG – was controlled by a privately-owned firm – PreussenElektra AG.

In his Opinion, Advocate General Jacobs embraced, in categorical terms, the *Van Tiggele–Sloman Neptun* approach to the interpretation of the notion of aid. His conclusions were based, first, on a literal reading of the provision, and, second, on the very evolution of the case law. As mentioned above, the letter of Article 107(1) TFEU refers to 'any aid' in 'any form whatsoever'. In addition, it expressly provides that the aid may be 'granted by a Member State or through State resources'. Contrary to what the Court suggested in *Crédit Agricole*, this wording, he claimed, cannot be interpreted as meaning that aid need not involve the use of State resources. According to the Advocate General, Article 107(1) TFEU is designed to address two scenarios: one in which State resources are directly 'granted by a Member State', and another where such resources are transferred through the intermediary of a public or private body.[30]

Advocate General Jacobs also expressed the view that the case law, by the time of his Opinion, had decisively moved in the direction he favoured. The judgments delivered in the wake of *Sloman Neptun*, including *Kirsammer-Hack*[31] and *Viscido*,[32] all assumed or made explicit that aid within the meaning of the regime involves, always and everywhere, the use of State resources. Therefore, a regulatory advantage such as the one at issue in *Kirsammer-Hack* (which exempted small enterprises from some labour law provisions) is not subject to the State aid regime.

---

[27] ibid, para 8.

[28] See in this sense Opinion of Advocate General Jacobs in Case C-379/98 *PreussenElektra AG v Schhleswag AG*, EU:C:2000:585, para 109.

[29] ibid, para 145.

[30] ibid, para 151.

[31] *Kirsammer-Hack* (n 17).

[32] *Viscido* (n 17).

Against this background, the question, from the Advocate General's perspective, was not so much whether State aid involves the use of State resources as whether the case law should be revisited so as to expand its substantive scope, as argued by the Commission.[33]

On this point, Advocate General Jacobs did not deem it justified to move away from the prevailing interpretation of the provision, even though he accepted the force of some of the counterarguments. In this sense, the Opinion addressed the procedural obligations stemming from Article 108 TFEU. He pointed out that they do not appear to be designed with the transfer of private resources in mind. After all, Article 108 TFEU (and the case law that expanded and fleshed out the obligations of the various actors[34]) suggests that the procedure is, in essence, a dialogue between the awarding EU Member State and the Commission, with interested parties confined to a relatively marginal role.[35] Such an institutional framework, he argued, would be inconsistent with an expansive interpretation of the notion of aid.

The aspects of the Opinion that examine the consequences of the formalistic approach he endorsed are no less interesting. Requiring the use of State resources to trigger Article 107(1) TFEU means that some measures may fall outside the scope of the regime merely by virtue of the regulatory technique on which the public authority relies. On this point, Advocate General Jacobs argued that the consequences of formalism need not be exaggerated.[36] In his view, the legal arsenal available to third parties is sufficiently broad to adequately address any distortions of competition and/or trade resulting from the regulatory advantages falling outside the scope of Article 107(1) TFEU. He noted, in particular, that measures having an equivalent effect to State aid are likely to infringe other EU law provisions.[37] More generally, Advocate General Jacobs noted that expanding the scope of the notion of aid was liable to give rise to legal uncertainty, insofar as it would cast doubt on the compatibility of vast swathes of regulatory measures adopted by EU Member States.[38]

---

[33] Opinion of AG Jacobs in *PreussenElektra* (n 28), para 146 ('The Commission expressly invites the Court to reconsider its existing case-law in view of recent developments in the Community legal order').

[34] ibid, para 156. See in this sense, in particular, the letter of Article 108(3) TFEU, according to which 'The Member State concerned shall not put its proposed measures into effect until this procedure has resulted in a final decision'.

[35] ibid. See in this sense Article 108(2) TFEU, which refers to the 'parties concerned' and invites them to 'submit their comments' and which imposes obligations on the granting EU Member State, which 'shall abolish or alter such aid within a period of time to be determined by the Commission'.

[36] ibid, para 158. According to Advocate General Jacobs, 'the danger of the Member States adopting on a large scale support measures for certain domestic undertakings which are financed through private resources, have the same anticompetitive effects as normal State aid and escape the Commission's control, should not be exaggerated'.

[37] ibid.

[38] ibid, para 157.

3.1.2. PreussenElektra: *Ruling*

The Court followed Advocate General Jacobs' Opinion and ruled that only measures involving the use of State resources qualify as aid.[39] The two scenarios enshrined in the Treaty ('aid granted by a Member State' and aid granted 'through State resources') were understood to concern, respectively, instances where the State resources are involved directly (the first scenario) and indirectly (the second scenario).[40] The Commission's teleological approach to the interpretation of Article 107(1) TFEU, based on the general duty of loyalty that EU Member States have vis-à-vis the Union,[41] was rejected by the Court. According to the judgment, there is no need to preserve the *effet utile* of Article 107(1) TFEU beyond the obligations already enshrined in the letter of the provision.[42] Unlike the rules on competition, the ECJ concluded, the State aid regime does not apply to undertakings.[43]

3.2. The Meaning and Scope of the Notion of State Resources

Even though the Court clarified in *PreussenElektra* that aid within the meaning of Article 107(1) TFEU only encompasses advantages that involve the (direct or indirect) use of State resources, it did not construe the latter concept in the judgment. Defining what counts as State resources is virtually as important as defining the scope of the provision at large. Under a narrow understanding, the concept would only comprise monies originating from public authorities' budgets. If one were to follow this approach, the measures at stake in cases like *Crédit Agricole* and *Van der Kooy* would fall outside the scope of Article 107(1) TFEU. The resources in both cases came from the firms' (respectively, a bank and a gas supplier) regular economic activities. If broadly construed, by contrast, the concept of State resources could encompass the selective advantages at issue in the two cases. Under this alternative understanding of the notion, the defining factor is not so much the origin of the resources as whether they can be deployed by the State to attain its aims.

---

[39] *PreussenElektra* (n 26), para 58.

[40] ibid: 'The distinction made in that provision between "aid granted by a Member State" and aid granted "through State resources" does not signify that all advantages granted by a State, whether financed through State resources or not, constitute aid but is intended merely to bring within that definition both advantages which are granted directly by the State and those granted by a public or private body designated or established by the State'. The duty of sincere cooperation is now enshrined in Article 4(3) TEU.

[41] ibid, para 63.

[42] ibid, para 65.

[43] ibid, para 64: 'it is sufficient to point out that, unlike Article [101] of the Treaty, which concerns only the conduct of undertakings, Article [107] of the Treaty refers directly to measures emanating from the Member States'.

Stardust Marine[44] provided the Court with the opportunity to clarify the meaning and scope of the concept of State resources. The factual scenario in the case was similar to the one considered in *Crédit Agricole*. It concerned, more precisely, a range of measures adopted by some of the subsidiaries of the (then) publicly owned Crédit Lyonnais in support of Stardust Marine.[45] The question was not approached in the same way as it had been in *Crédit Agricole* and *Van der Kooy*. Instead, the Court considered whether the monies of a publicly-owned firm (such as a bank or a public utility) could qualify as State resources within the meaning of Article 107(1) TFEU not because of their origin, but because they were available to the public authorities to pursue their economic policies.[46] In his Opinion, Advocate General Jacobs argued that the availability of the resources – as opposed to their origin – is indeed the key criterion in the assessment.[47]

The Court followed the Opinion and embraced the broad understanding of the concept of State resources. According to the judgment, whether or not the resources 'are permanent assets of the public sector' or part of the public authority's budget are not central considerations. Instead, the crucial factor when evaluating whether a measure falls within the scope of Article 107(1) TFEU is whether the resources 'remain under public control, and therefore available to the competent national authorities'.[48] Thus, where the State is 'capable', as a result of the 'dominant influence' it can exercise over a firm, of 'directing the use of their resources in order, as occasion arises, to finance specific advantages' in favour of other firms, Article 107(1) TFEU will be applicable.[49] The Court noted, in addition, that finding

---

[44] Case C-482/99 *France v Commission*, EU:C:2002:294 (hereinafter, '*Stardust Marine*'). For a comment, see Leigh Hancher, 'Case C-482/99, French Republic v. Commission ("Stardust Marine"), judgment of the full court of 16 May 2002' (2003) 40 Common Market Law Review 739.

[45] ibid, para 13.

[46] ibid, para 35: 'It therefore needs to be examined whether such a situation of State control allows the financial resources of the undertakings subject to that control to be regarded as "State resources", within the meaning of Article [107(1) TFEU], in a case such as the present, in which it is undisputed between the parties that the undertakings in question did not receive financial support from the French authorities before 30 June 1994, such as a guarantee or a specific transfer of funds'. See also the Opinion of Advocate General Jacobs in Case C-482/99 *France v Commission*, EU:C:2001:685, who identified the novelty of the point of law in para 33.

[47] Opinion of AG Jacobs in Stardust Marine (n 46), para 44.

[48] *Stardust Marine* (n 44), para 37: 'Second, it should be recalled that it has already been established in the case-law of the Court that Article [107(1) TFEU] covers all the financial means by which the public authorities may actually support undertakings, irrespective of whether or not those means are permanent assets of the public sector. Therefore, even if the sums corresponding to the measure in question are not permanently held by the Treasury, the fact that they constantly remain under public control, and therefore available to the competent national authorities, is sufficient for them to be categorised as State resources [...]'.

[49] ibid, para 38: 'It follows that, by holding in the contested decision that the resources of public undertakings, such as those of Crédit Lyonnais and its subsidiaries, fell within the control of the State and were therefore at its disposal, the Commission did not misinterpret the term "State resources" in Article [107(1) TFEU]. The State is perfectly capable, by exercising its dominant influence over such undertakings, of directing the use of their resources in order, as occasion arises, to finance specific advantages in favour of other undertakings'.

that aid may be granted through the intermediary of publicly-owned firms does not amount to discrimination within the meaning of Article 345 TFEU.[50]

3.3. Imputability to the State

It is implicit, to the point of being self-evident, that aid must be imputable to the State for it to fall within the scope of Article 107(1) TFEU. The initiative for the adoption of a measure, in other words, must come from a public authority. Even if it is sometimes assumed as a given, establishing imputability is not necessarily straightforward in all cases. It is true that in some instances the issue will be so obvious that it may not even be necessary to spell out explicitly that the criterion is met. Decisions to impose a levy and to award a tax exemption, for example, are, by their very nature, imputable to a public authority. These are measures that only the State can adopt. In other instances, such as those considered by the Court in both *Crédit Agricole* and *Van der Kooy*, the exercise may be more complex. By the same token, the definition that is attached to the concept of imputability may have a significant impact on the boundaries of Article 107(1) TFEU.

Consider a scenario like the one at stake in *Van der Kooy*. One could take the view that, in such a context, the measure is imputable to the Dutch State because it enjoys veto power within the supervisory board. Such an interpretation of the criterion would have significant implications for the State aid regime. It would mean that every decision adopted by a publicly-owned firm is potentially imputable to the State. Any measure it decides to implement, accordingly, could be potentially subject to scrutiny by the Commission and open to challenge by third parties. It is not difficult to see how such an interpretation could influence firms' everyday activities. This understanding of imputability would have an additional consequence: if it were to be followed, it would overlap with the State resources condition. In other words, the fact that the resources of the publicly-owned firm are available to attain its aims would be sufficient to establish that both criteria are met.

Stardust Marine gave a clean answer to the issue of imputability. The overarching idea behind the Court's interpretation is that the control exercised by the public authority over the organisation adopting the measure is insufficient, in and of itself, to show that the criterion is met. The judgment distinguished, in this sense, between the State resources condition (which can be established on the basis of the public authority's ability to influence the use of the relevant monies) and that of imputability. Unlike the former, imputability cannot be presumed to be met always and everywhere. The assessment, therefore, needs to be informed by the relevant legal context and by the economic reality within which the firm operates. The Court pointed out, in this sense, that not all firms are in the same

---

[50] ibid, para 40.

situation vis-à-vis the State and that they may be able to 'act with more or less independence' depending on the degree of autonomy they enjoy.[51]

At the same time, the Court was acutely aware of the difficulties associated with establishing imputability in practice. It addressed this concern by clarifying that the criterion can be shown to be met on the basis of indirect evidence. Accordingly, it is not necessary to show that the measure has been adopted 'on the instructions of the public authorities'.[52] The Commission, or a claimant, can rely on a set of indicators to substantiate its claims. It may be the case, for instance, that the firm cannot adopt any measure without the authorisation of the State or, similarly, that the firm is under a duty to take into account the directives given by a public authority.[53] Other indicators include the entity's 'integration into the structures of the public administration' (whereby a higher degree of integration makes it more likely that the measure is imputable to the State), the 'nature of its activities' (the underlying idea being that measures adopted by firms competing with private operators are less likely to be imputable to the State), and 'the intensity of the supervision exercised by the public authorities'.[54]

3.4. Aid Granted by the State and Through State Resources

The Treaty refers to aid 'granted by a Member State or through State resources'. Following the evolution of the case law, it is arguably more appropriate to say that a measure falls within the scope of Article 107(1) TFEU where it is both granted by the State and through State resources. Where the Treaty hinted at two alternative scenarios, the case law has clarified that the two elements ('granted by a Member State' and 'through State resources') are cumulative requirements. Aid must always be 'granted by a Member State' in the sense that it is necessary to show, on the basis of direct and/or indirect evidence, that the measure under consideration is 'imputable' to a public authority. In addition, an advantage must invariably involve the use of State resources for it to qualify as State aid. As clarified in *PreussenElektra*, not all selective advantages fall within the scope of Article 107(1) TFEU.

One may wonder, in light of the evolution of the case law, whether the rationalisation resulting from *PreussenElektra* and *Stardust Marine* (unduly) reduced

---

[51] ibid, para 52.

[52] ibid, para 54.

[53] ibid, para 55.

[54] ibid, para 56: 'Other indicators might, in certain circumstances, be relevant in concluding that an aid measure taken by a public undertaking is imputable to the State, such as, in particular, its integration into the structures of the public administration, the nature of its activities and the exercise of the latter on the market in normal conditions of competition with private operators, the legal status of the undertaking (in the sense of its being subject to public law or ordinary company law), the intensity of the supervision exercised by the public authorities over the management of the undertaking, or any other indicator showing, in the particular case, an involvement by the public authorities in the adoption of a measure or the unlikelihood of their not being involved, having regard also to the compass of the measure, its content or the conditions which it contains'.

the scope of Article 107(1) TFEU. There are compelling reasons to conclude that these two seminal judgments did not have the object or effect of narrowing the reach of the regime. Instead, they provided the coherent structure that pre-existing case law lacked and introduced a set of concepts that can be applied consistently. Contrary to how it may appear, the scope of Article 107(1) TFEU remained virtually unchanged. For instance, the measures at issue in both *Crédit Agricole* and *Van der Kooy* would still qualify as aid in the wake of *PreussenElektra* and *Stardust Marine*. The route to reach that conclusion would be a different one. However, the outcome would be the same. The novelty, if there is one, is methodological rather than substantive.

Figure 2.3 The rationalisation of the case law

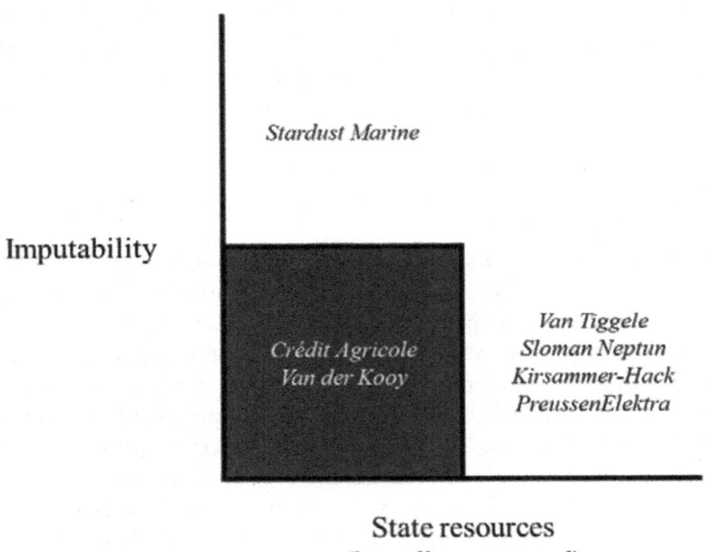

The way the case law was restructured and rationalised is best explained in light of the variables depicted in Figure 2.3. As far as the horizontal axis is concerned, *PreussenElektra* defined the outer boundary of the regime. Regulatory advantages can fall within the scope of Article 107(1) TFEU provided that they involve the use of State resources. *Stardust Marine*, in turn, made it clear that the relevant criterion to establish whether this condition is met rests on the public authority's ability to make use of the monies to attain its aims. Following this development, there should be little doubt that State resources were involved in *Crédit Agricole* and *Van der Kooy*. In both cases, the public authorities were able to direct the state-owned entities to support some firms. *Van Tiggele*, where the resources flowed from consumers to producers, would remain outside the scope of Article 107(1)

TFEU (but not EU law at large).[55] The same would be true of a regulatory advantage such as the one awarded in *Kirsammer-Hack*.

The vertical axis, in turn, relates to the imputability criterion. The relevant consideration, for Article 107(1) TFEU to come into play, is not the (public or private) status of the body adopting the measure. What matters is whether the measure can be attributed to the State. The degree of closeness to the State is what determines, in practice, the ease with which imputability can be established. Understood in this sense, there is little doubt that this criterion was met in both *Crédit Agricole* and *Van der Kooy*. The former is arguably the case that best illustrates this point. As explained above, there was evidence that the measures in the former had been expressly instigated by the French government. In *Van der Kooy*, the Court was not satisfied that the criterion was met merely because the gas supplier was owned by the Dutch State (which, incidentally, was the error of law committed by the Commission in *Stardust Marine*). The ECJ relied not just on the fact that the government had veto power over the tariffs but also on the fact that this veto power had been effectively exercised in the past, thereby showing that it was not merely hypothetical.[56]

4. The Case Law after Rationalisation

4.1. Mapping the Remaining Uncertainties

The rationalisation exercise undertaken in *PreussenElektra* and *Stardust Marine* drew clear, discernible boundaries around the notion of aid. The Court's approach could be readily applied in subsequent cases to provide a straightforward answer to some issues of law. In *ENEA*, for instance, the Court held that an obligation – placed on both public and private undertakings – to purchase electricity produced by cogeneration did not amount to aid.[57] The analysis in the judgment combines elements of both seminal rulings. The Court referred to *PreussenElektra* to point out that a mere purchasing requirement does not involve the use of State resources.[58] *Stardust Marine*, in turn, was relied upon to conclude that the purchasing behaviour of the public undertakings was not imputable to the State.[59] In *Poste Italiane*, to mention another example, the Court held that a regulatory duty to

---

[55] One could argue that, in such a context, State resources could be involved insofar as minimum prices might have an impact on the tax receipts for the State. This argument, however, has been expressly rejected by the Court. See in this sense *PreussenElektra* (n 26), para 62, which in turn refers to *Sloman Neptun* (n 15), para 21, and Case C-200/97 *Ecotrade Srl v Altiforni e Ferriere di Servola SpA*, EU:C:1998:402, para 36.

[56] *van der Kooy* (n 22), para 36: 'Gasunie and the Landbouwschap have on two occasions given effect to the Commission's representations to the Netherlands Government seeking an amendment of the horticultural tariff.'

[57] Case C-329/15 *ENEA SA v Prezes Urzędu Regulacji Energetyki*, EU:C:2017:671.

[58] ibid, para 24.

[59] ibid, para 21.

open an account with Poste Italiane did not involve, in and of itself, the use of State resources, even though it necessarily favoured the incumbent postal operator in the country.[60] There were, conversely, instances where it was unquestionable that a measure adopted by a publicly-owned firm involved the use of State resources and was imputable to the State.[61]

However, *PreussenElektra* and *Stardust Marine* did not and could not foresee all factual scenarios in which the meaning of imputability and State resources would be contentious. The subsequent refinements and clarifications of the case law revolve around two main themes. The first concerns instances where the measure is awarded by means of a private (or semi-private) organisation with regulatory or quasi-regulatory functions. It was clear from the early case law that such scenarios can be caught by Article 107(1) TFEU and that the provision had anticipated that governments might attempt to circumvent the regime by entrusting the award of measures to non-public bodies.[62] As mentioned above, *Sloman Neptun* made an express reference to 'public or private bodies designated or established by the State'.[63] As a result of the factual peculiarities of both *PreussenElektra* and *Stardust Marine*, however, the two seminal rulings did not shed light on the applicability of the rationalised framework beyond the public sector.

A second factual scenario on which *PreussenElektra* did not provide sufficient guidance, and which became perpetually contentious in the years that followed, revolves around instances where there is some form of charge, levy or tax involved. Suppose that, in a context such as the one at stake in *PreussenElektra*, the incentives to generate renewable electricity do not take the form of a fixed purchase price but are financed by means of a surcharge imposed on final consumers. Suppose, in addition, that the suppliers are compensated for the purchasing obligation via the said surcharge. *PreussenElektra* does not provide an unequivocal answer about the legal characterisation of these scenarios. One could argue, on the one hand, that the existence of a surcharge does not change the private nature of the transfer. It is possible to claim, on the other hand, that this form of intervention is not comparable to *PreussenElektra*. After all, the State directs how the funds are put to use. The tension between these two interpretations is at the origin of a stream of cases that reached the Court.

4.2. Measures Adopted by Private (or Semi-Private) Bodies

4.2.1. Background

Private (or semi-private) bodies with regulatory or quasi-regulatory functions are not rare in the EU Member States' legal order. These bodies interact with

---

governments to fulfil several roles, such as the regulation of professions, the definition of standards for products or services and the promotion of economic activities.
Even when they are nominally private, these bodies tend to be closely affiliated
with the State. Their very existence may be mandated by law, and they may be
subject to government supervision. In addition, it is not unusual that government
representatives provide advice or sit on the boards of these organisations alongside
private individuals sitting on behalf of a trade or activity. For the purposes of the
application of Article 107(1) TFEU, the grey area within which these bodies operate raises the question of whether the resources they manage can be characterised
as 'State resources' and, in the same vein, whether decisions about the allocation of
these resources are imputable to the State.

The Court was confronted with a scenario of this nature shortly after
Stardust Marine, in the preliminary reference in *Pearle*.[64] The case concerned a
levy imposed by a trade association for the purposes of funding an advertising
campaign promoting opticians' businesses. The facts show how blurred the line
between the private and the public sector can be in these scenarios: while the trade
association was governed by public law, the levy itself was imposed at the instiga-
tion of a private association.[65] Even though there was some degree of involvement
by public authorities, the Court concluded that the measures were neither imputable to the State,[66] nor did they involve the use of State resources.[67] As far as the
latter criterion is concerned, the Court noted that at no point were the resources
'made available to the national authorities'. As to imputability, the judgment briefly
points out, in a single paragraph, that the initiative was a private one, with the
trade association merely serving as a 'vehicle' for the collection and allocation of
the funds.[68] The Court was confronted with a similar scenario, and reached the
same conclusion, in *Doux Élevage*.[69]

4.2.2. Establishing Imputability

One of the lessons to draw from the case law that followed *Pearle* is that the essence
of the test laid down in *Stardust Marine*, which was conceived for publicly-owned
firms, can be transposed, *mutatis mutandis*, to measures adopted by private (or
semi-private) bodies with a regulatory or a quasi-regulatory function. Accordingly,
the ease with which imputability can be established depends on how close the

---

[64] Case C-345/02 *Pearle BV, Hans Prijs Optiek Franchise BV and Rinck Opticiëns BV v Hoofdbedrijfschap Ambachten*, EU:C:2004:448.

[65] ibid, para 27.

[66] ibid, para 37 ('the file clearly shows that the initiative for the organisation and operation of that advertising campaign was that of the NUVO, a private association of opticians, and not that of the Board').

[67] ibid, para 36 ('it does not in the circumstances of the case appear that the advertising campaign was funded by resources made available to the national authorities').

[68] ibid, paras 37 and 38.

[69] Case C-677/11 *Doux Élevage SNC and Coopérative agricole UKL-ARREE v Ministère de l'Agriculture, de l'Alimentation, de la Pêche, de la Ruralité et de l'Aménagement du territoire and Comité interprofessionnel de la dinde française (CIDEF)*, EU:C:2013:348.

body is to the State and the degree of autonomy it enjoys in relation to it. In some instances, the legislative framework and the degree of governmental oversight will mean that this criterion will be straightforward to establish. In *Salvat*,[70] for instance, a careful look at the arguments raised by the parties showed that they did not seriously question that the relevant measures (aimed at restructuring wine production in a region of the country) could be attributed to the French government.[71] The initiative to raise a parafiscal charge came from an inter-branch committee created by law, with an executive board made up of elected representatives and subject to supervision by the relevant Minister.[72]

Where the State does not exercise a comparable degree of control, it will be more difficult to prove that the imputability criterion is met. *Banca Tercas* eloquently illustrates how the analysis may need to be adjusted to the relevant circumstances.[73] The case concerned a decision adopted by a consortium of Italian banks, governed by private law. One of the core missions of this body is to guarantee its members' deposits.[74] The specific issue considered by the Court was whether the decision by the consortium to intervene in favour of a bank under special administration was imputable to the State. The analysis, which resulted in the dismissal of the appeal brought by the Commission, echoes *Stardust Marine*. The Court explained that the 'appropriate evidence' that is required to establish imputability to the requisite legal standard varies depending on the context.[75] In this sense, the fact that the body adopting the measure is a private entity necessarily affects the nature and quality of the evidence to be provided. This fact, however, does not mean that the standard of proof is a different one.[76]

4.2.3. *State Resources and Private Bodies*

One of the key ideas underpinning *PreussenElektra* and *Stardust Marine* is that a regulatory obligation requiring a transfer of private resources does not amount, in and of itself, to an aid. As *Pearle* showed, it does not matter whether this transfer takes the form of an obligation to purchase or a contribution financing the

---

[70] Case T-136/05 *EARL Salvat père & fils, Comité interprofessionnel des vins doux naturels et vins de liqueur à appellations contrôlées (CIVDN) and Comité national des interprofessions des vins à appellation d'origine (CNIV) v Commission*, EU:T:2007:295.

[71] ibid, para 134.

[72] ibid, para 141 ('An examination of Law No 200 of 2 April 1943 on the creation of an inter-branch committee for natural sweet wines and liqueur wines with a registered designation of origin, as amended by Decree No 55-1064 of 20 October 1956, confirms the predominant role of the State in that committee').

[73] Case C-425/19 P *Commission v Italy, Banca Popolare di Bari SCpA and Fondo interbancario di tutela dei depositi*, EU:C:2021:154.

[74] ibid, para 8.

[75] ibid, para 72: 'Thus, contrary to the Commission's assertions, in a situation where, as in the present case, the entity that provided the aid is a private entity, the appropriate evidence for the purpose of demonstrating that the measure is imputable to the State differs from that required in a situation where the entity providing the aid is a public undertaking'.

[76] ibid, para 73.

activities of a private body. The case law that followed went on to confirm that such measures escape Article 107(1) TFEU. *Eco TLC*, for instance, concerned a regulatory obligation, imposed upon sellers of some textile producers, to make a contribution to a waste management body approved by law or, in the alternative, to set up recycling facilities in-house.[77] Against this background, the Court concluded, in line with the Advocate General,[78] that the contributions were at no point 'under public control, and therefore available to the competent national authorities'. The resources in question remained in private hands throughout their entire 'life cycle'.[79]

4.3. The Legal Status of Contributions

4.3.1. Background

The Court's ruling in *Essent*, delivered in 2008,[80] revealed that the line between measures falling within the scope of Article 107(1) TFEU and those escaping it may be blurred. Relatively minor differences between two factual scenarios may have an impact on the characterisation of measures. There were similarities between *Essent* and *PreussenElektra*. Just like the latter, *Essent* related to a set of measures aimed at compensating electricity producers. These were incumbent generating companies that had incurred stranded costs prior to the liberalisation of the industry. Any costs were to be assumed by distributors, which passed them on to consumers in accordance with the relevant legislation.[81] The question, against this background, was whether the mechanism put in place by the Dutch legislature involved the use of State resources. One could have argued that the transfer resulting from the measure was not fundamentally different from the one at issue in *PreussenElektra* and thus warranted the same legal treatment.

The Court, however, reached the opposite conclusion. Some of the factual differences may explain the divergent outcomes. The first one is that the

---

[77] Case C-556/19 *Eco TLC v Ministre d'État, ministre de la Transition écologique et solidaire and Ministre de l'Économie et des Finances*, EU:C:2020:844.

[78] Opinion of Advocate General Pitruzzella in Case C-556/19 *Eco TLC v Ministre d'État, ministre de la Transition écologique et solidaire and Ministre de l'Économie et des Finances*, EU:C:2020:399.

[79] *Eco TLC* (n 77), para 33 ('As the Advocate General states at point 85 of his Opinion, these contributions remain private throughout their life cycle. The funds created by the payment of those contributions never pass through the State budget or that of another public entity, nor at any point do public authorities have access to them. Furthermore, it is apparent from the file before the Court that the Member State in question has not relinquished any resources, in whatever form, such as taxes, duties, charges and so on, which, according to national legislation, should have been paid into the State budget'). On the 'life cycle approach', see Leigh Hancher, '*Quo Vadis* notion of aid?' in Juan Jorge Piernas López, Leigh Hancher and Luca Rubini (eds), *The Future of EU State Aid Law: Consolidation and Expansion* (EU Law Live Press 2023).

[80] Case C-206/06 *Essent Netwerk Noord BV and others v Aluminium Delfzijl BV and others*, EU:C:2008:413.

[81] ibid, para 21.

contributions aimed at compensating for the stranded costs were directed to a subsidiary jointly owned by incumbent electricity generating companies, SEP.[82] Therefore, and contrary to what was true in *PreussenElektra*, there was something akin to a 'fund' where the resources were collected. A second difference is that the management of SEP's activities was tightly regulated by law. The State directed the use of the 'fund': it indicated which costs could be compensated and required that any monies exceeding the necessary amount be transferred to the government for its reallocation.[83] Concluding, against this background, that the resources in question remained 'constantly … under public control, and therefore available to the competent national authorities' seems consistent with the preceding case law.

While the outcome of the case may be in line with the relevant precedents, the facts in *Essent* do not fully dispel every ambiguity around the exact scope of *PreussenElektra*. It was not fully clear, in particular, whether it is necessary and/ or sufficient to characterise a contribution as a tax or levy for the funds to qualify as State resources. One could reasonably take the view that fiscal income falls by definition within the scope of Article 107(1) TFEU.[84] This fact does not mean, however, that every measure must involve a levy or tax. If anything, its status as a levy or tax increases the likelihood that the measure falls within the scope of Article 107(1) TFEU. The judgments that followed *Essent* confirmed these views and made it clear that the assessment revolves around the central question in *Stardust Marine*, namely whether the resources are, first, 'constantly under public control', and, second, thus 'available to the public authority'. These two aspects of the case law are examined in turn.

4.3.2. A Contribution Need not be Characterised as a Levy or Tax

The Court appears to have categorically excluded the idea that only (para)fiscal charges or levies trigger Article 107(1) TFEU. Provided that the *Stardust Marine* test is met, a measure involving other contributions will qualify as State resources. This point was expressly addressed by the Court in *EEG*.[85] The mechanism at issue[86] (hereinafter also referred to as the 'EEG') in this case can be (and was) depicted as the successor of the one considered in *PreussenElektra*.[87] It was, however, more

---

[82] ibid, para 66.

[83] ibid, para 69: 'It is apparent from the provisions of the OEPS that the designated company is not entitled to use the proceeds from the charge for purposes other than those provided for by the Law. Furthermore, it is strictly monitored in carrying out its task, since Article 9(5) of the OEPS requires it to have the detailed account of the sums received and transferred certified by an auditor'.

[84] This is, in fact, the point made by the Commission in the cases discussed in this section.

[85] Case C-405/16 P *Germany v Commission*, EU:C:2019:268. See also, in the same vein, Joined Cases C-790/21 P and C-791/21 P *Covestro Deutschland AG and Germany v Commission*, EU:C:2024:792.

[86] Case C-405/16 P *Germany v Commission* (n 85), para 3.

[87] ibid, para 37, where one of the parties argued the following: 'The EEG 2012 thus constitutes a continuation of the Stromeinspeisungsgesetz (Law on feeding electricity from renewable energy sources into the public grid, BGBl. 1990 I, p. 2633) which the Court of Justice did not classify as aid in [*PreussenElektra*] the only difference between the two schemes arising being that the electricity

complex in a number of respects. In addition to an obligation on network operators (typically, distributors) to purchase electricity from renewable sources at a fixed price, the EEG allowed the costs resulting from this obligation to be passed on to transmission operators. The latter, in turn, benefitted from a compensation mechanism aimed at placing an equal burden on all of them. Transmission operators were moreover allowed (but not required) to pass on to end consumers, by means of a surcharge, the costs that they would have been unable to recover when selling the electricity on the spot market.

The Court concluded that this mechanism did not involve the use of State resources within the meaning of *PreussenElektra*.[88] The fact that the funds in question were not obtained by means of a tax or levy was not a decisive factor in the analysis. In line with the preceding case law (including, most notably, *Stardust Marine*), the Court held that a measure may be characterised as aid even when the resources do not originate from such legal instruments. Therefore, the Commission (or a claimant) cannot be required to prove that a measure amounts to a levy or tax (or that it works, de facto, as such[89]) for Article 107(1) TFEU to come into play. In order to discharge its burden of proof, it is sufficient for the Commission (or claimant) to establish, pursuant to the principles laid down in *Stardust Marine*, that the funds generated by the surcharge 'constantly remain under public control' and are thus 'available' to the public authorities, irrespective of their origin.[90] It is insufficient, by contrast, to argue that the funds in question are under the 'dominant influence' of the said public authorities.[91]

Where a measure is financed by means of a levy or tax, on the other hand, it will involve the use of State resources provided that an additional condition is met.[92] This point, which is implied in *EEG*, would be confirmed in *FVE Holýšov I*[93] and *DOBELES HES*.[94] This line of case law suggests that the State resources condition will be deemed met where, first, there is a levy in place, and, second, the funds financed by means of the said levy are 'managed and apportioned' in accordance with the requirements of national legislation.[95] This is, in essence, the factual

---

suppliers buy not the physical electricity but the renewable nature of that electricity at a fixed price (EEG surcharge).

[88] ibid, para 87.

[89] ibid, para 72.

[90] ibid, para 73.

[91] ibid, paras 74 and 75. In the latter, the Court held that 'Without it being necessary to rule on the merits of the classification as a State concession thus applied by the General Court, it must be held that, although it is true that the factors thus accepted indicate the legal origin of the support for EEG electricity implemented by the EEG 2012, they are, however, not sufficient to conclude that the State nevertheless held a power of disposal over the funds managed and administered by the TSOs'.

[92] ibid, para 68.

[93] Case C-850/19 P *FVE Holýšov I s. r. o. and others v Commission*, EU:C:2021:740.

[94] Joined Cases C-702/20 and C-17/21 *'DOBELES HES' SIA and others v Sabiedrisko pakalpojumu regulēšanas komisija and others*, EU:C:2023:1.

[95] ibid, para 35: 'Funds must thus be regarded as "State resources" within the meaning of Article 107(1) TFEU if they derive from compulsory contributions imposed by the legislation of the Member State concerned and are managed and apportioned in accordance with that legislation [...]'. In support of

scenario considered in *Essent*, which was expressly distinguished by the Court from the one at issue in *EEG*.[96] This case law suggests that the characterisation of a charge as a tax or levy, while not necessary, will have an impact on the probability that the relevant funds qualify as 'State resources' within the meaning of the case law. In addition, the very existence of a levy can be relied upon to substantiate the claim that the measure is imputable to the State, as the Court held in *EEG*.[97]

4.3.3. *The* Stardust Marine *Test in Practice*

The *EEG* judgment also sheds light on the application of the two prongs of the *Stardust Marine* test. As far as the 'availability' prong is concerned, the Court held that it is not sufficient to show that the firms in charge of the management of a fund are subject to a regulatory obligation or that they act as if they had been awarded a 'concession' by the State.[98] The relevant question, instead, appears to be whether the public authorities have the ability to influence the allocation of the funds, either directly or through the control they can exercise over the body in charge of their administration.[99] Thus, where the funds in question are managed by a public authority or by a body under the control of public authorities, this prong of the test will be deemed met, as in *Vent De Colère!*[100] and *Achema*.[101] Where, as in *EEG*, the funds are managed by predominantly private operators, it will not.[102]

Concerning the 'public control' prong, in turn, the case law suggests that legislative mechanisms aimed at ensuring compliance with the various regulatory duties are not sufficient for the Commission (or a private claimant) to discharge its burden of proof.[103] The central consideration, instead, appears to be whether these mechanisms allow the State to determine how the funds are put to use. Where, as in *Vent De Colère!*, legislation prescribes in detail the way in which the resources

---

the cumulative understanding of these two conditions, see Case T-409/21 *Germany v Commission*, EU:T:2024:34. The appeal before the Court of Justice against this first-instance ruling is pending. See Case C-242/24 P *Commission v Germany*, pending.

[96] *EEG* (n 85), para 71: 'The fact, noted by the General Court in paragraph 95 of the judgment under appeal, that "in practice", the financial burden resulting from the EEG surcharge was passed on to the final customers and, consequently, could "be assimilated, from the point of view of its effects, to a levy on electricity consumption" is not sufficient for it to be concluded that the EEG surcharge had the same characteristics as the electricity price supplement examined by the Court of Justice in [*Essent*]'.

[97] ibid, para 50, which refers to Case T-47/15 *Germany v Commission*, EU:T:2016:281, para 40 and which is in turn referred to in *DOBELES HES* (n 94), para 33.

[98] ibid, para 75.

[99] ibid, para 73 ('It must, however, be noted that the General Court failed to establish that the State held a power of disposal over the funds generated by the EEG surcharge or even whether it exercised public control over the TSOs responsible for managing those funds').

[100] Case C-262/12 *Association Vent De Colère! Fédération nationale and others v Ministre de l'Écologie, du Développement durable, des Transports et du Logement and Ministre de l'Économie, des Finances et de l'Industrie*, EU:C:2013:851.

[101] Case C-706/17 *AB 'Achema', AB 'Orlen Lietuva' and AB 'Lifosa' v Valstybinė kainų ir energetikos kontrolės komisija (VKEKK)*, EU:C:2019:407.

[102] *EEG* (n 85), paras 78–82.

[103] ibid, para 76.

are to be administered (including questions such as whether the charges may be invested, how the remuneration resulting from these investments is used and whether the body managing them is entitled to make a profit from the management of the funds), the 'public control' prong will have been proved to the requisite legal standard.[104] The outcome would be the same in a scenario like the one at issue in *Achema*, where the administrator of the relevant fund had no discretion as to its allocation, which was established in detail by public authorities.[105]

5. Summary of the Principles Underpinning the Case Law

5.1. Introduction

The degree of maturity attained by the case law makes it possible to summarise the main principles in a systematic way. As is true of virtually any area of the law, it is difficult to draw precise boundaries around the 'State resources' and 'imputability' criteria or to state unequivocally whether a given measure would be characterised as an aid by the Court. The principles considered in the case law are best understood as providing a probability that Article 107(1) TFEU will come into play in a given case. The likelihood that the measure will be caught by the provision depends on the factual scenario at hand. The closer one gets to the core functions of the State, the more likely it is that intervention will be deemed to be imputable to the State and to involve the use of State resources. Conversely, the further one moves away from these core functions and the more one ventures into the private sphere, the less likely it is that the conditions for the application of Article 107(1) TFEU will be met.

5.2. Establishing Imputability

Figure 2.4 Likelihood of imputability

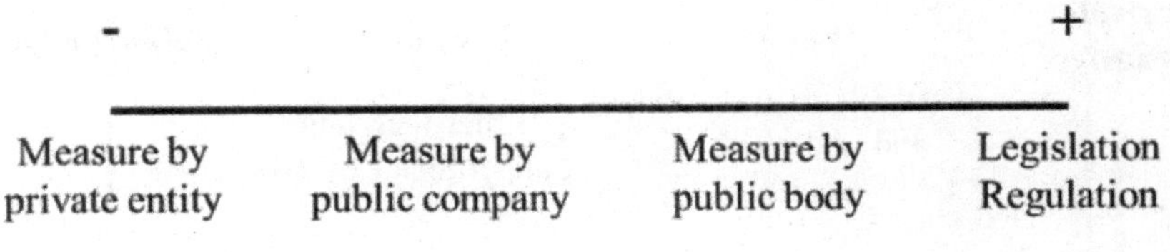

−			+
Measure by private entity	Measure by public company	Measure by public body	Legislation Regulation

---

[104] *Vent De Colère!* (n 100), paras 30 and 33.
[105] *Achema* (n 101), para 66.

Figure 2.4 seeks to capture the different factual scenarios, and the degree of likelihood that each of these scenarios will be found to meet the imputability criterion. One can identify, at the right end of the spectrum, instances where the measure directly originates from a legislative or a regulatory obligation. In such an instance, which is the default and most frequent one in the case law and administrative practice, it is self-evident that the measure is imputable to the State. At the other end of the spectrum, one can identify a private entity such as the one considered by the Court in *Banca Tercas*. As already discussed above, establishing imputability in the latter scenario is particularly demanding for the Commission or claimant. It may not be sufficient to show that the involvement of the State in the adoption of the measure was likely, but rather to offer positive, 'appropriate evidence' to that effect.[106]

In between these two factual scenarios, it will be more or less likely (and more or less difficult to establish) that the measure is imputable to the State depending on the degree of closeness to the core functions of government. One can identify, towards the right end of the spectrum, public bodies (such as regulatory agencies, which may be more or less independent of the executive), whose decisions can be deemed to be attributable to the State. Towards the left end of the spectrum, on the other hand, one can identify a State-owned company governed by private law and subject to competition from privately-owned firms. It is not difficult to think of scenarios that are somewhere in between, such as that of an entity governed by private law but benefitting from exclusive rights and subject to strict public service requirements (for instance, a water utility).

5.3. Establishing the Origin of the Resources

Figure 2.5 Likelihood that the resources qualify as State resources

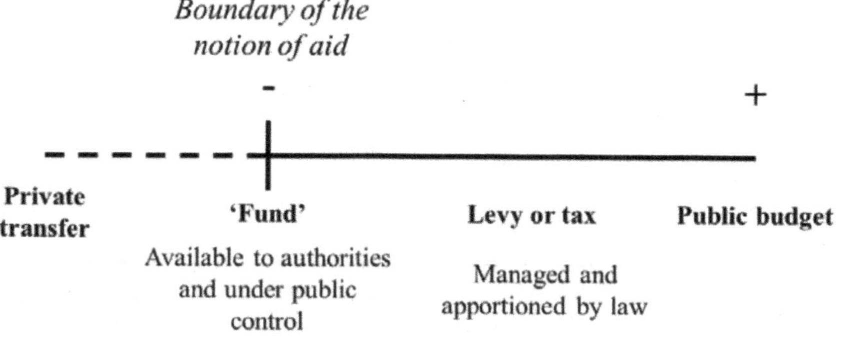

---

[106] *Banca Tercas* (n 73), para 72. See the contrast with the GC's approach in Joined Cases T-98/16, T-196/16 and T-198/16 *Italy, Banca Popolare di Bari SCpA and Fondo interbancario di tutela dei depositi v Commission*, EU:T:2019:167.

As shown in Figure 2.5, the case law suggests that a similar sliding scale applies when it comes to establishing whether the funds at issue in a given case qualify as State resources. The ease with which the Commission (or a claimant) can show that, pursuant to *Stardust Marine*, the funds are 'available' to authorities and constantly 'under public control' depends, again, on the degree of closeness to the core of the functions performed by the State. Thus, funds coming from the budget of a public authority – whether national, regional and local, and irrespective of whether the transfer is positive or negative – unquestionably qualify as 'State resources' within the meaning of *Stardust Marine*. The same is true of the monies obtained by means of a levy or tax, provided that they are 'managed and apportioned'[107] in line with the requirements of national legislation.

Establishing that State resources are involved becomes more difficult as one moves towards the left end of the spectrum. In borderline scenarios, it would appear that the decisive criterion for the purposes of the characterisation of a measure as aid is the existence of a fund (which could be the deposits of a State-owned bank or the cash flow of a public utility) that is allocated in accordance with criteria defined by, and under the supervision of, public authorities. Accordingly, Article 107(1) TFEU does not seem to be applicable where, instead of a fund, resources are transferred directly from one private entity to another. The fact that the transfer is the consequence of a legal obligation, as in *Eco TLC*, does not have an impact on its legal characterisation. Where there is a fund in place, Article 107(1) TFEU will come into play if it can be shown that the two prongs of the *Stardust Marine* test are met (and not simply the fact that the State exercises a 'dominant influence' over their use). If, by contrast, it can be shown that the funds remain private during throughout their entire 'life cycle', they will not qualify as State resources.[108]

6. Conclusions

The definition of the boundaries of the notion of aid has a significant impact on the ability of the EU State aid system to constrain regulatory competition and venture into regulatory harmonisation. If the scope of Article 107(1) TFEU is defined in such a way that any advantage given by a public authority can be potentially characterised as State aid, large swathes of targeted interventions in the economy (from the promotion of renewable energies and the definition of public transport strategies to the management of waste and bank insolvency proceedings) would be subject to scrutiny. A broad reading of Article 107(1) TFEU would turn the system into something akin to a master key giving the Commission jurisdiction to oversee anti-competitive regulation adopted by EU Member States. For the same reason, it would entail a significant transfer of power to the EU institutions.

---

[107] *DOBELES HES* (n 94), para 35.
[108] Hancher (n 79).

The balance eventually struck by the Court allows for relatively limited interference with EU Member States' economic policies. On the one hand, it is clear, at least since *PreussenElektra*, that only measures that involve the use of State resources can be characterised as State aid. This fact, alone, substantially reduces the reach of the regime. On the other hand, the very concept of State resources has been given a relatively expansive interpretation, in the sense that it encompasses not just the budget of public authorities but also any other funds that are available to authorities to attain their aims. They may include measures adopted via publicly-owned firms and, in some instances, via private bodies. In the latter scenarios, the extent to which the EU State aid regime will come into play will be modulated by the parallel concept of imputability.

An apparent feature of the interpretative choices made by the Court is formalism. By requiring that a measure involve State resources for it to be caught by Article 107(1) TFEU, it implicitly accepted that measures having an equivalent effect to State aid fall outside the scope of the regime. Coming back to some of the examples discussed above, there are no major differences between the measures considered in *Vent De Colère!*, which were characterised as State aid, and those at issue in *EEG*, which were not. Formalism, for all its virtues, opens the door to opportunistic conduct by EU Member States. As argued by the Commission in its submission in *PreussenElektra*, it makes it possible for public authorities to circumvent EU State aid law provision by relying on a particular regulatory technique. The substantive effects may be the same, but the legal implications are not.

The Court's approach can be easily rationalised when the broader constitutional context is considered. It is difficult to argue that Articles 107 and 108 TFEU were designed to give the Commission ample powers to oversee any regulatory advantage awarded by EU Member States. In this sense, an expansive interpretation of the notion of State aid might not have been easy to square with the nature of the competences granted to the EU (and, by the same token, might have negatively affected the perceived legitimacy of the EU State aid regime).[109] One should note, in addition, that the TFEU is not equipped to deal with every State measure negatively affecting trade and/or competition. The EU system of undistorted competition was not designed to be complete.[110] In this sense, leaving some regulatory advantages outside the scope of Article 107(1) TFEU is, rather than an exception, the expression of a broader compromise.

---

[109] This point, was, after all, the essence of the argument raised by AG Jacobs in *PreussenElektra* (n 28).

[110] This is an old debate. For an overview, see Giuliano Marenco, 'Competition Between National Economies and Competition Between Businesses – A Response to Judge Pescatore' (1986) 10 Fordham International Law Journal 420; Norbert Reich, 'The "November Revolution" of the European Court of Justice: Keck, Meng and Audi Revisited' (1994) 31 Common Market Law Review 459 and Julio Baquero Cruz, *Between Competition and Free Movement: The Economic Constitutional Law of the European Community* (Hart Publishing 2002).

3

The Concept of Advantage

1. Generalities on the Concept of Advantage

1.1. Advantage as a Departure from Normality

An advantage within the meaning of Article 107(1) TFEU can be aptly described as a measure that departs from normality. In *Steenkolenmijnen*, the Court of Justice (hereinafter, the 'Court' or the 'ECJ') referred to 'interventions which, in various forms, mitigate the charges which are normally included in the budget of an undertaking'.[1] This passage expressly alludes to measures which involve the use of State resources and which comprise not just subsidies in the narrow sense but also other initiatives that 'are similar in character and have the same effect'.[2] To begin with, and most obviously, an advantage equivalent to a subsidy encompasses instances where the public authority foregoes profits that would otherwise be due. Examples in this sense include tax exemptions[3] (or, similarly, the application of a lower tax rate[4]) and the sale of goods or services below market prices.[5]

State intervention also departs from normality in two other instances, which are implicit in *Steenkolenmijnen*. It does so where a public authority transfers to the recipient more resources than would be due under normal market conditions. Rather than reducing the charges to which it is subject, in other words, intervention in this sense artificially increases the firm's resources, thereby placing it at an advantage. For example, a local authority may purchase goods or services at a price exceeding the prevailing market rate. The concept also comprises, more generally, instances where the firm benefits from terms and conditions that would normally not be available to it. Consider in this sense, an unlimited guarantee given by the State. At the very least, there are reasons to presume that no rational operator in

---

[1] Case 30/59 *De Gezamenlijke Steenkolenmijnen in Limburg v High Authority*, EU:C:1961:2, 19.

[2] ibid: 'The concept of aid is nevertheless wider than that of a subsidy because it embraces not only positive benefits, such as subsidies themselves, but also interventions which, in various forms, mitigate the charges which are normally included in the budget of an undertaking and which, without, therefore, being subsidies in the strict meaning of the word, are similar in character and have the same effect'.

[3] Commission Notice on the notion of State aid as referred to in Article 107(1) of the Treaty on the Functioning of the European Union [2016] OJ C262/1, para 51.

[4] See for instance Case C-362/19 P *Commission v Fútbol Club Barcelona and Spain*, EU:C:2021:169, which concerned an instance where some undertakings were given a preferential tax treatment.

[5] Commission Notice on the notion of aid (n 3), para 52.

a market economy would be willing and able to provide such a guarantee.[6] The same would be true where the State acquires a stake in a company where no private investor would.[7]

Table 3.1 Four categories of advantage

Measure	Effect	Example
Subsidy (narrow sense)	Mitigation of normal charges to which a firm is subject	Grant
Negative subsidy (State foregoes profits)	Mitigation of normal charges to which a firm is subject	Tax exemption
Excessive transfer of resources	Artifical increase in the firm's budgetary position	Purchase of assets departing from market conditions
Unavailable transaction in the marketplace	Artifical improvement of the firm's position	Unlimited guarantee

The four categories of advantages within the meaning of Article 107(1) TFEU are depicted in Table 3.1. Whether or not a measure departs from normality will require consideration of the specificities of the case. There are two scenarios, examined in detail below, where State intervention will not amount to an advantage. The first one, addressed in Section 2, is an application of the so-called 'market economy operator' principle.[8] Pursuant to this doctrine, a transfer of State resources does not amount to an advantage if it does not deviate from the prevailing market conditions (that is, it is comparable to the behaviour of a rational private operator). The second scenario, explored in Section 3, relates to a compensation for the public service obligation imposed by the State. Such a measure only falls outside the scope of Article 107(1) TFEU where the conditions laid down by the Court in *Altmark* are met.[9]

1.2. Undertakings as Recipients

An advantage is only caught by Article 107(1) TFEU where it benefits one or several undertakings, which are defined as entities engaged in an economic

---

[6] ibid, para 110.

[7] Case C-142/87 *Belgium v Commission*, EU:C:1990:125 (hereinafter, *Tubemeuse*).

[8] Commission Notice on the notion of aid (n 3), paras 73–116. For a discussion of the principle, see Nicole Robins and Laura Puglisi, 'The market economy operator principle: an economic role model for assessing economic advantage' in Leigh Hancher and Juan J Piernas López (eds), *Research Handbook on European State Aid Law* (Edward Elgar Publishing 2021).

[9] Case C-280/00 *Altmark Trans GmbH and Regierungspräsidium Magdeburg v Nahverkehrsgesellschaft Altmark GmbH, and Oberbundesanwalt beim Bundesverwaltungsgericht*, EU:C:2003:415. See also Commission Notice on the notion of aid (n 3), para 70.

activity – irrespective of their legal status and the way they are financed.[10] A first consequence of this substantive boundary is that a measure does not amount to State aid where the only beneficiaries are end-users.[11] For example, subsidies aimed at incentivising consumption (such as social vouchers to promote the take-up of broadband services) would fall, in and of themselves, outside the scope of the provision.[12] A second consequence is that interventions that relate to the exercise of the core of EU Member States' powers (the so-called *fonctions régaliennes*[13]) are not caught by Article 107(1) TFEU. Examples in this sense include activities such as air traffic control and other forms of policing, whether they are exercised directly or indirectly by the State,[14] and the provision of healthcare services based on the principle of solidarity.[15]

Determining whether an entity qualifies as an undertaking is not always a straightforward exercise. The question may become particularly complex where a body performs economic and non-economic activities simultaneously. Such a duality may arise in a number of industries. Coming back to an example mentioned above, an airport operator may at the same time act as an undertaking (as far as its relationship with airlines is concerned) and as an entity falling outside the scope of Article 107(1) TFEU (regarding its policing role).[16] Uncertainty about this question is sometimes explained by the fact that a given activity may be economic in nature in one EU Member State, but not in another one. Variation from one jurisdiction to another depends on the manner in which the activity is organised. Thus, Article 107(1) TFEU will come into play insofar as it is possible to identify a market where goods or services are offered.[17]

The difficulties that might emerge when drawing the line between economic and non-economic activities have become apparent in the context of investments in infrastructure. It is reasonable to assume that the use of State resources to fund such projects falls outside the scope of Article 107(1) TFEU. Investments in, inter alia, railways, motorways and ports can be seen as a manifestation of the core functions of the State.[18] To the extent that access to the infrastructure is unrestricted and non-discriminatory, moreover, it is not immediately obvious to see the mechanism by which such investments provide an advantage.

---

[10] Case C-41/90 *Höfner and Elser v Macrotron*, EU:C:1991:161, para 21. For a discussion, see Juan Jorge Piernas López, 'When is a company not an undertaking under EU competition law? The contribution of the Dôvera judgment' (2021) 58 Common Market Law Review 529.

[11] Case C-403/10 P *Mediaset SpA v Commission*, EU:C:2011:533, para 81.

[12] See for instance Guidelines on State aid for broadband networks [2023] OJ C36/1, para 177.

[13] Commission Notice on the notion of aid (n 3), paras 17–18.

[14] Case C-364/92 *SAT Fluggesellschaft mbH v Eurocontrol*, EU:C:1994:7.

[15] See in particular Case C-244/94 *Fédération Française des Sociétés d'Assurance and others v Ministère de l'Agriculture et de la Pêche*, EU:C:1995:392 and Case C-205/03 *Federación Española de Empresas de Tecnología Sanitaria (FENIN) v Commission*, EU:C:2006:453.

[16] Case T-128/98 *Aéroports de Paris v Commission*, EU:T:2000:290.

[17] Commission Notice on the notion of aid (n 3), para 12.

[18] For a discussion, see Corinne Ruechardt, *EU State Aid Control of Infrastructure Funding* (Kluwer Law International 2018); and Michael Gayger, 'Infrastructure Funding at the Interface between the EU State Aid Rules and Member States' General Economic Policy' (2016) 15 European State Aid Law Quarterly 539.

As noted by the European Commission (hereinafter, the 'Commission') in its Notice on the notion of State aid, the picture changes once a potentially competitive market is liberalised. Where deregulation occurs, it may be possible to identify an economic activity. For example, there is competition among operators for the provision of broadband Internet services.[19] As a result, investment in the roll out of electronic communications networks will be subject to scrutiny under EU State aid law.[20]

The boundaries of the concept of advantage were tested and clarified in *Leipzig-Halle*.[21] On appeal, the Court held that there are circumstances where the expansion of airport infrastructure is an economic activity within the meaning of Article 107(1) TFEU.[22] This is so, the ECJ explained, where two conditions are met: first, the construction and operation activities cannot not be dissociated; and, second, the sector is open to competition.[23] In the specific circumstances of the case, the capital contributions supporting the expansion of the airport's runway could qualify as State aid, which was also the conclusion reached by the General Court (hereinafter, the 'GC') at first instance.[24] From the Court's perspective, the relevant question is not whether a private operator could have built the infrastructure, but whether the construction efforts can be linked to an economic activity (that is, the remunerated provision of services to airlines).[25] This is all the more so, the ruling suggests, where the fees collected from airport users fund the infrastructure in question.[26]

1.3. Direct and Indirect Advantages

Advantages within the meaning of Article 107(1) TFEU may be direct or indirect. Put differently, the recipient of State aid is not necessarily (or not only) the person or entity to which the resources are transferred. For instance, financial support to end-users (which do not qualify as undertakings) may have the indirect effect of benefitting the producers of the goods or services, the consumption of which is being subsidised. *Mediaset* provides an example in this sense.[27] The measure at issue was ostensibly aimed at supporting the acquisition, by households, of decoders for the reception of digital television. However, the intervention was not technologically neutral. Instead of subsidising the transition to digital systems irrespective of the transmission method, it covered only terrestrial television

---

[19] Directive (EU) 2018/1972 of the European Parliament and of the Council of 11 December 2018 establishing the European Electronic Communications Code (Recast) [2018] OJ L321/36.

[20] Guidelines on State aid for broadband networks (n 12).

[21] Case C-288/11 P *Mitteldeutsche Flughafen and Flughafen Leipzig-Halle v Commission*, EU:C:2012:821.

[22] ibid, para 44.

[23] ibid, paras 46–47.

[24] Joined Cases T-443/08 and T-455/08 *Freistaat Sachsen and others v Commission*, EU:T:2011:117.

[25] *Leipzig-Halle* (n 21), para 49.

[26] ibid, para 51.

[27] *Mediaset* (n 11).

(as opposed to, inter alia, cable, satellite and Internet). To the extent that it did, operators relying on terrestrial transmission received an advantage.[28]

One can also think of scenarios where the recipients of State aid are both the direct and the indirect beneficiaries of the measure. For example, a tax exemption aimed at incentivising investments in a particular activity will provide an advantage to two categories of undertakings. First, the investors directly benefitting from the exemption. Second, the economic operators engaged in the activity that is being incentivised. It is not difficult to find examples in the case law and administrative practice where there is a dual set of State aid recipients. In *Netherlands v Commission*, the measures at issue provided a direct advantage to service stations near the German border and were aimed at addressing the increase in excise duties in the Netherlands.[29] In addition, the scheme had the indirect effect of relieving oil suppliers from the need to compensate dealers for the consequences of extraordinary market conditions.[30] To the extent that this was the case, State intervention absorbed the costs that suppliers would normally bear and thus provided an advantage to them.[31]

2. The 'Market Economy Operator' Principle

2.1. Rationale(s) Underpinning the Principle

A corollary to *Steenkolenmijnen* is that State intervention that does not depart from the prevailing market conditions does not amount to an advantage within the meaning of Article 107(1) TFEU. This idea is encapsulated in the so-called 'market economy operator' principle.[32] Accordingly, where a public authority intervenes in the economy in the same way a private firm behaving rationally would, EU State aid law does not come into play.[33] The principle may be relevant in a variety of instances, and in particular where a public authority purchases or sells assets,[34] lends money,[35] invests in an economic venture[36] and acquires a stake in a

---

[28] ibid, para 76.

[29] Case C-382/99 *Netherlands v Commission*, EU:C:2002:363.

[30] ibid, para 62.

[31] ibid, para 66: 'In those circumstances, the aid granted to service stations linked to oil companies by PMS clauses had economic effects for the companies concerned since the effect of that aid was, in any event, to release those companies from their obligation to bear all or part of the costs of the forecourt discounts offered by dealers to prevent loss of market share'.

[32] Commission Notice on the notion of aid (n 3), paras 73–116.

[33] The origins of the doctrine can be traced back to Case C-234/84 *Belgium v Commission*, EU:C:1986:302 (hereinafter, *Meura*) and Case C-40/85 *Belgium v Commission*, EU:C:1986:93 (hereinafter, *Boch*).

[34] Joined Cases C-67/85, C-68/85 and C-70/85 *Kwekerij Gebroeders van der Kooy BV and others v Commission*, EU:C:1988:38; and Case C-39/94 *Syndicat français de l'Express international (SFEI) and others v La Poste and others*, EU:C:1996:285.

[35] Case C-342/96 *Spain v Commission*, EU:C:1999:164; and Case C-300/16 P *Commission v Frucona Košice a.s.*, EU:C:2017:706.

[36] Case C-305/89 *Italy v Commission*, EU:C:1991:142.

company.[37] One should note, in this sense, that, pursuant to Article 345 TFEU, the EU legal order is agnostic with regard to the 'system of property ownership' within EU Member States.[38] Therefore, it cannot place State intervention in the economy at a relative disadvantage.

2.2. The Applicability of the Principle

The applicability of the 'market economy operator' principle depends on substantive factors, not formal ones. Thus, the relevance of the doctrine in a given case should only depend on whether the measure at issue is comparable, in its nature and effects, to one that would have been adopted by a private firm. This point became apparent in *EDF*.[39] The Commission had dismissed the applicability of the principle on grounds that the measure related to a tax liability, which had been waived and converted into a stake in the publicly-owned incumbent.[40] The Commission argued that, insofar as taxation is a manifestation of the exercise of the State's regulatory powers, the intervention at issue could not be compared to the behaviour of a private investor. The exercise of these powers, by its very nature, could not be characterised as an economic activity.[41]

The Court, ruling on appeal, reached a different conclusion.[42] It agreed with the fundamental premise underpinning the Commission's analysis, whereby the roles of the State as a shareholder and as an authority exercising its coercive powers must be differentiated.[43] Similarly, it did not dispute that the 'market economy operator' principle is only relevant where the public body acts as the former. However, it drew different implications from these two premises. From the ECJ's perspective, the sole question that is relevant when considering the applicability of the principle is whether the State, intervening in its capacity as a private operator, grants, in substance, an advantage to the undertaking.[44] Accordingly, the Commission, in the context of the administrative procedure, cannot summarily dismiss 'objective and verifiable' arguments pertaining to the applicability of the principle.[45] Where the requisite evidence is produced in that context, the Commission is under a duty to 'carry out a global assessment' to determine whether the EU Member State was acting as a rational firm (as opposed to an authority exercising its prerogatives).[46]

---

[37] *Tubemeuse* (n 7).

[38] Pursuant to Article 345 TFEU: 'The Treaties shall in no way prejudice the rules in Member States governing the system of property ownership'.

[39] Case C-124/10 P *Commission v EDF*, EU:C:2012:318.

[40] Commission Decision of 16 December 2003 on the State aid granted by France to EDF and the electricity and gas industries [2005] OJ L49/9.

[41] ibid, paras 24–35.

[42] ibid, para 96.

[43] *EDF* (n 39), para 104.

[44] ibid, para 81.

[45] ibid, para 82.

[46] ibid, para 86. See also *Frucona Košice* (n 35) and Joined Cases C-331/20 P and C-343/20 P *Volotea SA and easyJet Airline Co Ltd v Commission*, EU:C:2022:886, para 120.

The Court was presented with a variation on the same question in *ING*.[47] That case concerned a restructuring plan in support of a financial institution in the aftermath of the financial crisis of the late 2000s.[48] The question was whether the 'market economy operator' principle could apply in the relevant circumstances, considering that the notified measure was a follow-up to a previous one – a capital injection – which, itself, had been found to fall within the scope of Article 107(1) TFEU.[49] The point of law that the Court had to address, in other words, was whether the characterisation of an initial measure as State aid means that every subsequent measure necessarily falls within the scope of the provision. The Court held that the latter are not inevitably tainted by the former. As a result, compliance with the 'market economy operator' principle will be assessed on their own merits.[50]

2.3. Practical Operation of the Principle: Presumptions

2.3.1. Unlimited Guarantees

There are some instances where one can safely presume that a measure would not have been adopted by a private investor. This is true of an unlimited guarantee (that is, one that does not place boundaries in terms of the amount, scope and/or the time), whether it is implicitly or explicitly granted.[51] As a matter of principle, it is possible to rule out that a rational operator would have agreed to such terms (all the more so, one may add, where the guarantee is not remunerated[52]). In *La Poste*, where the presumption was introduced, the Commission concluded that the incumbent postal operator in France was the beneficiary of an unlimited guarantee, which was found to be a de facto consequence of the relevant regulatory framework.[53] When quantifying the amount of the payable premium, the Commission deemed it impossible to estimate an amount, given that it covered all debts for an unlimited period. As a result, it explained, it was 'impossible to determine in advance the amount of aid granted at the time the guarantee is given.'[54] Such a scenario entails, by necessity, the award of an advantage to the undertaking.

---

[47] Case C-224/12 P *Commission v Netherlands and ING Groep NV*, EU:C:2014:213.

[48] ibid, paras 2–14.

[49] ibid, para 34.

[50] ibid, para 35: 'Indeed, as the Advocate General has stated in point 41 of her Opinion, any holder of securities, in whatever amount and of whatever nature, may wish or agree to renegotiate the conditions of their redemption. It is, consequently, meaningful to compare the behaviour of the State in that regard with that of a hypothetical private investor in a comparable position'; and para 36: 'What is decisive in the context of that comparison is whether the amendment to the repayment terms of the capital injection has satisfied an economic rationality test, so that a private investor might also be in a position to accept such an amendment, in particular by increasing the prospects of obtaining the repayment of that injection'.

[51] Case C-559/12 P *France v Commission*, EU:C:2014:217 (hereinafter, *La Poste*), paras 98 and 99. See also Case C-438/16 P *Commission v France and IFP Énergies nouvelles*, EU:C:2018:737, para 111.

[52] Commission Decision of 26 January 2010 on State aid C 56/07 (ex E 15/05) granted by France to La Poste [2010] OJ L274/1, para 254.

[53] ibid, paras 120–222. This point was confirmed on appeal. See *La Poste* (n 51), para 65.

[54] ibid, para 299.

2.3.2. Tender Procedures

Conversely, it is safe to presume that the sale or acquisition of assets by a public authority in the context of a genuine tender procedure does not amount to an advantage. The rationale behind this presumption is not difficult to grasp. Where suppliers or purchasers dealing with the State have been given a meaningful opportunity to take part in a public procurement procedure, the resulting price will be a faithful reflection of the prevailing market conditions.[55] That a presumption in this sense applies in this context was made explicit by the Court in *Land Burgerland*.[56] Accordingly, where the tender is 'open, transparent and unconditional', it is not necessary to rely on other direct or indirect indicators to rule out the existence of an advantage. The winning offer will be deemed to reflect the market price, the ECJ explained, provided that it 'is binding and credible' and that 'the consideration of economic factors other than the price is not justified'.[57]

A tender is considered to be open and transparent where, inter alia, it has been adequately publicised, is non-discriminatory and is competitive, in the sense that it gives genuine chances to all potential bidders to take part in it.[58] The Commission considers, in this regard, that these conditions are met where the EU Member State relies upon and complies with secondary legislation regulating public procurement procedures at the EU level.[59] Conversely, where the tender has been organised or designed in such a way that only a single firm is in a position to realistically bid for the contract, the presumption will no longer apply. In a decision concerning a series of measures adopted by Montpellier airport, for instance, the Commission found that one of the tenders for the provision of 'marketing services' had been tailored, in substance, to favour a specific airline.[60]

In addition, a tender must be unconditional for the presumption to come into play. What this criterion demands, in essence, is that the sale of assets by the public authority is not made contingent on the acquirer fulfilling additional obligations that a market economy operator would not have demanded in the same

---

[55] There are some markets where the market price is determined by means of a tender. See, generally, Paul Klemperer, 'Bidding Markets' (2007) 3 Journal of Competition Law & Economics 1.

[56] Joined Cases C-214/12 P, C-215/12 P and C-223/12 P *Land Burgenland, Grazer Wechselseitige Versicherung AG and Austria v Commission*, EU:C:2013:682, para 94: 'It follows that the General Court was correct to find [...] that, where a public authority proceeds to sell an undertaking belonging to it by way of an open, transparent and unconditional tender procedure, it can be presumed that the market price corresponds to the highest offer, provided that it is established, first, that that offer is binding and credible and, secondly, that the consideration of economic factors other than the price is not justified'. For an overview of the case law, see Cees Dekker, 'Does a Tender Exclude an Article 107(1) Advantage? An Investigation into the Different Approaches by the Court Of Justice and the European Commission' (2018) 17 European State Aid Law Quarterly 387.

[57] ibid.

[58] Commission Notice on the notion of aid (n 3), para 91.

[59] ibid, para 89.

[60] Case T-79/21 *Ryanair DAC and Airport Marketing Services Ltd v Commission*, EU:T:2023:334, para 296. Decision cited and discussed in Giuseppe Conte and Mohammed Khalil, 'Advantage' in Philipp Werner and Vincent Verouden (eds), *EU State Aid Control: Law and Economics* (2nd edn, Kluwer 2025).

circumstances.[61] The Notice on the notion of State aid explains, in this sense, that any conditions attached to the tender should be 'closely and objectively related to the subject matter and to the specific economic objective of the contract'.[62] A procedure would not meet the unconditionality criterion where the purchaser is required to refrain from subsequently restructuring the business as a rational private operator would (for instance, by requiring it to preserve a certain level of employment in the name of a policy objective unrelated to the object of the transaction[63]).

2.4. Practical Operation of the Principle: Case-by-Case Assessment

2.4.1. Generalities

If the abovementioned presumptions do not apply, it is necessary to engage in a case-by-case application of the principle. The assessment must be undertaken leaving aside all non-market related considerations that might have influenced the decision.[64] The only relevant factor is therefore whether a rational market operator would have behaved in the same way in the relevant circumstances. This is not to say that the EU Member State cannot be – or will never be – guided by public interest aims when taking part in an economic venture. As the Court clarified in *Volotea*, one can expect such considerations to permeate the action of public authorities. When a region takes part in an investment, for instance, one can expect it to be driven by economic development considerations, and not just in the profitability of the specific project.[65] This fact, however, does not rule out the applicability of the 'market economy operator' principle. The practical administration of the said principle simply requires that abstraction be made of such public interest considerations.[66]

Second, the question of whether a 'market economy operator' would have participated in a venture is to be undertaken ex ante, not ex post.[67] As the Court expressly held in *EDF*, it is not sufficient for the EU Member State to show, after the

---

[61] Commission Notice on the notion of aid (n 3), para 94.

[62] ibid, para 96.

[63] These ideas were already implicit in *Meura* (n 33), para 14 and *Boch* (n 33), para 13.

[64] *Meura* (n 33), para 14.

[65] This point was noted by the GC in Case T-607/17 *Volotea, SA v Commission*, EU:T:2020:180, para 124.

[66] ibid, para 120: 'The pursuit of public policy objectives is in fact inherent in most of the State measures which may be classified as "State aid" and examined, to that end, in the light of that principle [...]. The consequence of applying that principle, however, is that those measures must be examined while leaving aside such objectives [...] and the benefits linked to the State's situation as a public authority which the implementation of those objectives is liable to generate [...]'.

[67] Commission Notice on the notion of aid (n 3), para 78.

fact, that the project turned out to be profitable.[68] A rational firm operating under normal market conditions would have assessed the convenience of an economic transaction before engaging in it, typically on the basis of a business plan.[69] By the same token, the Commission would not be able to conclude that an advantage exists merely on the basis of the failure of the transaction to deliver the expected returns.[70] Consistently with the need to evaluate the operation ex ante, any decision about the existence of an advantage must be grounded in the information available at the time when participation in the venture was considered.[71]

2.4.2. Pari Passu *Transactions*

The question of whether State intervention in a given case is equivalent to that of a rational private operator can sometimes be ascertained directly. As the Commission explains in its Notice on the notion of State aid,[72] a measure does not amount to an advantage where public authorities and private firms take part in a transaction jointly and under the same terms and conditions (*pari passu*). Examining whether the terms and conditions of public and private actors are the same relies in practice upon a number of proxies, including the timing and significance of the involvement, the risks assumed (that is, whether the risk borne across the board is the same and whether the level stays consistent over time), the starting position (including factors such as the prior exposure to the economic activity in question or the potential for synergies) and whether there are other links between the parties.[73]

An example that has been frequently used in the literature[74] (and by the Commission itself[75]) provides an illustration of an instance where intervention by the public authority was found to take place *pari passu* and therefore did not amount to an advantage. In *Citynet*,[76] the Commission considered whether an economic venture (a fibre-to-the-home telecommunications network) in which the municipality of Amsterdam took part could be characterised as State aid. The local authority took part in the project alongside other investors (including a private bank and a telecommunications operator). The Commission applied a test based on four criteria (essentially similar to the ones already identified) to determine whether the 'market economy operator' principle was satisfied. It noted, in this sense, that the two private operators could be aptly characterised as 'market

---

[68] *EDF* (n 39), para 85.

[69] ibid, para 84.

[70] ibid, para 105.

[71] ibid.

[72] Commission Notice on the notion of aid (n 3), paras 86–88.

[73] ibid.

[74] See for instance Robins and Puglisi (n 8), and Conte and Khalil (n 60).

[75] Commission Notice on the notion of aid (n 3), para 87 and fn 142.

[76] Commission Decision of 11 December 2007 – Investment by the city of Amsterdam in a fibre-to-the home (FttH) network (Case C 53/2006).

investors' and that their involvement in the project was significant.[77] In addition, it pointed out that the terms and conditions (as well as the timing) were essentially similar across all investors.

These conditions were not met, by contrast, in another example that has been frequently discussed by commentators, namely *Agricultural Bank of Greece*.[78] This case concerned a series of measures aimed at the restructuring of a financial institution by means, inter alia, of a capital injection and a balance sheet reduction.[79] Even though some private operators participated in the transaction, the Commission concluded that their involvement was not comparable to that of the Greek State. It pointed out, in particular, that the capital contribution made by the latter was disproportionate relative to its stake in the financial institution – it was responsible for over 90% of the capital injection, whereas its shareholding remained at around 77%. In addition, the Commission put the intervention in context, noting that it occurred after a first round of measures that had already been characterised as State aid.[80]

2.4.3. *Benchmarking as an Indirect Method*

There are circumstances where it is not possible to ascertain directly whether the intervention at issue is comparable to that of a rational private operator. In such cases, it becomes necessary to resort to other methods. Benchmarking, cited in the Notice on the notion of State aid, is one such method.[81] The point of benchmarking is to ascertain whether the measure is in keeping with the behaviour of rational firms acting in similar circumstances and in relation to comparable transactions. Some examples can illustrate its usefulness in a wide range of scenarios. Where a publicly-owned bank lends money to a private firm, for instance, benchmarking can be used to determine whether the terms and conditions of the loan (and in particular the interest rate) reflect the prevailing market conditions.[82] The method may also be relevant, to give another example, where a public authority purchases or sells assets.[83]

The fundamental challenge that comes with this exercise has to do with the identification of the appropriate comparator (or comparators). Doing so means,

---

[77] ibid, paras 96–100.

[78] Commission Decision of 23 May 2011 – Agricultural Bank of Greece (ATE) (Case N 429/2010). For a discussion, see Conte and Khalil (n 60).

[79] ibid, paras 21–25.

[80] ibid, para 48: 'It must be noted that the measure does not respect the "concomitance" test, since the capital injected neither accompanies a comparable participation by a private shareholder nor is the capital injected proportionate to the number of shares held by the State. In fact, the participation of Greek authorities of up to EUR 1,144.5 million corresponds to up to 90.9% of the total capital increase (to be compared with the current shareholdership of the State in ATE of 77.3%), while the other shareholders are expected to contribute to a lower extent than their current shareholdership (i.e. for 9.1%)'.

[81] Commission Notice on the notion of aid (n 3), paras 98–100.

[82] Case C-457/00 *Belgium v Commission*, EU:C:2003:387, para 32.

[83] See for instance *SFEI* (n 34), para 61.

first and foremost, figuring out which 'market economy operator' is the one against which the intervention should be measured.[84] There is no such thing as a monolithic private firm. There is a difference, in this sense, between a venture capitalist, a property developer and the owner of telecommunications infrastructure. It is therefore necessary to identify the right variety of 'market economy operator' that best reflects the reality of the intervention. Similarly, the characteristics of the recipient (for instance, its creditworthiness, where debt instruments are at issue) are likely to play a role in the assessment.[85] Which benchmark to use is contingent on a number of additional (but related) factors, including, among others, the features of the relevant market (given that the behaviour of a rational private operator will adjust accordingly), the nature of the transaction at issue (there is a difference, coming back to the examples mentioned above, between a loan or a guarantee granted by a financial institution and the sale of real estate assets) or its timing.[86]

The Commission decision in *Péti Nitrogénművek Zrt* illustrates how the comparison exercise operates in practice.[87] The case concerned an intervention aimed at ensuring the viability of a firm in the form of two guarantees backing two loans given by a State-owned entity.[88] Hungary argued during the administrative proceedings that these measures were similar to the sort of support that would have been available under normal market conditions. It argued, in this sense, that the recipient had obtained equivalent terms and conditions from private operators. The Commission noted, however, that the allegedly comparable loans given by private entities were not appropriate benchmarks.[89] It pointed out, in this sense, that they were granted for lower amounts. The nature of the transaction was therefore different. In addition, the rates applied by the private banks were higher, thereby suggesting that the conditions offered by Hungary would not have been available under normal market conditions. Finally, the economic context was no longer the same, in the sense that the allegedly comparable loans had been given prior to the financial crisis.

2.4.4. Profitability Analysis

Benchmarking is not always available as a method. There may be circumstances where it is difficult, if not impossible, to find a genuine 'market economy operator' in the relevant industry. In some markets, existing players are influenced by non-market considerations to such an extent that their behaviour is not in keeping with

---

[84] Commission Notice on the notion of aid (n 3), para 99.

[85] Joined Cases T-228/99 and T-233/99 *Westdeutsche Landesbank Girozentrale and North Rhine-Westphalia v Commission*, EU:T:2003:57, para 251.

[86] Commission Notice on the notion of aid (n 3), para 99.

[87] Commission Decision of 27 October 2010 on State aid C 14/09 (ex NN 17/09) granted by Hungary to Péti Nitrogénművek Zrt. [2011] OJ L118/9. See also Case T-387/11 *Nitrogénművek Vegyipari Zrt. v Commission*, EU:T:2013:98.

[88] ibid, paras 9–12.

[89] ibid, para 45.

the conduct one would expect from a rational profit-maximising undertaking. For instance, benchmarking has been deemed to be an unreliable indicator when evaluating the behaviour of airport operators. In its 2014 Guidelines addressing the relationship between airports and airlines, the Commission expressed the view that a 'large majority' of airports within the EU are publicly owned and operated, with State resources covering both investments and even operating costs.[90] In such circumstances, their conduct was not deemed to provide a reliable approximation of the market price of the services they provide to airlines.[91]

Where benchmarking cannot be relied upon, it is necessary to resort to other methods. As is true of EU law at large,[92] any alternative approach must reflect the mainstream consensus, in the sense that it must be widely accepted as reliable by experts in the field.[93] In the same vein, it must rely on data that is not only complete, but objective and verifiable.[94] The evaluation of the profitability of the economic venture is one such alternative method. It makes it possible to determine whether the investment is a rational one from the perspective of a 'market economy operator'. The profitability assessment is conducted in two steps. It is necessary to determine, first, the rate of return expected by the public authority. The Commission identifies two possible (and overlapping) methods in this sense: the internal rate of return (or IRR)[95] and the net present value (or NPV).[96] The second step involves ascertaining whether the expected return is in keeping with normal market conditions (that is, the rate of return that a rational private operator would expect for a comparable investment).

An emblematic example of how profitability analysis is conducted in practice is provided by the *Ciudad de la Luz* case, concerning an investment in the construction of a major film studio in Spain.[97] The case reveals the rigour and nuance it brings to the assessment. Even though the expert reports commissioned by the regional authority had concluded that the investment would be profitable, the Commission decided that the project involved the award of State aid, which was, moreover, found to be incompatible with the internal market.[98] The fundamental reason why it ruled that the venture was not in keeping with the behaviour of a rational private investor had to do with the fact that, in spite of its seeming

---

[90] Guidelines on State aid to airports and airlines [2014] OJ C099/3, para 57.

[91] ibid, para 59.

[92] For a discussion on the mainstream consensus in other areas of EU law, see Pablo Ibáñez Colomo, 'Law, Policy, Expertise: Hallmarks of Effective Judicial Review in EU Competition Law' (2022) 24 Cambridge Yearbook of European Legal Studies 143.

[93] Commission Notice on the notion of aid (n 3), para 101.

[94] ibid.

[95] ibid, paras 102–103. Conte and Khalil (n 60) refer to the literature on the matter, and more precisely to Richard A Brealey, Stewart C Myers and Franklin Allen, *Principles of Corporate Finance* (McGraw-Hill 2014).

[96] As noted by Robins and Puglisi (n 8), both typically lead to the same results.

[97] Commission Decision of 8 May 2012 on State aid SA.22668 (C 8/08 (ex NN 4/08)) [2013] OJ L85/1. For an analysis of the case, see Robins and Puglisi (n 8) and Adina Claici, 'Ciudad de la Luz Judgement – An In-Depth Review of the Market Economy Investor Principle' in Caroline Buts and José Luis Buendía Sierra (eds), *Milestones in State Aid Case Law* (2nd edn, Lexxion 2022).

[98] ibid, Article 1.

profitability, the return expected by the regional authority was below the level that a private investor would have required in such circumstances.[99] A challenge against the decision was subsequently dismissed by the GC.[100]

2.5.   The Absence of a 'Market Economy Operator'

There are instances where it is not possible to identify a 'market economy operator', for the simple reason that such operator does not exist – and cannot exist – in the relevant economic and regulatory context. By their very nature, some projects are beyond the reach of the private sector. Therefore, they can only be realistically undertaken by a public authority. Some of the interventions that took place at the height of the financial crisis of the late 2000s provide an example in this sense.[101] In the face of systemic risk, only sovereign States may be in a position to step in and bring stability to the industry. When a public authority intervenes in such circumstances (for instance, by injecting capital in banks), it is difficult to argue that it does so in its capacity as an investor. Coming back to the criteria laid down in *EDF*, the aims and effects of intervention would arguably be a manifestation of the core of the State's powers.

A second scenario where a 'market economy operator' cannot be expected to emerge is one where the nature and scale of intervention is such that it could not have been undertaken or replicated by a rational private firm. It is not necessary to explain at length (the point being addressed in Chapter 1 and again in the subsequent section) that investments by public authorities may be driven by motives other than profit-maximisation. The example of airports, mentioned above, is one of them. In some instances, public investments aim at rolling out infrastructures that would never have been developed under normal market conditions. This may be true, for instance, of a network of railways which, in the name of social cohesion and effective participation in society, is not designed – and does not aspire – to be profitable (and, by the same token, would never be built or maintained by a rational private investor).

In a scenario that involves an infrastructure that would not have been replicated under normal market conditions, a question that may arise is that of whether granting access to it can be said to amount to the award of an advantage. One could argue that benefitting from such non-replicable assets departs by definition from normality. Accordingly, even if the relevant terms and conditions allowed the infrastructure operator to cover the costs involved in providing access, the very fact that the infrastructure cannot be compared to any private venture means that the parameters typically relied upon to ascertain the applicability of the 'market

---

[99] ibid, para 88.

[100] Joined Cases T-319/12 and T-321/12 *Spain, Ciudad de la Luz, SAU and Sociedad Proyectos Temáticos de la Comunidad Valenciana, SAU v Commission*, EU:T:2014:604.

[101] See in this sense Christian Ahlborn, 'Financial Sector' in Kelyn Bacon (ed), *European Union Law of State Aid* (2nd edn, Oxford University Press 2013).

economy operator' principle are irrelevant. One could argue in this sense that, where the State provides access to a non-replicable infrastructure, it is acting, always and everywhere, as a public authority, not a private undertaking.

Compelling as this conclusion may sound, the relevant case law suggests that the applicability of the 'market economy operator' principle is to be assessed on a case-by-case basis, in accordance with the approach and criteria spelled out in *EDF*. The 'market economy operator' principle is therefore applicable even when the relevant infrastructure would never have been rolled out by the private sector. In *Chronopost*, the ECJ conceded that the French postal network owned and operated by incumbent La Poste 'would never have been created by a private undertaking'.[102] In spite of this fact, the Court did not completely rule out the application of the 'market economy operator' principle to the terms and conditions of access to the (non-replicable) infrastructure. In this sense, it held that the analysis of whether access is provided on market terms 'must be assessed by reference to the objective and verifiable elements which are available'.[103] These elements include the costs borne by the incumbent when providing 'logistical and commercial assistance' to its subsidiary.[104]

Where the State acts in the exercise of its core powers, on the other hand, the measure will necessarily amount to State aid. One can come to this conclusion in light of the *ING* saga. The case discussed above concerned, strictly speaking, a follow-up of a capital injection that was approved at the peak of the financial crisis. It was accepted as given that the initial intervention (as opposed to the follow-up) amounted to State aid.[105] In her Opinion, Advocate General Sharpston expressed the view that, given the circumstances in which the capital injection occurred, it could not be otherwise. In her view, 'in the context of the serious financial crisis which broke in 2008, the Netherlands State was acting entirely in its capacity as supreme public authority concerned with the stability of the national economy as a whole'. This was not, therefore, 'a capacity in which any private investor would or could act'.[106]

3. Compensation for Public Service Obligations

3.1. The Status of Public Services in EU Law

Public intervention in the economy is often aimed at correcting the outcomes that would result from the normal operation of market forces. Such outcomes may

---

[102] Joined Cases C-83/01 P, C-93/01 P and C-94/01 P *Chronopost SA, La Poste and France v Union française de l'express (Ufex) and others*, EU:C:2003:388, para 36.

[103] ibid, para 38.

[104] ibid, para 39.

[105] *ING* (n 47), para 7.

[106] Opinion of Advocate General Sharpston in Case C-224/12 P *Commission v Netherlands and ING Groep NV*, EU:C:2013:870.

be deemed undesirable for non-economic reasons.[107] As explained in Chapter 1, some services are so central to meaningful participation in society that State action is deemed necessary to ensure that all citizens have access to them affordably, reliably and on non-discriminatory terms and conditions. For instance, performing indispensable bureaucratic tasks (such as paying taxes or requesting a permit from a public authority) often requires (or assumes) access to the Internet. Similarly, a citizen may find it difficult to go about their day-to-day activities without a bank account. Giving effect to demands of universal access to essential services requires the State to specify, inter alia, the nature of the services to be provided, the requisite levels of quality and the prices at which they are to be offered.

The TFEU respects and acknowledges the reality of these interventions and provides a framework for their interaction with the EU legal order.[108] Pursuant to Article 106(2) TFEU, firms 'entrusted with the operation of services of general economic interest' are subject to the rules of the TFEU (and in particular the rules of competition) only insofar as the application of the latter 'does not obstruct the performance, in law or in fact, of the particular tasks assigned to them' and provided that 'development of trade' is not 'affected to such an extent as would be contrary to the interests of the Union'. The very wording of the provision shows how much EU law accommodates efforts by EU Member States to ensure that services of general economic interest (hereinafter, 'SGEI') can be provided universally or without discrimination. The evolution of the case law suggests that, if anything, national authorities' leeway in relation to these services has probably increased over time.[109]

The TFEU does not define what amounts to an SGEI, and there is no finite or set list of services that qualify as such. By definition, what is necessary for effective participation in society may change and evolve over time. For instance, it is only relatively recently that access to broadband Internet became a major way to interact with public authorities and private firms; the importance of postal services,

---

[107] Cees Dekker and Vincent Verouden, 'Services of General Economic Interest' in Werner and Verouden (n 60).

[108] Pursuant to Article 14 TFEU: 'Without prejudice to Article 4 of the Treaty on European Union or to Articles 93, 106 and 107 of this Treaty, and given the place occupied by services of general economic interest in the shared values of the Union as well as their role in promoting social and territorial cohesion, the Union and the Member States, each within their respective powers and within the scope of application of the Treaties, shall take care that such services operate on the basis of principles and conditions, particularly economic and financial conditions, which enable them to fulfil their missions. The European Parliament and the Council, acting by means of regulations in accordance with the ordinary legislative procedure shall establish these principles and set these conditions without prejudice to the competence of Member States, in compliance with the Treaties, to provide, to commission and to fund such services'. On this issue, see generally José Luis Buendía Sierra, *Exclusive Rights and State Monopolies Under EC Law: Article 86 (Formerly Article 90) of the EC Treaty* (Oxford University Press 2000).

[109] As exemplified by the reference to Article 14 TFEU, successive revisions of the Treaties have progressively signalled the importance of SGEIs in the legal order of EU Member States. For an overview of the evolution of this case law, see Leigh Hancher and Pierre Larouche, 'The Coming of Age of EU Regulation of Network Industries and Services of General Economic Interest' in Paul Craig and Gráinne de Búrca (eds), *The Evolution of EU Law* (2nd edn, Oxford University Press 2011).

conversely, appears to be declining.[110] Moreover, the services deemed important or essential may vary from one society to another. It may therefore be difficult to introduce a common definition at the EU level. These features – and in particular their evolving and jurisdiction-specific nature – explain, first, why EU Member States are in principle free to decide which activities qualify as an SGEI, and, second, why such designation is only controlled for manifest errors by the EU institutions.[111]

Even though there is no formal definition of the concept, an overview of national legislation gives a sense both of what an SGEI is and of the circumstances where a service is likely to be designated as such. One of the overarching ideas to be drawn from the case law is that an SGEI exhibits 'special characteristics compared with that of other economic activities'.[112] Along the lines of what has been mentioned above, these are services that play a prominent role in citizens' daily lives. Utilities (including telecommunications, energy and transport) are – non-exhaustive – examples that come to mind immediately. A second overarching idea is that State intervention to guarantee the provision of an SGEI must be a response to the inability of the market to deliver the desired outcomes in terms of, inter alia, coverage, equality of treatment, affordability and continuity. Thus, where such outcomes can be expected from the normal play of market forces, the imposition of specific obligations to guarantee its provision is not warranted.[113]

The legal techniques on which EU Member States rely to guarantee the provision of an SGEI may come into conflict with the EU system of undistorted competition. The nature of the tensions between national and EU law became apparent in *Corbeau*. The case concerned the public service with which the Belgian postal operator (*Régie des Postes*) had been entrusted.[114] This undertaking was required, by law, to offer its services in the whole of the territory at the same price and equivalent levels of quality. The legal technique to achieve universal and non-discriminatory access was the award of an exclusive right (that is, a legal monopoly). The elimination of all competition enabled the postal operator to cross-subsidise the losses made in non-profitable areas (typically, remote and sparsely populated) with the excess monies obtained in profitable ones (typically, urban areas). The Court accepted that the award of exclusive rights could be justified in accordance with Article 106(2) TFEU, on the condition that it remained proportionate to the aims pursued.[115]

---

[110] See for instance the example of Denmark: Adrienne Murray and Paul Kirby, 'Denmark's postal service to stop delivering letters' *BBC News* (6 March 2025).

[111] Case T-17/02 *Fred Olsen, SA v Commission of the European Communities, supported by Spain*, EU:T:2005:218, para 216; and Case T-289/03 *BUPA and Others v Commission*, EU:T:2008:29, para 166.

[112] Case C-242/95 *GT-Link A/S and De Danske Statsbaner (DSB)*, EU:C:1997:376, para 53.

[113] Communication from the Commission on the application of the European Union State aid rules to compensation granted for the provision of services of general economic interest [2012] OJ C8/4, para 48.

[114] Case C-320/91 *Criminal proceedings against Paul Corbeau.*, EU:C:1993:198, para 15.

[115] ibid, para 19.

Instead of awarding exclusive rights, an EU Member State may choose to compensate the firm for the costs involved in the discharge of its public service duties. This legal technique impinges less on the EU system of undistorted competition – and is prima facie less problematic as a result – insofar as it allows for rivalry to emerge and be sustained in profitable areas that attract entry by new players. This fact does not mean that compensation as a technique is immune from scrutiny under EU law. A question that arises whenever a firm receives payments making up for the burden involved in the provision of an SGEI is whether the transfer of resources can be characterised as State aid and, specifically, whether it amounts to an advantage within the meaning of *Steenkolenmijnen*. A second question relates to the role of Article 106(2) TFEU in the assessment. and, more precisely, whether, and if so how, the provision can be relied upon to justify the award of aid.

3.2. Approaches to the Compensation for Public Service Obligations

As is true of the notion of aid, discussed in Chapter 2, the EU courts did not immediately provide an unequivocal answer concerning the question of whether compensations for public service obligations fall within the scope of Article 107(1) TFEU. Until after the turn of the century, two potential (and mutually inconsistent) approaches to the issue coexisted in the case law. These two interpretations were systematically contrasted by Advocate General Léger in his second Opinion in *Altmark*.[116] The Advocate General distinguished between the 'gross' and the 'net' theories of the concept of advantage. Under the former, compensating a firm for the discharge of its public service duties amounts to an advantage that may be justified where the conditions laid down in Article 106(2) TFEU are met.[117] Pursuant to the 'net' theory, by contrast, compensation for the discharge of public service duties only provides an advantage where it exceeds the costs involved in fulfilling the obligations.[118]

The 'gross' theory had been followed, prior to the Opinion, in *FFSA*[119] and *SIC*.[120] This interpretation of the concept of advantage draws a sharp distinction between the characterisation of a measure as State aid, on the one hand, and its justification under, inter alia, Articles 107(3) and 106(2) TFEU, on the other. As noted

---

[116] Opinion of Advocate General Léger in Case C-280/00 *Altmark Trans GmbH and Regierungspräsidium Magdeburg v Nahverkehrsgesellschaft Altmark GmbH, and Oberbundesanwalt beim Bundesverwaltungsgericht*, EU:C:2003:13.

[117] ibid, para 34.

[118] ibid, para 32.

[119] Case T-106/95 *Fédération française des sociétés d'assurances (FFSA) and others v Commission*, EU:T:1997:23.

[120] Case T-46/97 *SIC – Sociedade Independente de Comunicação SA v Commission*, EU:T:2000:123.

by Advocate General Léger, compatible State aid is never a gratuitous advantage.[121] By definition, it must make a contribution to a public interest objective, whether equity or efficiency related. Accordingly, the Advocate General argued, a transfer of State resources to make up for the cost of public service obligations is nothing but one potential justification for aid among others, and it is to be treated as such. From his perspective, embracing the 'net' theory would amount to conflating the characterisation and the justification stages of the assessment, thereby distorting the legal framework enshrined in the TFEU.[122]

By the time of the *Altmark* ruling, however, there was already support for the 'net' theory in the case law. In *ABDHU*,[123] for instance, the Court had already held, in a brief passage, that compensating an undertaking for the services provided to a public authority does not amount to State aid. The ECJ expressed the same view shortly before *Altmark*, in *Ferring*.[124] The case, mentioned in Chapter 4, concerned the fiscal treatment given to wholesalers distributing medicines, which was more favourable than that applying to laboratories. The exclusion of the former from the scope of a tax on direct sales sought to compensate them for the discharge of a public service obligation, namely the requirement to keep a minimum amount of medicines in stock.[125] The Court held (more clearly than in *ABDHU*, but without elaborating on the practical operation of the doctrine) that the differential treatment would only amount to an advantage where the amount foregone by the State exceeds the costs of complying with the regulatory duty.[126]

In addition to these precedents, one could argue that the principles governing the 'market economy operator' principle provide support for the 'net' theory. Compensating a firm for the discharge of a public service obligation, after all, is not fundamentally different from the acquisition or the sale of assets by a public authority. Indeed, it would not be unreasonable to characterise a payment for the provision of an SGEI as the purchase of a service by the State. To the extent that it takes place on market terms, such purchase would be comparable to other public-private sector interactions that escape scrutiny under EU State aid law. From this perspective, the 'net' theory would not be but a manifestation of the neutrality of the TFEU vis-à-vis the system of property ownership in the EU Member States, as well as an acknowledgement of the realities and complexities of mixed economies.

---

[121] Opinion of AG Léger in *Altmark* (n 116), paras 37–38.

[122] ibid, para 46.

[123] Case C-240/83 *Procureur de la République v Association de défense des brûleurs d'huiles usagées (ADBHU)*, EU:C:1985:59.

[124] Case C-53/00 *Ferring SA v Agence centrale des organismes de sécurité sociale (ACOSS)*, EU:C:2001:627.

[125] ibid, para 6.

[126] ibid, para 27.

3.3. The *Altmark* Criteria

The Court, in *Altmark*,[127] did not follow Advocate General Léger and embraced the essence of the 'net' theory. The ruling departed from *Ferring* and *ABDHU* insofar as it introduced a structured framework to evaluate, systematically and on the basis of objective criteria, whether compensation for the discharge of a public service obligation amounts to an advantage. Instead of leaving the definition of the relevant criteria to public authorities and/or recipients, the ECJ introduced four conditions to evaluate, as a matter of EU law, whether the transfer of resources falls within the scope of Article 107(1) TFEU. The common theme underlying the four conditions is that, where the relationship between the public authority and the firm is in substance comparable to the instances where the 'market economy operator' principle is applicable, the compensation will not be deemed to provide an advantage.

Pursuant to the first of the conditions, there must be clarity and transparency about the nature, duration and scope of the public service obligation.[128] In the words of the Court, the undertaking 'must actually have public service obligations to discharge'.[129] The obligations in question must, moreover, 'be clearly defined' (in, for instance, the applicable regulatory framework or in the agreement governing the relationship between the public authority and the recipient). If the public service obligations were vague or insufficiently specified, it would not be possible to determine whether the firm is or has been overcompensated. The case law and the administrative practice that followed suggest that the reference to 'public service' in *Altmark* must be interpreted as referring, in essence, to an SGEI within the meaning of Article 106(2) TFEU.[130] Accordingly, EU Member States enjoy 'wide discretion' when deciding 'the scope and organisation' of these services.[131] This discretion, however, is not unlimited.[132]

The second of the conditions refers to the definition of the criteria for the estimation of the compensation due. The Court held that 'the parameters on the basis of which the compensation is calculated must be established in advance in an objective and transparent manner, to avoid it conferring an economic advantage which may favour the recipient undertaking over competing undertakings'.[133] Accordingly, it is not sufficient to claim, as the EU Member State did in *Ferring*, that a particular measure seeks to make up for a regulatory burden. It is necessary to

---

[127] *Altmark* (n 9).

[128] ibid, para 89.

[129] ibid.

[130] Joined Cases C-66/16 P to C-69/16 P *Comunidad Autónoma del País Vasco and others v Commission*, EU:C:2017:999, para 56 ('the first *Altmark* condition, according to which the recipient undertaking must actually be required to discharge public service obligations which must be clearly defined, also applies where the derogation laid down in Article 106(2) TFEU has been invoked').

[131] ibid, para 70.

[132] ibid, para 71.

[133] *Altmark* (n 9), para 90.

show that the resources to be transferred or foregone by the State as consideration have been determined in advance. In *Enirisorse*, delivered shortly after *Altmark*, the ECJ noted that the EU Member State had failed to show how the allocation of infrastructure charges to an undertaking was 'linked to clearly defined public-service duties'. As a result, this second condition was not found to be met.[134]

In accordance with the third condition, 'the compensation cannot exceed what is necessary to cover all or part of the costs incurred in the discharge of public service obligations, taking into account the relevant receipts and a reasonable profit for discharging those obligations'.[135] This aspect of the *Altmark* ruling is self-explanatory, as it forms the core of the test. That said, there are two points to note about its meaning and operation. The first point to note is that a transfer of State resources that overcompensates the recipient would not just amount to an advantage within the meaning of Article 107(1) TFEU; it would also be, by its very nature, incompatible with the internal market.[136] This is primarily so because it would not make any contribution to a public interest objective. In other words – and coming back to the Opinion of Advocate General Léger – it would be the sort of gratuitous advantage for which there is no room in the EU legal order.

The second point to note is that any 'market economy operator' is expected to make a 'reasonable profit' when providing its services. From this perspective, it is unsurprising that the Court makes it explicit that the compensation can go beyond strictly making up for the costs involved in discharging the obligations. However, the ruling does not provide an interpretation of what a 'reasonable profit' is. The Commission, in its Communication on the matter, defines it as 'the rate of return on capital that would be required by a typical company considering whether or not to provide the service of general economic interest for the whole duration of the period of entrustment, taking into account the level of risk',[137] which seems in line with its approach to profitability analysis under the 'market economy operator' principle.

The fourth *Altmark* condition also follows the logic of the said principle. It requires, in essence, the EU Member State to ensure that the services are provided 'at the least cost to the community'.[138] The ruling provides two alternative routes to meet the condition. The preferred approach is to select the undertaking 'pursuant to a public procurement procedure'.[139] In line with the discussions above, where the recipient is selected on the basis of a genuine tender, one can safely presume that the services are provided at the most competitive price. Similarly, for

---

[134] Joined Cases C-34/01 to C-38/01 *Enirisorse SpA v Ministero delle Finanze*, EU:C:2003:640, para 40.

[135] *Altmark* (n 9), para 92.

[136] European Union framework for State aid in the form of public service compensation [2012] OJ C8/15, para 48.

[137] Communication from the Commission on the application of the European Union State aid rules to compensation granted for the provision of services of general economic interest [2012] OJ C8/4, para 61.

[138] *Altmark* (n 9), para 93.

[139] ibid.

this approach to be accepted in a particular case, the public procurement procedure organised by the EU Member State will have to be a genuine one, that is, one that is 'open, transparent and unconditional'. One of the rare examples where the Commission concluded that the fourth *Altmark* condition was fulfilled under this approach is *Tirrenia di Navigazione*.[140] As explained in the decision, there were sufficient safeguards in place to ensure that the tender would be competitive and non-discriminatory.[141]

In the absence of a public procurement procedure, the EU Member State will have to determine the level of compensation based on 'an analysis of the costs which a typical undertaking, well run and adequately provided with means of transport so as to be able to meet the necessary public service requirements, would have incurred'.[142] This alternative approach demands, in essence, a benchmarking exercise that is reminiscent of the indirect methods applied to identify the appropriate 'market economy operator'. For the same reason, the practical estimation can give rise to considerable complexities. Difficulties in this sense come to a significant extent from the fact that many, if not most, firms subject to public service obligations cannot be readily compared to a typical private undertaking. This reality, however, does not mean that the fourth condition should not apply.[143] It does not mean, either, that the said condition is satisfied just because the operator compares favourably with undertakings subject to similar obligations in other EU Member States.[144]

3.4. The Legal Framework Post-*Altmark*

3.4.1. *Commission Action Post-*Altmark

Altmark had major consequences, both from a substantive and an institutional standpoint. Where the four conditions are met, compensation for public service obligations falls outside the scope of Article 107(1) TFEU. By the same token, an *Altmark*-compliant intervention (or one that is believed to be *Altmark*-compliant) need not be notified pursuant to Article 108(3) TFEU. The substantive choice made by the Court in the ruling therefore had an impact on the Commission's ability to oversee financial support in relation to SGEIs and to develop EU-wide

---

[140] Commission Decision of 2 March 2020 on the measures SA.32014, SA.32015, SA.32016 (11/C) (ex 11/NN) implemented by Italy for Tirrenia di Navigazione and its acquirer Compagnia Italiana di Navigazione [2020] OJ L332/45, para 406. The case is discussed in Phedon Nicolaides, 'A Rare Case of *Altmark*-compliant SGEI (Part II)' (*State Aid Uncovered*, 8 December 2020), available at www.lexxion. eu/en/stateaidpost/a-rare-case-of-altmark-compliant-sgei-part-ii/.

[141] ibid, paras 386–390.

[142] *Altmark* (n 9), para 93.

[143] Communication from the Commission on the application of the European Union State aid rules to compensation granted for the provision of services of general economic interest (n 137), para 70. See also Case C-186/22 *Sad Trasporto Locale SpA v Provincia autonoma di Bolzano*, EU:C:2023:795.

[144] ibid, para 74.

policy in the area. Given how strict the conditions are (in particular the fourth), moreover, the ruling disincentivises the notification of a substantial number of measures potentially qualifying as State aid. As a result, *Altmark* could lead to the decentralised interpretation of Article 107(1) TFEU, thereby exacerbating the risk of legal uncertainty and substantive fragmentation.

The Commission addressed these risks in the immediate aftermath of *Altmark*. It adopted a package combining hard and soft law instruments. In its current (and second) incarnation, the package pursues two main objectives. First, it advances the Commission's interpretation of, and approach to, the four *Altmark* conditions (and, more generally, the meaning and scope of Article 107(1) TFEU where SGEIs are at issue).[145] Second, a series of instruments, comprising a Decision adopted pursuant to Article 106(3) TFEU,[146] a Regulation[147] and a Framework,[148] outline the Commission's approach to compensations that do not meet the *Altmark* conditions. These instruments deal extensively with the interpretation and application of Article 106(2) TFEU in relation to the discharge of public service obligations. This regulatory apparatus provides the basis for the steady stream of individual decisions that the Commission has issued in the course of the past two decades.[149]

The philosophy that guides the abovementioned package and the accompanying administrative practice is not fundamentally different from the principles introduced by the Court in *Altmark*. There is, on the one hand, a significant degree of overlap between the four conditions set out in the judgment and Article 106(2) TFEU. It has already been mentioned that a measure that fails the third *Altmark* condition would not just qualify as State aid; it would also be incompatible, by its very nature, with the internal market. In spite of the similarities, the analysis of compensations under Article 106(2) TFEU gives greater leeway to EU Member States than the *Altmark* straitjacket. This divergence is particularly apparent when it comes to the fourth condition set out in the latter. The Commission is ready to accept that State intervention that fails that criterion may be justified under Article 106(2) TFEU.

The Framework for State aid in the form of public service compensation explains that compensating a relatively inefficient undertaking may be compatible with the internal market where there are mechanisms to incentivise the efficient

---

[145] Commission on the application of the European Union State aid rules to compensation granted for the provision of services of general economic interest (n 137).

[146] Commission Decision of 20 December 2011 on the application of Article 106(2) of the Treaty on the Functioning of the European Union to State aid in the form of public service compensation granted to certain undertakings entrusted with the operation of services of general economic interest [2011] OJ L7/3.

[147] Commission Regulation (EU) 2023/2832 of 13 December 2023 on the application of Articles 107 and 108 of the Treaty on the Functioning of the European Union to de minimis aid granted to undertakings providing services of general economic interest [2023] OJ L 2023/2832.

[148] European Union framework for State aid in the form of public service compensation (n 136).

[149] For an overview of this practice, see in particular Conor Quigley, *European State Aid Law and Policy (and UK Subsidy Control)* (4th edn, Hart Publishing 2022) 451–478.

provision of the SGEI.[150] Under Article 106(2) TFEU, in other words, the fourth *Altmark* condition becomes an aspiration guiding the behaviour of the undertaking, rather than a strict requirement. In this sense, the Framework seeks to strike a balance between the leeway EU Member States enjoy when organising SGEIs, on the one hand, and the need to minimise the cost for the community, on the other. Accordingly, the Commission clarifies that the definition of the appropriate mechanisms to incentivise efficiency will vary from one sector to another, and that public authorities can choose between different approaches. What is more, it openly acknowledges that such mechanisms may not always be 'feasible or appropriate'.

Some examples from Commission practice usefully illustrate what these efficiency-related mechanisms may be, and how they adjust in practice to the nature and specificities of the SGEI at issue. *Post Office Limited*, first decided in 2012, related to compensation for the operation of a network of postal offices that was larger than the one the undertaking would have maintained as a rational private operator.[151] The Commission was satisfied with the 'yearly efficiency milestones' that the EU Member State had introduced. Funding was made contingent on these milestones being reached.[152] In a case concerning access to banking services, the Commission accepted a mechanism whereby compensation was progressively decreased year after year. What is more, the regime provided for the structural under-compensation for the services.[153]

3.4.2. Altmark *as a One-Size-Fits-All?*

One of the remaining questions, two decades after the ruling, is whether *Altmark* is sufficiently flexible so that it can meaningfully apply to every scenario involving compensation for public service obligations. The issue was raised early on, in a saga of cases involving public service broadcasting.[154] In some respects, television services are difficult to compare with sectors like rail, telecommunications or postal services, if only because of the role that the media plays in a democratic society.[155] As a result, public service broadcasters claimed (not unreasonably) that

---

[150] European Union framework for State aid in the form of public service compensation (n 136), paras 39–43.

[151] Commission Decision of 28 March 2012 – Post Office Limited (POL): Compensation for net costs incurred to keep a non-commercially viable network for the period 2012-15 and the continuation of a working capital facility (Case SA.33054).

[152] ibid, para 97.

[153] Commission Decision of 26 July 2021 – France Mission d'accessibilité bancaire pour la période 2021-2026 (Case SA.57570).

[154] Davide Grespan, 'A Busy Year for State Aid Control in the Field of Public Service Broadcasting' (2010) 9 European State Aid Law Quarterly 79; and Ansgar Held and Annette Kliemann, 'The 2009 Broadcasting Communication and the Commission's Decisional Practice Two Years after its Entry into Force' (2012) 11 European State Aid Law Quarterly 37.

[155] EU Member States have consistently signalled the importance of public service broadcasting in a democratic society. See in particular Resolution of the Council and of the Representatives of the

it is for them to decide which programming remains within the scope of their remit and the technologies upon which they rely to fulfil their mission. Even though the GC rejected the idea that the specificities of the sector justify departing from *Altmark*,[156] it expressed the view that such specificities must be taken into account as part of the assessment.[157]

BUPA, in turn, suggested that some of the assumptions underpinning *Altmark* may not be easily transposed to every regulatory scheme aimed at ensuring the effective provision of an SGEI. In this sense, the interpretation of Article 107(1) TFEU in *Altmark* seemingly assumed that the loss-making activities requiring compensation would be confined to discrete areas or activities that can be identified and distinguished from profitable ones. It also takes as given that a single firm would be in charge of the obligations. *BUPA* presented a different scenario. It concerned a risk equalisation scheme in the healthcare sector.[158] Instead of designating a single undertaking for the provision of loss-making activities, it introduced a scheme to ensure that all healthcare providers would bear the same risk profile. Thus, undertakings providing insurance to users with a healthier profile would compensate those with a less healthy one. In the circumstances of the case, the relative risk profile (and the resulting compensation) was to be determined by the Health Minister.

The risk equalisation scheme is an adaptation to the features of the sector. Absent State intervention, providers would compete for the healthier profiles, leaving less healthy ones uninsured. Risk equalisation creates a level playing field and ensures that access is universal.[159] This mechanism, however sensible, is not particularly well suited to the application of the *Altmark* conditions (and the assumptions underpinning them). The point of the scheme is not so much to avoid overcompensation and/or ensure that the service is provided at the lowest cost to the community as to spread risk evenly across the industry. Against this background, it would have been reasonable to introduce an ad hoc framework to evaluate whether such a scheme falls within the scope of Article 107(1) TFEU. After all, the Commission had issued its decision before *Altmark* had been delivered. The GC, however, chose to rely on an expansive interpretation of the four conditions instead.[160] On that basis, it dismissed the direct action brought against

Governments of the Member States, meeting within the Council of 25 January 1999 concerning public service broadcasting [1999] OJ C30/1.

[156] Case T-674/11 *TV2/Danmark A/S v European Commission*, EU:T:2015:684, paras 56–57.

[157] ibid, para 70.

[158] BUPA (n 111). See also Commission Decision of 13 May 2003 – Risk equalisation scheme in the Irish health insurance market (Case N 46/2003). For an analysis, see Wolf Sauter, 'Case T-289/03, *British United Provident Association Ltd (BUPA), BUPA Insurance Ltd, BUPA Ireland Ltd v. Commission of the European Communities*, Judgment of the Court of First Instance of 12 February 2008, nyr' (2009) 46 Common Market Law Review 269.

[159] *Risk equalisation scheme in the Irish health insurance market* (n 158), para 52.

[160] Sauter (n 158), 282.

the decision.[161] It remains to be seen how malleable the ruling is and whether its boundaries will again be tested in future cases.

4. Conclusions

At first glance, one may be tempted to argue that the 'market economy operator' principle and the *Altmark* doctrine have different and essentially complementary spheres of application. The former would be relevant where a public authority acts as a rational undertaking subject to market pressures, whereas the latter would come into play where the State seeks to correct the outcomes that would result from the unconstrained operation of market forces. Upon closer scrutiny, however, the two doctrines come across as the expression of a broader principle, namely one that acknowledges the economic and regulatory realities within which EU State aid law is enforced. According to this overarching principle, there is no advantage within the meaning of Article 107(1) TFEU where public authorities interact at arm's length with the private sector. The relevant question common to both doctrines is therefore whether the State is exercising its prerogatives to provide an advantage or whether, instead, it acts as a market player.

Seen in this light, the lines between *Altmark* and the 'market economy operator' principle are blurred, if not indistinguishable. On the one hand, the latter doctrine applies even when an infrastructure would not have been developed under normal market conditions. In *Chonopost*, the Court held that access to a non-replicable network does not amount, in and of itself, to an advantage – and this regardless of the fact that the network would not have been rolled out by a private firm. On the other hand, the ECJ clarified, in *Altmark*, that a compensation for a public service obligation is not caught by Article 107(1) TFEU where the State chooses the most cost-efficient option (that is, just like a 'market economy operator' would). The underlying economic reality is the same in both cases: the relevant market had been manufactured by the State. This fact, however, is not decisive. Both doctrines accept that there is no such thing as a 'pure' market in the mixed economies in the EU Member States. What counts, therefore, is the behaviour of the State, rather than the alleged artificiality of the activity under consideration.

The case law shaping the two doctrines has led to the progressive reduction of the scope of Article 107(1) TFEU (and therefore of the Commission's ability to manage regulatory competition among EU Member States). As far as the 'market economy operator' principle is concerned, the Court has decisively placed substance above form when ascertaining the applicability of the doctrine. This approach stands in stark contrast with the formalistic interpretation adopted in

---

[161] For an analysis, see Alfonso Lamadrid de Pablo, '*BUPA*: The Illusion of Flexibility that Strengthened *Altmark*', in Buts and Buendía Sierra (n 97).

relation to the notion of aid (discussed in Chapter 2) and the concept of selectivity (addressed in Chapter 4). As a result of this substantive choice, the potential reach of the 'market economy operator' principle is broader, as is apparent from *EDF* and *ING*. The adoption of the 'net' theory of the concept of advantage in *Altmark*, in turn, significantly reduced the powers of the Commission to oversee and shape the regulation of services of general economic interest.

4

When is an Advantage Selective?

1. The Concept of Selectivity

1.1. Generalities: Substantive and Geographic Selectivity

An advantage within the meaning of Article 107(1) TFEU must be selective for it to qualify as State aid. More precisely, it must distort (or threaten to distort) competition 'by favouring certain undertakings or the production of certain goods'. Advantages benefitting all firms without distinction (so-called general measures) therefore fall outside the scope of the provision. The selectivity condition places an important constraint on EU State aid law's ability to interfere with economic policy measures. The overarching logic underpinning Article 107(1) TFEU is that regulatory competition escapes scrutiny unless it relies, totally or partially, on targeted intervention. Thus, EU Member States are free to set, absent formal harmonisation at the EU level, the corporate tax rate at the level of their choice.[1] The use of economic policy tools that favour certain firms or certain activities (for instance by setting a tax break applicable to one sector of the economy), by contrast, will be subject to scrutiny by the European Commission (hereinafter, the 'Commission').

Establishing whether an advantage is indeed selective (as opposed to general) will in occasional instances be straightforward. So much so, in fact, that it is sometimes possible to infer the latter from the award of the former. For example, one can safely presume that an advantage granted by means of an individual measure is selective within the meaning of Article 107(1) TFEU.[2] In other instances, however, establishing selectivity to the requisite legal standard will prove to be a far more complex, uncertain and potentially controversial exercise. It is not surprising, in this sense, that the case law and administrative practice interpreting the condition have given rise to more commentary and discussion than any other element of the notion of State aid.[3] For the same reason, the boundaries of legitimate

---

[1] See Chapter 5 for an extensive discussion.

[2] Case C-15/14 P *Commission v MOL Magyar Olaj- és Gázipari Nyrt.*, EU:C:2015:362, para 60.

[3] Such commentary includes the following: José Luís da Cruz Vilaça, 'Material and geographic selectivity in state aid – recent developments' (2009) 8 European State Aid Law Quarterly 443; Andreas Bartosch, 'Is there a need for a rule of reason in European State aid law? Or how to arrive at a

regulatory competition (and, similarly, regulatory competition subject to scrutiny under Article 107(1) TFEU) remain unclear.

While it is true that establishing whether a measure is selective can sometimes raise practical challenges, the meaning of the condition itself is not particularly obscure. It is about targeted advantages, whether on the basis of substantive (or material)[4] criteria (that is, criteria pertaining to the firms' characteristics) or their geographic considerations instead. Accordingly, the selectivity condition will be met where an advantage benefits a single firm (for instance, there is a single recipient of an investment that departs from normal market conditions[5]). The same is true where a measure adopted by the central government favours a whole sector (or several sectors) of the economy (for instance, the textile industry[6] or manufacturing firms[7]) and, similarly, all firms operating in a given region.[8] In relation to the latter two examples, the Court of Justice (hereinafter, the 'Court' or the 'ECJ') has clarified that the wide availability of an advantage does not rule out the application of Article 107(1) TFEU.[9] A measure will also be deemed selective where the relevant regulatory framework gives the public authority the discretion to decide when to award the advantage.[10]

This assessment need not be conducted by reference to the relevant market in the antitrust law sense.[11] Accordingly, all rivals within a given product and geographic market may benefit from a measure and the selectivity condition may still be met. The fact that State intervention would have an arguably neutral effect on competition in the narrow antitrust sense is neither relevant nor sufficient to rule out the application of Article 107(1) TFEU. As explained in Chapter 1, State aid and subsidy control regimes are concerned, first and foremost, with competition

---

coherent concept of material selectivity?' (2010) 47 Common Market Law Review 729; Conor Quigley, 'Direct taxation and State aid: recent developments concerning the notion of selectivity' (2012) 40 Intertax 112; José Luis Buendía Sierra, 'Finding Selectivity or the Art of Comparison: Annotation on the Judgment of the Court of Justice of the European Union (First Chamber) of 8 September 2011 in Joined Cases C-78 to 80/08, *Paint Graphos*' (2018) 17 European State Aid Law Quarterly 85; Michael Honoré, 'Selectivity' in Philipp Werner and Vincent Verouden (eds), *EU State Aid Control: Law and Economics* (2nd edn, Kluwer 2025); and Christopher McMahon, 'Selectivity as discrimination: lessons from the case law on fiscal measures for identifying State aid' (2024) 43 Yearbook of European Law, forthcoming.

[4] The commentary typically refers to material selectivity, which is a literal (and misleading) translation of the French word *matériel*. The analysis that follows refers to substantive selectivity, which is a more accurate translation.

[5] See in this sense the examples discussed in Chapter 3 concerning the application of the 'market economy operator' principle and concerning measures such as, inter alia, capital injections or loans at preferential rates.

[6] Case C-173/73 *Italy v Commission*, EU:C:1974:71.

[7] Case C-143/99 *Adria-Wien Pipeline GmbH and Wietersdorfer & Peggauer Zementwerke GmbH v Finanzlandesdirektion für Kärnten*, EU:C:2001:598.

[8] Case C-88/03 *Portugal v Commission*, EU:C:2006:511 (hereinafter, '*Azores*').

[9] Case C-75/97 *Belgium v Commission*, EU:C:1999:311, para 32.

[10] Case C-256/97 *Déménagements-Manutention Transport SA (DMT)*, EU:C:1999:332, para 27.

[11] Honoré (n 3) 188–89.

between countries, rather than firms.[12] For the same reason, the assessment of selectivity revolves around a sui generis methodology (or methodologies) that has no obvious comparator beyond other models of subsidy control, and the essence of which is not always (or not necessarily) explicit.

2. Establishing Selectivity: Issues and Challenges

2.1. Introduction

Ascertaining whether an advantage favours certain undertakings or the production of certain goods presents a number of theoretical and practical challenges. Some of them relate to the choice of the appropriate methodology. One can think of at least three potential approaches to selectivity: one that relies on the formal aspects of the measure (that is, whether, on its face, it treats some firms more favourably than others); one that focuses on its effects; and, finally, one that revolves around the objective it pursues. These are examined in turn. A second challenge pertains to the refinement of the analysis. When it is claimed that some firms are favoured over others, it is at least implicit in the argument that there is an alternative 'but for' scenario where no such favouring exists. Irrespective of the methodology chosen, therefore, selectivity can only be established by reference to a benchmark (that is, an alternative where the advantage is general).

2.2. The Form-based (or De Iure) Approach to Selectivity

Figure 4.1 First variety of de iure advantage

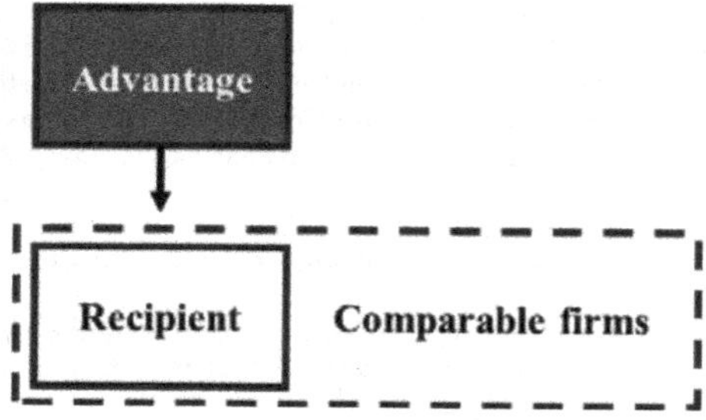

---

[12] José Luis Buendía Sierra and Ben Smulders, 'The Limited Role of the "Refined Economic Approach" in Achieving the Objectives of State Aid Control: Time for Some Realism' in *EC State Aid Law: Liber Amicorum in Honour Francisco Santaolalla* (Kluwer 2008).

A form-based approach to the assessment of selectivity is intuitively appealing and prima facie straightforward to administer. It revolves around ascertaining whether, as a matter of law, certain firms or the production of certain goods are targeted. De iure targeting along these lines comes in three different flavours, which are identified in Figures 4.1, 4.2 and 4.3. There would be selectivity in the formal sense, first, where there is a measure that positively favours a firm or a group thereof. The quintessential example of this category (depicted in Figure 4.1) is that of a direct transfer of State resources (that is, a subsidy in the narrow sense), or the sale of public assets at below-market prices. Formal targeting would also exist, second, where a firm or a group thereof is expressly dispensed from a set of obligations imposed on others (or, similarly, where its burden is alleviated relative to others). Such would be the case, for instance, where the relevant legislation provides that a sector of the economy (or firms established in a certain region) is subject to a lower corporate tax rate (or exempted altogether therefrom). Figure 4.2 captures this second scenario.

Figure 4.2 Second variety of de iure advantage

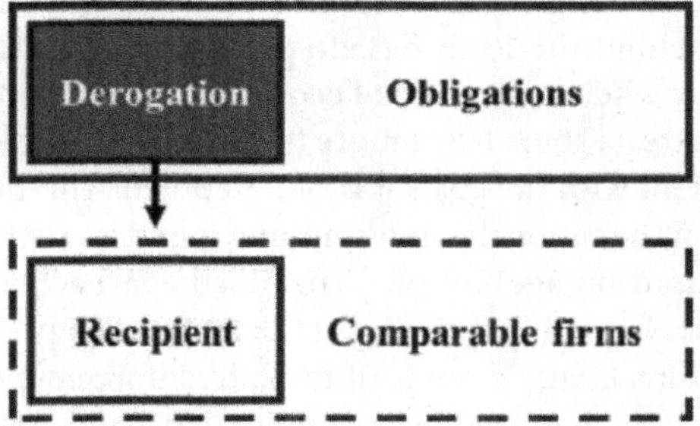

The third category is to some extent similar to the second one. It captures instances where, instead of an explicit carve out in the form of an exemption or more favourable treatment, the measure is crafted in such a way that some activities fall outside of its scope without the need to provide for an exemption or alleviate a burden. This category is probably best understood as a 'reverse derogation', in the sense that the difference in treatment comes from the fact that the measure imposes a burden on some firms, but not on others. It would amount to a selective advantage, therefore, insofar as it excludes from its scope undertakings that should have been subject to it. Consider the example of legislation aimed at taxing the pollution generated by extractive activities (such as mining for minerals and oil drilling). There would be a 'reverse derogation' within the meaning of Figure 4.3 if some extractive activities were expressly mentioned in the legislation, but comparable ones (say, gas drilling) were not subject to it.

Figure 4.3 Third variety of de iure advantage

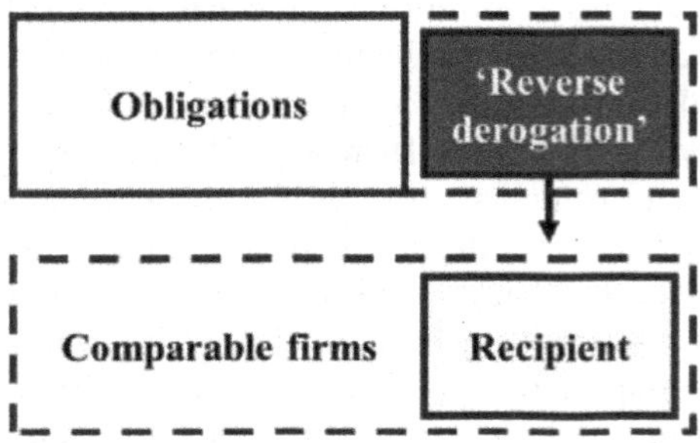

The advantages of a form-based approach to selectivity are apparent, at least at first glance. To begin with, it is a methodology that is seemingly straightforward to administer. Instead of relying on complex assessments, this approach would merely focus on the formal features of the measure under consideration. A second reason, in the same vein, relates to the legal certainty it provides to both public authorities – who would be able to design their measures to avoid scrutiny – and recipients. The implicit idea behind the form-based approach is that Article 107(1) TFEU only comes into play where a measure of economic policy is either discriminatory (in the sense that it treats some firms more favourably and/or less favourably than others) or inconsistent with the goals it is said to pursue (in the sense that there is a mismatch between the rationale underpinning it and its scope of application).

The potential disadvantages of the form-based approach are no less apparent upon closer scrutiny. Generally speaking, it is a methodology that can lead to both under- and overenforcement. It can lead to underenforcement (or type II errors) insofar as it does not contemplate the possibility that an advantage that is formally available to all firms may de facto only benefit a handful thereof. Consider the example of an EU Member State with a strong pharmaceutical industry that is interested in keeping and attracting investments in the sector. Public authorities in that country may attain their objective by providing for a generous exemption to investments in research and development. Formally speaking, the measure is of general application, in the sense that any firm qualifies for it. De facto, however, it necessarily favours research-intensive industries. More importantly, it allows the public authority to attain its goal, which is to benefit a specific sector of the economy.

The form-based approach may also be overinclusive and, as such, a source of type I errors. It is not necessarily the case that treating firms differently favours some firms over others. For instance, a levy that exempts renewable sources of electricity generation with a view to disincentivising non-renewable sources is not necessarily discriminatory. If the declared aim of the measure is to promote the adoption of the former and decarbonise the economy, it is in the nature of things that renewable sources are not subject to the levy. Formal discrimination, in other words, is not always inconsistent with the goals pursued by a regime. In some instances, in fact, consistency demands that objectively different activities be treated differently. One consequence to draw from this reality is that a form-based approach, if it is to be followed, must provide for corrective mechanisms to ensure that the broader context is considered and that errors (both type I and II) are minimised.

A second potential drawback of the form-based approach (and of formalism, more generally) is that it is not necessarily straightforward to implement in all cases. Whether or not a given measure is discriminatory, or whether it is inconsistent with the underlying aims, will in some instances be open to interpretation. Consider the example of a tax exemption that applies to every firm investing in a disadvantaged region.[13] It would be reasonable to argue that such a measure is not selective, insofar as the advantage is available to every potential investor. It would also be reasonable to argue – and this is the factor that complicates the analysis – that the measure is necessarily discriminatory, insofar as it is designed to promote investments in a certain region. One conclusion to draw, against this background, is that the form-based approach could well lead to arbitrary outcomes in the absence of a clear and coherent analytical framework spelled out in advance and applied consistently.

There are, third, scenarios where the application of the form-based approach may turn out to be unworkable and as such incapable of shedding light on the selective nature of the measure under consideration. This is the case, in particular, where a measure is discriminatory by design, that is, where the differential treatment is one of its constitutive features. The most obvious example in this sense is that of progressive taxation, whereby the amount paid depends on firms' income or turnover. Because the point of legislation is to achieve redistribution, one can expect it to favour some firms over others. It is not immediately obvious to see how a form-based approach can deal with such a reality satisfactorily. Taken to its logical consequences, the application of this methodology would lead to the prohibition, across the board, of progressive taxation, which may not be obvious to justify (whether as a matter of State aid law or one of EU law at large).

2.3. The Effects-based (or De Facto) Approach to Selectivity

The effects-based approach could remedy some of the potential flaws of formalism. The relevant question, under this methodology, is whether the measure under consideration – irrespective of its form – favours, de facto, certain firms or the production of certain goods. Coming back to one of the examples mentioned above, it would be immaterial that a tax exemption aimed at incentivising research and development is in principle open to every firm willing to engage in these

---

[13] See, by analogy, *Azores* (n 8).

activities. What would matter, instead, is the fact that, by definition, only a handful of industries would benefit from the measure (and, among those that would benefit, some would do so disproportionately more than others). Under this approach, formal discrimination is, at best, a preliminary first test, that is, one that is relied upon as a filter to identify the most egregious instances of selectivity.

One obvious advantage of the effects-based approach is that it safeguards the effectiveness of EU State aid law. It ensures that Member States are not able to circumvent Article 107(1) TFEU simply by choosing a regulatory technique that makes the measure seem, on surface, of general application. By placing substance over form, in fact, this methodology is consistent with the approach generally followed by the Court in other areas of EU law. The provisions dealing with the free movement of goods and services, for instance, encompass not just instances of overt discrimination but also measures having the effect of preventing market access.[14] The same approach permeates the enforcement of EU antitrust provisions.[15] For instance, an agreement within the meaning of Article 101(1) TFEU need not be a legally binding contract.[16]

In spite of these seeming advantages, this methodology has obvious drawbacks that raise the question of whether it is even workable. The single most important one is that it could lead to a finding of selectivity in virtually every instance. It is difficult to think of a measure – assuming that such a measure exists in the first place – that has a neutral impact on every firm and every sector of the economy. The example of a tax exemption to incentivise research and development activities has been mentioned above, but it is far from the only one. Consider, among the countless scenarios, legislation reducing labour costs across the board. This measure would not have the same impact on all industries. More precisely, labour-intensive industries would necessarily benefit from the measure more than capital-intensive ones. If one were to follow the effects-based approach to its logical consequences, such measures would be selective.

Because its potential scope would be virtually limitless, the effects-based approach, if implemented in an unfettered form, would be necessarily unpredictable. In practice, every advantage could be selective. In the absence of some corrective mechanisms, this methodology would turn an issue of law – does the measure amount to State aid within the meaning of Article 107(1) TFEU? – into one of discretion, where the Commission would have the leeway to decide when to take action against regulatory choices made by Member States. If only because such a reality would not be easy to reconcile with the allocation of powers between the Court and the Commission (it is for the former, not the latter, to state what the law is), it would not be obvious to accommodate in the EU legal order.

---

[14] See, for a discussion, Catherine Barnard, *The Substantive Law of the EU: The Four Freedoms* (4th edn, Oxford University Press 2022) 100–05.

[15] Pablo Ibáñez Colomo, 'Form and substance in EU competition law' (2023) 46 World Competition 401.

[16] Case 41/69 *ACF Chemiefarma NV v Commission*, EU:C:1970:71.

Accordingly, an effects-based approach that is aligned with basic constitutional premises underpinning EU law would have to rely on an analytical framework providing sufficient legal certainty. The role of such a framework would be, inter alia, to identify and flesh out a consistent method for the evaluation of the impact of measures on various firms and industries and, similarly, to establish a threshold below which the effects would be considered insignificant – or de minimis. Even then, it is not clear that the effects-based approach would be workable in practice or that it would necessarily be more predictable. Precisely because virtually every measure could be seen as potentially selective, the quantification exercise would inevitably interfere with large swathes of economic policy. For the same reason, enforcement would be resource consuming.

In a sense, the issues to which the effects-based approach gives rise are not fundamentally different from those that would have derived from an expansive understanding of the notion of aid as discussed in Chapter 2. Arguing that Article 107(1) TFEU should encompass both de iure and de facto instances of selectivity is not fundamentally different from claiming – as the Commission did in *PreussenElektra*[17] – that the notion of aid should comprise not just measures involving the use of State resources, but also regulatory advantages having an equivalent effect.[18] What is more, the reasons against an expansive interpretation of Article 107(1) TFEU advanced by Advocate General Jacobs in his Opinion in *PreussenElektra*[19] – such as the procedural implications or the impact of legal certainty – echo those advanced above. To the extent that they do, the discussion in Chapter 2 serves as a cautionary tale against an exclusive focus on the effectiveness of enforcement when shaping the concept of selectivity.

2.4. The Role of Objectives in the Assessment

2.4.1. *How the Objectives of the Regime can Assist the Analysis*

Taking into consideration the objectives pursued by a national regime can assist the assessment in several ways. To begin with, it could provide the basis for an alternative methodology to establish selectivity. Pursuant to this approach, the condition would be met where the measure is found to be designed to favour certain firms or the production of certain goods. Instead of focusing on the form or the effects of a measure, the assessment would revolve around its purpose. A tax advantage for research and development activities, for instance, would be selective where it is found to be expressly aimed at favouring certain sectors of the economy (as opposed to the promotion of innovation across the board). By shifting the centre

---

[17] Case C-379/98 *PreussenElektra AG v Schhleswag AG*, EU:C:2001:160.

[18] See Chapter 2.

[19] Opinion of Advocate General Jacobs in Case C-379/98 *PreussenElektra AG v Schhleswag AG*, EU:C:2000:585.

of gravity of the assessment, this methodology would capture both de iure and de facto instances of selectivity – and this without the need to consider the effects of a measure on the various operators.

This methodological approach would not be unprecedented. It could draw inspiration from other areas of EU law and, in particular, from the evaluation of the object of agreements under Article 101(1) TFEU. In line with the case law that applies to this provision, the assessment of the aim of a regime would revolve around objective factors, as opposed to subjective ones.[20] In this sense, it could take into consideration the relevant economic and legal context within which the measure is adopted. If it appears, in light of this analysis, that the advantage cannot be plausibly explained other than as a means to benefit a firm or group thereof, the selectivity condition would be deemed to be met.[21] Where, conversely, the measure can be rationalised as a means to attain a public interest objective, Article 107(1) TFEU would not come into play.

Taking into consideration the objectives pursued by the public authority can assist (and does assist) the analysis in a different way. It is apparent from the preceding sub-sections that, in some instances, it will only be possible to meaningfully establish selectivity by considering the aims underpinning the relevant regime. Two scenarios drawn from the case law illustrate this idea effectively. Whether or not the scope of a levy is broad enough to encompass all comparable activities, for instance, is a question that must take into account its underlying purpose. If the declared aim of the levy is to tax certain polluting activities but there is a mismatch between its declared goal and its formal boundaries, it will be found to be selective. In other instances, the objective of a measure will reveal that a formal difference in treatment is not a reliable indicator of selectivity, but a function of the appropriate operation of the regime. If, for example, the objective of a levy is to promote renewable energy sources, it is logical (as opposed to evidence of a selective advantage) that the said sources are left outside of its scope.

2.4.2. *Intrinsic and Extrinsic Objectives*

Relying on the aims of a measure to draw the line between selective and general advantages is not wholly uncontroversial. The fundamental objection one could raise is that it conflates the qualification (that is, whether an advantage amounts to State aid) and compatibility (whether the aid contributes to a public interest goal) stages of the assessment. One could argue, in this sense, that the objectives of the measure must only be considered once it has been shown to fall within the scope of Article 107(1) TFEU. Thus, the fact that an advantage aims at decarbonising the generation of electricity or to promote research and development activities should

---

[20] Pablo Ibáñez Colomo, 'Restrictions by object under Article 101 (1) TFEU: From dark art to administrable framework' (2024) 43 Yearbook of European Law, 224.

[21] See, by analogy, Case C-307/18 *Generics (UK) Ltd and others v Competition and Markets Authority*, EU:C:2020:52.

only be duly taken into account, according to this view, under Article 107(3) TFEU. Admittedly, it is not obvious to see why a question that is relevant at the compatibility stage can define the scope of Article 107(1) TFEU. As explained in Chapter 3, this was one of the arguments advanced by Advocate General Léger in *Altmark* in favour of the 'gross' theory of aid.[22] In fact, the Court declared, in *Italy v Commission*, that Article 107(1) TFEU 'does not distinguish between the measures of State intervention concerned by reference to their causes or aims but defines them in relation to their effects'.[23]

The Court has been confronted with this question. One of the contributions of the relevant case law is the distinction drawn the intrinsic and the extrinsic objectives of measures. As explained at length below, each category plays a distinct role in the assessment under Article 107(1) TFEU. The objectives that are intrinsic to the measure are best understood as the immediate, narrow aim behind the advantage and the role it plays within the overarching legal framework of which it is a part. This could be, for instance, the need to address double taxation within a tax regime.[24] Extrinsic aims, in turns, are the broader public interest objectives to which the measure contributes. The taxation of non-renewable electricity, for instance, would contribute to the decarbonisation of the economy. A special concession favouring investments in a particular region, in turn, would contribute to regional development.

2.5. The Definition of the Appropriate Benchmark (or Reference System)

The selective nature of a measure can only be assessed by reference to a benchmark, whether or not this benchmark is made explicit in the analysis. When it is claimed, for instance, that an ad hoc transfer of State resources to a particular firm amounts to a selective advantage, it is argued (or at least implied) that there is a wider pool of firms in a comparable position and that, out of this pool, only the recipient has benefitted from it. The same is true – to give another example – where it is argued that the scope of a levy is insufficiently broad and therefore gives an advantage to a group of firms that are not subject to it. Such an argument necessarily implies that there is a universe of undertakings with similar characteristics and that not all of them are subject to the same fiscal treatment. The definition of

---

[22] Opinion of Advocate General Léger in Case C-280/00 *Altmark Trans GmbH and Regierungspräsidium Magdeburg v Nahverkehrsgesellschaft Altmark GmbH, and Oberbundesanwalt beim Bundesverwaltungsgericht,* EU:C:2003:13.

[23] *Italy v Commission* (n 6), para 12.

[24] Commission Notice on the notion of State aid as referred to in Article 107(1) of the Treaty on the Functioning of the European Union [2016] OJ C262/1, para 139.

a benchmark (or reference system[25]) is an aspect of the assessment irrespective of the methodology followed to establish selectivity.

The identification of a universe of firms against which selectivity is assessed – the benchmark, that is – will sometimes be a straightforward exercise. If, for instance, the central authorities of an EU Member State decided to offer a reduced corporate tax rate to firms operating in a particular region, the relevant benchmark would be the tax regime that applies to all firms in the country as a whole. In other instances, on the other hand, the definition of the reference system can be left open, since the selective nature of a measure will be difficult to dispute. As already pointed out above, an ad hoc advantage granted to a single undertaking will be deemed to favour the recipient – and this without the need to establish in detail whether selectivity is assessed by reference to, inter alia, all firms based in the Member State, its rivals operating in the same sector or other potential recipients in a comparable position.[26]

There are other instances, however, where the definition of the relevant benchmark is not only open to interpretation but consequential for the outcome of the analysis. Suppose, for instance, that a particular activity – say, investing abroad – benefits from a corporate tax rebate. In such an instance, one could identify at least three potential universes of firms. It would be possible to argue, first, that the reference system comprises all firms subject to corporate taxation in the country. There would be grounds to claim, second, that the relevant pool is made up of firms investing, whether domestically or abroad. Alternatively, third, one could take the view that only firms investing abroad should be considered in the assessment. If the first two benchmarks were deemed to be the relevant ones, the advantage would be selective. By contrast, the third option would lead to the opposite conclusion.

3. Geographic Selectivity

3.1. Identifying the Reference System

It has been mentioned in the preceding sections that a measure can amount to a selective advantage where it favours firms on the basis of their geographic location. Whether such favouring exists is a function of the nature of the advantage and of the powers of the public authority that awards it. It is not because the charges to which firms are subject vary based on their geographic location that the selectivity condition is necessarily met. Whether regional (or local) differences are subject to

---

[25] This is the expression preferred by the Commission and relied upon in its Commission Notice on the notion of State aid (n 24). It has progressively found its way into the case law of the Court. See in particular Case C-6/12 P *Oy*, EU:C:2013:525; Joined Cases C-51/19 P and C-64/19 P *World Duty Free Group SA and Spain v Commission*, EU:C:2021:793; Case C-562/19 P *Commission v Poland*, EU:C:2021:201.

[26] *MOL* (n 2).

Article 107(1) TFEU depends on the relevant benchmark. Thus, where the universe against which selectivity is assessed comprises all the firms based within a given region, it is irrelevant that firms based in other regions are subject to higher (or lower) charges. The difference in treatment in that scenario would not amount to a selective advantage. The opposite is true when the appropriate reference system is the country as a whole. A finding of selectivity depends, in sum, on the level at which the decision is adopted.

It is not unusual for regional and local authorities to enjoy autonomous or devolved powers. For instance, a municipality may have jurisdiction to raise and determine the level of local taxes independently of the central government. It may also have the power to grant subsidies to businesses operating in the area. The fact that, as a result of the exercise of these competences, the level of local taxes varies from one municipality to another does not mean that some firms are favoured within the meaning of Article 107(1) TFEU. In such scenarios, geographic selectivity will be assessed by reference to the local authority exercising its powers. The same conclusion would follow where there are regional disparities attributable to the exercise by each region of its devolved powers to, inter alia, set the level of taxes or award subsidies. One could think, for example, of a situation where a fraction of the corporate tax rate is set at the national level and another fraction at the regional level.[27] Differences relating to the latter fraction would not amount to a selective advantage. Again, the benchmark would be the region, as opposed to the EU Member State as a whole.

The case law and the administrative practice have expressly recognised that the exercise by local and regional authorities of their autonomous or devolved powers does not amount to a selective advantage, even when they necessarily lead to local and/or regional disparities. In its decision in *Azores*, for instance, the Commission pointed out that 'the reference context for assessing the territorial selectivity of a measure is the territory in which it applies', therefore, 'measures that benefit all the firms in the territory would by definition become general measures'.[28] The Court confirmed this interpretation in its appeal judgment in the same case. It held that differences in terms of taxation would not be selective where there is 'a model for distribution of tax competences in which all the local authorities at the same level (regions, districts or others) have the autonomous power to decide, within the limit of the powers conferred on them, the tax rate applicable in the territory within their competence'.[29]

---

[27] One can consider, by analogy, the example of Spain, where competences in relation to personal income tax are shared between the State and the regional authorities. In this sense (and as an example), see Decreto Legislativo 1/2010, de 21 de octubre, del Consejo de Gobierno, por el que se aprueba el Texto Refundido de las Disposiciones Legales de la Comunidad de Madrid en materia de tributos cedidos por el Estado BOCM, n. 255, 25/10/2010.

[28] Commission Decision of 11 December 2002 on the part of the scheme adapting the national tax system to the specific characteristics of the Autonomous Region of the Azores which concerns reductions in the rates of income and corporation tax [2002] OJ L150/52, para 26.

[29] *Azores* (n 8), para 64.

Where, by contrast, differences in the level of regional or local taxes are attributable to a decision adopted by an authority operating at the national level, the selectivity condition will be met.[30] For instance, a central authority may seek to create special economic areas where the rate of corporate taxes is lower.[31] The same would be true where the initiative to award a subsidy to a specific region or municipality comes from the central authorities. In these scenarios, the reference system is the EU Member State considered as a whole. The latter scenario is far from uncommon in EU State aid law. Regional aid granted in accordance with Articles 107(3)(a) and 107(3)(c) TFEU (and codified in the Guidelines on regional aid[32]) is an obvious example in this sense.

3.2. Fiscal Autonomy and Selectivity

Figure 4.4 Geographic selectivity absent fiscal autonomy

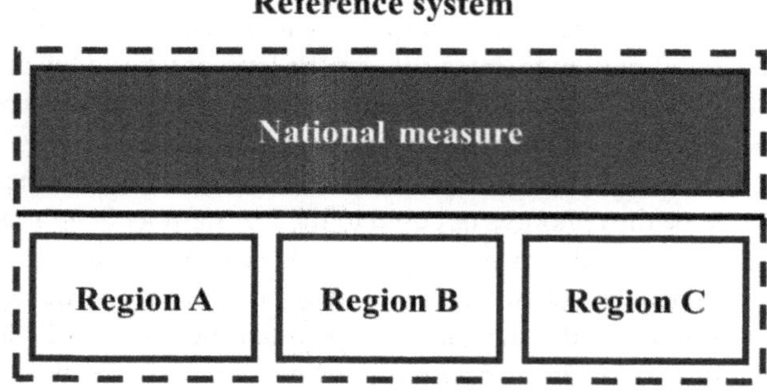

The examples discussed above relate to instances where differences exist at the same level of government – whether regional or local. One may be tempted to assume, against this background, that the selectivity condition is met, always and everywhere, where there is a disparity between the tax rates set at, respectively, the national and the regional levels. The same would be true of a tax exemption available only within a given region (but not nationwide). One may be tempted to conclude (as depicted in Figure 4.4) that, whenever there is such a discrepancy between two different levels of government, the assessment must be undertaken by reference to the EU Member State taken as a whole. There may be circumstances, however, where this assumption does not hold. It is not always the case, more precisely, that disparities between the national and regional tax policies are

---

[30] Opinion of Advocate General Geelhoed in Case C-88/03 *Portugal v Commission*, EU:C:2005:618, para 51.
[31] This was, in fact, the scenario at issue in *Azores* (n 8).
[32] Guidelines on regional State aid [2021] OJ C153/1.

attributable to the central government. A measure will thus not be selective (or at least not from a geographic standpoint) where it is attributable to the regional authority exercising its autonomy vis-à-vis the central government.

In *Azores*, the Court expressly acknowledged that a disparity between the tax rates set at the national and regional levels does not necessarily amount to a selective advantage. Where such disparity is the expression of the autonomy enjoyed by the region in question, Article 107(1) TFEU will not come into play. The autonomous region, as opposed to the EU Member State, will be the benchmark against which selectivity is assessed. That said, the judgment in *Azores* set strict conditions for the autonomy argument to rule out the application of State aid rules. In essence, the Court ruled that differences between national and regional rates are not deemed selective where the observed disparity is a genuine manifestation of the constitutional arrangements in place within the EU Member State and where, in addition, the autonomous region bears the financial consequences of its choices.

Pursuant to the first of the conditions set out by the Court in *Azores*, the region must have 'from a constitutional point of view, a political and administrative status separate from that of the central government'.[33] In other words, the institutional autonomy of the region must be recognised under the formal constitutional arrangements of the EU Member State. The case law that followed allowed the EU courts to flesh out this first condition. In the first-instance judgment in *Gibraltar*,[34] the (then) Court of First Instance concluded that, by virtue of Gibraltar's own constitutional order,[35] corporate taxation – at issue in the case – was subject to the competence of this British Overseas Territory. The fact that the UK Parliament enjoyed residual powers to legislate in Gibraltar did not alter this conclusion.[36] In *UGT-Rioja*, in turn, the Court ruled that the various aspects of the constitutional arrangement within the EU Member State must be considered together, not in isolation.[37]

The second condition in *Azores* relates to the decision-making mechanisms for the award of the advantage. In the words of the Court, the contentious measure 'must have been adopted without the central government being able to directly intervene as regards its content'.[38] This condition suggests, in essence, that autonomy must not only exist at the constitutional level but that there must be procedures in place that guarantee it at the decision-making stage (what was termed 'procedural autonomy' in *UGT-Rioja*[39]). In *Gibraltar*, for instance, the Court of First Instance found that the power to legislate in the area of corporate taxation was

---

[33] *Azores* (n 8), para 67.

[34] Cases T-211/04 and T-215/04 *Government of Gibraltar and United Kingdom v Commission*, EU:T:2008:595.

[35] ibid, para 93.

[36] ibid, para 95.

[37] Case C-428/06 to C-434/06 *Unión General de Trabajadores de La Rioja (UGT-Rioja), Comunidad Autónoma de La Rioja and Comunidad Autónoma de Castilla y León v Juntas Generales del Territorio Histórico de Vizcaya and others*, EU:C:2008:488, para 68.

[38] *Azores* (n 8), para 67.

[39] *UGT-Rioja* (n 37), paras 95–110.

exercised by the local legislature – and, more importantly, had been exercised to design the regime at issue in the case.[40] In *UGT-Rioja*, in turn, the Court clarified that this procedural autonomy condition may be met even when the autonomous region is required to take into account nationwide considerations when exercising its procedural autonomy.[41]

Finally, the Court clarified in *Azores* that 'the financial consequences of a reduction of the national tax rate for undertakings in the region must not be offset by aid or subsidies from other regions or central government'.[42] In other words, the region must be autonomous not just from a legal but also from an economic standpoint. Subsequent case law clarified that not every financial transfer from the central authority to the autonomous region amounts to an offset within the meaning of *Azores*. Specifically, the Court held that there must be a causal link between the transfer and the loss of revenue resulting from the tax policy under consideration.[43] Accordingly, the third condition may be fulfilled even when the central authorities provide financial assistance to the autonomous region for reasons unrelated to the measure.[44]

Figure 4.5 Geographic selectivity with fiscal autonomy (within the meaning of *Azores*)

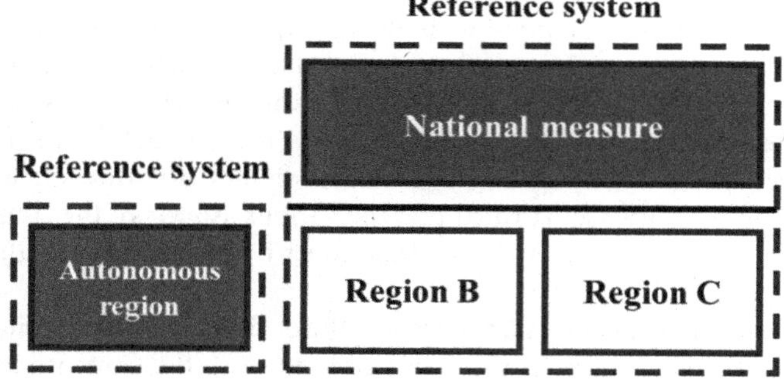

4. Substantive Selectivity: The Three-step Test as the Default Approach

4.1. Elements of the Three-step Test

The so-called three-step test is the default methodology followed by the Court when evaluating whether an advantage is selective from a substantive standpoint.

---

[40] Cases T-211/04 and T-215/04 *Gibraltar* (n 34), para 94.
[41] *UGT-Rioja* (n 37), para 104.
[42] *Azores* (n 8), para 67.
[43] ibid, para 76.
[44] *UGT-Rioja* (n 37), para 135.

This test is best described as one that takes the form-based approach described in Section 2 as a starting point. As a rule, it revolves around establishing whether the measure amounts to differential treatment. The test is refined in two ways. On the one hand, it acknowledges the need to identify, from the outset, the benchmark against which selectivity is assessed. On the other hand, it introduces corrective mechanisms to minimise the risk of type I and type II errors. As discussed in Section 2, formal discrimination against (or in favour of) certain firms is not necessarily the expression of a selective advantage, in the sense that it is sometimes an integral feature of the measure, but also in the sense that not all firms are in a comparable situation.

The Court has progressively incorporated the various elements of the three-step test into a coherent framework, which is now enunciated and implemented consistently. The first step of the test involves the definition, by the Commission (or the claimant in private proceedings), of the relevant benchmark, that is, the 'reference system'[45] (or 'normal' regime[46]). In line with the points made in Section 2, this analysis makes it possible to identify the universe of firms against which the selective nature of the advantage is assessed. The Commission codified the essence of the case law in its Notice on the notion of State aid and defined the reference system as 'a consistent set of rules that generally apply – on the basis of objective criteria – to all undertakings falling within its scope as defined by its objective'.[47] The point of the exercise, in other words, is to identify the relevant legal framework, its scope of application and its operation in ordinary circumstances.

The second step requires the Commission (or claimant) to show, against the relevant benchmark, whether firms that are in a 'comparable legal and factual situation'[48] are treated in the same way. The question, in other words, is whether the measure under consideration deals with like situations alike. If it does not, the advantage will be deemed to be prima facie selective. This assessment cannot be undertaken in the abstract. It must consider the objective pursued by the reference system. Whether or not producers of electricity are in a comparable factual and legal situation, for instance, depends on the underlying goals of the normal regime. If the stated aim of a levy is to disincentivise the use of fossil fuels in the generation of electricity, renewable producers, on the one hand, and gas producers, on the other, will not be in a comparable factual and legal situation. By the same token, leaving the former outside the scope of the levy would not amount to a selective advantage.

Once selectivity is established prima facie, the evidential burden shifts to the EU Member State, which has the chance to show, pursuant to the third step, that the difference in treatment is justified in the light of the 'nature and general scheme' of

---

[45] Joined Cases C-51/19 P and C-64/19 P *World Duty Free* (n 25) and accompanying text.

[46] Joined Cases C-78/08 to C-80/08 *Ministero dell'Economia e delle Finanze and Agenzia delle Entrate v Paint Graphos Soc. coop. arl and others*, EU:C:2011:550.

[47] Commission Notice on the notion of State aid (n 24), para 133.

[48] ibid, para 137. See also *Paint Graphos* (n 46), para 49.

the reference system concerned.[49] The Court has acknowledged that there may be circumstances where a difference in treatment within the meaning of the second step may be a faithful expression of 'the basic or guiding principles' underpinning the reference system, and as such not caught by Article 107(1) TFEU.[50] In this sense, the analysis under the third step can take into account the intrinsic objectives of the reference system. A difference in treatment could be justified, for instance, by the need to avoid double taxation.[51] Objectives that are extrinsic to the reference system, by contrast, cannot be taken into consideration under the third step. The EU Member State has the burden of showing and ensuring, in addition, that the advantage is not only consistent[52] with the logic underpinning the reference system, but also proportionate.[53]

4.2. First Step: The Definition of the Reference System

4.2.1. *The Powers of the Public Authority Determine the Boundaries of the Reference System*

The nature and scope of the powers enjoyed by public authorities vary widely in substantive terms – as much as they do from a geographic standpoint. For instance, the jurisdiction of some authorities may be confined to a particular industry. This could be the case, to mention a concrete example, of a sectoral agency that is empowered, inter alia, to compensate for the public service obligations discharged by an operator.[54] It would be difficult to argue, in that scenario, that the measures adopted by a body with sectoral powers are selective merely by virtue of the fact that other industries are not subject to them. By definition, the reference system in such a case can only encompass the range of activities that fall within the remit of the body in question. Just as the relevant benchmark varies depending on whether the advantage is granted at the national or the regional level, it is natural that it adjusts to the features and competences of the public authority.

The Court addressed this point of law in *Lübeck Airport*.[55] The case concerned a range of measures and potential beneficiaries,[56] including the schedule of charges applied by Flughafen Lübeck GmbH to the airlines using its services.[57] In its decision, the Commission concluded, in a single paragraph, that the said

---

[49] ibid, para 138.

[50] ibid, and para 160. See also *Paint Graphos* (n 46), paras 74–75.

[51] ibid, paras 139 and 162.

[52] ibid, para 140. See also *Paint Graphos* (n 46), para 73.

[53] ibid. See also *Paint Graphos* (n 46), para 73.

[54] One can think, for instance, of the financing of universal service obligations in the telecommunications sector. See in this sense Article 90 of Directive (EU) No 2018/1972 of 11 December 2018 establishing the European Electronic Communications Code (Recast) [2018] OJ L321/36.

[55] Case C-524/14 P *Commission v Hansestadt Lübeck*, EU:C:2016:971.

[56] ibid, paras 2–5.

[57] ibid, para 5.

charges amounted to a selective advantage insofar as they only applied to economic operators using Lübeck Airport.[58] The implicit idea behind this claim is that the reference system against which selectivity is assessed is broader and encompasses other German airports. In this sense, the Commission pointed out, when evaluating whether the schedule amounted to an economic advantage, that the charges applied at Lübeck Airport were lower than those applied at Hamburg Airport, with which there is a significant overlap in terms of passengers.[59]

The General Court (hereinafter, the 'GC' or the 'first-instance court') annulled the decision on grounds that the selectivity condition had been incorrectly interpreted.[60] The subsequent appeal by the Commission was dismissed. In line with the position expressed above, the EU courts concluded that the selective nature of the schedule had to be assessed by reference to Lübeck Airport, which provided the relevant benchmark.[61] Accordingly, the fact that other airlines fly to other airports, either by choice or by obligation, was not deemed to be a relevant consideration.[62] Similarly, the fact that the measure applies, by necessity, to a single sector of the economy does not mean that it is necessarily selective.[63] Whether the selectivity condition is fulfilled, accordingly, needs to take into account the nature and powers of the relevant public authority. One cannot compare a measure implemented by a body with nationwide powers, on the one hand, and an airport operator, on the other.[64]

4.2.2. The Scope of the Reference System may be Broader than that of the National Regime

In the absence of EU harmonisation, there is a potentially infinite range of economic activities that can be favoured – or, conversely, disincentivised – by EU Member States. Suppose that a public authority intends to promote the decarbonisation of transportation. It may choose to do so in myriad ways. For instance, public authorities may provide support for the acquisition of electric bicycles and/or electric buses, thereby providing a direct or indirect advantage to the manufacturers of these products. Alternatively, the EU Member State may choose to tweak the fiscal regime to penalise means of transport that rely on fossil fuels. Precisely because the potential array of measures that can be adopted to attain the objective is so large and diverse, one cannot expect an EU Member State to effectively promote every single one of them. Intervention will typically occur on a piecemeal basis – and will be subject to the typical constraints that policy-making encounters at the national level.

---

[58] As explained in Case T-461/12 *Hansestadt Lübeck v Commission*, EU:T:2014:758, para 47.
[59] Case C-524/14 P *Lübeck Airport* (n 55), para 36.
[60] Case T-461/12 *Lübeck Airport* (n 58).
[61] ibid, para 55; and Case C-524/14 P *Lübeck Airport* (n 55), paras 62 and 64.
[62] Case C-524/14 P *Lübeck Airport* (n 55), para 59.
[63] ibid, para 58.
[64] ibid, para 61.

From the perspective of EU State aid law, the fact that the State does not pursue every possible course of action to attain a particular objective does not mean that the measure it chooses to adopt is necessarily selective. Within the sphere of their competences – and, again, absent EU legislation addressing the matter – EU Member States are free to decide how to exercise their powers. The question that has emerged before the Court, against this background, is whether the national measure determines the boundaries of the reference system or whether, instead, the reference system may be broader in scope. If it is accepted that the relevant benchmark can indeed be broader, one could argue that the application of EU State aid rules interferes with EU Member States' competences. Consider the example of a tax measure. Concluding that the reference system encompasses more activities than those subject to the tax could be construed as an interference with a core area of State sovereignty. Article 107(1) TFEU would be, after all, dictating the scope of the national regime.

In spite of this fact, the Court has expressly ruled that the scope of the reference system is not necessarily defined by the national measure under consideration. EU State aid law does not simply defer to national legislation in this regard. Accordingly, it may be possible to conclude that a tax measure is selective insofar as it does not apply to all firms in a comparable factual and legal situation. Such was the conclusion reached by the Court in *Ferring*.[65] The preliminary reference concerned the lawfulness of a tax on direct sales imposed on pharmaceutical laboratories, but not on wholesalers. The aim of the differential treatment, according to the national legislature, was to rebalance the competitive relationship between the former and the latter. Only wholesalers were subject to an obligation to keep a minimum amount of medicines in stock. This factual scenario was equated by the Court to a tax exemption and, as such, potentially subject to Article 107(1) TFEU.[66]

The Court's position was confirmed (and more clearly formulated) in *British Aggregates*.[67] Just like *Ferring*, the case concerned an instance where only some activities were subject to a measure. National legislation had imposed a levy on the extraction of virgin aggregates. On the other hand, secondary aggregates – in other words, aggregates obtained as a by-product of other extractive activities – were not subject to it.[68] The Commission did not consider that the exclusion of the latter activities from the scope of the levy amounted to a selective advantage. Its decision emphasised the fact that, absent harmonisation at the EU level, EU Member States enjoy ample leeway to decide which polluting activities (such as the extraction of aggregates) they disincentivise by means of fiscal measures.[69] Accordingly, the

---

[65] Case C-53/00 *Ferring SA v Agence centrale des organismes de sécurité sociale (ACOSS)*, EU:C:2001:627.

[66] ibid, para 22: 'In the light of the foregoing, it must be held that, leaving aside the public service obligations laid down by French law, the tax on direct sales may in fact constitute State aid within the meaning of Article [107(1)] of the Treaty inasmuch as it does not apply to wholesale distributors'.

[67] Case C-487/06 P *British Aggregates Association v Commission*, EU:C:2008:757.

[68] ibid, para 2.

[69] Commission Decision of 24 April 2002 – United Kingdom/Aggregates Levy (Case N 863/01).

fact that other polluting activities could have been taxed would not be a sufficient reason to conclude that the measure is selective.

The GC (then Court of First Instance), in its first judgment in the case,[70] agreed with the Commission's analysis. Crucially, the first-instance court distinguished between a scenario where legislation provides for an exemption (in which case Article 107(1) TFEU could come into play) and the scenario at issue in *British Aggregates*, which relates to an instance where the scope of a measure is said to be insufficiently broad (in the sense that it should have encompassed other polluting activities). Contrary to the view expressed by the Court in *Ferring*, the GC did not consider that the two situations could be equated. It is therefore not surprising that the Court set aside the judgment and referred the case back to the first-instance court. Ruling on appeal, the ECJ held that the selective nature of an advantage does not depend on the regulatory technique on which the EU Member State relies to attain its aims, but on its effects.[71]

Figure 4.6 The scope of the reference system may be broader than that of the national regime

4.2.3. *The Reference System may be a Special Rule within a Broader Regime*

National legislation potentially subject to Article 107(1) TFEU is often complex. Regimes, in particular in the tax sphere, are often intricate, with special rules applying to certain activities and, occasionally, with carve-outs or exemptions derogating from the said special rules. The question that might arise in such circumstances, along the lines of what has been discussed above, is whether the benchmark is necessarily defined by reference to the overarching regime or whether, instead, the special measure (or, indeed, the exemptions to the special measure) can, in certain instances, be the system against which selectivity is assessed. Consider the example of corporate taxation. The question that may arise (and has arisen) before the Court is whether the reference system will be the taxation of corporations at large,

---

[70] Case T-210/02 *British Aggregates Association v Commission*, EU:T:2006:253. The General Court delivered a second ruling in the case after the Court referred the case back to it: Case T-210/02 RENV *British Aggregates Association v Commission*, EU:T:2012:110. The latter will be hereinafter referred to as *British Aggregates* (*renvoi*).

[71] Case C-487/06 P *British Aggregates* (n 67), para 89.

the treatment of a particular activity within the tax code or, indeed, a special rule or carve-out to the treatment of that activity.

What transpires from the case law is that the broad, overarching regime is not, always and everywhere, the benchmark against which selectivity is assessed. This conclusion was apparent even before the Court (or, indeed, the Commission) systematically defined the reference system in accordance with the three-step test. In *Germany v Commission*, for instance, the Court considered a special concession, within the German income tax code, aimed at favouring investments in the new Länder and in West Berlin.[72] This special concession was more generous that the general provision allowing corporations to offset the sale of assets against the cost of producing or acquiring certain assets. It was possible to identify three potential reference systems: first, the taxation of corporations; second, the rule allowing firms to offset their gains; and third, the special concession applying to the acquisition of assets in the new Länder and West Berlin. The Court's analysis assumed as given that the latter was the appropriate benchmark. It held that the special concession was not selective insofar as it applied 'without distinction to all economically active persons'.[73] In *3M Italia*, the Court held that a waiver applicable to some firms subject to tax proceedings was not necessarily selective, even though it derogated from the default rules that apply to the taxation of corporations.[74]

Subsequent case law was more explicit on this point. In *World Duty Free*, the Court formally declared that 'it cannot be ruled out that the reference framework to be taken into account may be more limited than that general system, or even that it may equate to the measure itself, where the latter appears as a rule having its own legal logic and it is not possible to identify a consistent body of rules external to that measure'.[75] The case concerned an advantage that allowed Spanish-based legal persons to deduct from their taxable base the goodwill resulting from the acquisition of at least a 5% stake in a foreign company.[76] As in *Germany v Commission*, there were three candidate reference systems in the case: the taxation of corporations, the tax treatment of goodwill in general and, finally, the tax treatment of goodwill in the context of the acquisition of stakes in foreign companies. The ECJ ultimately held that the GC had not erred in law when concluding that the tax treatment of goodwill, as opposed to the taxation of corporations at large, was the relevant benchmark against which selectivity was to be assessed.[77]

---

[72] Case C-156/98 *Germany v Commission*, EU:C:2000:467, relating to Commission Decision of 21 January 1998 on tax concessions under § 52(8) of the German Income Tax Act [1998] OJ L212/50.

[73] ibid, para 22.

[74] Case C-417/10 *Ministero dell'Economia e delle Finanze and Agenzia delle Entrate v 3M Italia SpA*, EU:C:2012:184, para 42.

[75] Joined Cases C-51/19 P and C-64/19 P *World Duty Free* (n 25), para 63.

[76] Commission Decision of 28 October 2009 on the tax amortisation of financial goodwill for foreign shareholding acquisitions [2009] OJ L7/48.

[77] Joined Cases C-51/19 P and C-64/19 P *World Duty Free* (n 25), paras 69–80. See also Case T-219/10 RENV *World Duty Free Group, SA v Commission*, EU:T:2018:784, para 140 ('It is clear from the foregoing that the reference system cannot be confined only to the measure at issue. This confirms that the

Figure 4.7 The reference system may be a special rule within a regime

4.2.4. *The Reference System of Progressive Tax Regimes*

Progressive taxation makes it difficult to identify the reference system. There is no such thing as a normal rate when the percentage varies based on income or turnover. Accordingly, the lower rates payable by some firms (or even the application of a 0% rate to some of them) cannot be seen, strictly speaking, as a derogation. Conversely, it would be equally inaccurate to present the higher rates paid by other firms as the default ones and therefore as the appropriate benchmark to establish selectivity. One could argue, alternatively, that the normal regime is made up of the average of the rates applied. Pursuant to this approach, firms paying a lower rate than the average would be receiving a selective advantage. This third approach would not be any more convincing. This is so not just because it is based on an artificial construct – a theoretical average of the rates applied – but because it challenges the very idea of progressive taxation. At the very least, it makes it inherently suspicious (if not presumptively incompatible with the internal market) under Article 107(1) TFEU.

The Court had the chance to address the definition of the reference system in the context of progressive taxation in two cases, *Commission v Poland*[78] and *Commission v Hungary*.[79] Both concerned progressive tax regimes applying to the turnover of firms. The Commission's analysis was based on the premise that such regimes are, by their very nature, selective. In its decision in the first of the cases, it argued, specifically, that the firms with a lower turnover were, by design, 'not subject to the retail tax or subject to the tax at substantially lower average effective rates.'[80] A progressive tax regime would only be justified, according to the decision, in 'exceptional circumstances' warranting the application of a different rate to firms with a higher turnover.[81] The burden of establishing that such exceptional circumstances are present, it suggested, lies with the EU Member State.[82]

---

tax treatment of goodwill is, as the Commission rightly held in the contested decision, the relevant reference framework in the present case').

[78] *Commission v Poland* (n 25).

[79] Case C-596/19 P *Commission v Hungary*, EU:C:2021:202.

[80] Commission Decision (EU) 2018/160 of 30 June 2017 on the State aid SA.44351 (2016/C) (ex 2016/NN) implemented by Poland for the tax on the retail sector [2018] OJ L29/38, para 47.

[81] ibid.

[82] ibid, para 56.

The Court dismissed the appeal brought by the Commission against the first-instance judgments in both *Commission v Poland* and *Commission v Hungary*. The Court held, in essence, that, absent harmonisation at the EU level, the definition of the appropriate tax rate and, indeed, the choice of a progressive tax structure remain within the sphere of EU Member States' competences.[83] It would be incorrect to make them inherently suspect, or to place the burden upon the public authority to provide a justification for its choices.[84] From the Court's perspective, progressivity is an inherent feature of the tax regime. As such, it cannot be ignored when defining the relevant benchmark. It is one of the characteristics that form 'in principle, the reference system or the "normal" tax regime for the purposes of analysing the condition of selectivity'.[85] The Commission would have the burden of showing why the progressivity of the tax is 'manifestly designed' to favour smaller firms over larger ones.[86]

4.2.5. *The Methodology for the Definition of the Reference System*

The preceding sub-sections show that the definition of the relevant benchmark does not defer to national regimes. The latter provides the basis for the assessment, but the exercise is ultimately undertaken autonomously, as a question of EU law.[87] As a result, the boundaries of the reference system will not always coincide with those of the regime under consideration. It is clear from the case law, moreover, that the scope of the relevant benchmark will sometimes be made up of the general system under consideration (for instance, the taxation of corporations) and sometimes of the special rules and/or exemptions within it (for instance, the ad hoc treatment of the re-investment abroad). On the other hand, the preceding sub-sections fail to shed light on the methodology that the Court follows to choose between the various candidate reference systems.

If one were to attempt to capture the essence of the approach followed in the case law, one could say that the exercise aims, in essence, at identifying the widest possible system of rules that is governed by the same principles.

---

[83] *Commission v Poland* (n 25), para 37.

[84] ibid, paras 38 and 40.

[85] ibid, para 42.

[86] ibid, para 43.

[87] Joined Cases C-885/19 P and C-898/19 P *Fiat Chrysler Finance Europe, Ireland and Grand Duchy of Luxembourg v Commission*, EU:C:2022:859, para 85: 'The question whether the General Court adequately defined the relevant reference system and, by extension, correctly applied a legal test, such as the arm's length principle, is a question of law which can be reviewed by the Court of Justice on appeal. The arguments aimed at calling into question the choice of reference system as part of the first step of the analysis of the existence of a selective advantage are admissible, since that analysis derives from a legal classification of national law on the basis of a provision of EU law'.

Accordingly, if it appears that a given measure is the expression of a broader universe of norms, the latter provides the relevant reference system. The Court has laid down a number of objective criteria, capable of being meaningfully reviewed,[88] to identify the reference system in a given case. The starting point of any assessment is the content, structure and specific effects of the system of rules under consideration,[89] as interpreted by the EU Member State.[90] This aspect of the evaluation will take into account factors such as the scope of the regime, its operation, as well as the conditions for the award of advantages (or, conversely, the imposition of obligations).[91]

CFC[92] provides an illustration of the application of these factors in practice. The question brought before the Court on appeal related, in essence, to whether the reference system was made up of the rules applicable to controlled foreign companies (CFCs) – as argued by the Commission in its decision[93] – or whether the appropriate benchmark was, instead, the corporate tax regime at large. The ECJ concluded that the latter provided the appropriate framework and set aside the first-instance judgment.[94] The analysis considered, in particular, that the CFC-specific rules followed the same principles and logic as those informing the operation of the overall regime.[95] It appeared, more precisely, that the former were, rather than an autonomous system, an ad hoc adjustment of the principle of territoriality (which governs the taxation of corporations) to the specificities of CFCs.[96]

3M Italia[97] is an example of an instance where the Court reached the opposite conclusion: the measure under consideration was not found to be a part of a broader set of rules. As mentioned above, the case concerned a fiscal waiver

---

[88] Joined Cases C-51/19 P and C-64/19 P *World Duty Free* (n 25), para 66 'the rules which must make up the reference system should be identified according to objective criteria, in particular to enable judicial review of the assessments on which that identification is based').

[89] *Fiat* (n 87), para 92. See also Case C-558/22 *Autorità di Regolazione per Energia Reti e Ambiente (ARERA) v Fallimento Esperia SpA and Gestore dei Servizi Energetici SpA – GSE*, EU:C:2024:209, para 84.

[90] Case C-451/21 P and C-454/21 P *Luxembourg and others v Commission*, EU:C:2023:948, para 120: 'It follows that, when determining the reference framework for the purpose of applying Article 107(1) TFEU to tax measures, the Commission is in principle required to accept the interpretation of the relevant provisions of national law given by the Member State concerned in the exchange of arguments referred to in paragraph 111 of this judgment, provided that that interpretation is compatible with the wording of those provisions'.

[91] Commission Notice on the notion of State aid (n 24), para 133.

[92] Case C-555/22 P, C-556/22 P and C-564/22 P *United Kingdom and others v Commission*, EU:C:2024:763 (hereinafter, *CFC*). For an analysis, see Stephen Daly, 'United Kingdom and ITV Plc v Commission: comparing apples with apples?' (2024) British Tax Review 725.

[93] Commission Decision of 2 April 2019 on the State aid SA.44896 implemented by the United Kingdom concerning CFC Group Financing Exemption [2019] OJ L216/1.

[94] Case T-363/19 and T-456/19 *United Kingdom and ITV plc v Commission*, EU:T:2022:349.

[95] *CFC* (n 92), para 127.

[96] ibid, para 128.

[97] *3M Italia* (n 74).

from which firms subject to tax proceedings could benefit. The ECJ understood this rule to be an ad hoc response to unusual circumstances, which are not comparable to those in which typical taxpayers find themselves.[98] Accordingly, it was found to follow a distinct logic that differs from that applying to the fiscal treatment of corporations at large. The Court concluded, in this sense, that the aim driving the waiver was to give effect to the principle whereby 'judgment must be given within a reasonable time'.[99] Insofar as all firms in similar circumstances were in a position to benefit from the waiver, the measure was not deemed selective.

As *3M Italia* shows,[100] the aims pursued by the public authority will often inform the analysis – whether implicitly or explicitly. In some instances, they play a major – if not indispensable – role.[101] This is so, in particular, where the scope of the national regime is insufficiently broad, in the sense that some activities are artificially left outside of its scope. In *British Aggregates*, for instance, the declared purpose of the legislation at issue was to address, by means of taxation, the environmental externalities relating to the commercial exploitation of aggregates.[102] It was against this background that the GC found that the scope of the levy was not far-reaching enough (and, by the same token, that the reference system encompassed a wider range of activities than the ones covered by the measure).[103] The Court identified a similar discrepancy between scope and objectives in *Commission v Netherlands*.[104] The aim of the measure was the introduction of a system allowing firms subject to NO_x emission restrictions to monetise the value of their allowances by means of a trading mechanism. It is therefore reasonable to assume, as the Court implicitly did, that selectivity had to be assessed against this broader benchmark.[105]

---

[98] ibid, para 42.

[99] ibid.

[100] The Court expressly referred in para 42 to the 'national legislature's objective of ensuring compliance with the principle that judgment must be given within a reasonable time'.

[101] This is true in spite of the occasionally equivocal statements in the case law regarding the role of objectives. As pointed out above, the Court, since *Italy v Commission* (n 6), has consistently held that Article 107(1) TFEU 'does not distinguish between the measures of State intervention concerned by reference to their causes or aims but defines them in relation to their effects'. See also Case C-487/06 P *British Aggregates* (n 67), para 75. In occasional instances, and in seeming contradiction with the rest of the case law, the Court has held that the determination of the reference system is undertaken, in principle, without having regard to the objective pursued by the legislature. See in this sense *Fallimento Speria* (n 89), para 85.

[102] Case T-210/02 *British Aggregates* (n 70), para 80.

[103] Case T 210/02 RENV *British Aggregates* (n 70).

[104] Case C-279/08 P *Commission v Netherlands*, EU:C:2011:551.

[105] ibid, para 64: 'It is agreed between the parties, as they confirmed at the hearing, that every undertaking the operations of which produce NO_x emissions must comply with obligations regarding the limitation or reduction of those emissions, whether or not it falls within the measure in question. In order to fulfil the obligations to which they are thus subject, under national law, only those undertakings covered by the measure in question have the opportunities described in the preceding paragraph,

Figure 4.8 Defining the reference system in practice

> *Overall aim*: identification, by means of objective criteria, of the widest possible system of rules that is governed by the same principles
>
> *First element*: content, structure and specific effects of the national regime (as interpreted by the EU Member State)
> *Factors*: scope and operation of the measure, as well as the conditions for the award of any advantages
>
> *Second element*: the objectives pursued assist in the definition of the boundaries of the reference system (*3M Italia*) and shed light on the consistency of the national regime (*British Aggregates*)

In spite of the evolution and refinement of the case law, the identification of the reference system remains contentious. The methodology incrementally introduced by the Court has not led to univocal or uncontroversial outcomes. It is not rare for the EU courts to annul Commission decisions for the incorrect definition of the appropriate benchmark.[106] Disagreements in this sense have been at the heart of lengthy sagas before the EU courts, including *British Aggregates*[107] and *World Duty Free*.[108] What is more, seeming discrepancies from one case to another are not always obvious to rationalise. One such discrepancy was central to *World Duty Free*. The measure in the case gave more advantageous treatment to the acquisition of stakes in foreign-based companies. One could have argued, in light of *Germany v Commission*, that the advantage itself provided the appropriate reference system and was therefore not selective.[109] After all, the measure in *Germany v Commission* also favoured investments in some areas. The Court, however, reached a different conclusion in *World Duty Free*.[110] *Miasta Mielca*,[111] raising similar questions, favoured an approach similar to the one embraced in

which constitutes an advantage in their favour not enjoyed by other undertakings in a comparable situation'.

[106] Cases in this sense include some judgments discussed in some detail above, and in particular *Lübeck Airport* (n 55), *Commission v Poland* (n 25), *Commission v Hungary* (n 79), *Fiat* (n 87), *Engie* (n 90) and *CFC* (n 92). See also Case C-203/16 P *Dirk Andres v Commission*, EU:C:2018:505.

[107] As mentioned above, the Court ruled on appeal and referred the case back to the GC.

[108] In *World Duty Free*, the case was appealed twice before the ECJ, resulting in two appeal rulings, one being Case C-20/15 P and C-21/15 P *Commission v World Duty Free Group SA, Banco Santander SA and Santusa Holding SL*, EU:C:2016:981 and the second in Joined Cases C-51/19 P and C-64/19 P *World Duty Free* (n 25). See also Joined Cases C-776/23 P to C-780/23 P *Commission v Banco Santander and others*, EU:C:2025:487.

[109] *Germany v Commission* (n 73), para 22.

[110] Joined Cases C-51/19 P and C-64/19 P *World Duty Free* (n 25), paras 69–80.

[111] Case C-453/23 *E. sp. z o.o. v Prezydent Miasta Mielca*, EU:C:2025:285. See, for a discussion, Dimitrios Kyriazis, 'Fiscal State Aid and Selectivity, or why we need a Keck Moment for Article 107 TFEU (*Case C-453/23, Prezydent Miasta Mielca*)' (EU Law Live, 26 May 2025).

Germany v Commission, thereby adding to the impression of uncertainty about the practical operation of the first step.

4.3. Second Step: Differential Treatment of Firms in a Comparable Factual and Legal Situation

4.3.1. Basic Operation of the Second Step

It is against the reference system that one can determine whether the advantage favours certain firms or the production of certain goods. This second point of law arguably forms the core of the three-step test.[112] The case law provides both a guide and a criterion to conduct the assessment. Selectivity is established in light of the objective pursued by the normal regime, which informs the question of whether firms that are in a 'comparable factual or legal situation' are treated differently. *Paint Graphos* provided an explicit articulation of this second step.[113] As pointed out above, the Court concluded that the taxation of corporations was the appropriate benchmark in the case. The question that followed was whether the difference in treatment, whereby cooperatives were exempted from corporation tax, amounted to a selective advantage. The Court hinted at a negative answer, given the many ways in which cooperative entities are not comparable to other legal persons.[114]

Subsequent case law provided concrete illustrations of the operation of the second step. In the second iteration of *British Aggregates* at first instance, the GC considered whether, in light of the environmental objective pursued by the relevant legislation, aggregates in a comparable factual and legal situation had been subject to the same treatment under the levy. It concluded that they had not on the basis of two factors. First, the GC noted that aggregates exempt from the scope of the legislation were exploited commercially in the same way and for the same purposes that taxed aggregates were.[115] Second, it pointed out that the extractive activities for the obtention of the exempt by-products were at least as harmful for the environment as the extraction of virgin aggregates, which were subject to the levy.[116] It was on this basis that the GC identified an inconsistency between the scope of the measure and its aim, thereby resulting in the award of a selective advantage.[117]

---

[112] Buendía Sierra (n 3).

[113] *Paint Graphos* (n 46). For a discussion, see Andrea Biondi, 'State aid is falling down, falling down: An analysis of the case law on the notion of aid' (2013) 50 Common Market Law Review 1719.

[114] ibid, para 61.

[115] Case T 210/02 RENV *British Aggregates* (n 70), para 72.

[116] ibid, para 73.

[117] ibid, para 74: 'In that regard, it must be stated that the Commission and the United Kingdom have failed to demonstrate to the requisite legal standard that it is precisely the – environmentally

The measure considered in the *ANGED* saga also related to the protection of the environment.[118] The tax at issue in the case applied to large distribution establishments. Smaller operations (that is, establishments with a sales area below 500 m^2 or with a basis of assessment below 2,000 m^2), on the other hand, were exempted from the tax. The Court concluded that large and small distribution establishments could not be said to be in a comparable factual and legal situation and thus that the dissimilar legal treatment did not amount to an aid. The contentious tax sought, in essence, to address the environmental externalities generated by retail operations.[119] Given that the level of such externalities varies significantly depending on the size of the establishment,[120] treating the two categories of retailers differently was found to be consistent with the declared objective of the system.

4.3.2. *The Guide: The Objective Pursued by the Normal Regime*

It is for the EU Member States, not the Commission, to decide which public interest objectives to pursue by means of economic regulation.[121] This is true not just of the selectivity assessment, but of EU State aid law at large.[122] The role of the Commission is not to dictate which goals are worth pursuing, but to evaluate whether they come into conflict with the EU legal order and, in the same vein, to ascertain whether the expected benefits outweigh any actual or potential effects on trade and competition. The leeway that national authorities enjoy in this regard means that the national understanding of the aims of the regime will always be the starting point of the comparability assessment under the second step.[123] By the same token, disagreements between the EU Member State and the Commission on this issue will in principle be decided in favour of the former.[124]

– particularly harmful nature of the extraction of the untaxed materials that distinguishes their situation from that of the taxed materials'.

[118] Joined Cases C-236/16 and C-237/16 *Asociación Nacional de Grandes Empresas de Distribución (ANGED) v Diputación General de Aragón*, EU:C:2018:291. This case is one of a series of preliminary references dealing with the same issue and will be used as a guide hereinafter. See also Case C-233/16 *Asociación Nacional de Grandes Empresas de Distribución (ANGED) v Generalitat de Catalunya*, EU:C:2018:280; and Joined Cases C-234/16 and C-235/16 *Asociación Nacional de Grandes Empresas de Distribución (ANGED) v Consejería de Economía y Hacienda del Principado de Asturias and Consejo de Gobierno del Principado de Asturias*, EU:C:2018:281.

[119] ibid, para 40.

[120] ibid, para 41.

[121] ibid, para 39, which refers to the Commission Notice on the notion of State aid (n 24), para 156: 'Member States are free to decide on the economic policy which they consider most appropriate and, in particular, to spread the tax burden as they see fit across the various factors of production. Nonetheless, Member States must exercise this competence in accordance with Union law'.

[122] Case C-594/18 P *Austria v Commission*, EU:C:2020:742. See also José Luis Buendía Sierra, '*Quo Vadis* compatibility?' in Juan Jorge Piernas López, Leigh Hancher and Luca Rubini (eds), *The Future of EU State Aid Law: Consolidation and Expansion* (EU Law Live Press 2023).

[123] *Fiat* (n 87).

[124] *Engie* (n 90).

The fact that EU Member States have leeway to decide which public interest objectives to pursue does not mean that all objectives are legitimate. As the case law shows, the very aim of a measure is sometimes inherently at odds with the EU internal market and, as such, the expression of a selective advantage. It is possible to draw this conclusion from, inter alia, *World Duty Free*. It has been explained above that the Court concluded that the GC had not erred in law when finding that the appropriate benchmark to assess selectivity was the regime for the acquisition of stakes in both foreign and domestic companies. Because both taxable events were found to be comparable, the advantage was deemed selective.[125] A more or less explicit issue permeating the proceedings (and, arguably, influencing the outcome) is the fact that the measure was treated as one akin to an export subsidy. As such, the Commission suggested that it was at odds, by its very nature, not just with the core of EU State aid law but with the internal market at large.[126] Maintaining 'international competitiveness', mentioned in *British Aggregates*,[127] would have been seen with the same scepticism if it had been ultimately considered in the selectivity assessment.[128]

The case law suggests, second, that compensating a firm for the fact that it is subject to a higher regulatory burden does not justify the award of an advantage. This idea was already implicit in *Italy v Commission*, where the EU Member State unsuccessfully claimed that the contentious measure was not caught by Article 107(1) TFEU insofar as it sought to 'make up for a handicap suffered by the Italian textile industry' vis-à-vis producers based in other countries.[129] Unsurprisingly, this argument, which runs counter to the EU legal order (and the underlying ambition of integrating Member States' economies), was rejected by the Court.[130] The need to compensate a group of firms for a regulatory disadvantage was invoked again in *Ferring*. In that case, it was advanced as an attempt to rationalise a measure aimed at levelling the playing field between wholesalers and pharmaceutical laboratories.[131]

4.3.3. *The Criterion: Comparability in the Case Law*

The case law gives indications about the factors that are relevant when conducting the comparability assessment. The first, and most obvious, of these relates to the characteristics of the economic activities at issue. In some instances (as is true

---

[125] Joined Cases C-51/19 P and C-64/19 P *World Duty Free* (n 25), para 128.

[126] Commission Decision on Spanish tax goodwill (n 76), paras 26 and 112.

[127] Case C-487/06 P *British Aggregates* (n 67), para 88.

[128] When referred back to the GC, this objective did not play a role in the assessment. See however Honoré (n 3), who expresses the view that the Court rejected international competitiveness as an objective.

[129] *Italy v Commission* (n 6), para 12.

[130] ibid, para 17.

[131] *Ferring* (n 65). As seen in Chapter 3, the question of whether this difference in treatment amounts to an advantage is a separate one.

of *British Aggregates*, mentioned above), the analysis will focus on the products concerned in the measure (for example, whether so-called virgin aggregates can be compared to those obtained as a by-product of other extractive operations). In other instances (including those at stake in *World Duty Free*), the issue will be whether two behaviours (such as the acquisition of shareholdings in, respectively, domestic and foreign companies) can be likened to one another. There are, finally, scenarios where the exercise turns to the characteristics of the relevant persons. This was the case in *Paint Graphos*, where the Court ascertained whether cooperatives and companies were comparable in law and fact.

The applicable regulatory framework is a second factor that may play a role in the assessment. The burden to which one of the activities is subject (or, conversely, the privileges from which they benefit) may have an impact on its comparability with other activities. *Eventech*[132] provides an apt illustration of the practical operation of this factor. One of the issues before the Court was whether traditional taxis (so-called black cabs) providing their services in London could be likened, for the purposes of the application of Article 107(1) TFEU, to private hire vehicles (so-called mini-cabs).[133] The ECJ's analysis suggested that the regulatory framework applicable to each of these activities was too distinct for them to be deemed comparable. It noted, in this regard, that only black cabs can 'ply for hire'.[134] Black cabs are bound, in addition, by a number of regulatory duties, including the 'compellability' rule and by the need to show a thorough knowledge of the London metropolitan area.[135]

The third factor relates to the effects of the economic activity. Two activities may not be deemed comparable where the disparity in this regard is such that a difference in treatment is appropriate. *ANGED*, discussed above, provides one such example. Given that the environmental impact of large distribution establishments is more significant than that of smaller ones, the former and the latter could not be considered to be in a comparable factual or legal situation.[136] *Kernkraftwerke Lippe-Ems*[137] provides an additional one. In this case, the Court took the view that national legislation levying a duty on the use of nuclear fuel did not amount to treating like situations in a different way. This is so, the ECJ explained, insofar as other forms of electricity generation do not produce nuclear waste.[138] Conversely, in *Commission v Netherlands*, the Court found no valid reason justifying the exclusion of small firms from the emissions trading scheme from which larger operations benefitted.[139]

---

[132] Case C-518/13 *Eventech Ltd v The Parking Adjudicator*, EU:C:2015:9.
[133] ibid, para 53.
[134] ibid, para 60.
[135] ibid.
[136] *ANGED* (n 118).
[137] Case C-5/14 *Kernkraftwerke Lippe-Ems GmbH v Hauptzollamt Osnabrück*, EU:C:2015:354.
[138] ibid, para 79.
[139] *Commission v Netherlands* (n 104).

Figure 4.9 The comparability assessment in practice

Overall aim: determining, in light of the objective pursued by the regime, whether firms are in a comparable factual and legal situation

First factor: characteristics of the economic activity.
Depending on the circumstances, the assessment may focus on the product (*British Aggregates*), the behaviour (*World Duty Free*) or the person (*Paint Graphos*)

Second factor: regulatory framework (*Eventech*)

Third factor: effects of the economic activity (*ANGED*, *Kernkraftwerke Lippe-Ems*)

There are two salient aspects about the assessment undertaken by the Court that are worth discussing. The first is a methodological one. The comparability assessment is not assisted by formal analytical tools, such as the ones relied upon in the area of competition law.[140] The approach is therefore less formal and may vary depending on the circumstances of the case. This difference should not come as a surprise. On the one hand, the systematic analysis of selectivity is relatively new in the case law.[141] As a result, methodological issues may not have reached the necessary maturity for such tools to emerge. On the other hand, the analytical apparatus used in competition law cannot be relied upon under Article 107(1) TFEU, no matter how tempted one may be to do so in certain scenarios. As already mentioned above, two economic activities may be deemed comparable even when they are not substitutable in the competition law sense.[142] Conversely, two substitutable activities in that sense may not necessarily be comparable when conducting the selectivity assessment.[143]

The second, somewhat related, point to note is that the Court does not appear to engage in a detailed, granular assessment of the extent of the comparability of the various economic activities under consideration. In *ANGED*, for instance, the ECJ did not find it necessary to ascertain whether the bright lines distinguishing between large and small distribution establishments were appropriate or proportionate in light of the objective pursued. Similarly, it did not call into question the legal technique relied upon to capture the differences between the two activities. One gets a similar impression from other cases discussed above, such as *Paint*

---

[140] In occasional instances (and in very specific contexts), the Court has hinted at a substitutability assessment. See in this sense Honoré (n 3) 188–89.

[141] As noted by Buendía Sierra (n 3).

[142] It is sufficient to think, in this sense, of Joined Cases C-51/19 P and C-64/19 P *World Duty Free* (n 25) and *Commission v Netherlands* (n 104).

[143] This is the conclusion one can draw from *Eventech* (n 132), at least insofar as the Court suggested that, irrespective of the substitutability between the two services, regulatory differences could justify the finding that they are not comparable under the three-step test.

Graphos. The evaluation remains relatively superficial. It would appear that, in practice, the degree of scrutiny will be confined to verifying whether the difference in treatment is reasonable and consistent with the aims of the regime.[144]

4.4. Third Step: Justification by the Nature and General Scheme of the System

A measure that is found to be prima facie selective pursuant to the first two steps of the test may nevertheless fall outside the scope of Article 107(1) TFEU where it is justified by the nature and general scheme of the system. As already pointed out, the EU Member State has the evidential burden of showing that the conditions for the justification are met. It is not different, in this sense, from similar mechanisms in other areas of EU law, including the free movement provisions[145] and competition law.[146] It makes sense to address two questions pertaining to this step. The first one relates to the rationale behind its introduction in the overall assessment of selectivity and the corrective role it plays. The second has to do with its substantive aspects. As already pointed out, the Court has made it clear that only intrinsic objectives may be considered at this stage of the assessment.

The introduction of a corrective mechanism can be seen as an acknowledgement that the complexities of some reference systems cannot be fully appreciated under the first two steps of the assessment. National regimes may need to introduce differential treatment, not for the sake of favouring certain firms or the production of certain goods, but as a means to ensure their overall coherence by addressing potential loopholes and/or addressing the specificities of certain scenarios. Measures dealing with double taxation, for instance, may come across as prima facie selective. Once their role in the overall system is taken into consideration, however, they may be understood for what they are: an indispensable adjustment to the situation faced by certain legal persons.[147] Similarly, the fact that some firms are subject to a special set of rules (for instance, by means of a flat rate or simplified procedures) may be necessary in the name of the manageability of the system.[148]

---

[144] *ANGED* (n 118), para 43: 'The determination of the threshold and of the methods for calculating the basis of assessment comes within the discretion of the national legislature and is based, in addition, on technical, complex assessments that the Court only has limited powers to review'.

[145] Barnard (n 14) 145–96.

[146] For instance, once an agreement is found to be restrictive of competition within the meaning of Article 101(1) TFEU, the burden of proof is reversed. For an analysis, see Andriani Kalintiri, 'The Allocation of the Legal Burden of Proof in Article 101 TFEU Cases: A "Clear" Rule with Not-So-Clear Implications' (2015) 34 Yearbook of European Law 232. The same is true in the context of Article 102 TFEU, once a practice is found to be prima facie abusive. Case C-413/14 P *Intel Corporation Inc v Commission*, EU:C:2017:632, para 140.

[147] Commission Notice on the notion of State aid (n 24), para 138. For a concrete example, see Case C-374/17 *Finanzamt B v A-Brauerei*, EU:C:2018:1024.

[148] ibid.

Some examples drawn from the case law illustrate this idea effectively. In *GIL Insurance*, the Court considered whether a difference in the tax rate applicable to insurance premiums (and, more precisely, the difference between a 'standard' and a 'higher rate') amounted to State aid.[149] It noted, in this sense, that even if one were to assume that it amounts to the award of a prima facie selective advantage favouring activities subject to the standard rate, the measure should not be seen in isolation from the broader regulatory apparatus of which it is a part. In the context of the preliminary reference procedure, the Court (and the Advocate General) noted that the 'the higher rate of IPT and VAT form part of an inseparable whole'. Once this factor was considered, it became clear that the difference in rates was a reasonable and proportionate means to prevent opportunistic conduct by taxpayers.[150]

In spite of its relevance in the overall framework, the case law significantly constrains the availability of this justification in practice.[151] The relatively high hurdles that EU Member States would have to overcome in practice are not just due to the shift in the evidential burden of proof. As outlined above, it is necessary for the public authority to show that the measure is both consistent with the overall regime and proportionate. More importantly, only objectives that are intrinsic to the reference system can be considered in the analysis. Accordingly, the public interest goals (such as the protection of the environment, at issue in both *British Aggregates* and *ANGED*) to which the measure may contribute cannot be accounted for under the third step. It is not difficult to rationalise the Court's substantive choices. Considering public interest goals (that is, extrinsic objectives) once a measure is found to be prima facie selective would amount to venturing into considerations that are only relevant under Article 107(3) TFEU. It would amount to conflating, in other words, the qualification and compatibility stages.

5. Substantive Selectivity: The *Gibraltar* Exception

5.1. Elements of the De Facto Approach to Selectivity

Under the three-step test, the fact that a measure has, in effect, a disparate impact on firms and/or economic sectors is not a relevant consideration. To come back to some examples discussed above, the fact that a generally applicable exemption for research and development activities will inevitably favour some industries over others – in the same way that lowering labour costs across the board would – does

---

[149] Case C-308/01 *GIL Insurance Ltd and others v Commissioners of Customs and Excise*, EU:C:2004:252.
[150] ibid, para 74.
[151] For a discussion of the implications of the reversal of the burden of proof, see Buendía Sierra (n 3). The author refers to Koen Lenaerts, 'State aid and direct taxation' in Heikki Kanninen, Nina Korjus and Allan Rosas (eds), *EU Competition Law in Context: Essays in Honour of Virpi Tiili* (Hart Publishing 2009), who makes a similar point.

not play a role in the selectivity assessment. The three-step test, in other words, is comfortable with the disparate effects of generally applicable measures, provided that there is consistency between the declared aims of a regime and its scope of application and provided that economic activities that are comparable in law and fact are subject to the same formal treatment.

The Court's default approach is reasonable and defensible. As already pointed out, advantages, even when generally applicable, rarely ever have the same impact on all economic actors. If one were to focus on the de facto impact of a measure, virtually every one of them would be selective. In this sense, the three-step test ensures that Article 107(1) TFEU can be readily administered by the Commission and national courts. The default approach is, moreover, in line with the manner in which the Court engages with national regimes. At various crucial stages of the selectivity assessment – including the definition of the reference system and the comparison of economic activities – it recognises some leeway in the interpretation and choices made by EU Member States. These substantive choices may be reasonable and present obvious advantages. On the other hand, they may incentivise opportunistic conduct in that they signal to Member States that Article 107(1) TFEU can be circumvented by crafting measures that are formally general in nature but that favour de facto certain firms or sectors.

Gibraltar exposed this risk eloquently. In addition to the geographic selectivity issues discussed above, the Commission took issue with the way in which the autonomous territory had designed a reformed corporate tax regime in its attempt to comply with best practices at the EU and OECD levels.[152] Unlike prior regimes, the one considered by the Commission avoided any discrimination between resident and non-resident entities, as well as between domestic and non-domestic economic activity. Formally speaking, the regime would apply equally to all companies established in Gibraltar. The system revolved around several taxes, namely a payroll tax (an annual amount payable per employee), a business property occupation tax and a registration fee, in addition to top-up taxes on certain sectors.[153] Combined liability to the first two taxes would have been capped, under the project, at 15% of profits.[154]

The Commission did not simply consider the formal aspects of these measures. In this sense, its assessment departed from the default three-step test. Instead of relying on the de iure features of the regime, it took account of the disparate impact it would have on various categories of economic operators. While the reformed regime eliminated the express distinction between offshore and onshore companies and was seemingly of general application, it continued to differentiate, de facto, between the former and the latter categories. The Commission explained in its decision that different types of companies would continue to pay different rates

---

[152] Commission Decision of 30 March 2004 on the aid scheme which the UK is planning to implement as regards the Government of Gibraltar Corporation Tax Reform [2004] OJ L85/1, para 5.

[153] ibid, para 7.

[154] ibid, para 13.

even after the legislative change.[155] It provided detailed estimations to substantiate its conclusions.[156] In particular, the decision noted, exempt companies outside the financial sector would continue to pay zero tax.[157]

The GC quashed the Commission decision.[158] The annulment can be primarily explained by the fact that, according to the first-instance court, the Commission did not apply the three-step test that the de iure approach to selectivity demands. The GC noted, in particular, that it had failed to identify the reference system against which the condition had been assessed.[159] In this sense, the fact that only firms making a profit were liable to the payroll tax and the business property occupation tax was deemed insufficient, in and of itself, to substantiate a finding of selectivity.[160] What is more, the GC found that the Commission had failed to challenge the characterisation of the regime by the Gibraltar authorities.[161] Crucially, the estimations relating to the de facto impact of the regime on the different economic actors were not deemed 'acceptable' for the purposes of the application of EU State aid law.[162] In this sense, whether or not the position of offshore companies varied over time was not considered to be a relevant factor in the analysis.[163]

On appeal, the Court set aside the first-instance judgment and dismissed the actions for annulment against the Commission decision.[164] Based on the *Italy v Commission* formula, whereby the EU State aid system does not 'distinguish between measures of State intervention by reference to their causes or their aims but defines them in relation to their effects', the ECJ concluded that the GC had erred in law by failing to consider the de facto impact of the regime on offshore companies.[165] It held, in this sense, that a finding of selectivity cannot be merely based on the 'regulatory technique' upon which the EU Member State relies.[166] Accordingly, a measure can amount to a selective advantage where it has been designed to impose a lighter burden on some firms or economic activities.[167] It is against this background that the Court concluded that the measure, even though

---

[155] ibid, para 148.

[156] ibid, para 147, which provides a detailed table.

[157] ibid, para 151.

[158] Cases T-211/04 and T-215/04 *Gibraltar* (n 34).

[159] ibid, para 170.

[160] ibid, para 177.

[161] ibid, para 179.

[162] ibid, para 186.

[163] ibid.

[164] Joined Cases C-106/09 P and C-107/09 P *Commission v Government of Gibraltar and United Kingdom*, EU:C:2011:732.

[165] ibid, para 108.

[166] ibid, para 88.

[167] ibid, para 101: 'In view of the features of that regime, outlined in the preceding paragraph, it is apparent that the regime at issue, by combining those bases, even though they are founded on criteria that are in themselves of a general nature, in practice discriminates between companies which are in a comparable situation with regard to the objective of the proposed tax reform, namely to introduce a general system of taxation for all companies established in Gibraltar'.

'founded on criteria that are in themselves of a general nature', amounted 'in practice' to discrimination between firms in a comparable factual and legal situation.[168]

5.2. Implications and Subsequent Clarification

The implications of *Gibraltar* cannot be overestimated. The Court held that a measure can be found to amount to a selective advantage even when it does not differentiate, de iure, between firms in a comparable factual and legal situation (that is, even when it is, formally speaking, a general measure). Above all, the introduction of a de facto approach to substantive selectivity is a potential source of legal uncertainty. This is so for two main reasons. First, and along the lines of what has already been discussed, a de facto approach is, by its very nature, more expansive, thereby catching a wider (and indeterminate) range of measures. Second, *Gibraltar* introduced an alternative legal avenue for a finding of selectivity. Following the judgment, the Commission (or a claimant before a national court) could rely on the default three-step test or, in the alternative, on the de facto approach to trigger Article 107(1) TFEU.

The subsequent case law addressed the potential uncertainty created by *Gibraltar*. In *Commission v Poland* and *Commission v Hungary*, the Court clarified that the de facto approach to selectivity would not co-exist on a par with the three-step step test. The case law, in other words, had not created two mutually incompatible methods from which the Commission and claimants could freely choose depending on what would be more convenient in the circumstances of the case. The Court held, more precisely, that the three-step test provides the default approach; and that *Gibraltar* is only available as a legal avenue in genuinely exceptional circumstances. More precisely, the Commission or a claimant can only resort to the de facto approach where the national regime has been designed 'according to manifestly discriminatory parameters intended to circumvent EU law on State aid'.[169]

The 'manifestly discriminatory' test set out in *Commission v Poland* and *Commission v Hungary* is difficult to meet for the Commission (or a private claimant). A reading of the two judgments suggests that it would be necessary to show not just that the measure de facto treats firms in a comparable factual and legal situation differently, but that it has been designed to circumvent EU State aid law. It is necessary to show, in other words, that both its object and effect are discriminatory. The extent to which meeting these substantive requirements is demanding became apparent in *Commission v Poland* and *Commission v Hungary*. A cursory reading of the Commission decisions in the two cases suggests that the contentious measures at issue had a strong protectionist flavour. In both cases, the higher

---

[168] ibid.
[169] *Commission v Poland* (n 25), para 43.

rates applied to foreign firms, while their domestic counterparts benefitted from a more favourable fiscal treatment.[170] One could have argued, against this background, that they were, by design, inherently inimical to the internal market. In spite of this fact, the Court held that the Commission had not sufficiently substantiated that *Gibraltar* was applicable.[171]

Commission v Poland and *Commission v Hungary* raise the question of what would need to be proved in order to show that the measure is both manifestly discriminatory and intended to circumvent the EU State aid rules. One potential approach is to draw an analogy with the case law on agreements within the meaning of Article 101(1) TFEU. The Court has held, in that context, that a practice will infringe the provision by its very nature (that is, by object) where it cannot be explained other than as a means to restrict competition.[172] One could apply the same substantive standard under Article 107(1) TFEU. Accordingly, the question would be whether the differential treatment of undertakings in a comparable factual and legal situation is the only plausible rationale for the design chosen by the public authority. As required by the case law, the assessment in this sense would be based on objective, rather than subjective, considerations.[173]

6. Making Sense of the Case Law: The Explicit and the Implicit

6.1. Objectives and Effects

Arguably, the most repeated formula in the case law interpreting the concept of selectivity is the one whereby Article 107(1) TFEU 'does not distinguish between the measures of State intervention concerned by reference to their causes or aims but defines them in relation to their effects'. This formula is somewhat equivocal, at least in the sense that it hints at an approach that does not capture the actual operation of the law. On the one hand, it cannot be seriously questioned that the objectives pursued by a measure play a pivotal role at several stages of the assessment. To the extent that they do, the 'causes or aims' of intervention are both relevant and consequential in practice. On the other hand, the formula suggests that the effects are the determinant factor when establishing selectivity. However, a cursory look at the case law shows that, in most instances, formal discrimination – irrespective of its

---

[170] Commission Decision on the State aid implemented by Poland for the tax on the retail sector (n 80), para 47.

[171] *Commission v Poland* (n 25), para 44.

[172] *Generics* (n 21).

[173] The same is true in the context of Article 101(1) TFEU. For an extensive analysis, see Ibáñez Colomo (n 20).

impact – will be sufficient, in and of itself, to prove the condition to the requisite legal standard.

The ambiguity of the formula must be understood, it is submitted, in light of the case law that followed. That the objectives underpinning intervention are a central element of the selectivity assessment seems difficult to dispute as the law stands. Aims often inform, if not determine, the first stage of the three-step test. It may be difficult to understand what the reference framework is without taking into account the point of the regime under consideration. The objective purpose of State intervention will frequently feature as an overarching criterion that helps understand the logic of the regime and the principles underpinning it. This conclusion is apparent, to mention just two examples, from cases such as *British Aggregates* and *CFC*. One should note, in this regard, that accounting for the aims of the regime does not necessitate venturing into subjective considerations. It is therefore fully compatible with the approach expressly favoured by the Court.

The role objectives play in the selectivity assessment is even more apparent at the second and third stages of the three-step test. It does not seem possible to systematically establish whether two firms (or categories thereof) are in a comparable factual and legal situation unless one relies upon the (legitimate) aims pursued by the regime. This point is particularly well exemplified by preliminary references like *ANGED* (and, more generally, intervention aimed at attaining an environmental goal). Objectives are no less crucial when evaluating whether a measure is de facto selective under the *Gibraltar* standard. As the Court would confirm in *Commission v Poland* and *Commission v Hungary*, this alternative test is as much about the manifestly discriminatory purpose of the measure, if not more, as it is about showing the disparate impact it has on various operators.

Given how prominent the aims of the regime are in the assessment, the meaning of the formula introduced in *Italy v Commission* must be put in context and revisited. Against the background of the current, actual operation of the law, the most reasonable interpretation of the passage whereby the Treaty 'does not distinguish between the measures of State intervention concerned by reference to their causes or aims' is that the award of an advantage does not escape scrutiny under Article 107(1) TFEU merely because it pursues a legitimate objective (which is, in fact, what Italy seemingly sought to argue in the context of the case). Accordingly, where the aim of the measure is pursued in a manner that involves awarding a selective advantage to a firm or sector (and, more generally, acting in a way that interferes with market integration), it will qualify as aid and will be subject to scrutiny. By the same token, the legitimate objectives pursued by a measure that awards a selective advantage will only be considered at the justification stage.

The second part of the *Italy v Commission* formula suggests that the characterisation of an advantage as State aid depends on its effects. The case law that followed this early judgment, however, shows that the evaluation of the impact of measures is piecemeal at best, and far from central to the assessment. The Court's default approach does not revolve around establishing the effects of economic advantages. Provided that, formally speaking, a measure treats all firms in a comparable factual and legal situation in the same way, it will generally escape scrutiny under Article 107(1) TFEU. Accordingly, whether an exemption for research and development benefits some economic activities more than others, for instance, will typically be an irrelevant consideration. The analysis of effects may come into play in genuinely exceptional circumstances, that is, where a measure has been designed with the purpose of circumventing EU State aid law.

A closer look at the case law suggests that, where the Court refers to the *Italy v Commission* formula, it does so, in the vast majority of instances, to clarify that the application of Article 107(1) TFEU does not depend on the regulatory technique on which the public authority relies.[174] References to the effects of measures, in other words, are typically made to point out that the scope of EU State aid law does not necessarily coincide with the boundaries of the national regime. This is the meaning that the Court attached to the formula, for instance, in *British Aggregates*, where the Court clarified that the scope of the reference system may be broader than that of the system of rules under consideration. More than anything, the formula is a valuable reminder that EU law consistently places substance above form when defining the scope of legal provisions.

6.2. Deference and Competence

6.2.1. *From Expansion to Deference*

The meaning and scope of any legal discipline depend to a significant extent on the allocation of the burden of proof between the relevant actors. Deciding which party needs to provide the evidence and, in the same vein, the nature and quality of the evidence that it needs to put forward greatly influences the shape and direction of the law. It is therefore not surprising that disagreements between the Commission and public authorities about issues of proof and evidence are a recurrent theme in the case law. What these disagreements reveal, above all, is the tension between the effective application of EU State aid law, on the one hand, and the preservation of the core of EU Member States' competences, on the other. The pursuit of the former has increasingly come into conflict with the latter. The tension became particularly apparent when the Commission applied Article 107(1) TFEU to tax measures.

One can distinguish between two periods in the case law. During the first period, the Court signalled both to the Commission and the GC that Article 107(1) TFEU was fully applicable to tax measures, and that the absence of harmonisation in the field did not absolve EU Member States from the need to ensure compliance

---

[174] This conclusion is apparent, in particular, from *Gibraltar* (n 164), Joined Cases C-51/19 P and C-64/19 P *World Duty Free* (n 25), *Fiat* (n 87).

with the EU legal order. Landmarks in this sense include *British Aggregates* (where the Court held that a public authority cannot circumvent Article 107(1) TFEU by excluding some activities from the scope of a levy) and *World Duty Free* (where it clarified that the Commission cannot be required to identify a universe of beneficiaries for EU State aid law to come into play). The single most significant (and symbolic) judgment of this period is arguably *Gibraltar*. The Court validated the Commission's approach, even though it amounted to challenging the very design of the corporate tax regime of a territory, and even though it amounted to qualifying as State aid a formally non-discriminatory system of rules.

The ECJ became markedly more cautious during the second period. Having paved the way for the application of Article 107(1) TFEU to the core of EU Member States' competences, it defined the boundaries of intervention under EU State aid law. Deference to EU Member States' choices is the dominant theme of this second period. Accordingly, the national regime, as designed by the public authority, is the starting point when defining the reference system within the meaning of the three-step test. By the same token, it will be for the Commission to prove why the scope of the national regime is inconsistent with its aim and/or underlying principles. Similarly, the design choices that EU Member States make when configuring their national regimes (including factors such as the level of tax rates and its progressive nature) cannot be called into question unless they are shown to meet the demanding test laid down in *Commission v Poland* and *Commission v Hungary*.

6.2.2. *The Interaction between EU and National Law*

Table 4.1 The interaction between EU and national law

Step of the assessment	Legal order	Deference to the Member State?	Authority
Definition of the reference system	EU law	No	*British Aggregates* *Fiat* *Miasta Mielca*
Design of the national regime	National law	Yes	*Commission v Poland* (and *v Hungary*)
Interpretation of the national regime	National law	Yes	*Fiat* *Engie*
Objective of the national regime	National law	Yes	*Fiat* *Engie* *Miasta Mielca*
Comparability and comparison	EU law	No	*Paint Graphos*
Criteria for the comparison	National law	Yes	*ANGED*

It makes sense to sum up the current state of the law by presenting systematically the interaction, in practice, between the EU and national legal orders. This interaction is summarised in Table 4.1. In and of itself, the definition of the reference system is a matter of EU law, not of national law. Accordingly, no deference to the EU Member State is warranted when performing the task. It is for the Commission (or court) to delineate the scope and boundaries of the relevant benchmark, which may or may not coincide with those of the system of national rules to which it relates.[175] When performing this assessment, however, the Commission must show deference to national law. In principle, it must assume as given the design (for instance, whether it is progressive or not), the operation and the interpretation (in the sense that the rules must be construed in light of the prevailing understanding at the national level) of the national regime. In the same vein, the case law suggests that, as a rule, the Commission cannot second-guess the objectives pursued by the EU Member State.

National authorities enjoy no deference when performing the comparison. Whether or not two economic activities are in a comparable factual and legal situation and, similarly, whether or not they are treated in the same way are points of EU law. If it is established that two activities are not comparable and therefore that a difference in treatment is not prima facie selective, the assessment under Article 107(1) TFEU will not interfere with the operation of the national regime that has been found to be prima facie non-selective. For instance, the Court has clarified that EU law does not go as far as to second-guess the factors on which the national regime relies to draw the line between two economic activities (such as the criteria to distinguish between two categories of firms) and does not question the extent and nature of the difference in treatment. The aim of the comparison is not to legislate on behalf of the EU Member State, but to check for consistency.

6.3. Searching for the 'Dark Matter'

An overview of the case law reveals that the Court does not rely on formal analytical tools to ascertain the selective nature of advantages. There are no instruments – adjusted to the nature, demands and specificities of EU State aid law – comparable to those upon which courts and authorities rely in the field of competition law. Similarly, some doctrines have not been fully developed. It is therefore only possible to speculate about their scope and meaning. This is true, for instance, of *Gibraltar*: it is not fully clear where it will come into play and what the substantive standard is. A second aspect of the case law, which can be attributed to some extent to the absence of formal analytical tools, is that disagreements about some aspects of the assessment – and in particular the definition of the reference system – are

---

[175] This point has been clear at least since Case C-487/06 P *British Aggregates* (n 67) and was confirmed in *Miasta Mielca* (n 111), para 60. However, it is not always apparent in the case law, which may occasionally convey the opposite impression.

relatively frequent. It has been mentioned above, in particular, that it is not always easy to reconcile different lines of case law (such as the seeming tension between *World Duty Free* and *Germany v Commission*).

There are reasons to wonder whether the observed gaps, tensions and inconsistencies could be rationalised or explained in light of a factor that looms over the case law, even when not explicitly acknowledged as such in the analysis – what one may call the 'dark matter'. It appears, more precisely, that a finding of selectivity is more likely where the objective pursued by the public authority is not deemed to be a legitimate one. This factor (implicit in the case) may be a useful guide to make sense of *Gibraltar* (and why the Court accepted intervention leading to the overhaul of the corporate tax regime in the territory). *Gibraltar* can only be fully understood against the background of the regulatory strategies developed by the autonomous territory over the years, and in particular the fact that it was permanently under scrutiny for the harmful nature of its taxation policies.[176] Seen through these lenses, it is easier to explain why the Court was willing to accept that, in this particular instance, the Commission was justified to look beneath the formal surface and ascertain whether, de facto, the regime had been crafted to favour the offshore sector.

These same analytical lenses may help explain the tension, identified above, between *World Duty Free*, on the one hand, and *Germany v Commission*, on the other. It has already been explained that the measures in both cases were similar, in the sense that that they treated more favourably certain kinds of investments (respectively, the acquisition of shares in foreign companies and the acquisition of assets in the new Länder and in West Berlin). The divergence in the definition of the reference system and, ultimately, in terms of outcome can be rationalised once objectives are factored into the assessment. As already pointed out, the advantage favouring the internationalisation of companies in *World Duty Free* was treated, from the outset, as one akin to an export subsidy and as such inherently inimical to the principles of the EU internal market (and thus Article 107(1) TFEU). The advantage at issue in *Germany v Commission*, by contrast, could be readily rationalised as one aimed at promoting regional development. Seen in this light, it may be easier to explain why the Commission (and the Court) were more inclined to conclude that investors in the designated region did not benefit from a selective advantage.

7. Conclusions

The nature of the debate around the interpretation of the concept of selectivity echoes the themes discussed in Chapter 2. As is true of the notion of aid, there

---

[176] The saga continued after the ruling, and right before Brexit. See in this sense Commission Decision of 19 December 2018 on the State aid SA.34914 (2013/C) implemented by the UK as regards the Gibraltar Corporate Income Tax Regime [2018] OJ L119/151 and Case C-705/20 *Fossil (Gibraltar) Limited v Commissioner of Income Tax*, EU:C:2022:680.

are essentially two approaches to determining whether a measure favours 'certain undertakings or the production of certain goods': a formalistic and a substantive one. Whereas the former hinges on the identification of a derogation from the relevant 'reference system', the latter focuses on the de facto impact of the intervention, irrespective of the regulatory technique on which it is based. An approach based on substance (or, if one prefers, an effects-based approach) provides some potential advantages relative to the alternative, at least in principle. First, it reduces the risk of false negatives and, in the same vein, maximises the potential reach of EU state aid law. Second, it ensures that like practices are treated alike, and this insofar as it minimises the scope for opportunistic conduct.

The drawbacks of the approach have become apparent throughout the chapter. From the outset, the Commission was aware that virtually every advantage would be caught by Article 107(1) TFEU if the analysis revolves around the effects of measures.[177] As already discussed, State intervention, even when formally neutral, tends to have a disparate impact on economic agents. For the same reason, the effects-based approach might become a source of legal uncertainty, as all potentially selective advantages would be subject to scrutiny by the Commission. The balance eventually struck by the Court in the case law reflects an implicit acknowledgement of these implications and confines the effects-based approach to exceptional circumstances. The Commission – or a claimant – would therefore need to show that the very design of the regime is 'manifestly discriminatory' for it to come into the picture. Accordingly, a form-based approach remains the rule when establishing selectivity.

One of the inevitable implications of relying on formalism when drawing the boundaries of Article 107(1) TFEU is the decreased ability of EU State aid law to manage regulatory competition among EU Member States (and, similarly, to engage in de facto harmonisation). Another implication is that a measure may fall outside the scope of Article 107(1) TFEU merely because of the regulatory technique chosen by the EU Member State. This second effect of formalism became apparent in both *Commission v Poland* and *Commission v Hungary*. The two rulings suggest that progressive tax regimes escape scrutiny unless the exceptional circumstances at issue in *Gibraltar* are shown to be met. This evolution of the case law is seemingly at odds with a consistent position expressed by the Court over the years, pursuant to which the characterisation of a measure as State aid cannot depend on the regulatory technique chosen by the EU Member State.

Even though this decades-old formula is repeated to this day, the reality of the case law seems to be evolving in the direction of increased formalism. This trend is manifested, in particular, in the deference that the Court is willing to give to EU Member States. Deference is manifested across several fronts when assessing selectivity. The national regime, for instance, will be the starting point when

---

[177] See in this sense the Commission Notice on the application of the State aid rules to measures relating to direct business taxation [1998] OJ C384/3.

defining the reference system against which an advantage is assessed. When deciding whether firms are in a comparable factual and legal situation, the ECJ appears unwilling to second-guess national legislation as long as it is prima facie consistent with the aims pursued. In *ANGED*, for instance, it was satisfied with the rough proxies introduced in national legislation to distinguish between large and small distribution establishments. In a similar vein, the Court has consistently held that the prevailing interpretations of domestic legislation at the national level bind the Commission.

Counterintuitive as it may sound, the parallel rise of formalism and deference is to a significant extent a function of the success of EU State aid law and testament to its effectiveness and reach. It is sufficient to compare the cases considered by the Court in the early years with the most recent ones to realise that enforcement has become increasingly ambitious. Before *British Aggregates*, it was not clear whether Article 107(1) TFEU could interfere with the scope of tax regimes as defined in national legislation. The most recent administrative practice, by contrast, routinely interferes with core aspects of EU Member States' taxation policies. This trend is illustrated, in particular, by the cases discussed in Chapter 5, which dive deep into the inner workings of national tax systems. To the extent that it does, formalism and deference come across as reasonable adjustments to more ambitious enforcement (and the resulting frictions with EU Member States' regimes).

PART II

Transformation and Expansion

5

State Aid and Tax Rulings

1. EU Law and Tax Competition

1.1. Taxation and Regulatory Competition in the EU

Regulatory competition is the rule rather than the exception in the EU legal order. The harmonisation of national laws is not a precondition for the integration of EU Member States' economies by means, inter alia, of the elimination of barriers to trade among them. This idea is symbolically encapsulated in the classic *Cassis de Dijon* formula, where the Court of Justice (hereinafter, the 'Court' or the 'ECJ') embraced the mutual recognition of regulatory standards as a guiding principle.[1] Pursuant to the doctrine, national systems (relating, for instance, to the characteristics of products and the approach to consumer protection) can coexist within the Union and compete with one another, provided that there are no 'mandatory requirements' justifying a restriction to cross-border trade.[2] By focusing on market access, subsequent case law on free movement has, if anything, confirmed that the EU legal order tolerates regulatory divergence. In principle, products lawfully manufactured in accordance with the requirements of an EU Member State can be commercialised in other EU Member States.[3]

The evolution of the case law discussed and mapped in Part I is consistent with the presumption in favour of regulatory competition. EU State aid law limits regulatory competition at the margins. It has been explained, to begin with, that advantages imputable to a public authority are only subject to Article 107(1) TFEU insofar as they involve the use of State resources. In addition, such advantages only amount to State aid where they are targeted to favour some firms or economic activities. Thus, generally applicable measures aimed at promoting and attracting investment across the board – such as an overall reduction of corporate tax rates – are not subject to scrutiny under Articles 107 and 108 TFEU. In this regard, the

---

[1] Case 120/78 *Rewe-Zentral AG v Bundesmonopolverwaltung für Branntwein*, EU:C:1979:42. See also Albertina Albors-Llorens, Catherine Barnard and Brigitte Leucht (eds), *Cassis de Dijon: 40 Years On* (Hart Publishing 2021).

[2] ibid, para 8.

[3] See, for a discussion, Catherine Barnard, *The Substantive Law of the EU: The Four Freedoms* (4th edn, Oxford University Press 2022).

Court has favoured an interpretative choice that reduces the likelihood that EU State aid law will interfere with regulatory competition.

Deference to EU Member States' choices is another theme that cuts across the various aspects of the case law discussed in Part I. The growing and more frequent tensions between EU State aid law and the legal order of EU Member States have increasingly been solved in favour of the latter, at least presumptively so. When defining the benchmark against which the selective nature of a measure is assessed, for instance, the national regime will be the starting point of the assessment. Similarly, the application of Article 107(1) TFEU cannot be based on an interpretation of domestic legislation departing from the one prevailing at the national level. The trend towards deference to national law is nowhere as apparent and consistent as it is in relation to taxation. In this sense, the Court has held that EU State aid law cannot second-guess the design of national regimes unless it is shown that they are 'manifestly discriminatory' by their very nature.

The Court's attitude vis-à-vis tax legislation is to be expected. Some of the reasons behind deference in this area have already been explored in Chapter 4. It has been pointed out, in particular, that taxation is probably the purest expression of the powers of a sovereign state.[4] One can think of a second reason, which is a function of the first. The TFEU, considered as a whole, interferes with national taxation regimes only in a limited and indirect way. When it does, it is, first and foremost, to allow the appropriate exercise by the EU of its competences. Setting up the customs union and ensuring the appropriate functioning of the internal market, namely by means of the elimination of customs duties on intra-EU trade[5] and prohibiting taxation discriminating against products from other EU Member States,[6] in particular, may demand the adjustment of national legislation in the area.

The TFEU, therefore, allows for the coexistence within the EU of different societal models. EU law does not prevent EU Member States from choosing between a system that relies on relatively low taxation levels and concomitantly low levels of social protection or, conversely, one that opts for a more generous welfare state.[7] The harmonisation of national taxation regimes – and thus the approximation of societal models – is not ruled out by the TFEU. It is, in fact, foreseen. The legal obstacles to such an occurrence are, however, notoriously high. Article 113 TFEU expressly addresses the harmonisation of indirect taxation 'to the extent that such harmonisation is necessary to ensure the establishment and the functioning of the internal market'. The provision, however, requires unanimity within the Council

---

[4] See Dimitrios Kyriazis, *Fiscal State Aid Law and Harmful Tax Competition in the European Union* (Oxford University Press 2023).

[5] Article 30 TFEU.

[6] Article 110 TFEU.

[7] This question has been a recurrent topic in the literature at various points in time. See in this sense Simon Deakin, 'Regulatory Competition after Laval' (2008) 10 Cambridge Yearbook of European Legal Studies 581; Pierre Larouche, 'Legal emulation between regulatory competition and comparative law' in Pierre Larouche and Péter Cserne (eds), *National Legal Systems and Globalization: New Role, Continuing Relevance* (Springer 2013); and Pieter Van Cleynenbreugel, 'Regulating tax competition in the internal market: is the European Commission changing course?' (2019) 4 European Papers 225.

of the EU (hereinafter, the 'Council') for legislation to be adopted. The EU VAT regime, for instance, was introduced on the basis of Article 113 TFEU.[8]

Article 114 TFEU, which is the default legal basis for the adoption of legislation having as its 'object the establishment and functioning of the internal market', cannot be relied upon for the harmonisation of so-called 'fiscal provisions'.[9] Accordingly, any attempts to develop a common set of rules in the area of direct taxation (and, in particular, corporate taxation) will have to rely on Article 115 TFEU. Just like Article 113 TFEU, legislation adopted pursuant to that provision requires unanimity at the level of the Council. Against this background, it is not surprising that the most ambitious proposals, which would have led to the adoption of a common corporate tax rate within the EU, have failed.[10] In spite of this fact, the Council has agreed over the years on a number of measures, in particular in the wake of the financial crisis of the late 2000s.[11] This steady stream of fiscal provisions is a response to concerns about harmful tax competition.

1.2. Harmful Tax Competition: Phenomenon and Manifestations

The phenomenon of harmful tax competition – as it has come to be known – is understood to be a side-effect of globalisation and other fundamental shifts, such as the growing importance of intangible property[12] and the development of global value chains.[13] These realities altered the incentives of both multinationals and tax jurisdictions. They paved the way for the implementation, by large corporate groups, of strategies aimed at minimising their tax burden. As capital has become more mobile, it is easier for these entities to choose the most convenient forum for fiscal purposes. Tax jurisdictions, in turn, have adjusted to the new landscape by implementing policies to attract and preserve inbound investment. While rational from the perspective of individual jurisdictions, the intensification of tax competition is viewed with concern insofar as it can lead to the erosion of tax income.[14] Just like subsidy races (discussed in Chapter 1), tax competition could potentially affect States' ability to invest in activities (such as education and innovation) that lead to long-term growth and the enhancement of welfare. It may, in addition, exacerbate social tensions.

---

[8] Council Directive 2006/112/EC of 28 November 2006 on the common system of value added tax [2006] OJ L347/1.

[9] Article 114(2) TFEU.

[10] For an overview, see Christiana HJI Panayi, *European Union Corporate Tax Law* (2nd edn, Cambridge University Press 2021) ch 1.

[11] See below for an overview.

[12] OECD, *Action Plan on Base Erosion and Profit Shifting* (2013), p 10.

[13] OECD, *Addressing Base Erosion and Profit Shifting* (2013), p 26.

[14] See, for a discussion, Reuven S Avi-Yonah, 'Globalization, tax competition, and the fiscal crisis of the welfare state' (2000) 113 Harvard Law Review 1573; Kimberly A Clausing, 'The effect of profit shifting on the corporate tax base in the United States and beyond' (2016) 69 National Tax Journal 905; and Reuven S Avi-Yonah, 'Globalization, tax competition and the fiscal crisis of the welfare state: a twentieth anniversary retrospective' University of Michigan Law & Econ Research Paper 19-002 (2019).

Tax planning strategies have attracted the attention of international organisations (in particular, the OECD) over the past three decades. The integration of multinationals' activities within a single global operation is at the heart of these strategies. Instead of treating the individual sub-units within a corporate group as self-contained entities fulfilling all or most functions in a particular jurisdiction, multinationals are run as a seamless cross-border operation.[15] In this model, individual sub-units typically have complementary functions and assist one another in the implementation of a single, overarching corporate policy. For instance, one sub-unit may be responsible for the licensing of the intangible assets, another one in charge of manufacturing, whereas a third may be responsible for providing intra-group financial assistance and services to other sub-units.

The interaction among the various sub-units is what enables the implementation of tax planning strategies. Corporate groups may minimise their tax burden by shifting profits from high- to low-tax jurisdictions and by exploiting legal frictions and loopholes. It makes sense to illustrate this idea by way of a simple example. As already mentioned, the interaction between sub-units based within a corporate group may involve the payment of royalties to the entity in charge of the exploitation of intangible property. In such a scenario, the tax payable in the jurisdiction of the licensee may be reduced or eliminated altogether by increasing royalty payments to the licensor. By shifting profits from the jurisdiction of the former to the jurisdiction of the licensor, the multinational may be able to minimise or eliminate altogether its tax liability. This may be the case where the country where the licensor is based charges low taxes across the board or provides for a specific exemption for the licensing of intangible property.

Figure 5.1 Profit shifting by means of intellectual property licensing

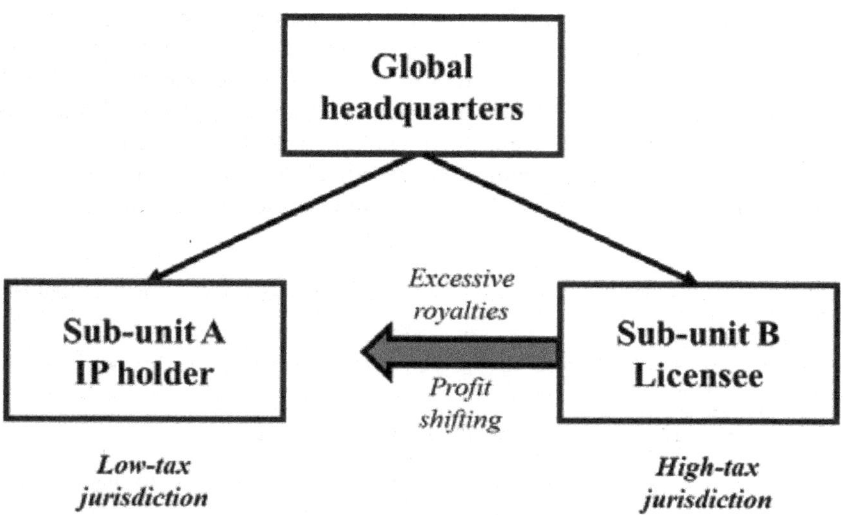

15 OECD (n 13), p 25.

The state may play a central role in the successful implementation of these strategies. Its involvement may be active or passive, depending on the circumstances. In some instances, the multinational may simply exploit frictions and gaps between national tax regimes (and, similarly, double taxation conventions concluded between jurisdictions). When the OECD turned its attention to harmful tax competition, it noted that legislation was often unfit for purpose, in the sense that it was based on assumptions that do not necessarily hold true in a world where multinationals design their strategies on a global scale.[16] Accordingly, some measures that might have been justified at a time when economies were less integrated (such as, for instance, an exemption applying to the exploitation of intellectual property rights) might have unintended consequences in the current technological and economic landscape.

One can think of different scenarios where the frictions between national tax regimes (or their legacy aspects) can be exploited by large corporate groups to their advantage. Suppose that the sub-unit of a multinational established in a low-tax jurisdiction provides a loan to its parent, which is based in a high-tax country. This strategy could lead to the minimisation of the corporate group's tax liability as a result of the combined operation of the two regimes. For example, the high-tax country may grant an exemption to foreign branches, whereas the low-tax country may levy little or no tax on income. In other instances, a multinational may rely on a conduit company in a third country that allows it to benefit from a double taxation treaty that would otherwise not have been applicable.[17] In this example, the conduit company makes it possible to act as a bridge between a high-tax and a low-tax jurisdiction.

A state may sometimes be actively involved in the implementation of multinationals' strategies. One of the scenarios discussed above was that of a corporate group shifting profits by means of (excessive) royalty payments. It is not obvious to see, at least at first glance, how the strategy would be in the interest of the country where the licensee is based. After all, profit-shifting would reduce its tax revenues. However, forbearance – if not active cooperation – by the tax authority can be easily rationalised once it is understood that it may be in the long-run interest of the country to attract (and preserve) investments by large multinationals. From this perspective, the relatively low tax revenue received from each corporation could be more than compensated by larger investment activity across the board. Tax authorities' tolerance and/or cooperation vis-à-vis these strategies, in other words, may be a manifestation of growing inter-jurisdiction competition.

It became apparent, in the wake of the financial crisis, that the phenomenon of harmful tax competition, if it is to be addressed, requires international cooperation on several fronts (however realistic the prospect). First, and most obviously, it was clear at the time that some of the abovementioned frictions, gaps and inconsistencies could only be tackled by amending, in a coordinated manner, tax legislation

---

[16] ibid, p 27.
[17] ibid, p 41.

at both the national and international levels.[18] Cooperation was understood to be necessary, second, to address some practices facilitating tax avoidance strategies. Third, further adjustments and clarifications were deemed indispensable in relation to the appropriate allocation of profits within multinationals. Deciding which country gets to tax profits has been a perpetually thorny problem in international tax law.[19] It has been further complicated by globalisation and the growing importance of intangible assets in the economy.

The third of these issues – the so-called transfer pricing problem – is at the heart of the European Commission's (hereinafter, the 'Commission') investigations under Articles 107 and 108 TFEU. The preferred approach to decide the appropriate allocation of profits has been, since the 1920s, the so-called arm's length standard (or principle), both at the national and international levels.[20] The idea behind the standard is straightforward: cross-border intra-group transactions within a multinational are to take place as if each sub-unit were an independent firm. From the perspective of an EU State aid lawyer, this criterion is reminiscent of the 'market economy operator' principle, discussed in Chapter 3. Where intra-group transactions occur on market terms (that is, at arm's length) one can safely presume that the allocation of profits across jurisdictions is the appropriate one.

The underlying intuition behind the arm's length standard may be easy to grasp. Its implementation, on the other hand, is fraught with difficulties, just like the application of the 'market economy operator' principle (and for similar reasons). Establishing whether an intra-group transaction occurs at arm's length requires authorities to perform complex assessments. The outcome of the assessment, moreover, may vary depending on the methodology upon which one relies. Discrepancies between the analysis performed by a company and a tax authority and, similarly, between two separate tax authorities are thus not only possible, but likely. The difficulty that is inherent in the exercise is a potential source of legal uncertainty from the multinationals' perspective. This same difficulty, however, may be exploited by the same multinationals to put their preferred tax planning strategies into effect.

The OECD has long led the efforts to provide methodological clarity and consistency in relation to the administration of the arm's length standard. Even though it lacks the power to legislate and impose legally binding obligations on its members, its soft law instruments are influential and shape domestic legislation. The arm's length standard is codified in the OECD Model Tax Convention.[21] In addition, the organisation issues a set of Guidelines, updated on a regular basis, intended to assist multinationals and tax authorities when estimating the

---

[18] ibid, p 47.

[19] Eduardo Baistrocchi, 'The Transfer Pricing Problem' in Eduardo Baistrocchi and Ian Roxan (eds), *Resolving Transfer Pricing Disputes: A Global Analysis* (Cambridge University Press 2012).

[20] ibid. See also Reuven S Avi-Yonah, 'The Rise and Fall of Arm's Length: A Study in the Evolution of US International Taxation' (1995) 15 Virginia Tax Review 89.

[21] See Article 9(1) of the OECD, *Model Tax Convention on Income and on Capital: Condensed Version* (2017).

tax profits due in a particular jurisdiction.[22] This instrument acknowledges the complexity that comes with the administration of the standard in practice, It notes, in this sense, that a one-size-fits-all approach would be unwarranted, and that the most appropriate method (or even multiplicity of methods) may vary depending on the peculiarities of each case.[23]

In the context of the relationship between multinationals and tax authorities, advanced pricing arrangements (hereinafter also referred to as 'tax rulings') are central to providing legal certainty and ensuring that the system remains administrable. Against a background of complexity where disputes are a perpetual threat, advanced pricing arrangements allow a taxpayer to come to a common understanding with the authority about the fiscal treatment of its activities. These rulings often address the criteria for the application of the arm's length standard (including the applicable method and the definition of the appropriate benchmarks and comparators). Crucially, they are issued in advance of the controlled transactions and can thus forestall litigation over a number of years.[24] The initiative to reach an advanced pricing arrangement lies with the company, which bears the burden of providing the criteria applied to the assessment and of showing why they are appropriate given the nature of the transactions.

The advantages of tax rulings, both for large corporate groups and tax authorities, are undeniable. At the same time, they could become an instrument of harmful tax competition. Where the incentives of a multinational and a jurisdiction are aligned, tax rulings provide an avenue for the former to minimise its fiscal burden. This risk may be exacerbated by several factors, identified by the OECD in its Guidelines.[25] Such factors include the level of detail (the more granular the arrangement, the higher the risk that it becomes a vehicle of harmful tax competition), transparency (since opaque arrangements are more likely to deviate from generally accepted practices), its duration (it is more probable that the assumptions underpinning the ruling prove incorrect where it applies over a longer period of time) and, finally, whether it is unilateral or multilateral (other things being equal, the involvement of more than one tax authority will tend to ensure that the outcome is fair to all administrations).

1.3. Addressing Harmful Tax Competition: International and EU Responses

The social, fiscal and economic malaise that followed the financial crisis created the conditions where ambitious large-scale action to constrain harmful tax competition could materialise. As mentioned above, the OECD took the lead. Its

---

[22] OECD, *Transfer Pricing Guidelines for Multinational Enterprises and Tax Administrations* (2022).
[23] ibid, pp 93–96.
[24] ibid, p 213.
[25] ibid, pp 219–22.

BEPS (base erosion and profit-shifting) project, backed by the G20, was intended to reshape the international tax regime so as to prevent instances of double non-taxation (or, similarly, little or no taxation) and ensure that, insofar as possible, taxation occurs in the jurisdiction where income is generated.[26] The first iteration of the initiative introduced a number of recommendations to turn these objectives into a reality. These covered three broad areas, namely the adjustment of national regimes to globalisation, the amendment of international treaties to address the potential for abuse and, finally, an increase in transparency.[27]

In relation to transfer pricing, BEPS recommended, first, the revision of national practices so as to adapt them to an economy dominated by intangibles and intra-group financial transactions, both of which favour profit-shifting.[28] From a transparency perspective, the project favoured the introduction of country-by-country reporting, which gives each authority the opportunity to oversee how tax is reported across jurisdictions.[29] By providing information about tax practices, this recommendation is best seen as an attempt to bridge the gap between government powers, which are by definition national in scope, and the global nature of multinationals' activities. To the extent that it does, it gives tax authorities the tools to assess more accurately whether transactions occur at arm's length and, specifically, to detect profit-shifting strategies. In a similar vein, BEPS recommends transparency in relation to the tax rulings issued by authorities, including by means of the compulsory exchange of arrangements.

The first round of efforts was followed by a second, more ambitious iteration – BEPS 2.0.[30] If the former sought to minimise the potential for profit-shifting by means of transparency measures and legal amendments, the latter focused on attaining concrete outcomes in the operation of the international tax regime. The aim of so-called Pillar One is the reallocation of profits among jurisdictions so that taxation and economic activity match more closely one another.[31] This aspect of the project would apply to the largest and most profitable multinationals,[32] which tend to operate in digital markets. The point of Pillar Two, in turn, is to put, in effect, a floor on tax competition by providing for a global minimum effective corporate tax rate of 15% on corporate groups with a certain turnover threshold.[33] The single most notable aspect of this initiative is that it opened the door to the imposition, in a coordinated manner, of a top-up tax where it appears that a

---

[26] OECD (n 13). For a discussion, see Ruth Mason, 'The transformation of international tax' (2020) 114 American Journal of International Law 353.

[27] OECD, *Action Plan on Base Erosion and Profit Shifting* (2013), pp 13–25.

[28] ibid, pp 15–16.

[29] ibid, pp 21–24.

[30] OECD, *Two-Pillar Solution to Address the Tax Challenges Arising from the Digitalisation of the Economy* (2021).

[31] ibid, p 4.

[32] ibid, p 14.

[33] ibid, p 15.

jurisdiction is taxing below 15%. It remains to be seen whether, and to what extent, BEPS 2.0 will lead to the desired outcomes.

The EU's position in relation to the reform of the international tax regime is somewhat ambiguous. On the one hand, it is arguably the entity that could most contribute to turning the BEPS project into a reality. Not only is it an influential player with the ability to shape regulatory developments on a global scale,[34] but it has the competence to enact binding legal instruments. On the other hand, and along the lines of what has been mentioned above, the harmonisation of direct taxation requires unanimity at the level of the Council. Given that EU Member States rely on different societal models – and, in particular, given that many of them had thrived in a world where tax competition was the norm – it was not a given that the EU would come to an internal agreement, let alone drive change at the international level. In light of this uncertainty, the Commission took the lead by following a two-pronged strategy.

The first prong of this strategy can be termed orthodox. In accordance with the allocation of powers under the TFEU, the Commission submitted legislative proposals for the Council to enact legislation on the basis of Article 115 TFEU. Inauspicious as it might have seemed, this route proved fruitful, and the EU has adopted, over the course of the past decade, a package of Directives codifying some core aspects of the BEPS project.[35] The second prong of the strategy consisted of exploring the extent to which some of the fundamental goals of the shift championed by the OECD could be achieved through the enforcement of EU State aid law provisions. This second prong, while less orthodox, presented the obvious advantage in that it did not require the involvement of either the Council or the Parliament. It is not unusual for the Commission to explore this second strategy in areas where the harmonisation of legislation may prove difficult, or likely to lead to suboptimal outcomes.[36]

2. Harmful Tax Competition as State Aid

2.1. Overview of the Investigations

The Commission opened a string of investigations into tax planning strategies at the same time as the BEPS project was taking shape at the OECD level. Between

---

[34] For an extensive discussion, see, generally, Anu Bradford, *The Brussels Effect: How the European Union Rules the World* (Oxford University Press 2020).

[35] Council Directive (EU) 2016/1164 of 12 July 2016 laying down rules against tax avoidance practices that directly affect the functioning of the internal market [2016] OJ L193/1; and Council Directive (EU) 2022/2523 of 14 December 2022 on ensuring a global minimum level of taxation for multinational enterprise groups and large-scale domestic groups in the Union [2022] OJ L328/1.

[36] For a discussion of similar strategies in the area of EU antitrust law, see Pablo Ibáñez Colomo, *The New EU Competition Law* (Hart Publishing 2023).

June and July 2013, it sent requests for information about the arrangements put in place by Ireland,[37] Luxembourg[38] and the Netherlands.[39] All three investigations would eventually crystallise into a decision concerning the agreements concluded between the authorities of these EU Member States and three multinationals, respectively Apple,[40] Fiat[41] and Starbucks.[42] The corpus of decisions on tax planning strategies was completed with three additional decisions concerning Luxembourg (and specifically tax rulings involving Amazon,[43] Engie[44] and McDonald's[45]) and an additional one relating to an Excess Profit mechanism put in place by Belgium (as well as the tax rulings deriving from it).[46] Three further investigations into arrangements with Nike,[47] Ikea[48] and Huhtamäki[49] were still ongoing at the time of writing.

Figure 5.2 Timeline of the tax rulings decisions adopted by the Commission

Fiat	*Starbucks*	*Excess Profit*	*Apple*	*Amazon*	*Engie*	*McDonald's*
21 Oct 2015	21 Oct 2015	11 Jan 2016	30 Aug 2016	4 Oct 2017	20 Jun 2018	19 Sep 2018

The precise timeline of the decisions is depicted in Figure 5.2. With the exception of *McDonald's*,[50] the Commission decided that the tax rulings issued by the tax authorities of Ireland, Luxembourg and the Netherlands amounted to unlawfully granted State aid, which was moreover found to be incompatible with the internal market.[51] As is the rule in such cases, the Commission ordered

[37] Commission Decision of 30 August 2016 on State aid SA.38373 (2014/C) (ex 2014/NN) (ex 2014/CP) implemented by Ireland to Apple [2017] OJ L187/1, para 1.

[38] Commission Decision of 21 October 2015 on State aid SA.38375 (2014/C ex 2014/NN) which Luxembourg granted to Fiat [2016] OJ L351/1, para 1.

[39] Commission Decision of 21 October 2015 on State aid SA.38374 (2014/C ex 2014/NN) implemented by the Netherlands to Starbucks [2017] OJ L83/38, para 1.

[40] Commission Decision in *Apple* (n 37).

[41] Commission Decision in *Fiat* (n 38).

[42] Commission Decision in *Starbucks* (n 39).

[43] Commission Decision of 4 October 2017 on State aid SA.38944 (2014/C) (ex 2014/NN) implemented by Luxembourg to Amazon [2018] OJ L153/1.

[44] Commission Decision of 20 June 2018 on State aid SA.44888 (2016/C) (ex 2016/NN) implemented by Luxembourg in favour of ENGIE [2019] OJ L78/1.

[45] Commission Decision of 19 September 2018 on tax rulings SA.38945 (2015/C) (ex 2015/NN) (ex 2014/CP) granted by Luxembourg in favour of McDonald's Europe [2019] OJ L195/20.

[46] Commission Decision of 11 January 2016 on the excess profit exemption State aid scheme SA.37667 (2015/C) (ex 2015/NN) implemented by Belgium [2016] OJ L260/61.

[47] Commission, 'State aid: Commission opens in-depth investigation into tax treatment of Nike in the Netherlands' IP/19/322 (Brussels, 10 January 2019).

[48] Commission, 'State aid: Commission opens in-depth investigation into the Netherlands' tax treatment of Inter IKEA' IP/17/5343 (Brussels, 18 December 2017).

[49] Commission, 'State aid: Luxembourg's tax treatment of Huhtamäki' IP/19/1591 (Brussels, 3 May 2019).

[50] Commission Decision in *McDonald's* (n 45), Article 1.

[51] See Article 1 of *Apple* (n 37), *Fiat* (n 38), *Starbucks* (n 39).

the EU Member States to recover the amounts involved.[52] The Belgian Excess Profit mechanism, in turn, was deemed an unlawful State aid scheme within the meaning of the Procedural Regulation.[53] As summarised in Table 5.1, these decisions suffered an uneven fate when challenged before the EU courts. While direct actions against the Commission decisions in *Belgian Excess Profit*[54] and *Apple*[55] were ultimately unsuccessful, the decisions in *Fiat*,[56] *Starbucks*,[57] *Engie*[58] and *Amazon*[59] were annulled, either at first instance before the General Court (hereinafter, the 'GC' or the 'first-instance court') or before the ECJ upon appeal.

Table 5.1 The fate of the tax rulings saga before the EU courts

Case	Outcome at first instance	Outcome upon appeal	Outcome upon referral
Fiat	Direct action dismissed	GC judgment set aside/ Commission decision annulled	n/a
Starbucks	Commission decision annulled	n/a	n/a
Excess Profit	Commission decision annulled	Case partially referred to the GC	Direct action dismissed
Apple	Commission decision annulled	GC judgment set aside/Direct action dismissed	n/a
Amazon	Commission decision annulled	Appeal (by Commission) dismissed	n/a
Engie	Direct action dismissed	GC judgment set aside/Commission decision annulled	n/a

[52] ibid, Article 2. The recovery of the aid, given the nature of the decisions, was often a source of difficulties. For a discussion, see Dimitrios Kyriazis, 'Tax rulings and State aid: Musings on recovery' in Leigh Hancher and Juan Jorge Piernas López (eds), *Research Handbook on European State Aid Law* (Edward Elgar Publishing 2021).

[53] *Belgian Excess Profit* (n 46), Article 1.

[54] Case T-131/16 RENV *Belgium v Commission*, EU:T:2023:561.

[55] Case C-465/20 P *Commission v Ireland and others*, EU:C:2024:724.

[56] Joined Cases C-885/19 P and C-898/19 P *Fiat Chrysler Finance Europe and Ireland v Commission*, EU:C:2022:859. Following the appeal judgment, the Commission adopted a new decision in the case, concluding that no aid had been granted. See Commission Decision of 28 November 2024 – Luxembourg, alleged aid to FFT on tax ruling (Case SA.38375).

[57] Cases T-760/15 and T-636/16 *Netherlands, Starbucks Corp and Starbucks Manufacturing Emea BV v Commission*, EU:T:2019:669. Following the judgment, the Commission adopted a 'no aid' decision in the case. See in this sense Commission Decision of 28 November 2024 – Netherlands, alleged aid to Starbucks (Case SA.38374).

[58] Joined Cases C-451/21 P and C-454/21 P *Luxembourg and others v Commission*, EU:C:2023:948.

[59] Judgment of the General Court of 12 May 2021, Joined Cases T-816/17 and T-318/18 *Luxembourg, Amazon EU Sàrl and Amazon.com, Inc v Commission*, EU:T:2021:252. See also the 'no aid' decision that followed the judgment: Commission Decision of 28 November 2024 – Luxembourg, alleged aid to Amazon (Case SA.38944).

This line of administrative practice is best understood as a response to the economic and technological transformations outlined in the preceding section. The decisions sought to address what the Commission saw as the combined effects of multinationals' strategies, on the one hand, and the disparities in the tax treatment of large corporate groups within the EU, on the other. If the rise of global value chains presents corporations with opportunities to exploit legal frictions, the absence of a harmonised response provides an avenue for regulatory arbitrage. In this sense, a common theme in all decisions is the fact that the tax rulings allowed multinationals to significantly reduce their effective tax rates relative to other entities. When announcing the recovery decision in *Apple*, for instance, Commissioner Vestager claimed that the tax ruling allowed the multinational 'to pay an effective corporate tax rate of 1 per cent on its European profits in 2003 down to 0.005 per cent in 2014'.[60]

All abovementioned recovery decisions are based on the premise that the corporate structures devised by the multinationals allowed them to engage in aggressive planning to minimise or eliminate their fiscal burden and (more importantly for the purposes of the application of Article 107(1) TFEU) that tax authorities had sanctioned the said strategies by means of a tax ruling. Some of the decisions – namely *Fiat*, *Starbucks* and *Amazon* – focused on the fact that the intra-group transactions had not been calculated in accordance with the arm's length standard; or that, to the extent that they had, the said standard had been misapplied.[61] The tax ruling was understood to be the mechanism by which the multinationals were allowed to depart from the criteria governing the reference system and applying to undertakings in a comparable factual and legal situation.

Starbucks illustrates the legal and factual issues addressed in the decisions that focused on transfer pricing. The Commission claimed, in essence, that Starbucks Manufacturing, a subsidiary of the US multinational, had been allowed to artificially reduce its tax base by means of a tax ruling issued by the Dutch authorities. According to the Commission decision, there were two prongs to the profit-shifting strategy pursued by the corporate group. First, Starbucks Manufacturing was found to have paid royalties to Alki (a UK-based member of the group) for the intangible property involved in the exercise of its coffee-roasting activities. Second, Starbucks Manufacturing compensated a Swiss subsidiary – Starbucks Coffee Trading – for the supply of coffee beans. The Commission concluded that these intra-group transactions had not taken place at arm's length, which resulted in Starbucks Manufacturing overpaying relative to a scenario in which it had negotiated, on market terms, with non-affiliated entities.

It is against this background that the Commission concluded that the Netherlands had awarded incompatible aid to Starbucks Manufacturing. The thrust

---

[60] Commission, 'State aid: Ireland gave illegal tax benefits to Apple worth up to €13 Billion' IP/16/2923 (Brussels, 30 August 2016).

[61] See in this sense Commission Decision in *Fiat* (n 38), paras 216–340; Commission Decision in *Starbucks* (n 39), paras 252–416; and Commission Decision in *Amazon* (n 43), paras 401–579.

of the decision revolves around an analysis of the tax ruling issued by the Dutch authorities, which had accepted, in essence, the approach proposed by the multinational's tax advisor.[62] The Commission did not just challenge the tax ruling on grounds that it was inconsistent with the arm's length standard. It also questioned the methodological choices made by the EU Member State when conducting its assessment. It pointed out, in particular, that the transfer pricing method relied upon by the tax authority was incapable of providing a reliable approximation of a market-based outcome. This was so in spite of the fact that the method in question had been expressly endorsed by the OECD in the iteration of the Transfer Pricing Guidelines in force at the time.[63]

The issues at stake in other cases dealing with transfer pricing are similar and can be seen as a variation on the scenarios identified in the preceding section. In *Fiat*, for instance, the subsidiary on which the investigation focused provided financial services to the rest of the members of the corporate group.[64] As in *Starbucks*, the Commission took issue with the method relied upon by the tax authority to assess compliance with the arm's length standard.[65] The investigation in *Apple*, in turn, revolved around the activities of Apple Operations Europe and Apple Sales International, two companies incorporated in Ireland.[66] The Commission challenged in that case some of the assumptions made by the tax authority when issuing tax rulings, and specifically the fact that the intellectual property licences held by the two companies had to be allocated outside of Ireland.[67]

Engie stands apart from these examples in that the finding of State aid did not relate to a failure to observe the arm's length standard by the tax authority. Instead, the multinational was alleged to have minimised its tax burden by means of two intra-group transactions which might not have been problematic when considered in isolation or in the abstract. After all, they relied upon exemptions or deductions foreseen in legislation and available to all undertakings. When taken together, however, they led to an outcome (all profit was left untaxed) that was, in the Commission's view, inconsistent with the objectives of the corporate tax regime (that is, the taxation of corporate profit).[68] It was on this basis that it concluded that the tax ruling sanctioning the corporate strategy involved the award of a selective advantage to Engie (both the group and its constituent units).[69] The decision relies on two supplementary lines of reasoning, one of which is based on the idea that the multinational's tax planning strategy amounted to an abuse of law and which will be discussed below.[70]

---

[62] Commission Decision in *Starbucks* (n 39), para 42.
[63] ibid, para 174.
[64] Commission Decision in *Fiat* (n 38), para 36.
[65] ibid, paras 234–240.
[66] Commission Decision in *Apple* (n 37), paras 40–58.
[67] ibid, para 260.
[68] Commission Decision in *Engie* (n 44), para 184.
[69] ibid, paras 236 and 288.
[70] ibid, para 313.

2.2. Article 107(1) TFEU and the Arm's Length Standard

The Commission's approach to the application of EU State aid law to tax rulings issued by national tax authorities rests on several assumptions about the meaning of Article 107(1) TFEU and how it applies to arrangements between tax authorities and multinationals. One of the overarching premises is that the arm's length standard is a creature of EU law, and therefore applicable to the scrutiny of tax rulings irrespective of whether the EU Member States have incorporated it into their national tax system. As stated in the Notice on the notion of State aid, the standard 'necessarily forms part of the Commission's assessment of tax measures granted to group companies under Article 107(1) of the Treaty'.[71] According to this interpretation of the provision, there is an overarching principle of equal treatment in taxation, of which the arm's length standard would be a manifestation.[72]

The idea that the Commission has the ability to assess compliance with the arm's length standard as a matter of EU State aid law is based on its interpretation of *Forum 187*.[73] This precedent concerned the legal status of the special tax regime applying to so-called coordination centres in Belgium. As is true of the tax rulings saga, multinationals investing in the country benefitted from this ad hoc scheme. It provided for some derogations and exemptions that were not available to other firms.[74] The Court held in the judgment that the regime gave an advantage to the relevant corporate groups insofar as the method relied upon for the calculation of intra-group transactions which – while ostensibly based on one endorsed by the OECD in its Transfer Pricing Guidelines – allowed them to exclude from the calculation of the taxable income some costs that an 'undertaking carrying on its activities in conditions of free competition' (that is, dealing at arm's length with other firms) would face.[75]

In the crucial passage from *Forum 187*, which is the one that would inform the administrative practice in the tax rulings saga, the Court held that '[i]n order to decide whether a method of assessment of taxable income such as that laid down under the regime for coordination centres confers an advantage on them, it is necessary, as the Commission suggests at point 95 of the contested decision, to compare that regime with the ordinary tax system, based on the difference between profits and outgoings of an undertaking carrying on its activities in conditions of

---

[71] Commission Notice on the notion of State aid as referred to in Article 107(1) of the Treaty on the Functioning of the European Union [2016] OJ C262/1, para 172.

[72] ibid: 'The arm's length principle the Commission applies in assessing transfer pricing rulings under the State aid rules is therefore an application of Article 107(1) of the Treaty, which prohibits unequal treatment in taxation of undertakings in a similar factual and legal situation. This principle binds the Member States and the national tax rules are not excluded from its scope'.

[73] Joined Cases C-182/03 and C-217/03 *Belgium and Forum 187 ASBL v Commission*, EU:C:2006:416.

[74] In fact, some authors identify this case as the expression of a first State aid wave of the application of Article 107(1) TFEU to aggressive tax planning practices. See in this sense Kyriazis (n 4) 98–100.

[75] *Forum 187* (n 73), para 95.

free competition'.[76] The Commission inferred from that passage a general principle pursuant to which an intra-group transaction that departs from the arm's length standard necessarily confers an advantage on the beneficiary of the measure. As a matter of EU law, therefore, members of the same corporate group would be under an obligation to deal with one another as if they were independent firms.

The Commission's interpretation of *Forum 187* was not devoid of controversy and has been widely discussed.[77] A plain reading of the judgment (and the administrative decision[78] that was annulled as a result) suggests that the relevant passages could be interpreted in different ways. One could convincingly argue, to begin with, that, in *Forum 187*, the Commission had not really taken issue with the application of the arm's length standard by the EU Member State, but with the fact that multinationals relying on the scheme benefitted from a number of derogations and special rules (such the exclusion of staff costs and financial costs from the calculation of the taxable income and the application of a flat tax) that were not available to other firms in a comparable factual and legal situation. The arm's length standard, if anything, was little more than a distraction from the questions that actually determined the outcome of the case.

In fact, neither the contested decision nor the judgment dealt with the administration of the arm's length standard as such, or in the abstract. They did so only insofar as the said standard was relevant for the assessment of the national tax regime through the lens of Article 107(1) TFEU.[79] Transfer pricing issues (and the alleged compatibility with the OECD Guidelines) had not been introduced by the Commission. They had been invoked by the EU Member State as a defence, in an attempt to argue that the derogations were a side-effect of the (OECD-approved) transfer pricing methodology applied.[80] It appears, in fact, that the point of the paragraph on which the Commission relied in its tax ruling cases was to stress that the ad hoc adjustments applying to coordination centres were selective insofar as they excluded some costs from the calculation of the tax base. Contrary to what Belgium argued, therefore, they could not be seen as an inescapable consequence of the application of the OECD Guidelines.

The interpretation of *Forum 187* in the tax rulings saga might not have reflected a wide consensus about its meaning and implications. However, it was instrumental in allowing the Commission to summarily dismiss arguments pertaining to the operation of national tax regimes and their relationship with the arm's length

---

[76] ibid.

[77] See in this regard Kyriazis (n 4); Tony Joris and Wout De Cock, 'Is Belgium and *Forum 187 v. Commission* a Suitable Legal Source for an EU "At Arm's Length Principle"?' (2017) 16 European State Aid Law Quarterly 607; Pierpaolo Rossi-Maccanico, 'A new framework for State aid review of tax rulings' (2015) 14 European State Aid Law Quarterly 371; and Phedon Nicolaides, 'State aid rules and Tax Rulings' (2016) 15 European State Aid Law Quarterly 416.

[78] Commission Decision of 17 February 2003 on the aid scheme implemented by Belgium for coordination centres established in Belgium [2003] OJ L282/25.

[79] See in this sense Kyriazis (n 4) 158–62.

[80] Commission Decision in *Forum 187* (n 78), paras 43–47.

standard. Generally speaking, the Commission consistently relied on *Forum 187* to claim that its analysis was not an application of the OECD Model Tax Convention (or, similarly, an attempt to make it legally binding upon the EU Member States), but a manifestation of the exercise of its powers under Articles 107 and 108 TFEU.[81] Similarly, it rejected arguments suggesting that its analysis was an interpretation of the domestic tax regime or that it was an attempt to overrule national authorities.[82]

Apple illustrates the Commission's understanding of the relationship between EU State aid law and the arm's length standard. Ireland argued, in reaction to the decision opening the formal investigation procedure, that there was no scope for the incorporation of the framework developed at the OECD level unless it had been expressly codified in domestic legislation.[83] It claimed, in a similar vein, that taxes could not be imposed on the basis of general principles.[84] To the extent that the national tax regime did not make any reference to the arm's length standard at the time of the tax rulings, the EU Member State argued that the said standard could not provide the basis for assessing the allocation of profits to an Irish branch.[85] The Commission rejected these arguments summarily. While accepting that the OECD framework is not legally binding, it claimed that it provides 'useful guidance' when ascertaining whether a given tax ruling involves the award of a selective advantage within the meaning of Article 107(1) TFEU.[86]

2.3. The Scope and Standard of Review of National Legislation

Because the Commission relied on the exercise of its powers under EU State aid law, it assumed as given that EU Member States' obligations flowing from Article 107(1) TFEU take precedence over national legislation. A first implication of its interpretation of the primacy of EU law is that it gave it the implicit power to oversee – and, in effect, construe – all aspects of the domestic tax regime. In fact, the various

---

[81] See for instance Commission Decision in *Starbucks* (n 39), para 265: 'The arm's-length principle therefore necessarily forms part of the Commission's assessment under Article 107(1) of the Treaty of tax measures granted to group companies independently of whether a Member State has incorporated this principle into its national legal system. [...] Thus, for any avoidance of doubt, the arm's-length principle that the Commission applies in its State aid assessment is not that derived from Article 9 of the OECD Model Tax Convention, which is a non-binding instrument, but is a general principle of equal treatment in taxation falling within the application of Article 107(1) of the Treaty, which binds the Member States and from whose scope the national tax rules are not excluded'.

[82] ibid, para 265: 'Consequently, in response to the Netherlands' argument that the Commission, in undertaking such an assessment, replaces the national tax administration in its interpretation of their national law, the Commission recalls that is not examining whether the SMBV APA complies with the arm's-length principle as laid down in Article 8b(1) of the CIT or the Decree, but whether the Dutch tax administration conferred a selective advantage on SMBV for the purposes of Article 107(1) of the Treaty [...]'.

[83] Commission Decision in *Apple* (n 37), para 153.

[84] ibid, para 257.

[85] ibid, para 155.

[86] ibid, para 255.

decisions in the saga are peppered with instances where the EU Member States argued that the Commission's interpretation of their obligations under EU State aid law contradicted not just the prevailing case law and administrative practice at the national level, but also a plain reading of the relevant provisions. In *Engie*, for instance, Luxembourg maintained, inter alia, that the analysis of the selectivity of the measure was based on a *contra legem* interpretation of the domestic tax regime and, similarly, that the Commission's understanding of the relevant provisions had no basis in the law.[87] In *Apple*, Ireland argued that, contrary to what the decision opening the proceedings suggested, there was no basis for computing the tax liability of the relevant entities other than the one enshrined in national law.[88]

A second implication of the Commission's position is that Article 107(1) TFEU can be an autonomous source of principles and obligations in the area of taxation, and that these principles and obligations can be imposed above and beyond domestic legislation. The most consequential manifestation of this aspect of the administrative practice is the approach that the Commission took to the application of the arm's length standard. As is apparent from the decisions, it did not merely argue that a transaction departing from a market-based outcome provides a selective advantage. It assumed that, in the exercise of its competences under the TFEU, it could rely on the transfer pricing method which, among those endorsed by the OECD, provides the most reliable approximation of an arm's length negotiation. In the event of a conflict with the method applied by the EU Member State in its tax ruling, moreover, the Commission's own method would prevail. This was so in spite of the fact that, as discussed in Section 1, the OECD acknowledges that the application of the arm's length standard is case-specific and that the selection of a method is rarely straightforward.

In *Starbucks*, for instance, the Commission took issue with the transfer pricing method chosen by the Dutch tax authority (TNMM[89]), even though it had been sanctioned by the OECD in its Guidelines.[90] This methodological choice was problematic, according to the decision, insofar as the OECD itself had expressed a preference for another method – CUP.[91] The Commission argued, in this sense, that the duty of EU Member States under Article 107(1) TFEU involves ascertaining whether the transfer pricing method proposed by a multinational in the context of a tax ruling is capable of providing a reliable approximation of a market-based outcome.[92] From this perspective, the fact that the national regime does not require the tax authority to observe a particular approach (or, similarly, that its approach is consistent with the OECD's openness about the issue) does not absolve the EU Member State from its obligations under EU law, which, again, would be

---

[87] Commission Decision in *Engie* (n 44), para 194.

[88] Commission Decision in *Apple* (n 37), para 153.

[89] Commission Decision in *Starbucks* (n 39), para 55.

[90] ibid, para 67.

[91] ibid, para 68.

[92] ibid, para 266.

independent from, and imposed in addition to, those flowing from domestic legislation.[93]

A third implication of the Commission's interpretation of the scope of its powers is that EU Member States do not benefit from a margin of discretion or appreciation when evaluating whether a given intra-group transaction is concluded at arm's length. Considering the nature of transfer pricing, this aspect is of particular relevance. As explained in Section 1, transfer pricing estimations are sensitive not just to the method used, but to the assumptions made when performing the analysis. The arm's length standard is therefore incapable of producing an exact figure: rather than a specific price, it yields a range of outcomes that can be considered to be reasonable approximations of a market-based one. One could argue, against this background, that the control exercised by the Commission under Article 107(1) TFEU should be confined to manifest errors of assessment by the EU Member State.

Exchanges about the appropriate standard of review of tax rulings feature in the various decisions. In *Fiat*, for instance, Luxembourg reminded the Commission of the fact that the OECD itself had acknowledged that transfer pricing is not an 'exact science'.[94] The exercise of judgement is, as discussed above, inherent in the assessment. By the same token, the EU Member State suggested, a mere disagreement about the methodological choices underpinning the analysis cannot lead to a finding of a selective advantage. Divergence in terms of outcomes does not necessarily mean that the Commission's approximation to a market-based outcome is to be preferred to (or that it is necessarily more accurate or less prone to errors than) the EU Member State's. In *Apple*, Ireland argued, in a similar vein, that a finding that a measure amounts to unlawful and incompatible State aid should not lead to recovery.[95]

The various decisions of the tax rulings saga did not appear to attach significant relevance to the requisite standard of review or, similarly, to the fact that disagreements in terms of outcome between the analysis performed by, respectively, the Commission and the national tax authorities are not necessarily an indicator of a selective advantage. The former's approach appears to imply that it is entitled to substitute its own assessment for that of the EU Member State when applying Article 107(1) TFEU. From the Commission's perspective, what matters, more than the fact that transfer pricing is incapable of providing a correct, indisputable answer, is the objective pursued by the exercise, namely ensuring that intra-group transactions occur at arm's length. Accordingly, if it is in a position to show that the methodology followed by the tax authority does not provide a reliable approximation of a market-based outcome, other considerations would not be decisive.[96]

---

[93] ibid, para 267.

[94] Commission Decision in *Fiat* (n 38), para 149.

[95] Commission Decision in *Apple* (n 37), para 160.

[96] Commission Decision in *Fiat* (n 38), para 227.

2.4. Selectivity and Advantage

There are several aspects about the selectivity assessment by the Commission in the tax rulings saga that stand out when compared to the framework discussed in Chapters 3 and 4, if only because of the novelty of some of the legal approaches. The first distinctive aspect of the decisions is that they do not distinguish neatly between the advantage and the selectivity stages of the analysis. Invariably, the Commission ascertained whether these two conditions were met in a single analytical step.[97] The conflation of the two stages is justified in light of the *MOL* doctrine[98] (discussed in Chapter 4), pursuant to which the selective nature of a measure can be presumed once the award of an advantage is proved to the requisite legal standard.[99] The substance of the analysis, however, did not focus on the concept of advantage. Instead, it revolved around the criteria to establish selectivity, namely the definition of the reference system, the identification of a derogation and the potential for a justification.[100]

Where transfer pricing was the central aspect of the assessment (as it was in *Fiat*, *Starbucks* and *Amazon*), the Commission assumed as given that a selective advantage can be inferred from the fact that the transaction deviates from a reasonable market-based outcome.[101] The application of the arm's length standard and the interpretation of Article 107(1) TFEU, in other words, became one and the same issue. The legal interpretation underlying the Commission's assumption is that, by sanctioning transactions that do not take place at arm's length, the EU Member State necessarily places integrated multinationals benefitting from the tax ruling in a more favourable position vis-à-vis non-integrated firms (given that the latter are required to deal with third parties in the open market).[102] Accordingly, the finding of a selective advantage was not contingent on showing that other tax rulings issued by the tax authority offered less generous terms to those extended to the beneficiary of the measure. The idea, instead, is that the normal tax burden is that supported by the typical non-integrated firm.

The latter point already hints at the way in which the Commission construed the three-step test in the tax rulings saga. Its default angle (and primary line of reasoning) was to take the corporate tax regime at large as the relevant reference system.[103] Against this benchmark, the Commission considered that all undertakings, whether integrated or not, are in a comparable factual and legal situation.

---

[97] ibid, para 218. See also Commission Decision in *Starbucks* (n 39), para 254 and Commission Decision in *Apple* (n 37), para 224.

[98] Case C-15/14 P *Commission v MOL Magyar Olaj- és Gázipari Nyrt.*, EU:C:2015:362.

[99] ibid, para 60.

[100] For an extensive discussion, see Chapter 4.

[101] See for instance Commission Decision in *Starbucks* (n 39), paras 415–416; and Commission Decision in *Fiat* (n 38), paras 339–340.

[102] Commission Decision in *Fiat* (n 38), para 198; Commission Decision in *Apple* (n 37), para 150.

[103] See for instance Commission Decision in *Starbucks* (n 39), para 244; Commission Decision in *Apple* (n 37), paras 242–243; and Commission Decision in *Fiat* (n 38), para 209.

This conclusion is not necessarily straightforward. It would not be unreasonable to claim, in fact, that multinationals cannot be readily likened to other undertakings. The allocation of profits across the sub-units of a large corporate group is a source of complexity that only arises when firms operate across borders. From this perspective, the very fact that tax rulings are common currency among such entities can be seen as evidence that integrated and non-integrated entities are not in a comparable situation.[104]

This point of law is consequential both from a substantive and an institutional standpoint. As noted by commentators, establishing the award of a selective advantage under a broader reference system – that is, the corporate tax regime at large – is comparatively simpler and less resource-intensive for the Commission, which bears the burden of proving that an aid has been granted.[105] If such an approach is embraced, it is sufficient to show, as the Commission did in its decisions, that the intra-group transactions had not taken place at arm's length. Under a narrower reference system, by contrast, it would have been required to establish that the tax ruling treats the undertaking in question more favourably than other multinationals. Such an exercise involves, in practice, comparing the various tax rulings and ascertaining whether they treat like situations alike. Even though there was support in the Commission's past administrative practice for the latter,[106] the approach was not endorsed (and was expressly rejected in *Starbucks*[107] and *Apple*[108]).

Engie, which did not revolve around the administration of the arm's length standard, gave rise to unique challenges as far as the assessment of selectivity is concerned. The corporate tax structure on which the multinational had relied to minimise its tax burden was not unique to it. In principle, any corporate group could devise a similar optimisation strategy, which did not even require a tax ruling for its implementation.[109] Against this background, it is open to question whether the cumulation of advantages that were available without distinction to all firms meeting the requisite conditions really amounted to a selective advantage.[110]

---

[104] See in this sense Commission Decision in *Fiat* (n 38), para 201.

[105] José Luis Buendía Sierra and Nieves Bayón Fernández, '*Fiat, Starbucks, Apple, Amazon* and *Engie*: Do Individual Tax Rulings Confer a Selective Advantage?' in Caroline Buts and José Luis Buendía Sierra (eds), *Milestones in State Aid Case Law* (2nd edn, Lexxion 2022).

[106] Commission Decision of 8 July 2009 on the groepsrentebox scheme which the Netherlands is planning to implement (C 4/07 (ex N 465/06)) [2009] OJ L288/26; and Commission Decision of 28 October 2009 on State aid C 10/07 (ex NN 13/07) implemented by Hungary for tax deductions for intra-group interest [2010] OJ L42/3.

[107] Commission Decision in *Starbucks* (n 39), para 236.

[108] Commission Decision in *Apple* (n 37), paras 231–235. In *Apple*, the Commission followed a subsidiary line of reasoning that suggested that, even if the reference system were understood to comprise other multinationals, the tax ruling issued by the tax authority provided a selective advantage that was not available to other corporate groups in a comparable factual and legal situation. See *Apple* (n 37), paras 379–403.

[109] Commission Decision in *Engie* (n 44), para 184.

[110] See, by analogy, some cases discussed in Chapter 4, including Case C-156/98 *Germany v Commission*, EU:C:2000:467; and Case C-417/10 *Ministero dell'Economia e delle Finanze and Agenzia delle Entrate v 3M Italia SpA*, EU:C:2012:184.

The Commission rejected the relevance of these arguments. It did not do so by reference to *Gibraltar*[111] – that is, by arguing that the measures, even if generally available to all undertakings, favoured de facto some large corporate groups. Instead, the Commission claimed that such a position goes against some foundational principles of tax systems, whereby taxpayers cannot unilaterally determine their fiscal burden.[112] In addition, it would affect EU Member States' ability to raise revenue and thus fulfil their functions.[113]

It is worth highlighting the alternative line of reasoning pursued by the Commission in *Engie*, if only because it featured prominently before the EU courts. According to this subsidiary approach, Luxembourg had granted a selective advantage to the multinational insofar as it had failed to apply the domestic anti-abuse provisions. In its decision, the Commission concluded that the corporate structure designed by Engie amounted to an abuse of law within the meaning of Luxembourg law.[114] It concluded, by the same token, that the tax authorities had failed to abide by their duties under Article 107(1) TFEU by issuing a tax ruling endorsing the legal construct presented by the multinational. More precisely, the EU Member State would have allowed the multinational to circumvent the 'main objective of the reference system', which is the taxation of corporate profit.[115]

3. Tax Rulings before the Court of Justice

3.1. Overview

One could aptly characterise the Commission's interpretation of Article 107(1) TFEU in the tax rulings saga as a set of principles and rules harmonising, in effect, some aspects of national tax regimes. From a substantive perspective, this conclusion is most apparent in relation to the arm's length standard, which EU Member States would be under a duty to apply when assessing intra-group transactions – and this regardless of whether it has been incorporated into domestic legislation. As pointed out in the literature, this line of administrative practice made binding

---

[111] Joined Cases C-106/09 P and C-107/09 P *Commission v Government of Gibraltar and United Kingdom*, EU:C:2011:732.

[112] Commission Decision in *Engie* (n 44), para 184 ('The Commission cannot accept this conclusion. Not only would it contravene the general feature of any tax system according to which the amount of taxes to be paid cannot unilaterally be determined by the taxpayer, but also the basic principle – common to every Member State – that income taxes should be levied according a taxpayer's ability to pay').

[113] ibid ('Moreover, [accepting the argument] would put at risk the capacity by the State to mobilise the necessary resources to finance its budget, thus rendering ineffective its tax system').

[114] ibid, para 313. See also the discussion above.

[115] ibid, para 291.

upon EU Member States the soft law issued by the OECD.[116] The creation of an EU law of transfer pricing via Article 107(1) TFEU is not the only example of de facto harmonisation. Most notably, *Engie* introduced something akin to an EU-wide anti-avoidance safeguard, whereby EU Member States would be under an obligation to take action whenever corporate groups exploit gaps and loopholes in national legislation to minimise their tax burden.

From an institutional perspective, the Commission's interpretation of the scope of its powers under Articles 107(1) and 108 TFEU would confer it with jurisdiction to enforce the new set of rules and principles. The tax rulings saga suggests that the application of EU State aid law would provide a framework allowing it to rectify some of the methodological choices made by EU Member States when applying the arm's length standard (as well as other aspects of the OECD framework). Similarly, the substantive overlap between Article 107(1) TFEU and the national tax regime would give it the power to enforce, on behalf of the national tax authorities, some aspects of domestic legislation. Such was the practical consequence, for instance, of the subsidiary argument raised by the Commission in *Engie*. Finally, and more generally, EU State aid law would become, under this approach, a general tool – or, if one prefers, a safety net – to identify and amend legislation facilitating instances of tax avoidance within the EU.

Going back to the framework devised in Chapter 1, the interpretation of Article 107(1) TFEU underpinning the tax rulings saga placed the EU State aid regime close to its outer, most far-reaching boundary (what was labelled the 'cross-border harmonisation' variety of subsidy control). The fact that commentators were divided about whether the Commission had indeed acted within the confines of its powers under EU State aid law should therefore not come as a surprise.[117] Sceptical views about the Commission's approach were expressed not just by specialists in the discipline, but by a growing number of tax lawyers who developed an interest in it. Some of the latter questioned the basis of the sui generis arm's length standard developed by the Commission,[118] whereas others perceived the standard of review of tax authorities' enforcement to be unduly strict.[119]

When challenged before the EU courts, the core aspects of the Commission's approach to the assessment of tax rulings did not survive. As already pointed out, while the direct actions against some of the decisions were ultimately unsuccessful,

---

[116] See in this sense Werner Haslehner, 'Double Taxation Relief, Transfer Pricing Adjustments and State Aid Law' in Isabelle Richelle, Wolfgang Schön and Edoardo Traversa (eds), *State Aid Law and Business Taxation* (Springer 2016); and Edoardo Traversa and Alessandra Flamini. 'Fighting Harmful Tax Competition through EU State Aid Law: Will the Hardening of Soft Law Suffice?' (2015) European State Aid law Quarterly 323.

[117] See among other contributions Richard Lyal, 'Transfer pricing rules and State aid' (2015) 38 Fordham International Law Journal 1017; Liza Lovdahl Gormsen, *European State Aid and Tax Rulings* (Edward Elgar Publishing 2019); Kyriazis (n 4); Hugo López and Aitor Navarro, 'EU State aid and the tax allocation of multinationals' profits' (2024) 61 Common Market Law Review 1255.

[118] Ruth Mason, 'Tax Rulings as State Aid – Part 4: Whose Arm's-Length Standard?' (2017) Tax Notes, 15 May 2017, p 947.

[119] Stephen Daly, 'The power to get it wrong' (2021) 137 Law Quarterly Review 280.

the idea of EU State aid law as a source of an autonomous set of rules and principles applying above and beyond national tax regimes was not endorsed by the Court. The latter found, in particular, that the Commission had erred in law when claiming that the arm's length standard is a creature of EU law. Similarly, the Court held that the application of Article 107(1) TFEU cannot depart from the interpretation of tax legislation prevailing at the national level. What is more, the standard of review of the complex assessments undertaken by tax authorities was not endorsed. The Commission's ultimate success in the *Apple* saga owed more to the specificities of the case (at least formally speaking) than to the overarching framework, which was not accepted by the Court. These various aspects are considered in turn.

3.2. Article 107(1) TFEU and the Arm's Length Standard

The Court held, in the appeal against the GC judgment in *Fiat*,[120] that the Commission had erred in law when assessing, in light of its own interpretation of the arm's length standard, whether Luxembourg had conferred a selective advantage on the multinational by means of a tax ruling.[121] More than the legal characterisation of facts, the error related to the interpretation of Article 107(1) TFEU. According to the ECJ, the arm's length standard can only form part of the analysis under EU State aid law insofar as it has been incorporated into national law. More importantly, the Commission must accept the interpretation of the standard prevailing in the domestic tax regime, at least as a matter of principle. It cannot therefore ground its assessment in its preferred methodology or approach unless it can show, in light of the *Gibraltar* line of case law,[122] that national legislation is designed in a manifestly discriminatory way that leads to a systematic undervaluation of intra-group transactions.[123]

In its appeal judgment in *Fiat*, the ECJ also departed from the ruling delivered at first instance. The GC did not accept the idea that the arm's length standard is a manifestation of an overarching principle of equal treatment in taxation that, as such, necessarily forms part of the assessment of the selectivity of measures under Article 107(1) TFEU.[124] However, it did not completely reject the Commission's theory.[125] According to the first-instance court, the arm's length

---

[120] Joined Cases T-755/15 and T-759/15 *Grand Duchy of Luxembourg and Fiat Chrysler Finance Europe v Commission*, EU:T:2019:670. See also Joined Cases T-816/17 and T-318/18 *Grand Duchy of Luxembourg, Amazon EU Sàrl and Amazon.com, Inc v Commission*, EU:T:2021:252.

[121] Joined Cases C-885/19 P and C-898/19 P *Fiat* (n 56). See also Case C-457/21 P *Commission v Grand Duchy of Luxembourg, Amazon.com Inc and Amazon EU Sàrl*, EU:C:2023:985.

[122] ibid, para 95 ('without harmonisation in that regard, any fixing of the methods and criteria for determining an "arm's length" outcome falls within the discretion of the Member States').

[123] ibid, para 70.

[124] Joined Cases T-755/15 and T-759/15 *Fiat* (n 120), para 143.

[125] For a discussion, see Buendía Sierra and Bayón Fernández (n 105).

standard can be used as a 'tool' when assessing whether a tax ruling confers a selective advantage.[126] In the same vein, the GC ultimately accepted that, to the extent that the EU Member State does not formally differentiate between integrated and non-integrated entities, the Commission was entitled to review whether the tax authorities had complied with the arm's length standard when issuing a tax ruling. Crucially, the first-instance court held that the Commission could do so – and this is where the disagreement with the ECJ lies – on the basis of the methods developed by the OECD, which were understood to have been developed by experts and captured the consensus on the matter.[127]

The Court held that the GC had erred in law by concluding that the Commission was entitled to rely on an interpretation of the arm's length standard deriving directly from the instruments issued by the OECD instruments. Like the Commission, the first-instance court considered that the relevant benchmark can be defined without taking into consideration the domestic tax regime and, more precisely, the way in which (and the extent to which) national law incorporates the arm's length standard.[128] As suggested above, the Commission's approach would amount to harmonising, in effect, national legislation in the area of taxation. It was rejected by the ECJ for that very reason. The Court held, in this sense, that 'in the absence of harmonisation in EU law, the specific detailed rules for the application' of the arm's length standard 'are defined by national law and must be taken into account in order to identify the reference framework'.[129]

It is implicit in this conclusion that the Commission had erroneously construed *Forum 187*. That precedent, the Court held, cannot be relied upon in support of the proposition that the arm's length standard is applicable in the area of EU State aid law irrespective of whether – and if so how – it has been incorporated into national legislation.[130] In line with what has already been pointed out, transfer pricing methods only arose in the context of that judgment because the national tax regime made an express reference to them and only insofar as the ad hoc methodological choices made by the EU Member State alleviated the burden of the undertakings benefitting from the special regime.[131] This conclusion is consistent with the analytical framework outlined in Chapter 4 (and in particular the deference to the interpretation of national legislation by the Court). In a sense, *Commission v Poland* and *Commission v Hungary* heralded the outcome in *Fiat*.[132]

The rejection of the Commission's interpretation of Article 107(1) TFEU must be understood against the background of the allocation of competences between the EU and its Member States. The Court explicitly held in *Fiat* that the

---

[126] Joined Cases T-755/15 and T-759/15 *Fiat* (n 120), para 151.
[127] ibid, para 147.
[128] Joined Cases C-885/19 P and C-898/19 P *Fiat* (n 56), para 92.
[129] ibid, para 93.
[130] ibid, para 102.
[131] ibid, para 103.
[132] See Case C-562/19 P *Commission v Poland*, EU:C:2021:201 and Case C-596/19 P *Commission v Hungary*, EU:C:2021:202 and the accompanying discussion in Chapter 4.

Commission's analysis, by erring in law, infringed the TFEU rules that provide the legal basis for the harmonisation of legislation in the area of taxation, and in particular Article 114(2) TFEU (which excludes taxation from the default harmonisation mechanism) and Article 115 TFEU (which is the residual provision to approximate national regimes, including in the area of direct taxation, and demands unanimity within the Council).[133] In other words, the Court implied that the Commission had sought to harmonise national legislation via the enforcement of Article 107(1) TFEU, thereby circumventing the appropriate legal routes enshrined in the TFEU.

3.3. The Scope and Standard of Review of National Legislation

The position of the Court in relation to the status of the arm's length standard under Article 107(1) TFEU determined the fate of other aspects of the Commission's approach to the review of non-harmonised tax legislation. Contrary to what the decisions suggested, the enforcement of EU state aid law can only interfere with the design and operation of domestic regimes at the margins, that is, where it can be shown that the 'manifestly discriminatory' test defined in *Gibraltar* is met. Put differently, national tax systems are subject, if at all, to marginal review. To give a concrete example, the Commission would not be in a position to substitute its own assessment for that of the tax authority when evaluating whether an intra-group transaction has taken place at arm's length. Similarly, it would not be able to second-guess the transfer pricing method applied in a tax ruling.

These conclusions come across as an inevitable consequence of the Court's judgment in *Fiat*, but they were already heralded at first instance in *Starbucks*, in which the GC annulled the Commission decision.[134] In essence, the first-instance court held in *Starbucks* that a mere discrepancy with the tax authority in terms of methods and outcomes cannot justify, in and of itself, a finding of a selective advantage. The GC emphasised that the crucial consideration when applying Article 107(1) TFEU is whether the contentious measure mitigates the charges to which a firm is normally subject. As the judgment puts it, 'non-compliance with methodological requirements does not necessarily lead to a reduction of the tax burden.'[135] Similarly, 'the mere finding by the Commission of errors in the choice or application of the transfer pricing method' is insufficient to substantiate

---

[133] Joined Cases C-885/19 P and C-898/19 P *Fiat* (n 56), para 117: 'the decision at issue must be annulled in so far as the Commission erred in law in finding that there was a selective advantage in the light of a reference framework comprising an arm's length principle which does not derive from a full examination of the relevant national tax law, following an exchange of arguments on that subject with the Member State concerned, and that, in so doing, it also infringed the provisions of the FEU Treaty relating to the adoption by the European Union of measures for the approximation of Member State legislation relating to direct taxation, in particular Article 114(2) TFEU and Article 115 TFEU'.

[134] Cases T-760/15 and T-636/16 *Starbucks* (n 57).

[135] ibid, para 201.

a finding of an advantage.[136] The GC reached similar conclusions in its judgment in *Apple*.[137]

Fiat appeared to dismiss completely the idea that Article 107(1) TFEU can be relied upon as a basis to introduce principles and objectives applying above and beyond those stemming from domestic legislation. Fiscal duties have to be expressly derived from the national regime. What is more, the Court acknowledged that the very nature of taxation (and its impact on, inter alia, fundamental rights) means that tax authorities – including those concerned in the tax rulings saga – do not allow the imposition of fiscal measures merely on the basis of principles or objectives. According to a tradition that is common to EU Member States – and which the ECJ found to be a part of the EU legal order – any obligation to pay tax, as well as the rationale underpinning any such obligation, must be explicitly enshrined in law, thereby giving the taxpayer the ability to estimate the amount and timing of the obligation.[138]

The appeal judgment in *Engie* exemplifies well the impact of the Court's course correction on the scope and standard of review of national tax regimes.[139] As pointed out above, one of the arguments raised by the EU Member State in that case related to the interpretation of domestic legislation, which it deemed *contra legem*. In this regard, the ECJ held that the Commission, when assessing the selectivity of a measure, is required to defer to the interpretation of the relevant tax regime put forward by the EU Member State in the context of the administrative proceedings, at least as a matter of principle.[140] Accordingly, it may only depart from the alleged understanding of national legislation where it is able to show, 'on the basis of reliable and consistent evidence', and following an exchange of arguments, that the prevailing interpretation at the national level is a different one.[141]

It has been mentioned above that the Commission pursued an alternative line of reasoning in *Engie*, pursuant to which Luxembourg had conferred a selective advantage by failing to apply the relevant domestic provisions on abuse of law to the corporate structure devised by the multinational. Again, the Court held that the Commission could not come to this conclusion without assessing how the tax authority's failure to enforce the anti-abuse regime entailed a departure from the case law and administrative practice prevailing at the national level.[142] Crucially, the appeal judgment explained that, if the Commission were to be dispensed of the need to provide evidence in this sense, it would allow itself 'to define what does or does not constitute a correct application of such a provision, which would

---

[136] ibid.

[137] Joined Cases T-778/16 and T-892/16 *Ireland, Apple Sales International and Apple Operations Europe v Commission*, EU:T:2020:338.

[138] Joined Cases C-885/19 P and C-898/19 P *Fiat* (n 56), para 97.

[139] Joined Cases C-451/21 P and C-454/21 P Engie (n 58).

[140] ibid, para 120.

[141] ibid, para 121.

[142] ibid, para 155.

exceed the limits of the powers conferred on it by the Treaties in the field of State aid review'.[143]

3.4. Selectivity and Advantage

Because the Commission's analysis was found to be erroneous at a relatively early stage, the judgments that followed the tax rulings saga fail to shed much light on the interpretation of the concepts of selectivity and advantage. That said, some of the most salient aspects of the Commission's approach featured in the direct actions brought against the decisions. The conflation of selectivity and advantage, which are in principle two separate conditions, was challenged by *Apple* before the GC.[144] The first-instance court, with some support in the case law (selectivity and advantage have indeed been presented as a single condition in some of the canonical rulings considered in Part I[145]), dismissed the relevance of the claim, arguing that the joint examination of the two concepts is not 'inconceivable', and particularly so in the area of taxation, where the analysis revolves around establishing whether a measure leads to a reduction in the charges to which an undertaking would be normally subject.[146]

In relation specifically to the concept of advantage, the judgments that follow the tax rulings saga are valuable as a reminder that the administration of the arm's length standard is not an end in itself, and that it must be neatly distinguished from the question of whether a given tax ruling amounts to State aid. In this sense, the GC pointed out that the Commission bears the burden of proving the existence of an advantage, which cannot merely be inferred from the fact that an EU Member State had relied on incorrect assumptions or, similarly, the fact that it had committed methodological errors.[147] It would be necessary to show how such assumptions and/or errors led to a reduction in the burden that would normally have been supported by the undertaking. As explained above, the Commission was found to have failed at this stage in the first-instance rulings in both *Amazon* and *Apple*.

3.5. Making Sense of the Appeal Judgment in *Apple*

The last Court judgment on the tax rulings saga to be delivered by the Court related to the appeal in *Apple*. Against the background of the above, the outcome

---

[143] ibid.

[144] Joined Cases T-778/16 and T-892/16 *Apple* (n 137).

[145] *MOL* (n 98).

[146] Joined Cases T-778/16 and T-892/16 *Apple* (n 137), para 135.

[147] Article 108(2) TFEU makes a reference to the 'parties concerned' and the possibility for them to 'submit their comments'.

might have seemed a foregone conclusion. The *Apple* decision had been annulled at first instance,[148] even though the GC had not dismissed outright the substantive and methodological choices made by the Commission – including, for example, its reliance on the OECD soft law framework as a reasonably accurate analytical proxy for the evaluation of national legislation.[149] That said, the first-instance court showed more deference than the Commission to the tax authority's assessment. From an analytical perspective, the GC judgment suggests, a finding of a selective advantage requires more than a mistaken assumption or a disparity of views.[150] From a substantive perspective, the first-instance court held that the Commission must ground its assessment in national law, not in an abstract construct.[151]

The appeal judgments in *Fiat* and *Engie* made it more likely that the Commission's appeal against the first-instance ruling in *Apple* would be dismissed. The latter differed from the preceding two in that the arm's length standard had not been incorporated into the Irish legal order at the time of the contentious tax rulings. One could argue, as a result, that not even the tenuous links that the GC had found between the national tax regime and the standard would be of relevance for the assessment.[152] In *Apple*, the Commission had not deferred to the EU Member State's interpretation of its own legislation. In fact, the interpretation of the key provision in the Irish tax regime had become a central bone of contention.[153] As explained above, Ireland resisted the idea that one could infer anything akin to the arm's length standard from it. After *Engie*, one would have been forgiven for assuming that such an approach would have proved conclusive for the decision's fate on appeal.

However, the ECJ set aside the first-instance ruling in *Apple* and gave final judgment in the matter – instead of referring the case back to the GC (which Advocate General Pitruzzella had proposed in his Opinion[154]). The Court dismissed the applications brought by Ireland and Apple.[155] The judgment differs significantly from *Fiat* and *Engie*, and not just in terms of outcome. If the analysis in the latter two had focused on issues of law in the strict sense of the word (that is, on the interpretation of the meaning and scope of Article 107(1) TFEU) and on the framework for the assessment of State aid, the appeal judgment in *Apple* revolved around the legal characterisation of facts by the GC. It therefore ventured into the details of tax-related issues, ultimately concluding that the first-instance court

[148] Joined Cases T-778/16 and T-892/16 *Apple* (n 137).

[149] ibid, paras 218–220.

[150] ibid, para 348.

[151] ibid, para 207.

[152] As mentioned above (n 149), the GC considered that something akin to the arm's length standard could be inferred from national legislation.

[153] Commission Decision in *Apple* (n 37), paras 152–160. See also Joined Cases T-778/16 and T-892/16 *Apple* (n 137), paras 173–188.

[154] Opinion of Advocate General Pitruzzella in Case C-465/20 P *Commission v Ireland and others*, EU:C:2023:840.

[155] Case C-465/20 P *Apple* (n 55).

had erred in law when reviewing the Commission's assessment of the intra-group transactions.[156]

From the perspective of tax law, one disputed issue revolved around whether the intellectual property licences held by Apple Operations Europe and Apple Sales International had to be allocated to their Irish branches. There was a divergence of views, in this regard, between the Court and the GC. The ECJ held that the first-instance court had erred in law when it held that the Commission, in its decision, had allocated the licensing income to the Irish branches 'by exclusion'.[157] The second point of contention had to do with the relevance of the activities of Apple Inc (the parent company, incorporated in the US) in the analysis. The Court concluded that the GC had erred when it held that the parent's activities (and, more precisely, the role it had in relation to the management of the group's intellectual property) could be taken into account when deciding whether to allocate the relevant income to the Irish branches.[158]

The single most notable feature of the appeal judgment from an EU State aid law perspective is that the Court's analytical approach appears to depart from the one followed in both *Fiat* and *Engie*. In the latter, the ECJ had annulled the decision because the Commission had failed to defer to the interpretation of the arm's length standard prevailing in national law. In *Apple*, by contrast, the ECJ accepted as given the Commission's premise, according to which the national tax regime corresponded 'in essence' to an aspect of the OECD framework that had not been incorporated into domestic law.[159] The tension between the two lines of case law and the eventual departure from *Fiat* and *Engie* in *Apple* can be explained on procedural grounds and is case-specific. The Court held that it could not examine whether the arm's length standard could serve as a basis for the interpretation of the national tax regime insofar as the issue had not been raised in a cross-appeal either by Ireland or by Apple. As a result, the question had force of *res judicata* and could not be reviewed.[160]

Because the issues addressed in *Apple* are so case-specific, and because the Court did not revisit some of the fundamental premises underpinning the GC's analysis, it would be inaccurate to argue that the judgment in the case overruled *Fiat* and *Engie*. The Court did not engage with the meaning and scope of Article 107(1) TFEU. Therefore, the deference of EU State aid law vis-à-vis national legislation

---

[156] ibid, para 259.

[157] ibid, paras 117–131.

[158] ibid, para 220.

[159] ibid, para 123.

[160] ibid, paras 272–281, in particular para 278: '[…] Ireland and ASI and AOE claimed […] that, in view of the Irish tax authorities' application of section 25 of the TCA 97, the Commission could not check by reference to the arm's length principle whether the level of profit allocated to the branches for their trade in Ireland, as accepted in the contested tax rulings, corresponded to the level of profit that would have been obtained through carrying on that trade under market conditions. [I]n so far as the judgment under appeal rejected those arguments on the grounds set out in paragraphs 192 to 225 thereof, and in the absence of a cross-appeal, the judgment under appeal has the force of *res judicata*. There is therefore no need to rule on those arguments'.

(in the absence of harmonisation) remains an accurate characterisation of the relationship between the two legal orders. In this sense, *Apple* is best understood as a one-off arising from a particular set of procedural circumstances. It is not alone in this regard, whether in the context of EU State aid law or EU law at large. *Gibraltar*, discussed in Chapter 4, is another example. The path to reach the outcome might have been different, but both are testament to the malleability of EU law.

It is against this background that one can make sense of the relevance and place of *Apple*. The value of the judgment, it is submitted, is threefold. First, *Apple* is a reminder that administrative action in the area of tax rulings will sometimes remain within the confines of Article 107(1) TFEU. The Court signals, in other words, that there will be circumstances where the sanctioning of tax planning strategies will amount to unlawful and incompatible State aid. In this sense, *Apple* could be read as a vindication of the Commission's attempt to explore the limits of its powers in the area. Second, the judgment may be understood as an acknowledgement, by the Court, of the reality of tax avoidance and its potential to distort competition in the internal market. Leaving aside EU State aid law considerations, tax scholars had taken the view that there were compelling reasons to regard with concern some tax arrangements concluded between multinationals and EU Member States.[161]

One could argue, third, that the judgment, in a sense, is indicative of the way forward. In many ways, the tax rulings saga dealt with the days of yore. *Apple*, for instance, related to an era where the arm's length standard had not even been incorporated into national legislation. The appeal ruling in the case could be more relevant moving forward, that is, as EU Member States' regimes become progressively aligned and the OECD standards find their way into the EU and the national legal orders. In this new context, the sort of analysis into which the Court ventured could be more relevant and commonplace. More importantly, it would be fully in keeping with *Fiat* and *Engie*. From this perspective, the judgment could be read as an indication that enforcement in the area of tax rulings will have a place, albeit diminished, in the EU legal landscape.

4. Conclusions

The tax rulings saga can only be fully understood if one takes into account the specificities of the EU as an organisation and the nature of its competences and powers. When looking at the behaviour of the various institutional actors, one can identify a consistent pattern over the years, in particular at critical junctures requiring intervention at the EU level. Disagreements between the Commission

---

[161] See for instance Ruth Mason and Stephen Daly, 'Rotten to the Core: The EU's Court of Justice Decision in Apple' (2024) 116 Tax Notes International 987. These authors, while critical with the Court's analysis, argue that the Commission 'could have launched a legally stronger case against Apple'.

and the Council about the speed and breadth of integration are far from unusual. Experience shows that the former typically favours faster and more ambitious action, whereas the latter tends to tilt towards cautious and incremental measures. Where such frictions are observed, the Commission has frequently sought to break the impasse by testing the limits of its powers under the TFEU, and in particular in the area of competition law (including under Regulation 1/2003[162] and Article 106(3) TFEU[163]).

Examples in this sense abound. The liberalisation of the telecommunications sector, for instance, followed this pattern. Given the EU Member States' initial reluctance to open these activities to competition, the Commission tested the extent to which it could do so by means of Directives within the meaning of Article 106(3) TFEU.[164] At a subsequent stage, and on the back of the (partial) success of this strategy, the EU legislature was brought on board.[165] A similar strategy was followed in relation to the integration of energy markets. The enforcement of Articles 101 and 102 TFEU complemented, and occasionally went beyond, the liberalisation efforts introduced by means of legislation.[166] In relation specifically to EU State aid law, a sector inquiry launched by the Commission into capacity mechanisms[167] anticipated the ad hoc legislation that would be subsequently adopted.[168]

These examples help put the tax rulings saga in perspective. One lesson to draw from them is that intervention under Articles 107 and 108 TFEU cannot be examined in isolation. It must be evaluated together with other initiatives overlapping, totally or partially, with EU State aid enforcement. Considered in this way, the fact that some core substantive choices underpinning the tax rulings saga (and in particular the idea that the arm's length standard flows directly from Article 107(1) TFEU) were not endorsed by the Court does not seem decisive. The crucial factor, instead, is the fact that the EU appears to have moved decisively, and on various fronts, to address tax avoidance and promote tax fairness.[169] By signalling the salience of the issue and the Commission's resolve to explore ways to address it, EU State aid law will have played its part. And the unexpected outcome in *Apple* suggests that, at least to some degree, it will continue to do so.

---

[162] Council Regulation (EC) No 1/2003 of 16 December 2002 on the implementation of the rules on competition laid down in Articles 81 and 82 of the Treaty [2003] OJ L1/1.

[163] Pursuant to Article 106(3) TFEU, 'The Commission shall ensure the application of the provisions of this Article and shall, where necessary, address appropriate directives or decisions to Member States'.

[164] Case C-202/88 *France v Commission*, EU:C:1991:120.

[165] For a discussion of the process, see Pierre Larouche, *Competition Law and Regulation in European Telecommunications* (Hart Publishing 2000).

[166] See in this sense Ibáñez Colomo (n 36).

[167] Commission, 'State aid: Sector Inquiry report gives guidance on capacity mechanisms' IP/16/4021 (Brussels, 30 November 2016).

[168] Regulation (EU) 2019/943 of the European Parliament and of the Council of 5 June 2019 on the internal market for electricity (recast) [2019] OJ L158/54.

[169] Koen Lenaerts, 'The Role of the Court of Justice in Enhancing Tax Fairness in the EU' (2025) 34 EC Tax Review 78.

6

The Permacrisis of EU
State Aid Policy

---

1. Introduction

Because State aid can contribute to public interest objectives, it would be inappropriate to prohibit it whenever it is found to distort competition and affect trade. Due to the ambivalent effects of subsidies and similar measures, it is indispensable to develop criteria to identify the instances where action by the State makes a contribution that is, on the whole, positive for society. As mentioned in Chapter 1, the balancing of the positive and negative effects of measures remains the fundamental challenge of any subsidy control regime, including the EU one. A substantive apparatus that allows for such balancing needs to be fleshed out in the form of rules and standards so it can be readily administered by the European Commission (hereinafter, the 'Commission') and applied by the EU Member States. One of the distinctive features of the EU model is precisely that it expressly provides for a legal avenue for this balancing to be undertaken.

However, Articles 107(2) and 107(3) TFEU lack, in and of themselves, the requisite degree of specificity and detail to provide a structured framework for weighing the positive and negative aspects of State aid. If at all, these two provisions identify the public interest objectives that will – as far as Article 107(2) TFEU is concerned[1] – or may – in the case of Article 107(3) TFEU[2] – lead to a finding of compatibility. For instance, Article 107(3)(c) TFEU, which is by far the most frequent legal basis in practice and the one on which the remainder of the chapter focuses, merely refers, without more, to 'aid to facilitate the development of certain economic activities or of certain economic areas'. The task has fallen upon the Commission to provide meaning and structure to these two provisions. It has done so, as mentioned in passing across all chapters in Part I, by means of a variety of hard and soft law instruments,

---

[1] Article 107(2) TFEU refers to aid that 'shall be compatible with the internal market'.

[2] Article 107(3) TFEU, in turn, refers to aid that 'may be considered to be compatible with the internal market'.

including Regulations,[3] Decisions,[4] and a combination of Frameworks[5] and Guidelines.[6]

These various instruments reveal the extent to which it is difficult to engage in the balancing of the positive and negative dimensions of State aid. The Environment and Energy Guidelines,[7] for instance, run to dozens of pages, laying down in painstaking detail the criteria under which different interventions (such as support for renewable sources of electricity, the energy performance of buildings, and clean mobility) will be deemed compatible with the internal market.[8] Similarly, the Guidelines on regional aid[9] elaborate at length on how Articles 107(3)(a) and 107(3)(c) TFEU are to be fleshed out when State intervention is aimed at promoting the development of certain economic regions. The Commission, inter alia, explains what is meant by an 'abnormally low' standard of living within the meaning of sub-paragraph (a) of the provision,[10] and introduces rules for the allocation of aid in so-called (c) regions.[11]

The balancing exercise and the development of administrable proxies are complex endeavours during the best of times. At times of crisis, these tasks may become close to impossible. In the event of a pandemic or a serious economic disruption, some of the assumptions underpinning the ordinary assessment of the compatibility of State aid may no longer hold. For instance, the range of positive effects that can be taken into consideration may change. If intervention to promote renewable sources of electricity is typically rationalised as a response to a market failure, action in the context of a serious economic crisis may provide additional justifications for the award of State aid. Where economic protectionism is rampant across the world, for instance, the question of whether industrial policy considerations provide such a justification emerges. More generally, unusual times may require more tolerance vis-à-vis

---

[3] See in particular the so-called General Block Exemption Regulation: Commission Regulation (EU) No 651/2014 of 17 June 2014 declaring certain categories of aid compatible with the internal market in application of Articles 107 and 108 of the Treaty [2014] OJ L187/1.

[4] For instance, and in particular, Commission Decision of 20 December 2011 on the application of Article 106(2) of the Treaty on the Functioning of the European Union to State aid in the form of public service compensation granted to certain undertakings entrusted with the operation of services of general economic interest [2011] OJ L7/3.

[5] See, among the frameworks discussed in the preceding chapters, the Framework for State aid in the form of public service compensation [2012] OJ C8/1 and the Framework for State aid for research and development and innovation [2022] OJ C414/1.

[6] Guidelines on regional State aid [2021] OJ C153/1 and Guidelines on State aid for climate, environmental protection and energy 2022 [2022] OJ C80/1.

[7] Environment and Energy Guidelines (n 6).

[8] For an analysis, see Antonis Metaxas, 'The new State Aid Guidelines on Climate, Environmental Protection and Energy: what changes do they bring?' in Leigh Hancher and Ignacio Herrera Anchustegui (eds), *Research Handbook on EU Competition Law and the Energy Transition* (Edward Elgar 2024).

[9] Guidelines on regional aid (n 6).

[10] Article 107(3)(a) TFEU refers to 'aid to promote the economic development of areas where the standard of living is abnormally low or where there is serious underemployment, and of the regions referred to in Article 349, in view of their structural, economic and social situation'.

[11] Article 107(3)(c) TFEU, in turn, refers to 'aid to facilitate the development of certain economic activities or of certain economic areas'.

distortions of competition and trade. At the height of a pandemic, for instance, the ordinary balancing exercise may become a straitjacket limiting firms' ability to adjust to an unusual reality, thereby jeopardising their very viability.

It is not a secret that the EU State aid system has been placed under considerable stress since 2020. The rapid succession of the Covid-19 pandemic and the invasion of Ukraine required the Commission to adjust the instruments around which the compatibility assessment relies so as to ensure that EU Member States have the necessary leeway to respond to unprecedented challenges. The changing geopolitical landscape is an additional factor that contributes to the sense that EU State aid policy cannot be implemented in the established way. According to this view, the crisis in the rules-based international order and the rise of protectionism, both described in Chapter 1, mean that the system may no longer be applied as originally designed. As a result, some interventions that might not necessarily have been deemed compatible with the internal market (such as the subsidisation of economic activity to prevent displacement to a non-EU country) might need to be accommodated in the new economic and regulatory landscape.

The fundamental question that these developments raise is whether they might have transformed EU State aid policy for good. There are reasons to believe, in this sense, that it may no longer be feasible or realistic to turn back the clock to the days preceding the Covid-19 pandemic. It is undeniable that the EU State aid system has been subject to considerable stress at particular points in time – an obvious instance being the financial crisis of the late 2000s.[12] However, the scale and the persistence of the exceptional circumstances surrounding the implementation of the regime since 2020 are unprecedented. As a result, it is submitted, it seems unlikely that the system will return to the old ways. It is probable, in this sense, that the expectations and incentives around the permacrisis in policymaking will lead to a new equilibrium and, by extension, a new balance between the positive and negative aspects of State aid.

2. Principles Underpinning the Compatibility Assessment

2.1. The Scope of the Commission's Discretion: Theory and Practice

Unlike Article 107(2) TFEU, Article 107(3) TFEU vests the Commission with genuine discretion to define the circumstances where State aid is compatible with

---

[12] For a detailed analysis, see Christian Ahlborn and Daniel Piccinin, 'The application of the principles of restructuring aid to banks during the financial crisis' (2010) 9 European State Aid Law Quarterly 47; and Christian Ahlborn, 'Financial Sector' in Kelyn Bacon (ed), *European Union Law of State Aid* (2nd edn, Oxford University Press 2013).

the internal market. Accordingly, the Commission has the power to shape the relevant legal notions enshrined in the provision. For instance (and coming back to one of the examples mentioned in the introduction), its role is to define what an 'abnormally low' standard of living is.[13] Similarly, it can lay down the criteria to establish whether the intervention under consideration 'does not adversely affect trading conditions to an extent contrary to the common interest'. A corollary to the discretion enjoyed by the Commission is the limited review to which the interpretation and application of Article 107(3) TFEU is subject before the EU courts. Judicial review is thus confined to manifest errors of assessment.[14]

A second corollary is that the Commission is not bound by its past decisions.[15] As the Court of Justice (hereinafter, the 'Court' or the 'ECJ') held in *Freistaat Sachsen*, the past interpretation given in the context of the compatibility assessment 'cannot affect the correctness of the Commission's interpretation [of a decision] and hence its validity'.[16] Such a position could be reasonably seen as problematic from the perspective of legal certainty. Its primary implication, after all, is that administrative action does not necessarily provide a reliable indication about the direction of future enforcement. The Court's position in *Freistaat Sachsen* can be easily rationalised, however, the moment one takes into consideration that Article 107(3) TFEU is a vehicle for the formulation of policy and that policy should necessarily be allowed to fluctuate and evolve in a way and at a pace that the law cannot.[17]

Discretion is a double-edged sword for the Commission.[18] On the one hand, it gives it ample leeway to determine the criteria for the compatibility of State aid with the internal market. What is more, its assessment will be controlled, if at all, for manifest errors alone. However, this very leeway might turn out to be problematic, in particular considering that it is not bound by previous decisions. The implication, in practice, is that, at least in theory, the Commission can declare the compatibility of a vast array of measures. For that very reason, it may find itself vulnerable to lobbying by EU Member States and recipients. As explained in Chapter 1, public authorities may find it difficult to withstand short-term pressures to award aid, even when they are aware that the measure is not in their long-term interest. These pressures may be passed on to the Commission.

It is against this background that one must make sense of the techniques on which the Commission relies to flesh out Article 107(3) TFEU. What the various

---

[13] Case 730/79 *Philip Morris Holland BV v Commission*, EU:C:1980:209.

[14] ibid, para 17.

[15] This point is extensively discussed in José Luis Buendía Sierra, '*Quo Vadis* Compatibility?' in Juan Jorge Piernas López, Leigh Hancher and Luca Rubini (eds), *The Future of EU State Aid Law: Consolidation and Expansion* (EU Law Live Press 2023).

[16] ibid, who cites Joined Cases C-57/00 P and C-61/00 P *Freistaat Sachsen, Volkswagen AG and Volkswagen Sachsen GmbH v Commission*, EU:C:2003:510, para 52.

[17] See, for a discussion of the different paces of law and policy, Pablo Ibáñez Colomo, 'Law, Policy, Expertise: Hallmarks of Effective Judicial Review in EU Competition Law' (2022) 24 Cambridge Yearbook of European Legal Studies 143.

[18] As noted in Buendía Sierra (n 15).

hard and soft law instruments mentioned above reveal is an awareness of the risk that the effective formulation of its policy may be endangered by stakeholders' attempts to influence outcomes in individual cases. Accordingly, the Commission typically relies on rigid bright lines, rather than flexible standards, when establishing the conditions under which State aid is compatible with the internal market. It is sufficient to take a look, in this sense, at the General Block Exemption Regulation (hereinafter, the 'GBER')[19] or the Guidelines on regional aid to realise the extent to which the practical operation of the system revolves around such hard boundaries. The Guidelines on regional aid, for instance, define fixed percentages of aid intensity depending on the characteristics of the region at issue.[20] This technique is best understood as a pre-commitment device, whereby the Commission minimises its own ability to depart from the course of action it has previously set for itself.

2.2. State Aid must Contribute to a Public Interest Objective

2.2.1. *State Aid is not a Gratuitous Advantage*

The fundamental principles around which the assessment revolves were outlined by the Court in *Philip Morris*.[21] One of these principles was discussed at some length in Chapter 3. The ECJ held, in essence, that State aid can only be declared to be compatible with the internal market where it makes a contribution to a public interest objective. As pointed out by Advocate General Léger in *Altmark*, State aid cannot be a gratuitous advantage if it is to meet the conditions of Article 107(3) TFEU.[22] There must be, always and everywhere, a quid pro quo in exchange for the award, whether it relates to efficiency or equity. Accordingly, the mere improvement of the position enjoyed by the recipient – or, similarly, the fact that State intervention allows it to remain in business – would not be sufficient to declare the compatibility of the measure with the internal market. Something else – a benefit to society at large, that is – must be shown to result from the measure.

This principle helps explain why some types of interventions have always been viewed with reticence both by the Commission and are only deemed compatible with the internal market where very strict conditions are met. This is true, in particular, of so-called operating aid and of support to ailing firms. It is in principle difficult to see what the contribution to a public interest objective might be in such instances. To the extent that operating aid is aimed at covering a firm's current expenditures, for instance, it seems to do nothing other than help it remain

---

[19] GBER (n 3).

[20] Guidelines on regional aid (n 6).

[21] *Philip Morris* (n 13).

[22] Opinion of Advocate General Léger in Case C-280/00 *Altmark Trans GmbH and Regierungspräsidium Magdeburg v Nahverkehrsgesellschaft Altmark GmbH, and Oberbundesanwalt beim Bundesverwaltungsgericht*, EU:C:2003:13, paras 37–38.

in business. The same could be said of aid in support of ailing undertakings, the object of which is, prima facie, to avoid their bankruptcy. In such scenarios, it will be for the EU Member State to substantiate how the measure contributes to a public interest objective. It could be the case, for instance, that operating aid is indispensable to keep economic activity within a remote or seriously deprived region[23] or that financial assistance for the purpose of restructuring a business addresses the social consequences of a disorderly closure.[24]

The public interest objectives that might justify the award of State aid have been systematically defined by the Commission in its administrative practice. Since the launch of the so-called State aid Action Plan in the mid-2000s,[25] it has consistently required that EU Member States identify the positive effect that is expected to result from the intervention. In line with the discussion in Chapter 1, the public interest objective to which the measure contributes may relate to efficiency or equity. The various soft law instruments systematically identify the market failures that may justify the award of State aid in a particular economic sector (for instance, energy[26]) or in relation to a particular activity (for instance, employee training[27]) and thus respond to instances where markets fail to deliver efficient outcomes. Solidarity and redistribution feature no less prominently in the Commission's practice – including services of general economic interest, addressed in Chapter 3.

2.2.2. *State Aid must Bring about Change: The Incentive Effect*

A second principle stemming directly from *Philip Morris* is that State aid must lead to an outcome that departs from the one that would have resulted from the normal operation of market forces.[28] Accordingly, intervention will be deemed to be incompatible with the internal market where it supports an activity that would have occurred in its absence. If, as in *Philip Morris*, an investment would have been undertaken irrespective of the involvement of the public authority, it would be difficult to argue that the latter makes a meaningful contribution to a public interest objective. This same philosophy underpins the Commission's interpretation and application of Article 107(3) TFEU. It is best captured by two features of the analytical framework it consistently applies to the assessment of State aid.[29] The first is the need to identify the equity or efficiency objective sought. This point has

---

[23] In this case, Article 107(3)(a) TFEU would provide a legal basis. See also the Guidelines on regional aid (n 6).

[24] See in this sense the Guidelines on State aid for rescuing and restructuring non-financial undertakings in difficulty [2014] OJ C249/1.

[25] State Aid Action Plan: Less and better targeted state aid: a roadmap for state aid reform 2005–2009 COM(2005) 107 final.

[26] Environment and Energy Guidelines (n 6).

[27] Criteria for the analysis of the compatibility of State aid for training subject to individual notification [2009] OJ C188/1.

[28] *Philip Morris* (n 13), para 26.

[29] For an illustration of this framework, see for instance the Environment and Energy Guidelines (n 6).

already been addressed in the preceding sub-section. The second is the requirement to demonstrate the so-called 'incentive effect' – that is, that intervention brings about change that would otherwise not have occurred.[30]

Proving the incentive effect of State aid makes it necessary to evaluate intervention against the relevant counterfactual. The Commission applies some rules of thumb to ensure that interventions have such an effect. Generally speaking, the larger the investment by the undertaking, the more reluctant it will be to find that aid supporting it is compatible with the internal market. Accordingly, soft law instruments provide for additional safeguards applying to investments exceeding a certain amount.[31] These safeguards will require the EU Member State to notify the measure individually so that the Commission can establish, on the basis of specific evidence, that intervention can be expected to bring about the desired change. If, for instance, an EU Member State intends to show that an investment would not have been undertaken within the EU in the absence of State aid, they will have to do on the basis of a profitability analysis like the ones described in Chapter 3.[32]

In the same vein, where there is evidence that investments do occur (or are likely to occur) even in the absence of market intervention, State aid is unlikely to be deemed compatible with the internal market. This idea is best illustrated in light of the Guidelines on State aid for broadband networks. In this context, the Commission takes the view that financial support for the rollout of infrastructure will lack an incentive effect where the available evidence reveals that the 'stakeholders have invested or intend to invest in, respectively, fixed or mobile networks in the target areas within the relevant time horizon' and that an 'equivalent investment' would have been committed by the recipient.[33] In such circumstances, the measure will only be deemed to bring about change and thus potentially meet the conditions of Article 107(3) TFEU, where it can be expected to alter the nature or scale of the investment involved.[34]

2.2.3. *State Aid must be Proportionate*

State aid must not only have an incentive effect but must remain proportionate to bring about the desired change. Accordingly, where the transfer of resources exceeds what is necessary to attain the public interest objective pursued, it will be deemed to be incompatible with the internal market. Chapter 3 provided an illustration of this point, albeit concerning the application of Article 106(2) TFEU.

---

[30] ibid, para 26: 'Aid can be considered as facilitating an economic activity only if it has an incentive effect. An incentive effect occurs when the aid induces the beneficiary to change its behaviour, to engage in additional economic activity or in more environmentally-friendly economic activity, which it would not carry out without the aid or would carry out in a restricted or different manner'.

[31] Guidelines on regional aid (n 6), paras 20–23.

[32] See Chapter 3, in particular Section 2.4.4.

[33] Guidelines on State aid for broadband networks [2023] OJ C36/1, para 40.

[34] ibid: 'State aid may, however, be considered compatible where and to the extent necessary to provide a quality of service going beyond the requirements resulting from such obligations'.

It was mentioned that financial support that exceeds what is required to compensate for the costs of discharging the public service obligations imposed upon an undertaking – including a 'reasonable profit' – does not meet the *Altmark* conditions and therefore provides an advantage within the meaning of Article 107(1) TFEU.[35] More importantly for the purposes of the present chapter, a measure that overcompensates for the obligation would also lead to a finding of incompatibility under Article 106(2) TFEU.[36]

The same logic applies when a measure is assessed under Article 107(3) TFEU. *BMW*[37] illustrates well the practical operation of the proportionality assessment. The case concerned a regional aid measure that was intended to incentivise the shift of production from BMW's headquarters in Munich to a relatively less developed location that could benefit from regional aid under Article 107(3)(c) TFEU – Leipzig.[38] The Commission evaluated, in the context of an individual notification, the amount that was necessary to attain the desired change. This amount was found to represent 'the difference between the net costs for the beneficiary company to invest in the assisted region and the net costs to invest in the alternative region(s)'.[39] It is in light of this analysis that the Commission concluded that the measure, as originally notified, was disproportionate, insofar as it exceeded the requisite figure.[40]

2.3. The Public Interest Objective is Defined by the EU Member State

The Commission has the exclusive competence to determine whether or not State aid is compatible with the internal market. It lacks the power, however, to dictate which objectives EU Member States are allowed to pursue. Accordingly, the Commission will have to evaluate whether the conditions set out in Article 107(3) TFEU are met – namely whether the goal of the measure is consistent with the EU legal order and whether the contribution it makes to the public interest is on balance positive. At most, the Commission can influence, indirectly, the way in which expenditure decisions are adopted by EU Member States. By eliminating the notification obligation in relation to measures that fall below the notification thresholds, for instance, the GBER effectively nudges the behaviour of public

---

[35] Case C-280/00 *Altmark Trans GmbH and Regierungspräsidium Magdeburg v Nahverkehrsgesellschaft Altmark GmbH, and Oberbundesanwalt beim Bundesverwaltungsgericht*, EU:C:2003:415, para 92.

[36] Framework for State aid in the form of public service compensation (n 5), para 48.

[37] Case C-654/17 P *Bayerische Motoren Werke AG v Commission*, EU:C:2019:634.

[38] ibid, para 14.

[39] ibid, para 58.

[40] ibid, para 75: 'the General Court noted [...] that the incentive effect and the proportionality of the aid in question, which amounted to EUR 49 million, corresponded to the difference between the net costs of investing in Munich (Germany) and in Leipzig [...]. In the present case, this was equivalent to EUR 17 million [...]'.

authorities towards certain measures. Its soft law instruments can have the same effect, if only because they provide a sense of the instances when, and the likelihood that, a particular measure will be declared compatible with the internal market.

A question that emerged in *Hinkley Point*[41] is that of whether the public interest objective pursued by an EU Member States must be shared by all other EU Member States. This issue is not a trivial one if one considers, as discussed in Chapters 3 and 5, that disparities may emerge within the EU in the absence of harmonisation. Different societal choices inevitably lead to divergent perceptions about the sort of aims that are capable of advancing the public interest. In *Hinkley Point*, the specific question raised before the Court was whether an investment in nuclear energy could be deemed to be a legitimate one under Article 107(3) TFEU. Insofar as some EU Member States are staunchly opposed to this form of electricity generation, Austria argued, one could not consider that State aid supporting it pursues an objective in the common interest of the EU as a whole.[42]

Hinkley Point cannot be fully understood without taking into consideration the analytical framework applied at the time. When the action was brought, the Commission required EU Member States to show, among other things, that State aid 'be aimed at an objective of common interest' for it to be compatible with the internal market.[43] One could reasonably have interpreted this requirement as meaning that intervention must contribute to the interest of society at large, and not merely benefit the recipient. Such an interpretation was not, however, the one favoured by Austria. Instead, the EU Member State claimed that the 'objective of common interest' condition is only met where the measure is the expression of a set of values that is shared by all EU Member States. After all, Article 107(3)(c) TFEU expressly demands that intervention should 'not adversely affect trading conditions to an extent contrary to the common interest', which could be construed as providing support for this reading.

The Court ruled in *Hinkley Point* that nothing in the letter of Article 107(3)(c) TFEU and the case law interpreting this notion (including *Philip Morris*[44]) requires that the objective pursued by the EU Member State be in the common interest.[45] In this regard, the ECJ drew a clear distinction between the balancing assessment by the Commission, which must take into account, by necessity, the EU at large, and the goals underpinning the aid measure under consideration. It also distinguished between the public interest objectives that may be sought by virtue of Article 107(3)(b) TFEU and those falling within the scope

---

[41] Case C-594/18 P *Austria v Commission*, EU:C:2020:742.

[42] ibid, para 16. According to Austria, 'all aid must, in principle, pursue an objective of common interest, or even an objective of common interest of the European Union, that is to say, an interest which corresponds to the common interest of all the Member States'.

[43] 'State aid modernisation – a major revamp of EU State aid control' (2014) Competition Policy Brief, available at https://competition-policy.ec.europa.eu/.

[44] *Philip Morris* (n 13), paras 24–26.

[45] *Hinkley Point* (n 41), para 21.

of sub-paragraph (c). Unlike the former, which expressly refers to 'the execution of an important project of common European interest', the latter are not necessarily informed by the common goals of the EU.[46] It would be sufficient to show, accordingly, that the aid can 'facilitate the development of certain economic activities'.[47]

2.4. The Displacement of Economic Activity is not a Public Interest Objective

One of the principles underpinning the compatibility assessment is so central that it is frequently assumed as given. The fact that it is for EU Member States to determine which objective to pursue does not mean that every objective will be legitimate from an EU law perspective. As discussed at some length in Chapter 4, there are some aims which, by their very nature, are inherently at odds with the internal market. It seems clear, in particular, that a measure the only effect of which is to displace economic activity does not make a contribution to a public interest objective and thus does not meet the conditions of Article 107(3) TFEU. Consider the example of financial support for a large investment, mentioned above. If the only change brought about by the measure is a change in the location of the economic activity (that is, that the investment is undertaken in the awarding country or region, as opposed to a different one), it will be deemed incompatible with the internal market.

The logic of this principle need not be explained at length. If economic displacement alone were to be considered a legitimate objective for the award of State aid, the system would lack the necessary tools to prevent the very harmful subsidy races that it is in principle designed to avoid. As pointed out in Chapter 1, such subsidy races are harmful not just because they tilt the game in favour of EU Member States that are larger and have deeper pockets, but because they divert resources away from more productive uses. The principle will be of particular relevance where planned investment is large – in which case the incentive effect, as mentioned above, will be typically more difficult to establish – and where a sector suffers from structural overcapacity. In the latter scenario, State aid might have no other effect than distorting the process by which the industry progressively becomes viable again.[48]

---

[46] Article 107(2)(b) TFEU reads: 'aid to promote the execution of an important project of common European interest or to remedy a serious disturbance in the economy of a Member State'.

[47] *Hinkley Point* (n 41), para 19: 'Thus, in order to be capable of being considered compatible with the internal market under that provision, State aid must meet two conditions, the first being that it must be intended to facilitate the development of certain economic activities or of certain economic areas and the second, expressed in negative terms, being that it must not adversely affect trading conditions to an extent contrary to the common interest'.

[48] See for instance Case C-301/87 *France v Commission*, EU:C:1990:67.

2.5. Compatibility Assessment and the EU Interest

Hinkley Point drew a clear divide between the aims of the aid, on the one hand, and the compatibility assessment strictly speaking, on the other. While the first is the exclusive province of the EU Member State, in the sense that it has the leeway to decide which objectives to pursue, it is for the Commission to ascertain whether intervention is in the EU interest. This assessment involves two separate questions. The first is the balancing assessment itself, which revolves around whether the expected benefits resulting from the aid do not distort trade and competition to an extent contrary to the common interest – as the very letter of Article 107(3)(c) TFEU provides. The second involves ascertaining whether the measure amounts to a breach of another provision of EU law – including, in particular, legislation in the area of public procurement, competition law and free movement – or, indeed, a general principle of EU law.

The idea that a measure must not infringe other EU law provisions or principles has a long pedigree in the case law, dating back to *Ianelli v Meroni*.[49] In some respects, it comes across as self-evident. It would be difficult to justify how a measure could be deemed compatible with Article 107(3) TFEU where it is at odds with other aspects of the EU legal order. This idea, long accepted as uncontroversial, has experienced a revival since *Hinkley Point*. The renewed interest in the question raises a number of theoretical and practical issues. As the case law that followed shows,[50] the principle could have significant implications on the way the Commission conducts its assessment. It could, more specifically, place a significant burden on the administrative authority if it were required to systematically evaluate whether the aid infringes other EU law provisions – let alone the general principles of EU law. Unsurprisingly, subsequent case law acknowledged that the principle must be reconciled with the need to preserve the effectiveness of the EU State aid system.[51]

2.6. The Codification by the Commission of the Principles

The principles described in this section have been codified by the Commission in its post-*Hinkley Point* practice. As exemplified in its Environment and Energy Guidelines,[52] issued in 2022, the compatibility assessment under Article 107(3)(c) TFEU follows closely the letter of the provision and, indeed, the Court judgment.

---

[49] Case 74/76 *Iannelli & Volpi SpA v Ditta Paolo Meroni*, EU:C:1977:51.

[50] See in this sense Case C-284/21 P *Commission v Anthony Braesch and others*, EU:C:2023:58; Case C-28/23 *NFŠ a.s. v Slovenská republika konajúca prostredníctvom Ministerstva školstva, vedy, výskumu a športu Slovenskej republiky and Ministerstvo školstva, vedy, výskumu a športu Slovenskej republiky*, EU:C:2024:893; and Case C-490/23 P *Neos SpA v Commission*, EU:C:2025:32. For a discussion, see Phedon Nicolaides, 'A Test for Determining Whether State Aid Infringes Other Provisions of EU Law' (2025) 24 European State Aid Law Quarterly 43.

[51] *Neos* (n 50), para 59. But see Case C-59/23 P *Austria v Commission*, ECLI:EU:C:2025:686.

[52] Environment and Energy Guidelines (n 6), paras 20–76.

Accordingly, the analytical framework is broken down into the evaluation of the 'positive condition', on the one hand, and the 'negative condition', on the other. The positive condition is the contribution to the development of an economic activity and/or to regional development (and regional cohesion). The evaluation of this aspect of the analysis comprises the identification of the benefit *stricto sensu*, establishing the incentive effect of the measure and the absence of a breach of another EU law provision. The negative condition, in turn, revolves around the necessity of the measure (that is, the efficiency or equity rationale underpinning it), its appropriateness (that is, whether State aid is the appropriate policy instrument), and, finally, the balance of the positive and negative effects on competition and trade.

3. Mapping the Permacrisis

3.1. The COVID Temporary Framework

3.1.1. Description

The Covid-19 pandemic forced EU Member States to adopt unprecedented measures – such as social distancing and lockdowns – aimed at preventing the spread of the virus. Given the inevitable and substantial impact of some of these measures on the economy at large, the situation required the rapid and widespread award of State aid to preserve activity and employment and avoid large scale closures and disruptions. The Commission rose to the challenge by adopting a temporary framework in March 2020.[53] This instrument was primarily based on Article 107(3)(b) TFEU, which allows EU Member States to take action, inter alia, 'to remedy a serious disturbance' in their economies.[54] In this sense, it was conceived, from the outset, as a complement to the avenues for the support of economic activity pursuant to Article 107(3)(c) TFEU.[55] In addition, the instrument clarified that Article 107(2)(b) TFEU, which deals with 'natural disasters and exceptional occurrences', provides an appropriate basis to compensate some sectors (in particular 'transport, tourism, culture, hospitality and retail') that can be deemed to have been 'particularly hit' by the pandemic.[56]

The original incarnation of the COVID Temporary Framework signalled that it would deem compatible with the internal market, in accordance with Article 107(3)(b) TFEU, four categories of measures, namely 'direct grants,

---

[53] Communication from the Commission Temporary Framework for State aid measures to support the economy in the current COVID-19 outbreak [2020] OJ C91I/1.

[54] This legal basis was the same on which the Commission relied during the peak of the financial crisis. For an analysis, see Ahlborn (n 12).

[55] COVID Temporary Framework (n 53), para 14.

[56] ibid, para 15.

repayable advances or tax advantages',[57] support 'in the form of guarantees on loans',[58] intervention by means of 'subsidised interest rates for loans'[59] and, finally, 'short-term export credit insurance'.[60] The underlying philosophy in all four instances was the same. First and foremost, the COVID Temporary Framework was an immediate response to the liquidity problems that firms could face in the midst of the Covid-19 pandemic.[61] Second, the Commission sought to ensure that financial support would be directed only at undertakings that either faced no difficulties prior to the outbreak of the disease or that faced them in its aftermath,[62] as opposed to ailing firms requiring rescue and restructuring aid.[63] Third, the instrument introduced an upper limit, which varied from the original figure, set at EUR 800,000.[64]

The COVID Temporary Framework was amended several times and its application extended until June 2022.[65] These amendments expanded the reach of the instrument in two ways. First, they added to its scope of application, in the sense that they provided for a wider range of mechanisms to offer liquidity and relief, including selective advantages in the form of 'deferrals of tax and/or of social security contributions',[66] 'wage subsidies for employees to avoid lay-offs'[67] and 'recapitalisation'.[68] Second, the Commission introduced a number of scenarios where Article 107(3)(c) TFEU was deemed to provide the appropriate legal basis and which were not captured at the time by the available instruments. The latter included State aid in support of investments in areas such as Covid-19-specific research and development,[69] the testing and upscaling of relevant infrastructures[70] and the production of related products.[71]

3.1.2. Impact

For most measures, the COVID Temporary Framework applied until the end of June 2022. During the period of its application, it provided the basis for a

---

[57] ibid, paras 21–23 (as the instrument was originally adopted).

[58] ibid, paras 24–25 (as the instrument was originally adopted).

[59] ibid, paras 26–27 (as the instrument was originally adopted).

[60] ibid, paras 32–33 (as the instrument was originally adopted).

[61] ibid, para 4: 'In the exceptional circumstances created by the COVID-19 outbreak, undertakings of all kinds may face a severe lack of liquidity. Solvent or less solvent undertakings alike may face a sudden shortage or even unavailability of liquidity'.

[62] ibid, paras 22, 25 and 27.

[63] Guidelines on rescue and restructuring aid (n 24).

[64] COVID Temporary Framework (n 53). It is sufficient to compare the original figure, set at EUR 800,000 to the final version, which allowed for the award of grants and similar measures of up to EUR 1.8 million per undertaking.

[65] ibid, paras 22, 25, 27 and 35.

[66] ibid, paras 40–41.

[67] ibid, paras 42–43.

[68] ibid, paras 44–85.

[69] ibid, paras 34–35.

[70] ibid, paras 36–37.

[71] ibid, paras 38–39.

large amount of State aid, whether this is measured in terms of the number of awards or in terms of GDP percentage. In its retrospective analysis of the implementation of the package, the Commission noted that, between 2020 and 2021, it adopted 1,185 decisions and amendment decisions relating to 865 national measures and representing over EUR 3 trillion – or 11.4% of the GDP of the EU Member States.[72] There was, however, a considerable discrepancy between the measures notified and those actually implemented (at least at the time of the analysis). The latter figure remained below the EUR 1 trillion figure – at EUR 940 billion, in excess of 3% of the GDP of the EU 27.[73] The Commission's State aid scoreboard reveals the extent to which these figures represent a departure from the norm of the preceding years.[74]

The most remarkable aspect of the retrospective analysis conducted by the Commission – and the most relevant for the discussion that follows – has to do with the considerable discrepancies in terms of amount from one country to another. The State aid actually granted by the four largest EU Member States – namely Germany, France, Italy and Spain – amounted to over 80% of the total granted during the period considered in the analysis.[75] One should note, to put this figure in context, that the total population of these four countries represents around 60% of the EU total. The discrepancy between support relative to population can be usefully illustrated by reference to the amount of aid relative to the EU Member States' GDP. Italy, for instance, awarded measures amounting to 6% of its GDP.[76] Spain's and France's efforts amounted, respectively, to 5.3% and 4.7% of their GDP.[77] Against this background, it is not a surprise that questions were raised about the impact of the COVID Temporary Framework on the internal market. As noted by commentators, it is almost inevitable that larger EU Member States with deeper pockets stand to gain the most from an ad hoc instrument relaxing rules on an interim basis.[78]

---

[72] See Giuseppina Cannas and others, 'Looking back at the State aid COVID Temporary Framework: the take-up of measures in the EU' (2022) Competition State Aid Brief, available at https://competition-policy.ec.europa.eu/.

[73] ibid: 'The overall budget that Member States notified to the Commission under such State aid measures is worth a total of nearly €3.1 trillion, representing 11.4% of EU27 annual GDP'.

[74] Commission, 'State aid Scoreboard 2024' (April 2025), available at https://competition-policy.ec.europa.eu/.

[75] Cannas and others (n 72): 'Germany and France have granted around a fourth of the total aid provided each: Germany granted 24.1% of the total (€226 billion) and France 23.8% (€223 billion). They are followed by Italy with 21.8% (€205 billion) and Spain with 13.1% (€123 billion). These four Member States have collectively granted more than 80% of the total State aid support for COVID-19 measures'.

[76] ibid.

[77] ibid.

[78] See in particular Alfonso Lamadrid de Pablo and José Luis Buendía Sierra, 'A Moment of Truth for the EU: A Proposal for a State Aid Solidarity Fund' (2020) 11 Journal of European Competition Law & Practice 1.

3.1.3. Compatibility Assessment

It is unsurprising, considering the amounts involved, that the award of State aid in accordance with the COVID Temporary Framework gave rise to litigation.[79] The fundamental point of law that arose as a result of the challenges brought against Commission decisions related to whether the compatibility of State aid is contingent on adherence by the EU Member State to a general principle of non-discrimination. This argument was raised by Ryanair in several of the actions brought against the legality of aid aimed at keeping airlines afloat at a time of severe travel restrictions.[80] The Irish firm claimed, in essence, that, while EU Member States are not required to award State aid, they are bound by the general principle of non-discrimination when they choose to do so.[81] From Ryanair's perspective, the compatibility assessment must necessarily ascertain whether all competing undertakings operating within a market exposed to an 'exceptional occurrence' have received support on equivalent terms and conditions.

Ryanair's argument is inspired by the idea that a measure assessed under Article 107 TFEU must not be in breach of other provisions of EU law – or, indeed, a general principle of EU law. The Court, ruling on appeal, rejected the different variations of the airline's claim. The core of the reasoning developed focuses on the effectiveness of the EU State aid system. The ECJ held, in this sense, that a measure cannot be declared to be incompatible with the internal market merely because of the negative effects it may have on competition and trade.[82] In other words, the balancing exercise that is inherent in the assessment under Articles 107(2) and 107(3) TFEU is based on the premise that such negative effects exist and need to be weighed against the contributions the aid makes to a public interest objective. Arguably, the very idea of discrimination is inherent in the notion of aid. As discussed at length in Chapter 4, a precondition for the application of Article 107(1) TFEU is a finding that the advantage treats firms in a comparable factual and legal situation differently.[83]

---

[79] For an exhaustive overview of these challenges, see Alfonso Lamadrid de Pablo, Virginia Romero Algarra and Adina Claici, 'State Aid in Times of Crisis: Temporary Frameworks and the Boundaries of State Aid Policy' in Philipp Werner and Vincent Verouden (eds), *EU State Aid Control: Law and Economics* (2nd edn, Kluwer 2025).

[80] See in particular Case C-591/21 P *Ryanair DAC and Laudamotion GmbH v Commission*, EU:C:2024:635.

[81] ibid, paras 38 ('While Member States are indeed not obliged to grant State aid, they should, when they decide to do so, comply with the conditions laid down in the FEU Treaty, including the principle of non-discrimination') and 56.

[82] ibid, para 76: 'State aid [...] cannot be held to be incompatible with the internal market having regard solely to the characteristics or effects'.

[83] ibid, para 72.

3.2. The Temporary Crisis (and Transition) Framework

3.2.1. Description

As the application of the COVID Temporary Framework was coming to an end, the invasion of Ukraine upset, again, the economies of EU Member States. The impact of the aggression was felt particularly acutely in the price of gas, which increased substantially and had the potential to affect electricity markets and energy-intensive industries across the EU. What is more, the adoption of sanctions against Russia had the potential to disrupt supply chains and trade with third countries. In this landscape, the Commission reacted by adopting the so-called Temporary Crisis (and Transition[84]) Framework (hereinafter, the 'TCT Framework').[85] The purpose of the various incarnations of the instrument was twofold. As much as its COVID counterpart, it sought, first, to provide liquidity and access to finance to undertakings facing challenges as a result of the impact of the invasion.[86] In this sense, the TCT Framework laid down criteria for the provision of liquidity support in the form of guarantees[87] and subsidised loans.[88]

Second, the instrument sought to address the consequences of the 'exceptionally severe increases in the price of natural gas and electricity'.[89] What is notable about the policy developed by the Commission in the TCT Framework is the introduction of incentives aimed at reducing energy dependence from third countries. There was, in this sense, a nascent industrial policy dimension that would feature even more prominently in subsequent policy instruments. The Commission invited EU Member States to set environmental and/or security of supply requirements as part of the conditions for the award of aid. Such measures comprised, inter alia, the obligation to draw a proportion of recipients' electricity needs from renewable sources, to invest in energy efficiency measures aimed at reducing consumption and to diversify sources of supply to avoid overdependence from a particular supplier.[90]

Just like its COVID counterpart, the TCT Framework was subsequently amended – the latter no fewer than six times[91] – and its application extended in

---

[84] The expression 'Transition' was added in one of the amendments to the Framework. See Commission, 'State aid: Commission prolongs and amends Temporary Crisis Framework' IP/22/6468 (Brussels, 27 October 2022).

[85] Temporary Crisis Framework for State Aid measures to support the economy following the aggression against Ukraine by Russia' [2022] OJ C 131 I/01. The document will be referred to hereinafter as the 'TCT Framework'. Any subsequent references are made to the final consolidated version.

[86] ibid, para 3.

[87] ibid, paras 65–67.

[88] ibid, paras 68–69.

[89] ibid, paras 71–73.

[90] ibid, paras 80–81.

[91] Commission, 'Extension of the application of state aid measures to manage the crisis for a limited period' IP/24/2332 (Brussels, 1 May 2024).

time, in some cases until the end of 2025.[92] The industrial policy dimension at which the original iteration hinted became more apparent with every new incarnation of the instrument. The March 2023 version, for instance, expressly linked the prolongation of the TCT Framework to the wider ambition of decarbonising the economy across the EU. Therefore, it focused on measures aimed at transitioning towards net zero – such as the deployment of renewable energy and the funding of energy storage solutions.[93] In addition, it introduced several avenues to allow for investment in technologies allowing for the green transition to be accelerated. The aim of these new avenues was to streamline and expand the range of instances where State aid can be allowed.

The single most remarkable feature of the March 2023 iteration of the framework is the introduction of a so-called 'matching clause' and a 'funding gap' criterion in the TCT Framework. The point of this feature is to provide for flexibility in instances where there would be a risk of diversion of investments in green technologies to third countries outside the EEA. Accordingly, the Commission accepted that, in exceptional circumstances and on the basis of an individual notification, an EU Member State could offer support corresponding to the amount that the undertaking 'could demonstrably receive for an equivalent investment in a third country jurisdiction outside the EEA'.[94] As part of the conditions, the EU Member State must establish that the financial support received either incentivises the choice of the location or triggers the investment project.[95]

At the same time, the TCT Framework revealed the extent to which such a 'matching clause' has the potential to distort trade and competition within the internal market. It has been mentioned above that, the higher the amount granted, the greater the potential for negative effects and the less likely it is that the measure has an incentive effect. It was also mentioned, in the same vein, that the displacement of economic activity does not count as a legitimate aim under the compatibility assessment. The Commission introduced, in this sense, several safeguards to minimise the negative effects aid may have. First, the instrument makes it clear that matching aid must benefit so-called 'assisted areas', that is, areas that would qualify for the award of regional aid within the meaning of Articles 107(3)(a) TFEU or 107(3)(c) TFEU.[96] Second, the Commission expressly provided that the aid may not be granted to 'facilitate relocation' of production activities within the

---

[92] ibid: 'Sections 2.5, 2.6 and 2.8 aimed at accelerating the green transition and reducing fuel dependencies will remain available until 31 December 2025'.

[93] Commission, 'State aid: Commission adopts Temporary Crisis and Transition Framework to further support transition towards net-zero economy' IP/23/1563 (Brussels, 8 March 2023).

[94] TCT Framework (n 85), para 86: 'Exceptionally, by derogation from point 85(b) and on the basis of individual notifications, for the production of the relevant goods for the transition towards a net-zero economy as defined in point 85(a) of this Communication, the Commission may approve on the basis of Article 107(3)(c) TFEU individual aid up to the amount of subsidy, which the beneficiary could demonstrably receive for an equivalent investment in a third country jurisdiction outside the EEA, provided the following conditions are met'.

[95] ibid.

[95] ibid. See also Guidelines on regional aid (n 6).

EU.[97] As part of the information gathering exercise, therefore, it committed to evaluating the impact on economic activity in other EU Member States.[98]

In a decision adopted in January 2024, the Commission relied on the 'matching clause' for the first time to approve State aid granted by Germany in support of Northvolt.[99] The aim of the measure, which amounted to EUR 902 million, was to incentivise the construction of a plant manufacturing batteries for electric vehicles in Heide, which is a location that would have qualified for the award of regional aid under Article 107(3)(c) TFEU.[100] The decision is explicit about the fact that the US Inflation Reduction Act incentivised investments in green technologies, and could therefore lead to the displacement of economic activity away from the EU.[101] In fact, one of the key arguments raised by Germany in the context of the administrative procedure was that, in the absence of intervention, the investment would be undertaken in a specific region in the US.[102] In this regard, the Commission was satisfied with the evidence produced and concluded that the 'calculations and the underlying parameters' were 'realistic'.[103]

The Commission was also satisfied that the positive effects would outweigh any negative impact resulting from the award of the measure. While it acknowledged that a substantial investment – approaching the EUR 1 billion figure – has a significant potential to cause distortions of competition and trade,[104] it relied on several industry-specific factors to conclude that such an outcome was not to be expected. It noted in this sense, first, that the market was a nascent one and that the recipient, Northvolt, had a small presence therein, both at the EU and the global level.[105] Second, the addition to manufacturing capacity would represent a modest fraction of European demand for batteries, which was moreover expected to grow significantly.[106] Finally, the Commission ruled out the possibility that the project

[97] ibid: 'The aid may not be provided to facilitate relocation of production activities between Member States'.

[98] ibid: 'When evaluating the notifiable measures, the Commission will request all necessary information to consider whether the State aid is likely to result in a substantial loss of jobs in existing locations within the EEA. In this situation, and if the investment enables the aid beneficiary to relocate an activity to the target area, if there is a causal link between the aid and the relocation, this constitutes a negative effect that is unlikely to be compensated by any positive effects'.

[99] Commission Decision of 8 January 2024 – TCTF: Aid to Northvolt Germany GmbH (Case SA.107936).

[100] ibid, para 3.

[101] ibid, para 44: 'The doubts regarding the European expansion business case increased when in August 2022 the Inflation Reduction Act ('IRA') was signed to law. It created very favourable investment conditions in the USA, both from a regulatory and a subsidy point of view'.

[102] ibid, para 54.

[103] ibid, para 103.

[104] ibid, para 111.

[105] ibid, para 124: 'the market share of NV is currently very limited in the EEA and, in particular, globally'.

[106] ibid: 'while the production facility at NV Drei with an annual capacity of 60 GWh would constitute a significant addition to the European battery cell capacity in light of currently very low manufacturing levels in Europe'.

would have a 'crowding out' effect, and this on account of the significant gap in terms of output between, respectively, batteries and electric vehicles.[107]

3.2.2. Impact

According to the analysis by the Commission,[108] the impact of the TCT Framework has not been as significant as that of the COVID one. In the period between March 2022 and June 2024, it approved State aid – either under the instrument or directly under the TFEU but on the basis of the principles underpinning the instrument – amounting to EUR 795.69 billion, of which EUR 218.86 (that is, a third of the total cleared or 0.52% of the GDP of the EU 27) was actually awarded to undertakings. Again, there was significant disparity across EU Member States in terms of expenditure. Germany's actual awards amount to 38% of the total aid granted under the TCT Framework (while its population represents less than 20% of the EU total).[109] Taken together, the three EU Member States granting the most aid – Italy and Spain, in addition to Germany – were responsible for 74% of the awards.

3.3. The Clean Industrial Deal: The Exceptional as the New Normal

The most significant impact of the TCT Framework is the fact that it appears to have changed the face of EU State aid control for good. What looked like a temporary instrument addressing the impact of the invasion of Ukraine progressively morphed into a mechanism that provided the basis for the streamlined award of aid for the decarbonisation of the economy. The various incarnations of the TCT Framework heralded the introduction of a new normality in the EU State aid system. The process would be ultimately completed with the adoption of the Framework for State aid measures to support the Clean Industrial Deal, announced in June 2025.[110] Unlike its predecessor, which was (at least initially) designed to be a one-off response to a particular set of circumstances, the new Framework has been conceived as a lasting instrument that will provide legal certainty to EU Member States and stakeholders. Instead of regular amendments and extensions, it will apply, from the outset, until the end of 2030.[111]

---

[107] ibid, paras 126–128.

[108] Sara Ferraro and Alessandra Landa, 'The use of crisis State aid measures in response to the Russian invasion of Ukraine' (2025) Competition State Aid Brief, available at https://competition-policy.ec.europa.eu/.

[109] ibid: 'Germany has provided €81.9 billion, representing 38% of all the aid granted. The second largest spender, Italy, has granted €57.8 billion, followed by Spain, with €21.2 billion. Romania has granted €8.8 billion and Hungary €8.4 billion. In absolute terms, the three countries that have granted the most, Germany, Italy, and Spain, have granted 74% of all the aid'.

[110] Framework for State Aid measures to support the Clean Industrial Deal [2025] OJ C/2025/3602.

[111] ibid, para 216.

The spirit of the Clean Industrial Deal Framework (hereinafter, the 'CID Framework') is similar to that of its predecessor. To begin with, the industrial policy dimension that slowly emerged under the TCT Framework features prominently in the new instrument. What is more, this policy is presented as having an EU-wide dimension. In this sense, the CID Framework points out that the decarbonisation ambitions of the Clean Industrial Deal can only be achieved by incentivising 'the roll-out of renewable energy, to deploy industrial decarbonisation, and to ensure sufficient manufacturing capacity of clean tech'.[112] The role of the instrument as an aspect of a broader industrial policy strategy is also apparent from the reference to the Net Zero Industry Act,[113] aimed at eliminating barriers to the development of European manufacturing capacity and presented as a complement to it.[114]

4. The Permacrisis and the Compatibility Assessment

4.1. The 'Ratchet Effect' of the Permacrisis

With the Covid-19 pandemic, the EU State aid system entered a continuous period of emergency that lasted five years. There are reasons to believe, as suggested in the preceding section, that policy-making has changed for good. This idea is symbolised by the transition from the TCT to the CID Framework, which turned the (perpetually) temporary into a permanent state of affairs, both in terms of substance and procedure. As a result of this change (and the broader transformations within the EU and beyond), it may not be possible for the Commission to turn back the clock to the way it conducted policy prior to the rapid succession of crises. It may be true that, as an administrative authority in charge of policy-making, it is not bound by its previous decisions. That said, there are reasons to believe that the new reality has led to a new equilibrium that may turn out to be stable in the medium term.

Several factors might contribute to the 'ratchet effect' of the permacrisis in EU State aid policy. The first and arguably most relevant one is that, while the Covid-19 pandemic might have passed, and while energy prices might have returned to relative normality in spite of the (ongoing at the time of writing) aggression against Ukraine, the world no longer appears to be reverting to the old order. Changes in the geopolitical landscape suggest that the role that EU State aid

---

[112] ibid, para 4.

[113] ibid, para 5. The Net Zero Industry Act is Regulation (EU) 2024/1735 of the European Parliament and of the Council of 13 June 2024 on establishing a framework of measures for strengthening Europe's net-zero technology manufacturing ecosystem [2024] OJ L 2024/1735.

[114] ibid: 'While the NZIA will increase the competitiveness of the net-zero technology sector, attract investments, and improve market access for clean tech in the EU, certain clean tech investments may require additional support to make sure that capacity is increased in the Union, thereby allowing the acceleration of the net-zero transition and increasing European resilience in this area'.

policy used to fulfil must be complemented with other responses. The system may have been conceived as a mechanism to reduce intra-EU distortions of trade and competition, and to balance these against the positive effects expected from some forms of intervention. There are reasons to believe, however, that it may no longer be possible to think about the system in these same terms (and, similarly, that failing to acknowledge the changes may not be feasible).

The very CID Framework shows that EU State aid policy appears to be introducing other considerations – such as the need to attract and preserve investment into the European continent and the need to enhance economic security – that were not relevant before (or at least not to a comparable extent). Pre-Covid-19 policy-making was underpinned by a number of regulatory and economic realities that were taken as given and that made it possible for the Commission to focus on intra-EU dynamics. In essence, EU State aid policy relied on a global rules-based order that revolved around free trade and where large-scale industrial policy initiatives to attract economic activity would be the exception, rather than the rule. As the decision in *Northvolt* shows, it may no longer be possible for the Commission to ignore in its analysis how proactive strategies pursued by third countries may be affecting investment decisions in Europe – and, more importantly, how the orthodox balancing assessment may have to be complemented and enriched by other considerations.

A second reason suggesting that the EU State aid system might have reached a new equilibrium has to do with the change in the dynamics between the Commission and the EU Member States. The streamlining of the compatibility assessment, and the signalling by the Commission that it was receptive to the award of aid in the sectors identified, has an impact on assumptions made about the operation of the system. These changes may be reflected in EU Member States' expectations and, by the same token, in the scale of the projects that are notified for approval. *Northvolt*, which involved an amount approaching the EUR 1 billion figure, is an apt illustration in this sense. In the context of the CID Framework, the Commission has placed relatively generous thresholds (of up to EUR 200 million[115]) in a variety of scenarios, which can be exceeded in certain circumstances if it can be shown to be necessary to incentivise the relevant activity.[116]

4.2. The Potential for Increased Distortions

The new equilibrium in the EU State aid regime may be the emerging and inevitable reality. It is not, however, without major practical consequences. The

---

[115] See for instance, Section 5 concerning aid for the decarbonisation of industry, where the Commission applies a streamlined analytical framework for aid amounts of up to EUR 200 million. See in this sense paras 154–155, and also para 157 (which concerns the funding gap). See also, in a similar vein, para 167, which applies an EUR 200 million threshold in relation to aid to ensure manufacturing capacity in clean technologies.

[116] ibid, paras 156–158.

combination of more frequent awards and a predisposition towards a more lenient treatment thereof – even large-scale ones – means that the potential for distortions of competition and trade will be necessarily more pronounced moving forward. As the figures discussed above show, there are significant discrepancies in terms of EU Member States' ability to award State aid, with some countries representing a substantial proportion of the support provided. Over the long run, the relative leniency of the Commission could have the effect of displacing economic activity towards the largest and wealthiest EU Member States. From this perspective, the reorientation of EU State aid policy may be beneficial at an aggregate level – in the sense that it may be successful in attracting or preserving economic activity within the continent – but may entail sacrifices for individual EU Member States, insofar as it may come at the price of paving the way for the sort of displacement that the system is in principle designed to prevent.

One should note, in addition, that the EU State aid system, as designed, may not necessarily be in a position to fully account for the impact of the new equilibrium on trade and competition. Articles 107 and 108 TFEU are well equipped to assess, ex ante, the likely effects of individual measures. In addition, the provisions, as they have been developed in secondary legislation, allow for existing aid to be subject to constant review to avoid any distortions. The Commission has, in fact, conducted follow-up studies measuring, ex post, the impact of interventions over time.[117] These studies, while insightful and complementary to the ex ante review of aid, focus on individual cases.[118] The remaining blind spot in the EU State aid system relates to its inability to consider the cumulative effect that interventions might have on the internal market. Assessed individually, measures may come across as positive on balance. Taken together, however, they may pave the way for the very distortions that Articles 107 and 108 TFEU were conceived to address and minimise.

It is not difficult to imagine how the cumulative effect of individual measures may alter the economic landscape within the Union and favour larger and wealthier EU Member States. One cannot be surprised, against this background, that the long-term consequences of the relaxation of the compatibility assessment of aid for the internal market were identified in the so-called Letta Report.[119] The document expressly mentioned the 'risk that over time such an approach amplifies distortions of the level playing field within the Single Market due to the difference in fiscal space available to Member States'.[120] The document eloquently identified

---

[117] See in this sense Commission, *Ex post assessment of the impact of state aid on competition* (November 2017), available at https://op.europa.eu/. For a critical analysis of these ex post studies, see Xavier Boutin, Zsolt Udvari and Daniele Vidoni, 'Ex Post Evaluation of Aid' in Werner and Verouden (n 79).

[118] ibid, This assessment considered four case studies: regional aid to an airport in the UK, R&D&I aid to a substrates manufacturer in France, SGEI aid and measures applied to a postal operator in Italy and, finally, an instance of environmental aid to a starch producer in France.

[119] Enrico Letta, *Much More than a Market* (April 2024), available at www.consilium.europa.eu/.

[120] ibid, 11.

the mismatch between the industrial policy ambitions of the new iteration of EU State aid control and the locus of decision-making. While acknowledging that the new geopolitical realities might require EU-wide responses, it noted that expenditures are not similarly EU-wide.

4.3. The Change in the Nature of the Assessment

The emerging incarnation of EU State aid policy entails a change in the nature and scope of the compatibility assessment, at least in instances where industrial policy features prominently. In such cases (that is, where intervention seeks, among other things, to incentivise the location of economic activity within the EU and to promote economic security by limiting dependence from third countries), the criteria and parameters that are considered necessarily vary. It is possible to identify two analytical adjustments in this regard. One has to do, first, with the geographic level at which the positive and the negative conditions are evaluated. Specifically, the global dimension is introduced into the equation. Second, the range of positive effects that can be considered as part of the assessment also changes. The approach heralded in the TCT Framework and subsequently incorporated into the CID Framework places relocation effects front and centre of the analysis insofar as they contribute to an economic activity within the meaning of Article 107(3) TFEU.

It makes sense to elaborate on these two transformations. A close look at the CID Framework, and, indeed, decisions like *Northvolt*, suggests that the assessment has added a global layer to the assessment that was typically absent from the more traditional iteration of the evaluation under Article 107(3) TFEU and, more precisely, sub-paragraph (c). The fundamental contribution of the Court judgment in *Hinkley Point* suggests that the benefits expected from the measure will be identified by the EU Member State, whereas the balancing exercise will be undertaken at the EU level. The emerging analytical framework, by contrast, weighs the positive and negative effects of EU-wide benefits not just by reference to the EU but also to the global level. Accordingly, the fact that a measure attracts investment into the EU or that it reduces reliance on third countries will be factored into the assessment.

Such a transformation is not without consequences. As already mentioned above, it is an analytical approach under which the displacement of economic activity can be factored into the analysis as a public interest objective. To the extent that such relocation effects benefit the EU – as in *Northvolt* – they will be considered to be a contribution to an economic activity within the meaning of Article 107(3)(c) TFEU. This aspect of the analysis is not obvious to reconcile with the canonical principles of *Philip Morris*, insofar as it suggests that what is true at the EU level about the displacement of economic activity is not necessarily true at the global one. In this sense, the system appears to be concerned with the prevention of subsidy races in relation to intra-EU trade, but not necessarily in the relationship with third countries. This discrepancy can be easily rationalised in a context where the rules-based order has come under increased pressure and where protectionism is on the rise.

While easy to rationalise, one should not lose sight of the fact that the observed transformation would turn EU State aid policy into a fundamentally different animal. From a system aimed at minimising distortions of competition and trade within the EU and ensuring that any such distortions are outweighed by contributions to a public interest goal, it would be morphing into one aimed at directing the EU Member States towards investments increasing the competitiveness of the EU and increasing its economic autonomy. This chapter has focused on measures aimed at supporting investments in energy-related activities. However, the same trend can be identified in other areas. This is true of, inter alia, State aid in support of so-called Important Projects of Common European Interest,[121] or in support of the development of manufacturing capacity in the area of semiconductors.[122] As these two examples show, administrative practice in the area is typically coupled with legislation pursuing the same aims.

4.4. Discussing the Way Forward

The ongoing transformation of EU State aid policy in response to changes in the geopolitical landscape exposes, as suggested above, a mismatch between the nature of the challenges faced by the EU and its Member States, which require a Union-wide response, and the fact that the bulk of the expenditure occurs at the national level. The main consequence of this mismatch, which seemingly alters the nature and scope of the compatibility assessment, is that distortions of trade and competition are likely to become more pronounced and pervasive under the new iteration of the system. It is not clear that this new reality will prove sustainable in the medium to long term. The perpetuation of such distortions would give rise to the tensions that the EU State aid system is designed to remedy, not exacerbate. It remains to be seen how the EU institutions and its Member States respond to the adjustment to the new reality.

Some amendments to the system have been floated to address the increased potential for distortions. Lamadrid de Pablo and Buendía Sierra floated the idea of a 'European solidarity fund' that would be fed by contributions made by the

---

[121] Communication from the Commission Criteria for the analysis of the compatibility with the internal market of State aid to promote the execution of important projects of common European interest [2021] OJ C528/10.

[122] Commission, 'Commission approves €5 billion German State aid measure to support ESMC in setting up a new semiconductor manufacturing facility' IP/24/4287 (Brussels, 19 August 2024). State aid intervention in this area must be understood in the context of broader initiatives by the EU in the area. See in particular Communication from the Commission: A Chips Act for Europe COM(2022) 45 final and the so-called Chips Act, Regulation (EU) 2023/1781 of the European Parliament and of the Council of 13 September 2023 establishing a framework of measures for strengthening Europe's semiconductor ecosystem and amending Regulation (EU) 2021/694 (Chips Act) [2023] OJ L229/1.

awarding countries.[123] Thus, a fraction (for instance, 15%) of the aid granted would be redirected so it can benefit other EU Member States in the process. This proposal was deemed valuable enough to be embraced in the Letta Report.[124] The other, more obvious but politically more complex solution is to shift expenditure to the EU level, so that the responses can be more effectively coordinated and the institutional set up matches the challenges faced by the Union. The ability to adopt strategic decisions swiftly and effectively is, in fact, one of the themes cutting across the Draghi Report.[125] Over the medium term, what seems politically challenging may become inevitable.[126]

5. Conclusions

Legal disciplines sometimes undergo fundamental transformations in a seamless, organic way. Such major changes are all the more likely where an administrative authority enjoys discretion to formulate policy. It is submitted that the apparent relaxation of the compatibility assessment during the permacrisis that started with the Covid-19 pandemic has led to one such mutation. There are, in fact, reasons to wonder whether the core goal of the system may be changing – or has in fact changed. The vocabulary used by the Commission in the most recent instruments hints at a regime that may progressively become a tool aimed at coordinating and steering EU Member States' expenditure towards certain EU-wide initiatives. As a result of this shift in the level of analysis, the system may become more tolerant towards distortions of competition and trade. The attraction of investments towards Europe and the economic resilience of the Union may take precedence, at least in some instances, over the traditional concerns underpinning the enforcement of Articles 107 and 108 TFEU.

The observed transformation may be an inevitable function of the major geopolitical landslides. One of the conclusions to draw from the evolution of policy-making in the field is that the traditional enforcement of the discipline

---

[123] Lamadrid de Pablo and Buendía Sierra (n 78).

[124] Letta Report (n 119), 11: 'we could envision a State aid contribution mechanism, requiring Member States to allocate a portion of their national funding to financing pan-European initiatives and investments'.

[125] Draghi Report, *The future of European competitiveness: Part B | In-depth analysis and recommendations* (September 2024), 298–306. This section provides, inter alia, proposals to 'Accelerate the decision-making processes and increase the predictability of decisions' and which expressly refer to State aid. In addition, the Report advances ideas on how 'State aid control' may be used as a tool for 'efficiency enhancing industrial policies'.

[126] See in this sense the eternal discussion about the introduction of permanent joint borrowing by EU Member States (the so-called Eurobonds). Martin Sandbu, 'European common debt is the way to topple the dollar' *Financial Times* (London, 19 June 2025). See also, in this sense, the Letta Report (n 119) 36, which argue that 'Putting bonds issued at the EU level firmly at the centre of the EU's financial architecture would be crucial for the stability and integration of financial markets and for strengthening innovation and growth across the whole EU internal market'.

was more fragile than originally assumed. Indeed, it may have been contingent on a consensus on the global stage that has not proved to be a lasting one. In an era of growing protectionism and active industrial policies by large trade blocs, transforming the calculus when performing the compatibility assessment under Article 107(3) TFEU may be necessary. It is submitted that the shift may well be necessary, but it will not prove sufficient, in itself, to address emerging challenges. In this sense, it is not a surprise that, as a complement to the shift in the intra-EU enforcement of EU State aid rules, the Commission has now been empowered to monitor the impact on the internal market of subsidies awarded by non-EU countries. This legal development is addressed at length in Chapter 7.

It is equally unsurprising that the consequences for the internal market have given rise to discussions and proposals to prevent undue distortions of competition and trade. If it is the case that the current landscape requires the EU to assert more firmly its economic independence vis-à-vis third countries by means of, inter alia, the award of State aid, ensuring that the benefits of intervention are shared widely and fairly across the Union – as opposed to concentrated within some EU Member States (or areas therein) – is paramount to preserve cohesion and trust in the underlying project of integration. It remains to be seen how the potential for increased distortions will be addressed, and in particular whether greater coordination and minor tweaks to the regime will be sufficient, or whether, in the long run, the institutional apparatus will adjust to the new reality so that the locus of expenditure and compatibility assessment become one and the same.

7

Cross-border Convergence – The UK Subsidy Control Act 2022

1. The Subsidy Control Act 2022 as Partial Legal Convergence

The EU-UK Trade and Cooperation Agreement (hereinafter, the 'TCA' or the 'Agreement')[1] is an unusual creature in the European landscape. Until its adoption, the growing number of agreements between the EU and other jurisdictions within the continent had had, as their primary aim, the deepening of (legal and economic) ties. In some instances, the treaty prepared the ground for eventual accession of a State to the EU.[2] In other instances, it allowed third countries to take part in the EU internal market.[3] The TCA, by contrast, established a new relationship between the EU and the UK that was not premised on eventual accession of the latter into the former or, more generally, the approximation of the legal orders of the two partners. Instead, it affirmed the UK's desire to carve its own path as a sovereign trading nation. Accordingly, it did not go much beyond a basic trade deal providing for the elimination of tariffs and quotas among the two parties.

Geography (or, if one prefers, economic gravity[4]) could not be wished away, however. Neither could decades of economic integration, which had led to the close intertwinement of firms (and within firms) on the two sides of the Channel. These factors have a significant impact on the scope and reach of some of the legal obligations imposed upon both parties. In several areas, the TCA ventures well beyond what one might have expected, considering the limited ambition of what is, after all,

---

[1] Trade and Cooperation Agreement between the European Union and the European Atomic Energy Community, of the one part, and the United Kingdom of Great Britain and Northern Ireland, of the other part [2021] OJ L149/10.

[2] See for instance Association Agreement between the European Union and its Member States, of the one part, and Ukraine, of the other part [2014] OJ L161/3; and Stabilisation and Association Agreement between the European Communities and their Member States, of the one part, and the Republic of Serbia, of the other part [2013] OJ L278/16.

[3] Agreement on the European Economic Area [1994] OJ L1/3.

[4] See, for a discussion, James Anderson and Eric Van Wincoop, 'Gravity with Gravitas: A Solution to the Border Puzzle' (2003) 93 American Economic Review 170; and Scott Baier and Jeffrey Bergstrand, 'The Growth of World Trade: Tariffs, Transport Costs, and Income Similarity' (2001) 53 Journal of International Economics 1.

not much more than a 'bare bones' free trade agreement.[5] Such a mismatch is particularly apparent in the area of subsidy regulation. As mentioned in Chapter 1, the typical free trade deal rarely ever provides for more obligations than those enshrined in the Agreement on Subsidies and Countervailing Measures (hereinafter, the 'SCM Agreement'), whether from a substantive or an institutional standpoint.

By contrast, the TCA has a dedicated chapter on subsidy control that stands out not just because of the level of detail into which it goes but because of the nature of the legal constraints it imposes upon both parties. In particular, the Agreement engages with the principles that the EU and the UK must observe when contemplating the award of subsidies. These principles identify, in effect, the efficiency and equity instances where State intervention is deemed to contribute to a public interest objective.[6] In addition, the TCA addresses at length several issue-specific questions, including those relating to the support of the so-called services of public economic interest,[7] the award of rescue and restructuring aid,[3] as well as the criteria to follow when adopting measures in the energy and environmental industries.[9] This level of detail goes well beyond that found in primary EU law.

The institutional framework is, in any event, the area where the contrast with the typical free trade agreement (and, indeed, the SCM Agreement) is most apparent. In addition to the obligations in terms of transparency[10] and consultation[11] (which are relatively frequent[12]), the TCA demands that the

---

[5] TCA (n 1), in particular Articles 15–36. For an analysis, see Steve Peers 'So close, yet so far: the EU/UK trade and cooperation agreement' (2022) 59 Common Market Law Review 49.

[6] Pursuant to Article 366(1) TCA:

'With a view to ensuring that subsidies are not granted where they have or could have a material effect on trade or investment between the Parties, each Party shall have in place and maintain an effective system of subsidy control that ensures that the granting of a subsidy respects the following principles:

(a) subsidies pursue a specific public policy objective to remedy an identified market failure or to address an equity rationale such as social difficulties or distributional concerns ("the objective");
(b) subsidies are proportionate and limited to what is necessary to achieve the objective;
(c) subsidies are designed to bring about a change of economic behaviour of the beneficiary that is conducive to achieving the objective and that would not be achieved in the absence of subsidies being provided;
(d) subsidies should not normally compensate for the costs the beneficiary would have funded in the absence of any subsidy;
(e) subsidies are an appropriate policy instrument to achieve a public policy objective and that objective cannot be achieved through other less distortive means;
(f) subsidies' positive contributions to achieving the objective outweigh any negative effects, in particular the negative effects on trade or investment between the Parties'.

[7] Article 365 TCA.

[8] Article 367(3) TCA.

[9] Article 367(14) TCA.

[10] Article 369 TCA.

[11] Article 370 TCA.

[12] See for instance Free Trade Agreement between the European Union and its Member States, of the one part, and the Republic of Korea, of the other part [2011] OJ L127/6; and Agreement between the European Union and Japan for an Economic Partnership [2018] OJ L330/3.

parties set up a dedicated 'operationally independent authority or body' with 'the necessary guarantees of independence' and with an 'appropriate role' within the regime.[13] Similarly, the Agreement mandates the introduction of an enforcement apparatus entrusting courts and tribunals with the power to review, among others, subsidy decisions (whether adopted by the awarding public body or by the 'independent authority')[14] and to impose effective remedies, which comprise not just the suspension or the prohibition of the subsidy measure, but also the recovery of awards.[15]

It is against the background of the obligations imposed on the UK by virtue of the TCA that one must make sense of the Subsidy Control Act 2022 (hereinafter, the 'Act'). This regime, as defined by the legislature, is as much an instrument aimed at complying with the international duties deriving from the Agreement, as it is one that seeks to ensure that awards within the UK (in particular those granted by local authorities and other sub-national entities) contribute to a public interest objective. Thus, a subsidy within the meaning of the Act is not just one that has an impact on cross-border trade and/or investment between the EU and the UK, but also, and more generally, one that affects 'competition or investment' within the latter.[16] From this perspective, the Act is unique in that it is hard-wired to promote best practices at the domestic level. To the extent that it does (and coming back to the potential justifications for subsidy control discussed in Chapter 1), it reflects concerns, such as the protection of inter-firm competition and the prevention of subsidy races, that go beyond strictly trade-related ones.

The Act is an intriguing instrument from a comparative perspective. As far as its substantive dimension is concerned, it could be aptly described as a codification of the EU acquis around Article 107(1) TFEU and, as such, a prime example of convergence around the EU model. Just like the TCA, the Act studiously avoids any formal references to the EU legal order. Such references would have implied a duty to interpret the former in light of the latter. Thus, the UK regime is built around the notion of subsidy, as opposed to that of State aid; similarly, it demands that a measure be specific,[17] as opposed to selective. On the other hand, traces of the case law of the Court of Justice (hereinafter, the 'ECJ') are apparent throughout. As will be explained at length hereinafter, a reader of Chapters 2 to 4

---

[13] Pursuant to Article 371(1) TCA, 'Each Party shall establish or maintain an operationally independent authority or body with an appropriate role in its subsidy control regime. That independent authority or body shall have the necessary guarantees of independence in exercising its operational functions and shall act impartially'.

[14] Article 372 TCA.

[15] Articles 373 and 374 TCA.

[16] Section 2(1)(d) of the Act.

[17] Pursuant to s 2(1)(c), a subsidy within the meaning of the Act 'is specific, that is, is such that it benefits one or more enterprises over one or more other enterprises with respect to the production of goods or the provision of services'.

will not fail to identify the judgments that inspired the drafting of the provision, from *PreussenElektra*[18] and *Pearle*[19] to *British Aggregates*[20] and *Azores*.[21]

As far as the institutional dimension is concerned, the Act departs markedly from EU State aid law. The role and powers of the Competition and Markets Authority (hereinafter, the 'CMA'), which has been designated as the 'independent authority' within the meaning of the TCA, cannot be compared in any way with those enjoyed by the European Commission in the EU legal order. Unlike the latter, the former has essentially an advisory role, the point of which is to ensure that the public authorities awarding subsidies comply with the subsidy control principles mentioned above. Thus, the CMA lacks the power to construe the notion of subsidy, decide on the compatibility of the measure with the regime and to take remedial action (including recovery). These functions are entrusted to other actors, namely the Secretary of State and the Competition Appeal Tribunal (hereinafter, the 'CAT' or the 'Tribunal').

The pages that follow explore the interplay between the substantive and institutional dimensions of the Act. It seems difficult to overstate the impact that the latter have on the evolution of the former. An idea that cuts across Chapters 2 to 6 is that the European Commission has been the driving force behind the broadening of the reach of Article 107(1) TFEU. The tax rulings saga epitomises, better than any other, how the EU system creates incentives for the broadening of the scope of the notion of State aid. The institutional framework created by the UK regime, by contrast, does not favour an expansive understanding of the boundaries of the Act. The strictly advisory role of the CMA, on the one hand, and the self-assessment of practices by awarding public authorities, on the other, mean that no actor in the institutional framework has either the ability or the incentive to test the boundaries of the regime and push it towards the outer variations of subsidy control depicted in Chapter 1.

2. Substantive Aspects of the Act

2.1. The Boundaries of the Notion of Subsidy

A subsidy within the meaning of the Act must involve 'financial assistance' from 'public resources' for it to fall within the scope of the regime. It does not depart in this regard from EU State aid law, which unambiguously and consistently requires (at least since *PreussenElektra*) that a measure involve the use of State resources

---

[18] Case C-379/98 *PreussenElektra AG v Schhleswag AG*, EU:C:2001:160.

[19] Case C-345/02 *Pearle BV, Hans Prijs Optiek Franchise BV and Rinck Opticiëns BV v Hoofdbedrijfschap Ambachten*, EU:C:2004:448.

[20] Case C-487/06 P *British Aggregates Association v Commission*, EU:C:2008:757.

[21] Case C-88/03 *Portugal v Commission*, EU:C:2006:511 (hereinafter, '*Azores*').

if it is to be caught by Article 107(1) TFEU.[22] The two systems are also aligned as far as the imputability condition is concerned. Pursuant to s 2(1)(a) of the Act, a 'subsidy' involves a measure which, inter alia, 'is given, directly or indirectly' by a 'public authority'. The extensive analysis in Chapter 2 has made it clear that the practical application of these conditions is not invariably straightforward. It may not always be obvious to draw the line between public and private resources, just as it may be challenging to establish whether a given measure is imputable to (or given by) a public authority.

The approach taken in s 2 of the Act is not fundamentally different from the rationalisation exercise undertaken by the ECJ in *PreussenElektra* and *Stardust Marine*. Accordingly, a measure may fall within the scope of the regime even when it is not adopted by a public authority.[23] Pursuant to s 2(3), financial assistance given from the resources of a person that is not a public authority is to be treated as a measure awarded by means of public resources where 'the involvement of a public authority in the decision to give financial assistance is such that the decision is, in substance, the decision of the public authority'. One can only interpret this provision as meaning that a subsidy within the meaning of the Act may involve resources flowing from the likes of a State-owned bank or utility, which may not exercise functions of a public nature but may be tied to a public authority.[24] It would seem that the relevant question, in practice, is whether the public authority is in a position to attain its aims by relying upon the person's resources.

Section 2(4) introduces the criteria to determine whether the decision to provide financial assistance is, 'in substance', that of the public authority. It captures the essence of the set of indicators introduced by the ECJ in *Stardust Marine* to determine, indirectly, the attributability[25] (what one may term imputability[26] in EU law parlance) of the measure to the public authority. Section 2(4) identifies, specifically, factors relating to the 'the control exercised over that person by that public authority' and the 'the relationship between that person and that public authority'. As is true in the context of Article 107(1) TFEU, the higher the degree of integration of the person with the structures of the authority, the more likely it is that the decision is, in substance, adopted by the latter. Conversely, the looser the ties (as would be true where the person in question is incorporated as a private company and operates in competition with privately owned firms), the less likely it is that the decision will be deemed to be, in substance, that of a public body.

---

[22] See Chapter 2 for an extensive analysis.

[23] The concept of public authority under the Act has a very specific meaning, which – pursuant to s 6(1) of the Act – expressly excludes the UK Parliament as well as the devolved legislatures but which encompasses 'a person who exercises functions of a public nature'. This chapter will therefore rely on the concept to convey the specific meaning attached to it in the Act. The issue is addressed in detail below, in Section 4.

[24] Case C-482/99 *France v Commission*, EU:C:2002:294 (hereinafter, '*Stardust Marine*').

[25] This is the vocabulary used in Department for Business and Trade, *Statutory Guidance for the United Kingdom Subsidy Control Regime – Subsidy Control Act 2022* (4th edn, January 2025), paras 15.8–15.11. This document is hereinafter referred to as the 'Subsidy Control Guidance'.

[26] *Stardust Marine* (n 24), paras 37–38.

2.2. The Concept of Advantage under the Act

As is true of State aid, an advantage for the purposes of the Act may be awarded not just by means of positive transfers of public resources (such as a grant or a loan) but also by means of other measures which, borrowing from *Steenkolenmijnen*, mitigate the charges to which a firm is normally subject. Financial assistance in this sense may be granted by means of instruments which, pursuant to s 2(2), include a 'contingent transfer of funds' (such as a guarantee), the 'forgoing of revenue that is otherwise due' (which may be at issue where a public authority exempts some firms from a tax or levy), as well as the acquisition or sale of goods or services. The subsidy control regime only comes into play where the advantage is given to one or more enterprises (as opposed to end-users), the definition of which is reminiscent (although not necessarily identical[27]) to that of an undertaking under EU law. Section 7(1) defines an enterprise as 'a person who is engaged in an economic activity that entails offering goods or services on a market'.

Section 3(2) of the Act expressly codifies in UK law the 'market economy operator principle' as developed in the EU legal order and discussed in Chapter 3. Thus, financial assistance is not to be treated as conferring an economic advantage where the conditions are not more favourable than those that 'might reasonably have been expected to have been available on the market to the enterprise'. Such might be the case, for instance, where the purchase (or sale) of assets or, similarly, the terms and conditions of a loan (including the interest rates applied) reflect the prevailing market conditions. The Subsidy Control Guidance (hereinafter, the 'Guidance') issued by the Secretary of State refers to the principle as the 'commercial market operator' (or 'CMO') principle[28] and outlines a number of methodological approaches with a view to its concrete application.

The Act is silent, by contrast, in relation to whether, and if so under what circumstances, compensation for public service obligations amounts to an economic advantage. Put differently, it has not expressly incorporated the *Altmark* doctrine,[29] whereby such compensations do not qualify as State aid where four cumulative conditions are met. It is true that s 29 reflects the fundamental principles underpinning the doctrine, in the sense that it identifies the requirements that apply where a public authority provides financial assistance to an 'SPEI enterprise' (that is, a firm that has been entrusted with a service of public economic interest, or SPEI).[30] However, s 29 applies to measures that qualify as subsidies within the meaning of s 2, and are

---

[27] See in this sense *The Durham Company Limited v Durham County Council* [2023] CAT 50.

[28] Subsidy Control Guidance (n 25), para 2.20: '[…] Financial assistance will not confer an economic advantage if it could reasonably be considered to have been given on the same terms as it could have been obtained on the market. This is known as the "commercial market operator" (CMO) principle'.

[29] Case C-280/00 *Altmark Trans GmbH and Regierungspräsidium Magdeburg v Nahverkehrsgesellschaft Altmark GmbH, and Oberbundesanwalt beim Bundesverwaltungsgericht*, EU:C:2003:415.

[30] See in particular s 29(2).

therefore deemed to provide an economic advantage. Article 106(2) TFEU is, therefore, the most appropriate analogy for this provision.[31]

The Guidance, however, sheds some light on the potential application of the *Altmark* doctrine in the UK legal order. When dealing with services of public economic interest, it expressly mentions that, prior to the application of the subsidy control requirements applying to such services, it is necessary to determine whether the financial assistance confers an economic advantage on the recipient in the first place. The Guidance points out, in this regard, that, as a rule, intervention will not qualify as a subsidy where the SPEI enterprise is selected by means of a competitive tender (just like a competitive tender typically suggests that the 'CMO' principle is met). Such an instance corresponds to the default scenario in *Altmark* (and more precisely the fourth condition). It remains to be seen whether the case law will endorse the doctrine. Given the institutional peculiarities of the UK regime (which will be discussed below), however, the need for the development of something akin to the *Altmark* conditions is less pressing.

2.3. Financial Assistance which is Specific

2.3.1. *The Substantive (or Material) Dimension of Specificity*

The effort to codify EU law is more explicit and exhaustive in relation to the concept of specificity, which seeks to capture the essence of the EU acquis on selectivity (even if not fully aligned with it). To begin with, s 4 incorporates into the UK legal order the default approach to the substantive (or material) dimension of the question, namely the so-called three-step test. The analysis comprises, as discussed at length in Chapter 4, first, the identification of a benchmark (or 'reference system')[32] against which selectivity is assessed; second, establishing whether, in light of the objective pursued, the contentious measure treats differently firms in a comparable factual and legal situation (that is, whether it treats like situations alike);[33] and, finally, determining whether such difference in treatment may be rationalised by the nature and general scheme of the system.[34]

Section 4(5) is an attempt to codify the first of these steps. Instead of referring to a benchmark or reference system, the letter of the Act alludes to the 'normal

---

[31] See, by analogy, European Union framework for State aid in the form of public service compensation [2012] OJ C8/1.

[32] See in this sense the case law discussed in Chapter 4, in particular Case C-6/12 *P Oy*, EU:C:2013:525; Joined Cases C-51/19 P and C-64/19 P *World Duty Free Group SA and Spain v Commission*, EU:C:2021:793; Case C-562/19 P *Commission v Poland*, EU:C:2021:201.

[33] Joined Cases C-78/08 to C-80/08 *Ministero dell'Economia e delle Finanze and Agenzia delle Entrate v Paint Graphos Soc. coop. arl and others*, EU:C:2011:550.

[34] ibid. See also Case C-308/01 *GIL Insurance Ltd and others v Commissioners of Customs and Excise*, EU:C:2004:252.

taxation regime'.[35] To the extent that it does, it lacks the degree of generality of its EU counterpart. While it is true that the 'three-step test' is particularly helpful to establish the selectivity of fiscal measures, it is applied across the board (both by the European Commission and the ECJ), irrespective of the mechanism by which the economic advantage is awarded. It would indeed be difficult to justify a different methodological choice depending on the nature of the measure. It is unsurprising, against this background, that the Guidance issued by the Secretary of State appears to extend the scope of the three-step test beyond the narrow realm of fiscal measures and treats it as the general approach.[36] One would expect the case law to evolve in a similar direction, just like it did in EU law.[37]

There is a second point where the Act could be read as diverging from the three-step test as interpreted and applied by the ECJ. Pursuant to s 4(5)(a), the 'normal taxation regime' (or benchmark) is identified in light, inter alia, of its 'internal objective'. It would be reasonable to interpret this provision as suggesting that only the objectives that are intrinsic to the system (that is, the immediate, narrow aim pursued by the measure within the regime of which it is a part) can be taken into consideration. The extrinsic objectives (that is, broader public interest aims) would not be relevant in the analysis. Such an interpretation would be at odds with EU law. As discussed extensively in Chapter 4 (and as the ECJ itself has repeatedly acknowledged), the underlying goals will often be indispensable to make sense of the boundaries of the normal regime.[38]

Since the wording of the provision is ambiguous and does not borrow directly from EU law, one cannot immediately conclude that 'internal' and 'intrinsic' are analogous terms, or that the former should necessarily be interpreted in light of the latter. It remains to be seen how s 4(5)(a) will be construed by the courts. The Guidance suggests that the definition of the reference system might take into consideration the broader ('extrinsic') policy objectives pursued by the regime.[39] This interpretation is consistent with the spirit of the Act. Sections 4(6) and 6(7), which codify the EU *British Aggregates* saga (which deals with special purpose levies), provide that specificity may be considered in light of the 'non-economic public policy objectives' pursued by the levy. As the case law evolves, a single, unifying approach may naturally emerge as the most reasonable and defensible interpretation of the Act. The experience of EU law may also be valuable insofar as it shows that considering the extrinsic objectives of the measure may be indispensable to the meaningful application of the three-step test.

---

[35] Pursuant to s 4(5) of the Act, the 'normal taxation regime' must be 'identified from' factors such as 'the internal objective of the regime' and 'the features of the regime (such as the tax base, the taxable person, the taxable event or the tax rate)'.

[36] Subsidy Control Guidance (n 25), para 15.88.

[37] Commission Notice on the notion of State aid as referred to in Article 107(1) of the Treaty on the Functioning of the European Union [2016] OJ C262/1, para 128.

[38] See for instance *British Aggregates* (n 20) and Case C-417/10 *Ministero dell'Economia e delle Finanze and Agenzia delle Entrate v 3M Italia SpA*, EU:C:2012:184, para 42 and the discussion in Chapter 4.

[39] Subsidy Control Guidance (n 25), para 15.89.

The second of the three steps (again, formally confined to tax measures) is codified in s 4(4). As much as its counterpart in EU law, it is broken down into two sub-steps. Pursuant to the first, it is necessary to ascertain whether the measure amounts to a derogation relative to the normal regime (that is, whether the economic advantage allows an enterprise or group thereof to 'obtain a reduction in the tax liability that it or they would otherwise have borne under the normal taxation regime'). The second sub-step, in turn, revolves around whether the derogation leads to the treatment of similar situations differently (in other words, that the recipients of the economic advantage 'are treated more advantageously than one or more other enterprises in a comparable position under the normal taxation regime'). While not explicit in the Act, the Guidance provides that the comparability assessment is undertaken in light of the objective pursued by the normal regime, which is the same methodological approach followed under Article 107(1) TFEU.

Finally, the third step of the test is enshrined in s 2(2), which provides the principle ('[f]inancial assistance is not to be regarded as being specific if the distinction in the treatment of enterprises is justified by principles inherent to the design of the arrangements of which that financial assistance is part') and s 2(3), which identifies the sort of principles that might justify the differential treatment of enterprises in a comparable factual and legal situation. These include, among others, the 'the need to fight fraud or tax evasion', 'administrative manageability' and 'the avoidance of double taxation'. Such objectives, or principles, are directly inspired by the ECJ case law (including cases such as *GIL Insurance*[40]) and by the European Commission Notice on the notion of State aid, which compiled them systematically.[41]

When examined from a comparative perspective, there are two questions that stand out about the notion of specificity. The Act departs from EU law insofar as it does not appear to leave any room for a de facto or effects-based approach to ascertain whether a formally general measure has been designed in such a way that it favours a firm or select group thereof. This subsidiary approach, which was accepted by the ECJ in *Gibraltar*,[42] makes it possible to take action in exceptional circumstances, that is, where a measure is manifestly discriminatory.[43] It would be reasonable to assume that the legislature has opted against introducing two mutually contradictory approaches to the assessment of specificity in the Act. As a choice, it may have an impact on the effectiveness of the system, insofar as some measures will fall outside of its scope simply because of the regulatory technique selected by the public authority. On the other hand, embracing a single approach provides greater legal certainty.

---

[40] *GIL Insurance* (n 34).

[41] Commission Notice on the notion of State aid (n 37), para 139.

[42] Joined Cases C-106/09 P and C-107/09 P *Commission v Government of Gibraltar and United Kingdom*, EU:C:2011:732.

[43] *Commission v Poland* (n 32).

2.3.2. *The Geographic Dimension of Specificity*

In EU State aid law, the issue of geographic selectivity has been settled since *Azores*.[44] As a general rule, the question of whether a measure favours certain firms on the basis of their location depends on the powers of the public authority that adopts the said measure. Thus, a regional or local authority which, in the exercise of its competences, decides to reduce taxes across the board does not provide a selective advantage within the meaning of Article 107(1) TFEU. Insofar as the body in question is acting within the scope of its powers, it will be the geographic benchmark against which selectivity is assessed. The Act codifies this case law. It provides, in s 4(5)(c), that the definition of the normal regime, from a geographic standpoint, must consider the status of the public authority adopting the measure. The exercise involves ascertaining, first, whether the said authority is 'autonomous institutionally, procedurally, economically and financially as regards the regime' and, second, whether it 'has the competence to design the features of the regime'.

2.4. The Subsidy Control Principles

Pursuant to s 12, a public authority must consider the subsidy control principles prior to the implementation of a measure (whether an individual one or a scheme), and, similarly, it must take any steps in this sense 'unless it is of the view that the subsidy is consistent with those principles'. The subsidy control principles, which are enunciated in Sch 1 of the Act, incorporate into UK law the obligations acquired by virtue of the TCA, and more precisely its Article 366.[45] This provision, in turn, codifies into a legally binding instrument the administrative practice followed by the European Commission over the past two decades (that is, since the advent of the so-called State Aid Action Plan[46]). The fundamental point of the subsidy control principles is to ensure that any contributions to a public interest objective resulting from the award of the measure outweigh any actual or potential distortive effects on competition, trade and/or investment.

Accordingly, the subsidy control principles demand that the subsidy pursue a interest policy objective, whether efficiency-related (such as a response to a market failure)or equity-related (such as the promotion of regional cohesion). In particular,

---

[44] *Azores* (n 21).

[45] Pursuant to para A of Sch 1 of the Act: 'Subsidies should pursue a specific policy objective in order to–

    (a) remedy an identified market failure, or

    (b) address an equity rationale (such as local or regional disadvantage, social difficulties or distributional concerns)'.

[46] Neelie Kroes, 'The State Aid Action Plan – Delivering Less and Better Targeted Aid' (UK Presidency Seminar on State Aid, London, 14th July 2005). For an example of the interpretation and operation of these principles in practice, see Guidelines on State aid for climate, environmental protection and energy 2022 [2022] OJ C80/1.

compliance with the principle presupposes that the measure is capable of bringing about the desired change in the economic behaviour of the recipient (what is known as the 'incentive effect'[47] in EU law parlance).[48] Thus, it must be shown that the expected benefit would not have occurred in the absence of the award (and, similarly, that the latter is capable of delivering the public interest objective pursued). Public authorities must evaluate, in addition, that the subsidy is the appropriate policy measure to attain the desired goal and that it remains proportionate (which involves ascertaining whether there are less distortive measures and, more generally, confining the measure to what is necessary to fulfil the objectives of the public authority).

Chapter 2 of Part 2 of the Act fleshes out these principles. It identifies a number of instances where subsidies are deemed prohibited (or may be prohibited unless some conditions are met). Sections 15 to 18 provide for the prohibition of measures that have either the object or effect of distorting competition and/or trade or that can be safely presumed to have a net negative impact. Section 15, for instance, refers to unlimited guarantees. It has been explained in Chapter 3 why such a measure is exceedingly unlikely to be awarded by a rational private operator and can therefore be deemed distortive of competition by its very nature. Sections 16 and 17, in turn, deal with measures that have, as their very object, the alteration of trade patterns (that is, subsidies contingent on export performance and on the use of domestic content), whereas s 18 deals with intervention aimed at distorting investment decisions. Finally, ss 19 and 20 lay down the conditions under which rescue and restructuring aid may be acceptable.

3. The Institutional Features of the Regime

3.1. The Role of the CMA

Even though it is the designated 'independent authority' within the meaning of the TCA, the role of the CMA under the UK subsidy control regime cannot be compared to that which the European Commission plays in the EU legal order. The powers of the latter can be broken down into three main areas. First, the

---

[47] Energy and Environment Guidelines (n 46), para 26: 'Aid can be considered as facilitating an economic activity only if it has an incentive effect. An incentive effect occurs when the aid induces the beneficiary to change its behaviour, to engage in additional economic activity or in more environmentally-friendly economic activity, which it would not carry out without the aid or would carry out in a restricted or different manner'. See also, in general, Chapter 6.

[48] Paragraph C of Sch 1 of the Act reads as follows: '(1) Subsidies should be designed to bring about a change of economic behaviour of the beneficiary.

(2) That change, in relation to a subsidy, should be–

(a) conducive to achieving its specific policy objective, and
(b) something that would not happen without the subsidy'.

European Commission enjoys jurisdiction to interpret Article 107(1) TFEU and thus to determine whether or not a given measure amounts to aid. Second, it is empowered to enforce the regime. More specifically, it can investigate, gather information and receive complaints regarding potentially unlawful awards. It also has the (exclusive) competence to rule on the compatibility of aid with the internal market and, where necessary, order recovery from EU Member States. Third, the European Commission formulates policy in the area. It does so by means of a combination of hard (decisions[49] and regulations[50]) and soft (Notices,[51] Guidelines[52] and Frameworks[53]) law instruments.

The CMA does not enjoy comparable powers under the Act. It fulfils advisory and monitoring functions. What is more, the instances where it can intervene are determined, and constrained, by the Secretary of State. The point of the CMA's involvement in the process, generally speaking, is to assist public authorities awarding subsidies and, similarly, to promote best practices under the regime. Pursuant to s 59, it must evaluate, by means of an individual report,[54] how the body providing financial assistance has assessed the measure's conformity with the subsidy control principles, including its impact on competition or investment within the UK.[55] It can, in the same vein, provide advice on how the public authority's analysis can be improved and how the subsidy could potentially be amended or modified to ensure compliance with the said principles. The awarding body, however, is under no duty to follow this advice.

As already mentioned, the instances where the CMA becomes involved in the evaluation process are determined by the Secretary of State. It is for the latter to adopt secondary legislation identifying the instances where measures qualify, respectively, as subsidies (or schemes) of 'interest' and of 'particular interest'.[56] Pursuant to the Act, the latter are subject to a mandatory referral to the CMA,[57] whereas the latter are subject to a voluntary referral.[58] In addition, the Secretary of State has the discretion to mandate the referral of a particular measure.[59] The

---

[49] See Articles 4 and 9 of Council Regulation (EU) 2015/1589 of 13 July 2015 laying down detailed rules for the application of Article 108 of the Treaty on the Functioning of the European Union (codification) [2015] OJ L248/9.

[50] Commission Regulation (EU) No 651/2014 of 17 June 2014 declaring certain categories of aid compatible with the internal market in application of Articles 107 and 108 of the Treaty [2014] OJ L187/1.

[51] See for instance Commission Notice on the notion of State aid (n 37).

[52] See for instance Framework for State aid in the form of public service compensation (n 31).

[53] See for instance Energy and Environment Guidelines (n 46).

[54] Pursuant to s 59(1) of the Act: 'The CMA's report under section 53 or 57 must include an evaluation of the public authority's assessment under section 52(2)(d) or 56(2)(d)'.

[55] In accordance with s 59(2) of the Act: 'The evaluation must take into account any effects of the proposed subsidy or scheme on competition or investment within the United Kingdom'.

[56] Section 11 of the Act. See also the Subsidy Control (Subsidies and Schemes of Interest or Particular Interest) Regulations 2022, as amended by the The Subsidy Control (Subsidies and Schemes of Interest or Particular Interest) (Amendment) Regulations 2025.

[57] Section 52(1)(a) of the Act.

[58] Section 56(1) of the Act.

[59] Section 52(1)(b) of the Act.

constraints that the Act places upon public authorities referring subsidies to the CMA are procedural, not substantive. They must comply, in particular, with the information obligations set out in s 52 and respect the so-called 'reporting'[60] and 'cooling off' periods[61] prior to the award of the subsidy or scheme. Failure to comply with these obligations entails the prohibition of the subsidy.[62]

The limited powers of the CMA under the Act mean that it lacks the means not just to interpret the scope of the notion of subsidy (let alone the enforcement of the provision) but to engage in any form of policy making, including by means of Guidelines and other soft law instruments. It has already been pointed out that it is ultimately for the public authority to decide whether to implement the subsidy. More than shaping or nudging decisions taken by awarding bodies to ensure that they act in the public interest, the CMA is entrusted with a monitoring function to oversee the operation of the regime at large and thus assist the Secretary of State in the exercise of their powers. The Act requires it, in this sense, to report, for a specified period, on the effectiveness of the system and its impact on competition and investment within the UK.[63]

3.2. The Role of the Secretary of State

The Secretary of State fulfils many of the functions with which the European Commission is entrusted in the EU legal order. The overview of the substantive aspects of the regime in the preceding section of this chapter has already made it apparent that they can provide guidance (subject to interpretation by the courts) about the notion of subsidy, the subsidy control principles and other aspects of the operation of the regime.[64] The Guidance, which is kept under regular review, fulfils, among other things, the role of the European Commission Notice on the notion of State aid.[65] While public authorities 'must have regard' to it when giving a subsidy or making a subsidy scheme, the Secretary of State is careful to note that, as a soft law instrument, it is not an authoritative statement of the law.[66] In practice, however, it may be more relevant and influential than the EU Notice, if only because the CMA, unlike its EU counterpart, lacks jurisdiction to interpret the notion of subsidy. Given the paucity of the case law, the Guidance may therefore become the primary instrument to navigate the substantive aspects of the Act.

The management of the system by means of secondary legislation is a second function where the Secretary of State fulfils a pre-eminent role. Some aspects of this function have already been discussed above, when outlining the advisory

---

[60] Section 53(3) of the Act.
[61] Section 54 of the Act.
[62] Section 31 of the Act.
[63] Section 65 of the Act.
[64] Section 79 of the Act.
[65] Subsidy Control Guidance (n 25).
[66] ibid, para 1.3.

and monitoring functions of the CMA. Under the Act, it is for the Secretary of State to lay down legal instruments defining the instances where measures falling within the scope of s 2 qualify as subsidies 'of interest' or 'of particular interest'. The Subsidy Control (Subsidies and Schemes of Interest or Particular Interest) Regulations 2022 rely on quantitative thresholds (that is, the amount of the subsidy) to characterise the two categories of subsidy.[67] As already mentioned, the Secretary of State has the discretion to require that a particular measure be referred, whether prior to[68] or after its implementation.[69]

As decades of experience under the EU system show, limiting the instances where a measure is subject to an individual referral comes across as indispensable to ensure that the system remains manageable. There are circumstances where the modest (or de minimis) amount of the measure is sufficient, in and of itself, to dispense with the need to refer it to an independent authority. One can presume that, in such cases, the effect on competition, trade or investment will not be significant (or be comfortably outweighed by any public interest goals pursued). The European Commission has adopted several iterations of the De Minimis Regulation over the decades.[70] A similar approach is followed in the UK regime, which, in s 36 of the Act (which deals with 'minimal financial assistance'), provides that the subsidy control requirements do not apply to measures below a certain quantitative threshold.[71] Section 42 of the Act empowers the Secretary of State to alter these amounts by means of secondary legislation.

There is a third feature of the system, which allows the Secretary of State to engage in policy-making (and which adds to its management function). One of the instruments that ensures the administrability of the EU regime is the (General) Block Exemption Regulation.[72] This instrument defines the instances in which State aid is deemed compatible with the internal market and therefore not subject to a notification obligation.[73] It is estimated that, in practice, a very substantial percentage of measures (sometimes estimated to represent over 90% of all aid) fall

---

[67] What amounts to a subsidy or subsidy scheme of particular interest is defined in reg 3 of the Subsidy Control Regulations (n 56). This provision identifies a number of quantitative thresholds, which vary depending on the circumstances. For instance, the default scenario, enshrined in reg 3(2), applies where the subsidy exceeds £1 million and the total amount of subsidy over a given period (the 'applicable period' within the meaning of the Regulations, or three financial years) does not exceed a certain amount (£25 million after the review of the thresholds in 2025). The threshold is lower, pursuant to reg 3(3), where the subsidy is awarded in a 'sensitive sector'.

[68] Section 55(1) of the Act.

[69] Section 60(1) of the Act.

[70] For the current version of the Regulation, see Commission Regulation (EU) 2023/2832 of 13 December 2023 on the application of Articles 107 and 108 of the Treaty on the Functioning of the European Union to de minimis aid granted to undertakings providing services of general economic interest [2023] OJ L 2023/2832.

[71] In accordance with s 36(1) of the Act, 'The subsidy control requirements do not apply to minimal financial assistance given to an enterprise if the total amount of minimal or SPEI financial assistance given to the enterprise within the applicable period does not exceed £315,000'.

[72] General Block Exemption Regulation (n 50).

[73] ibid, Article 3.

within its scope.[74] The Block Exemption Regulation is a powerful – albeit subtle – policy-making tool. Activities falling within its scope unquestionably contribute to a public interest objective, whether efficiency- or equity-related. Signalling that they are subject to more lenient treatment, both from a substantive and a procedural standpoint, effectively steers the EU Member States' expenditure decisions towards these activities.

While there is not a direct equivalent in the UK regime, the role of the Block Exemption Regulation appears to have been fulfilled, in practice, by the so-called streamlined subsidy scheme. Section 10(4) defines it as a subsidy scheme[75] which is both 'made by a Minister of the Crown' and 'specifies it is made for the purposes of this Act as a streamlined subsidy scheme'. Pursuant to s 10(6), such instruments (including any subsequent modifications) must be laid before Parliament before they are made. Parliament may resolve not to approve the scheme.[76] At the time of writing, all three streamlined subsidy schemes (or streamlined routes) within the meaning of s 10(5) have been made by the Secretary of State. It is not surprising that the areas covered by these instruments (respectively, research, development and innovation;[77] energy usage;[78] and local growth[79]) are roughly the same as those covered in the European Commission's Block Exemption Regulation.

3.3. The Role of the CAT

The place of the CAT in the UK regime is more central than that of the EU courts under the EU State aid system. Some of the functions assumed by the Commission under the EU regime are exercised by the Tribunal. In the absence of an administrative apparatus allowing interested parties to bring complaints against measures granted in breach of the Act's requirements, the CAT provides the only avenue for them to seek relief. When performing this function, the Tribunal may be called upon to interpret the notion of subsidy within the meaning of s 2 of the Act. As Chapters 2 to 5 show, disputes around the boundaries of the notion are far from unusual. It is therefore inevitable that some public authorities will implement

---

[74] European Commission, *State aid Scoreboard 2024* (April 2025).

[75] Pursuant to s 10(1) of the Act, a 'subsidy scheme' is 'a scheme made by a public authority providing for the giving of subsidies under the scheme'.

[76] Section 10(7) of the Act: 'If, within the 40-day period, either House of Parliament resolves not to approve the scheme, or the scheme as modified, then, with effect from the end of the day on which the resolution is passed, the scheme, or the scheme as modified, is to be treated as not having been made'.

[77] Research, Development and Innovation Streamlined Subsidy Scheme, available at www.gov.uk/government/publications/subsidy-control-act-2022-streamlined-routes. See also the Research, Development and Innovation Streamlined Route Guidance.

[78] Energy Usage Streamlined Subsidy Scheme, available at www.gov.uk/government/publications/subsidy-control-act-2022-streamlined-routes. See also the Energy Usage Streamlined Route Guidance.

[79] Local Growth Streamlined Subsidy Scheme, available at www.gov.uk/government/publications/subsidy-control-act-2022-streamlined-routes. See also the Local Growth Streamlined Route Guidance.

subsidies without treating them as such. This impression is confirmed by the first disputes brought before the CAT. In them, the claimant alleged a failure to recognise that the contentious measure was caught by the Act.[80]

Under the UK regime, it is also for the CAT to exercise the sort of enforcement powers that the European Commission enjoys by virtue of Articles 107 and 108 TFEU. On an application for review (whether on grounds that are specific to public authorities' duties under the Act or on general public law grounds), the Tribunal has jurisdiction not just to issue a declaration characterising a measure as a subsidy within the meaning of s 2, but also to review whether the said measure is in keeping with the subsidy control principles and, where justified, grant relief, including a prohibiting or a quashing order.[81] Where the CAT issues a judgment providing for the latter, it may refer the issue back to the public authority for it to reconsider and adopt a new decision.[82] Crucially, the range of remedies also comprises the possibility to order the public authority to recover the subsidy from the recipient.[83]

3.4. Summary and Conclusions

Table 7.1 The dispersion of power in the UK system

System	Interpretation	Policy-making	Compliance with the principles	Enforcement
EU State aid	Commission and national courts (ultimately ECJ)	Commission	Commission (subject to marginal review)	Commission (and private enforcement)
UK Subsidy control	Secretary of State (and ultimately courts)	Secretary of State	Self-assessment (CMA input and judicial review)	Private enforcement

[80] See in particular the Notice of Appeal in *The Durham Company Limited v Durham County Council*, where the appellant sought from the CAT, inter alia, a declaration that the respondent had 'granted a subsidy to its Trade Waste Collection Business'. Similarly, in *Mr Aubrey Weis v Greater Manchester Combined Authority*, the appellant sought, inter alia, a declaration to the effect that 'the Respondent has granted a subsidy to Trinity and/or Jackson'. See also the Notice of Appeal in the third case brought before the CAT, namely *The New Lottery Company Ltd and Others v The Gambling Commission*. Both of these notice of appeal documents are available at www.catribunal.org.uk/.

[81] The powers are specified by reference to the relevant jurisdiction. Section 72(2) specifies the relief available in England and Wales or Northern Ireland (and which includes a 'mandatory order', a 'prohibiting order', a 'quashing order', a 'declaration' and an 'injunction'). Section 73(2), in turn, deals with the powers of the CAT in Scotland, which are the same as the powers of review of the Court of Session.

[82] See in this sense s 72(3), which relates to the powers of the CAT in England and Wales. In relation to Scotland, the Subsidy Control Guidance (n 25) clarifies, in para 13.18, that the Tribunal may adopt 'an order requiring the public authority to perform a specified act, for example an order requiring the public authority to perform its legal duties'.

[83] Section 74 of the Act.

The extent to which the EU and UK models differ from one another is summarised in Table 7.1. While the EU model chose to concentrate power within the European Commission, its UK counterpart disperses it across several actors. As far as the latter is concerned, the policy-making functions lie firmly with the Secretary of State, as the representative of a democratically-elected government. In this capacity, they can steer the award of subsidies by public authorities towards the activities that will have a net positive impact and also ensure that the system remains effective and manageable. The CMA, as an 'independent authority', has the functions that are typical of an expert agency, namely to provide advice and promote best practices. Ultimately, the Act is based on the self-assessment by awarding bodies of the measures they adopt (in contrast with the exclusive competence of the European Commission to ascertain the compatibility of State aid with the internal market).

As an advisory agency, the CMA is also stripped of the enforcement functions that the European Commission enjoys. The latter has investigative powers, which it can exercise on its own motion or following a complaint. The UK model, by contrast, relies, by and large, on private claimants seeking relief before the Tribunal. As a result of this difference, the latter will primarily evolve in the context of disputes between interested parties and public authorities. The expert body testing the boundaries of the regime, without which the evolution of EU State aid law cannot be understood (suffice it to think, as mentioned in the introduction, of the tax rulings saga or the disagreements preceding *PreussenElektra* and *Stardust Marine*), will be absent from the UK landscape. How this institutional difference can be expected to affect the substantive aspects of the regime will be explored in Section 5 of this chapter.

4. The Scope of the Subsidy Control Requirements

4.1. The Notion of Public Authority under the Act

The notion of public authority has a specific meaning under the Act. Pursuant to s 6, it is a 'person who exercises functions of a public nature'. Crucially, the Act expressly excludes from the definition both Houses of Parliament as well as the devolved legislatures.[84] This substantive choice implies that financial assistance granted by means of primary legislation is subject to the Act only to the extent determined in Sch 3. This part of the instrument adjusts the definitions to accommodate the specificities of legislatures and determines the aspects of the regime that apply to them. In particular, it provides that a subsidy within the meaning of s 2(1) of the Act must be understood as financial assistance that is given, directly

---

[84] See s 6(1).

or indirectly, from public resources provided by means of primary legislation.[85] It also clarifies that subsidies granted by a public authority under a duty imposed by primary legislation are also regulated by Sch 3.[86]

4.2. Subsidy Control and Acts of Parliament

Generally speaking, Acts of Parliament are only subject to the subsidy control regime insofar as it is necessary for the UK to comply with its obligations under the TCA. The virtually complete exemption of UK-wide legislation is an expression of the principle of parliamentary sovereignty,[87] which would sit at odds with several of the substantive and institutional requirements enshrined in the Act.[88] In fact, the TCA itself acknowledges the constitutional arrangements within the UK, and expressly provides that nothing in the subsidy control chapter must be interpreted as questioning them or requiring that they be adjusted to meet the parties' obligations. This point is particularly relevant in relation to the judicial review of awards. Article 372 TCA, which deals with courts and tribunals, provides that the Agreement does not require the EU or the UK to widen the scope or grounds of judicial review. The consequence, in the case of the latter, is that Acts of Parliament providing for the award of a subsidy cannot be challenged before a court or tribunal.[89]

As a result of these constitutional factors, subsidies provided by means of primary legislation are only subject to the transparency obligations enshrined in Chapter 3 of Part 2 of the Act (that is, ss 32 to 34 thereof). These obligations derive from Article 369 TCA and seem indispensable for the appropriate functioning of the Agreement. It is difficult to see how consultations within the meaning of Article 370 TCA[90] could be performed and, similarly, how remedial measures under Article 374 TCA[91] could otherwise be adopted. Subsidies

---

[85] See para 3(1) of Sch 3: 'The definition of "subsidy" in section 2 applies for the purposes of this Schedule (so far as the context requires) as if the reference in subsection (1)(a) of that section to financial assistance given by a public authority were a reference to financial assistance provided by means of primary legislation.'

[86] Pursuant to para 4 of Sch 3, 'In this Schedule references to a subsidy provided by means of primary legislation–

    (a) include references to a subsidy given by a public authority under a duty imposed by that legislation.'

[87] On sovereignty, see, generally, Martin Loughlin and Stephen Tierney, 'The shibboleth of sovereignty' (2018) 81 The Modern Law Review 989.

[88] Subsidy Control Guidance (n 25), para 14.15: 'The substantive subsidy control requirements do not apply to subsidies given or schemes made in Acts of Parliament. This is because of the constitutional principle that Parliament is sovereign and one Act of Parliament cannot bind another'.

[89] ibid, para 14.19. As clarified in the Subsidy Control Guidance, however, they may be challenged under WTO law or under the terms of another international agreement.

[90] One should note, in this sense, that, pursuant to Article 370(2) TCA, one of the parties to the agreement may request the information gathered in accordance with the transparency obligations enshrined in Article 369 TCA.

[91] Pursuant to Article 374(1), 'A Party may deliver to the other Party a written request for information and consultations regarding a subsidy that it considers causes, or there is a serious risk that it will cause, a significant negative effect on trade or investment between the Parties [...]'.

provided by means of primary legislation must therefore feature in the database that the Secretary of State is required under the Act to provide.[92] The duty to include information in the subsidy database, which is laid down in s 33, is to be fulfilled by the 'appropriate authority' within the meaning of Sch 3, which, in relation to Acts of Parliament, is 'a Minister of the Crown or the Commissioners for [His] Majesty's Revenue and Customs'.[93]

The constitutional arrangements within the UK are not an obstacle for the 'appropriate authority' within the meaning of the Act (and, if different, the promoter of the proposed primary legislation) to follow best practices and seek the advice of the CMA. Accordingly, para 9 of Sch 3 provides for the possibility of a voluntary referral to the expert agency of a subsidy (or subsidy scheme) of interest or of particular interest. To this date (and as will be explained in detail in the subsequent section of this chapter), there has not been a single voluntary referral of proposed primary legislation to the CMA. Irrespective of whether such a voluntary referral occurs, one must bear in mind that the UK at large is under a duty to observe the subsidy control principles (together with other substantive requirements) as a matter of international law (and more precisely Articles 366 and 367 TCA).

It is hard to overestimate the implications of shielding Acts of Parliament from scrutiny under the regime. Decades of EU State aid law enforcement show that the most significant and potentially distortive measures tend to be precisely those introduced by means of primary legislation. While this conclusion would be true in any jurisdiction, it is particularly apparent in a highly centralised State like the UK, where the power to tax and the power to spend lie firmly with Parliament. In particular, the exclusion of fiscal measures introduced by means of primary legislation is likely to have a significant impact on the effectiveness of the regime. It is sufficient to point out, in this sense, that the concept of selectivity, as discussed in Chapter 4, has evolved, to a significant extent, in the context of challenges against State-wide legislation (including UK-wide legislation, as in *CFC*[94] and *GIL Insurance*,[95] to mention two emblematic examples).

4.3. Subsidy Control and Devolved Legislation

Devolved primary legislation is subject to a greater degree of scrutiny under the Act. Unlike appropriate authorities in relation to Acts of Parliament, devolved legislatures are not just subject to the transparency requirements of ss 32 to 34. In accordance with para 6 of Sch 3, they must also observe, as a matter of domestic law, the subsidy control principles and the energy and environment principles laid down in ss 12

---

[92] Section 32(1): 'The Secretary of State must make arrangements for the provision of a database of subsidies and subsidy schemes for the purposes of this Part ("the subsidy database")'.

[93] Paragraph 2(1) of Sch 3.

[94] Joined Cases C-555/22 P, C-556/22 P and C-564/22 P *United Kingdom and others v Commission*, EU:C:2024:763.

[95] *GIL Insurance* (n 34).

and 13, and this prior to the award of a subsidy. The same is true of the prohibitions and requirements enshrined in Chapter 2 of Part 2 and which, as mentioned above, comprise the prohibition of, inter alia, export subsidies and those contingent on the use of domestic content. These obligations are without prejudice to the possibility of a voluntary referral to the CMA for a report (an option that has not been exercised so far by an appropriate authority or promoter of devolved legislation).

The most important difference from Acts of Parliament, in any event, has to do with the fact that devolved primary legislation can be subject to judicial review. Challenges against subsidies provided in this way, however, are not brought before the CAT, but before the appropriate court within the meaning of para 2(1) of Sch 3, which varies depending on the devolved legislature.[96] As part of the judicial review of legislation, claimants can seek the recovery of subsidies that fail to comply with the subsidy control principles and/or with the prohibitions and additional requirements enshrined in Part 2. Paragraph 10 expressly provides for this remedy, in that it clarifies that s 74 of the Act applies in subsidy proceedings brought against devolved primary legislation. No challenge has been brought against primary devolved legislation to date.

5. The Interaction between the Substantive and Institutional Dimensions

5.1. Means and Incentives in the UK and EU Regimes

The fact that there is a high degree of convergence between the EU and UK regimes does not mean that the two will necessarily evolve in a similar direction from a substantive standpoint. Both systems significantly diverge from one another as far as the institutional dimension is concerned. EU State aid law gives the European Commission the means and the incentives to maximise the effectiveness of the regime and minimise the distortive effects of subsidies and other measures having an equivalent effect. As pointed out above, these institutional features are likely to be reflected, inter alia, in the (expansive) way in which Article 107(1) TFEU is construed. The dispersion of power that is the hallmark of the UK regime creates a different set of incentives. What is more, no single institutional actor has the means to ensure the effectiveness of the regime to the same extent as the European Commission. As a result, it would not be surprising if the UK system carved its own substantive path.

---

[96] In accordance with para 2(1) of Sch 3, an 'appropriate court' means the Court of Session in relation to a subsidy provided by means of an Act of the Scottish Parliament; the High Court in England and Wales in relation to a subsidy provided by means of an Act or Measure of Senedd Cymru; and, finally, the High Court in Northern Ireland in relation to a subsidy provided by means of an Act of the Northern Ireland Assembly.

5.1.1. *Means and Incentives in the EU Regime*

It makes sense to develop these ideas at some length. When it is mentioned that the European Commission has the means to maximise the effectiveness of the regime, one must bear in mind that the powers with which it is entrusted under Article 108 TFEU and related secondary legislation, which have already been discussed at some length, are only a part of the picture. The ability to, inter alia, investigate the award of State aid on its own motion, to declare the incompatibility of aid and to order the recovery of unlawful and incompatible awards is complemented by other aspects of the system. The European Commission can become involved in State aid proceedings other than by means of its own administrative proceedings. In particular, it may become involved in preliminary reference proceedings before the ECJ.[97] In that context, it can submit its observations about the issues raised by the national court. The latter, moreover, can seek guidance from the European Commission when interpreting Article 107(1) TFEU in the context of ordinary proceedings.[98]

Other factors strengthen the powers that the European Commission enjoys, and allow it to maximise the effectiveness of the regime. These additional factors are best seen as a side-effect of the formal powers it enjoys. One should consider, in this sense, the depth and breadth of its expertise, which is not easy to replicate in any public or private context.[99] A second factor relates to the experience that it has accumulated over decades as the body in charge of making policy and enforcing the law in the area. These legal and extra-legal means, combined together, give the European Commission a unique role as the only genuine repeat player in the system.[100] As such, it is able not just to navigate effectively legal proceedings (both at the EU and the national levels), but also to design its strategies with a view to shaping the evolution of the law over the long term.

From the European Commission's perspective, the most effective way to maximise the effectiveness of the regime (and, in the same vein, minimise the distortions of trade and competition caused by the award of subsidies and similar measures) is to favour as expansive an interpretation as possible of the scope of Article 107(1) TFEU. A relatively broad understanding of the reach of the provision gives the European Commission ample discretion to engage in policy-making, in particular when acting in accordance with Article 107(3) TFEU. In addition, an expansive understanding of the notion of State aid allows the European Commission to fill temporary gaps in regulatory regimes or to induce legislative change in other areas of EU law. Intervention in the area of tax rulings, addressed in Chapter 5, is an example in this sense.

---

[97] See Article 23 of the Statute of the Court of Justice of the European Union [2012] OJ C326/210.

[98] Commission Notice on the enforcement of State aid rules by national courts [2021] OJ C305/1.

[99] See in this sense the figures provided in the Introduction.

[100] The expression is borrowed from Marc Galanter, 'Why the "haves" come out ahead: Speculations on the limits of legal change' (1974) 9 Law & Society Review 95.

5.1.2. *Means and Incentives in the UK Regime*

There is no institutional actor in the UK legal order with means comparable to those that the European Commission has at its disposal. Just like powers, means are dispersed across the UK regime. Part of the expertise and the experience lies with the CMA. This expertise, however, is limited by its technocratic role, which is confined to the provision of expert advice. The Secretary of State is another repository of expertise under the regime. Their role in providing guidance about the meaning and scope of the regime (and more precisely the notion of subsidy) complements the CMA's. Insofar as the system revolves around the self-assessment of the financial assistance they provide, it creates the conditions for public authorities (at least those frequently referring measures to the expert agency) to become an additional vector of expertise over time (albeit a fragmented one). One should mention, finally, the CAT, which was designed as an area-specific judicial body and which can be expected to develop specialist knowledge as subsidy decisions are challenged before it.

More importantly, the role and strategies of these institutional actors are not the same as those of the European Commission. For the reasons explained above, the latter has an apparent incentive in expanding the scope of Article 107(1) TFEU. It is not obvious to see which actor in the UK regime would have the same motivation. From the perspective of public authorities, the referral of subsidies entails the diversion of resources, and might make their decisions vulnerable to legal challenge. It is therefore uncertain that they would have an interest in expanding the notion of subsidy. In the absence of any policy-making functions, and given its relatively narrow remit, the same conclusion applies to the CMA. From the perspective of the Secretary of State, while a broad reading of the scope of the regime might allow them to oversee more effectively financial assistance at the local and regional levels, it may also expose their own awards.

The only set of actors that may have a marked interest in expanding the reach of the Act are claimants that compete with recipients of subsidies. Unlike the European Commission, however, these private claimants are unlikely to have the expertise and the experience that the former has been able to accumulate over the years. In other words, they are typically one-shotters, as opposed to repeat players. For the same reason, their litigation strategies may be oriented towards the short term. One should note, moreover, that they face at least two structural disadvantages vis-à-vis the European Commission. The latter, as an administrative body with decision-making functions, can interpret the scope of the provision without having recourse to a judge. In addition, the Act provides that subsidy decisions are subject to a judicial review standard, which is known to be deferential to authorities.[101]

---

[101] Section 70(5). See also the Subsidy Control Guidance (n 25), para 13.15. See also *Durham Company Limited* (n 27), where the review standard is discussed.

5.2. The Regime in Practice: Early Indicators

The differences between the UK and the EU regimes in terms of means and incentives are likely to be reflected across a number of fronts. The first of these relates to the nature of the cases that shape the law. One can expect the UK system to revolve around more clear-cut cases (in the sense that the status of the measure as a subsidy is not seriously questioned) and fewer frontier cases (that is, cases where there may be a reasonable disagreement about the status of the measure). A second front where institutional divergence may be observed is the sheer volume of cases considered. Where expertise and incentives are dispersed, both claims before courts and referrals to the CMA are likely to be lower than in a system where an administrative body combining investigative and decision-making functions has been expressly entrusted with the mission to develop law and policy. The fact that the standard of review is deferential to authorities means that the probability of a challenge is even lower.

Indicators about the early evolution of the system, while imperfect, are consistent with these intuitions. One aspect that stands out immediately relates to referrals to the CMA. As explained above, subsidies of particular interest are subject to a mandatory referral, whereas subsidies of interest may be subject to a voluntary one. Since January 2023 and out of a total of 103 referrals closed by the end of December 2025, there has not been a single voluntary referral to the CMA. The potential advantages of such a move (such as the legal certainty that it may provide or the fact that it is a signal of good governance) do not seem to have played a role. Mandatory referrals, moreover, concern relatively clear-cut measures, with a clear majority (76%) involving exclusively (69%) or in part (7%) financial assistance in the form of a positive transfer of public resources, such as a grant. Other forms of intervention include (whether exclusively or partially) loans (7%) and capital injections (6%). The most sophisticated cases (arising, in particular, in the energy sector) are legacy EU ones.[102] None of these cases can be categorised as frontier cases that made up the core of the analysis in Chapters 2 and 4.

The paucity of the case law is a second indicator of the potential evolution of the system. Only six challenges (four of them pending at the time of writing) have been brought before the CAT since the entry into force of the regime.[103] One may add two additional cases brought before the High Court of England and Wales for an alleged breach of the obligations assumed by the UK under the TCA.[104]

---

[102] This is true, in particular, of capacity mechanisms in the energy sector. See for instance CMA, *Subsidy Advice Unit Report on the Capacity Market Scheme (as amended in 2025)* (28 March 2025) and so-called contracts for difference. See for instance CMA, *Subsidy Advice Unit Report on the proposed Contracts for Difference Clean Industry Bonus Subsidy Scheme* (20 December 2024).

[103] These are *Durham Company Limited* (n 27); *Mr Aubrey Weis v Greater Manchester Combined Authority* [2025] CAT 41; *The New Lottery Company Ltd and Others v The Gambling Commission* (Case 1730/12/13/25), pending; *Bristol Airport v Welsh Ministers* (Case 1740/12/13/25), pending; *Zenobē Energy Limited v Gas and Electricity Markets Authority* (Case 1754/12/13/25); and *BEK Developments Ltd and Others v Durham County Council* (Case 1760/12/13/25).

[104] *R (British Sugar Plc) v Secretary of State for International Trade* [2022] EWHC 393 (Admin); and *R (British Gas Trading) v Secretary of State for Energy Security and Net Zero* [2023] EWHC 737 (Admin).

The ruling in one of them, *Bulb*, was subsequently appealed before the Court of Appeal.[105] From a substantive standpoint, these cases complement referrals to the CMA. Unlike the latter, they concern genuine frontier cases where it is not clear whether the measure amounts to a subsidy. *Durham Company Limited*, for instance, had to do with the alleged cross-subsidisation of activities within a public body and thus gave rise to the sort of issues considered by the ECJ in *Chronopost*.[106] *Weis*, in turn, revolved around the application of the 'commercial market operator' (or CMO) principle.

6. Conclusions

The UK subsidy control regime exemplifies, first and foremost, the success of the EU model. To a greater or lesser degree, most European countries have now implemented a regime in the area that bears the hallmarks of EU State aid law, a framework for the justification of measures (whether for efficiency or equity reasons) and, in addition, the involvement – at least to some degree – of an independent authority. In several respects, the introduction of the UK regime can be seen as a landmark in the process of convergence around the EU model. First, and as mentioned in the introduction, it is an example of an instance where this process has occurred without the concomitant development of closer legal and economic ties across the board. Second, the UK model, while inspired and informed by its EU counterpart, departs from it in several important respects.

Against this background, the evolution of the UK regime may provide valuable lessons about the EU model, and about the features that make it so distinctive in practice. On the one hand, the substantive dimensions of the Act codify, by and large, the EU regime. While the formal concepts upon which it relies are drawn from the WTO regime, a close reading of the relevant provisions reveals the extent to which it incorporates into UK law the case law of the ECJ. The institutional framework, on the other hand, departs markedly from EU State aid law, which places the European Commission at the centre of the system and provides it with the means to develop its various legal and policy-related dimensions. Under the UK regime, power and expertise are fragmented and shared by several institutional actors. More importantly, none of these actors has both the means and the incentives to test the outer boundaries of the core legal notions. It would therefore not be unreasonable to expect that the UK regime will drift away from its EU counterpart.

It remains to be seen whether institutional divergence will actually result in the UK system moving progressively away, as far as its substantive aspects are

---

[105] *R (British Gas Trading and E.ON) v Secretary of State for Energy Security and Net Zero* [2025] EWCA Civ 209.

[106] Joined Cases C-83/01 P, C-93/01 P and C-94/01 P *Chronopost SA, La Poste and France v Union française de l'express (Ufex) and others*, EU:C:2003:388.

concerned, from the EU regime. If this phenomenon happens, and gaps open up between both sides of the Channel in terms of scope and/or effectiveness, it is not clear whether it will lead to adjustments in the supranational regime or to legal disputes under the TCA. In light of the points addressed in Chapter 6, this aspect of the EU-UK relationship may depend, at least in part, on how the EU State aid regime evolves. If enforcement within the EU permanently adjusts to reflect the new geopolitical reality, observable differences with the UK model would be unlikely to give rise to tensions. One cannot rule out, on the other hand, the deepening of the EU-UK relationship over time. In such a scenario, greater institutional convergence would be one of the most immediate consequences of such a rapprochement.

8

Unilateral Expansion – The EU Foreign Subsidies Regulation

1. State Aid Control for a New World

The success of the system of EU State aid control cannot be seriously questioned. The substantive and institutional choices enshrined in the TFEU, combined with the expertise and experience accumulated over time by the European Commission (hereinafter, the 'Commission'), have created the conditions whereby EU Member States are subject to effective and meaningful constraints in their ability to provide selective advantages to firms. There is no comparable system (with the potential exception of the EEA regime, which is, in essence, an extension of the EU one) in terms of depth, reach and sophistication. A combination of hard and soft law instruments steers EU Member States' expenditure away from measures that only have as their object or effect the distortion of trade and competition (such as operating subsidies). The system also prevents, in a similar vein, the sort of destructive subsidy races described in Chapter 1.

As the evolution of the compatibility assessment traced in Chapter 6 suggests, the continued operation of the regime at full speed cannot be taken for granted. The constraints that EU State aid law places upon public authorities mean that firms based in the EU may not always receive the same degree of support (or in the same circumstances) as their rivals based in third countries. The process of legal convergence discussed in the preceding chapter, where a common acquis organically emerges across the European continent, can only provide a partial response to this challenge. It is unrealistic to expect that the substantive and institutional aspects of the EU system will be extended beyond the immediate vicinity of the EU. It has been discussed in Chapter 1 that the typical free trade agreement concluded by the bloc with a non-European country goes barely beyond the international obligations binding the two partners.

In a sense, the rise and rise of EU State aid law over the past decades might have been the result of a particular set of economic and legal circumstances that cannot be assumed as given – or that they will necessarily last in time. One could argue, from an economic perspective, that the EU system was designed for a world that was both larger and less integrated. The EEC Treaty, after all, was adopted at a time when the integration of EU Member States' economies was ambitious in its own right. With the progress of globalisation, the significant constraints on EU-based firms that facilitated the original objectives of the EU may be progressively more difficult to sustain or justify. In the new landscape, the obligations arising from the WTO regime – much less stringent than its EU counterpart – may prove insufficient to alleviate the anxieties that might result from the absence of a level playing field worldwide. In this sense, the operation of the public sector in China has been a permanent source of concern among Western countries.[1]

These anxieties can only be exacerbated when the WTO regime itself comes under pressure and the spectre of dysfunction looms over its core institutions. The progressive weakening of the rules-based multilateral system, placing legal limits on countries' ability to distort trade by means of, inter alia, subsidies, is one of the most significant developments of the past decade. First the actors that sustained the WTO system – such as its Appellate Body – are no longer in a position to fulfil their function.[2] More importantly, there appears to be no political willingness to turn back the clock to the times when the regime was fully operational.[3] Second, some of the policies implemented by major economic players are in open defiance of the core tenets of the WTO regime. As mentioned in Chapter 1, some aspects of the US Inflation Reduction Act were blatantly in breach of the Agreement on Subsidies and Countervailing Measures (hereinafter, the 'SCM Agreement').[4] The same can be said of the tariff policy introduced by the Trump Administration.[5]

It is against this new technological, economic and legal background that one must make sense of the EU Foreign Subsidies Regulation (hereinafter, the 'Regulation' or the 'regime').[6] This instrument could be accurately described as a unilateral expansion of the core aspects of the EU model to third countries, and this with a view to preventing distortions of competition within the EU internal market. The Regulation empowers the Commission to oversee the award of subsidies by non-EU States, balance their positive and negative effects and take remedial action to ensure that the former outweigh the latter (including, where necessary, divestitures and the repayment of the financial contribution by the recipient). The regime gives the Commission general powers to investigate, on its own motion,

---

[1] See, generally, Usha CV Haley and George T Haley, *Subsidies to Chinese Industry: State Capitalism, Business Strategy, and Trade Policy* (Oxford University Press 2013); and Chad P Bown and Jennifer A Hillman, 'WTO'ing a Resolution to the China Subsidy Problem' (2019) 22 Journal of International Economic Law 557.

[2] For an in-depth analysis, see Petros C Mavroidis, *Industrial Policy, National Security, and the Perilous Plight of the WTO* (Oxford University Press 2025).

[3] Alan Beattie, 'A crumbling system of trade rules awaits Trump's wrecking ball' *Financial Times* (14 November 2024).

[4] Giulia Claudia Leonelli and Francesco Clora, 'Retooling the regulation of net-zero subsidies: lessons from the US Inflation Reduction Act' (2024) 27 Journal of International Economic Law 441.

[5] Nicolas Lamp, 'What President Trump's "Reciprocal" Tariffs Mean for International (Trade) Law' (EJIL: Talk! Blog of the European Journal of International Law, 30 April 2025).

[6] Regulation (EU) 2022/2560 of the European Parliament and of the Council of 14 December 2022 on foreign subsidies distorting the internal market [2022] OJ L330/1.

actual or potential distortions of competition resulting from these measures.[7] In addition, it introduces ad hoc procedures that apply in the context of concentrations and public procurement procedures involving a recipient of foreign subsidies.

The Preamble to the Regulation does not hide the fact that its adoption is in part a response to the substantive and institutional limits of the WTO regime. From a substantive perspective, the effectiveness of the SCM Agreement will always be handicapped by the fact that it only applies to trade in goods. Therefore, distortions arising from the subsidisation of investments, services and financial flows would fall outside of its scope.[8] From an institutional standpoint, and as mentioned in Chapter 1, the WTO regime revolves around State-to-State disputes, the adequate functioning of which is contingent on the continued operation of a set of enforcement structures that are under growing pressure. As the multilateral rules-based order comes under pressure, the Preamble justifies the adoption of the Regulation as an assertion of the EU's open strategic autonomy.[9]

What follows seeks to present systematically the features of the Regulation in light of the EU State aid system, upon which it is modelled, and the WTO regime, from which it also draws inspiration, albeit to a lesser extent. The picture that emerges from the analysis is one of ambitious expansion. In spite of some adjustments that are in some instances inevitable (insofar as the Regulation can only bind recipients operating within the EU internal market) and in other instances desirable (to manage the flow of cases), the foreign subsidies regime captures a broad range of economic activities, as reflected in the large number of notifications received following its adoption.[10] In addition, it allows for the imposition of far-reaching remedies, which give the Commission ample powers to tackle distortions

[7] ibid, Recital 8: 'To ensure a level playing field throughout the internal market and consistency in the application of this Regulation, the Commission is the sole authority competent to apply this Regulation. The Commission should have the power to examine any foreign subsidy, to the extent it is in the scope of this Regulation, in any sector of the economy on its own initiative, relying thereby on information from all available sources [...]'.

[8] ibid, Recital 5: 'No existing Union instruments address distortions caused by foreign subsidies. Trade defence instruments enable the Commission to act when subsidised goods are imported into the Union, but not when foreign subsidies take the form of subsidised investments, or when services and financial flows are concerned [...]'.

[9] ibid, Recital 7, where the EU legislature states that: 'The proper application and enforcement of this Regulation are to contribute to the resilience of the internal market against distortions caused by foreign subsidies and thereby contribute to the Union's open strategic autonomy'. See also Joan Miró, 'Responding to the global disorder: the EU's quest for open strategic autonomy' (2023) 37 Global Society 315.

[10] See Axel Gutermuth, Charlotte Simphal and Sara Routsi, 'The Foreign Subsidies Regulation: Where Do We Stand 18 Months Into Implementation of the Notification Obligations' (Arnold & Porter Advisories, 30 May 2025), available at www.arnoldporter.com. According to the authors, 'By early April 2025, the Commission had received approximately 140 notifications related to M&A transactions, and by the end of April 2025, over 2,000 submissions related to public procurement procedures (the vast majority of which – precisely 1,734 – were declarations, with only 322 being notifications, which are required when foreign subsidies exceed a EUR 4 million threshold)'.

of competition (including the possibility of ordering divestitures or a compulsory licensing duty).

From a broader EU law perspective, the question is whether, and if so to what extent, the foreign subsidies regime will influence its internal EU counterpart, and thus whether substantive convergence will result from the expansion of the EU model to third countries. While the legislature designed two different systems with similar, but not identical, scope and operation, dynamics may change as soon as the body of administrative law and practice issued under the Regulation becomes an integral and growing element of the landscape. In practice, it might not be easy to sustain the application of two substantive standards depending on whether the awarding authority is an EU or a non-EU one. In the same vein, cross-fertilisation between regimes could potentially make it possible to remedy potential frictions and inconsistencies and, as part of the process, correct some aspects of EU State aid law.

2. Mapping the Differences with EU State Aid Law

2.1. From Awarding Bodies to Recipients

EU State aid law applies to, and binds, the EU Member States. This conclusion is apparent from a plain reading of Article 107(1) TFEU (which introduces the principle of incompatibility of State aid with the internal market) and Article 108 TFEU (which provides for the kernel of an institutional framework). In addition, the EU courts have regularly reminded that the procedure revolves around a dialogue between the Commission and the EU Member State concerned. Similarly, any obligations (in particular, the duty to inform the former of any plans to grant or alter aid and, where necessary, to recover unlawful and incompatible aid) are imposed on the latter. The beneficiary of the aid is treated as any other of the 'parties concerned' (or 'interested parties') and will become involved at the formal stage of the procedure only to the extent that is necessary for the purposes of the investigation.

The foreign subsidies regime, by contrast, places the recipient of the financial contribution at its heart. For instance, it is for the undertaking concerned to notify the Commission in advance of any plans to conclude a concentration and to take part in a public procurement procedure. Similarly, if the enforcement of EU State aid law revolves around a dialogue between the Commission and the EU Member State, procedural obligations under the Regulation are imposed, by and large, on the recipient of a financial contribution by a third country.[11] This difference, in any event, is most apparent in relation to the remedies that might be imposed where it appears that they are necessary to address the distortion of

---

[11] Foreign Subsidies Regulation (n 6), in particular Articles 13, 14, 15, 21, 25, 29, 36 and 39.

competition resulting from the foreign subsidy. Redressive measures within the meaning of Article 7 of the Regulation may be imposed on the recipient.

This difference between the foreign subsidies regime and EU State aid law is, as mentioned in the preceding section, an inevitability. EU law may be imposed on undertakings operating within the internal market but not directly on third countries. Any aspect of the investigation involving the latter must be undertaken with its consent or, alternatively, must be confined to non-binding, high-level dialogue. In this sense, Article 15 provides that the Commission may, in order to carry out its duties under the Regulation, conduct inspections outside the territory of the EU.[12] This possibility, however, may only materialise where the third country has been 'officially notified' and 'raises no objections'. Pursuant to Article 37, in turn, the Commission may engage in a dialogue with a third country that is either suspected of the award of 'repeated foreign subsidies' or where there are several enforcement actions identifying measures originating in the said third country.

2.2. Structure and Operation of the Substantive Provisions

One of the most apparent differences between the Regulation and its EU counterpart relates to the way in which the core substantive provision is structured. As explained in Chapter 1, the conditions for a measure to be subject to EU State aid control are all contained in Article 107(1) TFEU. This is true not just of the substantive conditions considered at length in Part I of this volume (the imputability to the State of a selective advantage that involves the use of State resources), but also of what are sometimes called the jurisdictional conditions (that is, the distortion of competition and the effect on trade between Member States conditions, briefly addressed in Chapter 1). According to a consistent line of case law, the characterisation of a measure as State aid within the meaning of Article 107(1) TFEU requires that all these elements be present in a given case.[13]

The foreign subsidies regime, by contrast, disentangles the two sets of conditions. Accordingly, the characterisation of a measure as a foreign subsidy within the meaning of the Regulation is considered in light of the substantive elements set out in Article 3 (and which, as explained below, are similar in their scope and operation to their rough equivalents in EU State aid law). The question of whether a foreign subsidy within the meaning of Article 3 leads, or could lead,

---

[12] ibid, Article 15: 'In order to carry out the duties assigned to it by this Regulation, the Commission may conduct inspections in the territory of a third country, provided that the government of that third country has been officially notified and raises no objection to the inspection [...]'.

[13] Case C-280/00 *Altmark Trans GmbH and Regierungspräsidium Magdeburg v Nahverkehrsgesellschaft Altmark GmbH, and Oberbundesanwalt beim Bundesverwaltungsgericht*, EU:C:2003:415, para 74; Case C-300/16 P *Commission v Frucona Košice a.s.*, EU:C:2017:706, para 19; Case C C-128/16 P *Commission v Spain and others*, EU:C:2018:591, para 35.

to a distortion in the internal market (and therefore, whether remedial intervention is warranted) is considered at a subsequent stage, in light of the conditions defined in Articles 4 and 5 of the Regulation. The distinction between the two stages of the analysis (classification, on the one hand, and assessment of whether it has the potential to negatively affect competition within the internal market, on the other) became apparent in the Commission decision in *e&/PPF Telecom Group*.[14]

The bifurcated treatment of the substantive and jurisdictional dimensions of a financial contribution betrays the hybrid origins of the foreign subsidies regime. While the Regulation seeks to export, in essence, the operation of EU State aid law, some of its features are directly inspired by the WTO Regime. From a formal standpoint, the definition of subsidy within the meaning of Article 3 borrows directly from Article 1 of the SCM Agreement. The concepts (such as 'financial contribution', as opposed to 'aid'; and 'benefit', as opposed to 'advantage' or 'favouring') can be traced back to that legal provision. The same can be said of the very bifurcation of the substantive and jurisdictional conditions. Under the WTO regime, the questions of whether a measure amounts to a subsidy and whether the said subsidy is either prohibited or actionable are considered separately.

Unlike the WTO regime, however, the Regulation expressly allows for the balancing of the positive and negative effects of the subsidy and, on that basis, for the Commission to decide whether it may be justified to impose redressive measures. It is, in this regard, in line with the law and practice under the EU State aid system. Pursuant to Article 6, the Commission may engage in this balancing exercise, taking into account the policy interest objectives to which the foreign subsidy may contribute. While the provision itself is silent about the considerations that might be taken into account as part of this assessment, the Preamble suggests that these are efficiency- and equity-related objectives similar to the ones that are accounted for under both Articles 107(1) and 106(2) TFEU. Recital 21 refers, more precisely, to a 'high level of environmental protection' and of 'social standards', in addition to the promotion of 'research and development'.

Table 8.1 is an attempt to summarise the hybrid nature of the foreign subsidies regime. It shares features with both the EU and WTO systems. The lineage it shares with the latter (which, as explained above, is most apparent in the bifurcation of the substantive and jurisdictional elements and in the formal aspects of the legal concepts around which the notion of subsidy revolves) cannot come as a surprise. The SCM Agreement is the gold standard that features in trade agreements around the world, including those concluded by the EU. In that sense, embracing the concepts enshrined in WTO law signals not just the application of a set of notions with which governments and stakeholders are familiar, but avoids the impression that it is exporting its own substantive approach beyond its borders.

---

[14] Commission Decision of 24 September 2024 in Case FS.100011 – *e&/PPF Telecom Group*.

The commonalities with the EU regime, on the other hand, allow the Commission to manage the flow of cases and address potential distortions more effectively than under the SCM Agreement.

Table 8.1 The hybrid origins of the EU Foreign Subsidies Regulation

System	Substantive conditions	Bifurcation of conditions	Balancing
EU State aid law	State resources Imputability Selective advantage	No	Yes
WTO law	Financial contribution 'by a government' Specific benefit	Yes	No
Foreign subsidies regime	Financial contribution Attributability Limited benefit	Yes	Yes

2.3. Trigger of the Procedural Obligations

The EU State aid system is designed to ensure that incompatible aid is never put into effect.[15] The administrative procedure before the Commission is expressly crafted to attain this aim.[16] What triggers intervention, therefore, is the very award of measures falling within the scope of Article 107(1) TFEU, whether implementation takes place lawfully or unlawfully. The Regulation, by contrast, does not come into play whenever a foreign subsidy is awarded. The primary purpose of the regime is instead to prevent distortions of the internal market. This point of divergence is reflected in the design and wording of the provisions. It appears, in particular, that there is no obligation to systematically notify all measures qualifying as a foreign subsidy within the meaning of Article 3 and, similarly, there is no procedure to systematically consider, ex post, financial contributions by third parties.

In line with this difference in focus, the Regulation provides for two specific ex ante procedures relating, as mentioned above, to concentrations and public tenders. The trigger, in both cases, is not the award of the foreign subsidy as such, but the transaction with which it is associated, and which might lead to a distortion in the internal market. What is more, the said distortion cannot simply be presumed to be present in every instance a foreign subsidy is awarded. As a general

---

[15] Case C-199/06 *CELF and others v Société internationale de diffusion et d'édition (SIDE)*, EU:C:2008:79, para 47.

[16] See in this sense Article 16 of Council Regulation (EU) 2015/1589 of 13 July 2015 laying down detailed rules for the application of Article 108 of the Treaty on the Functioning of the European Union (codification) [2015] OJ L248/9.

rule, and pursuant to Article 4, the negative impact on the internal market will have to be established on a case-by-case basis, and this in light of the indicators set out in the provision. Accordingly, only a subset of foreign subsidies, identified in Article 5, is deemed to have sufficient distortive potential for the presumption to apply. The analysis of distortions of competition is considered at length below.

2.4. Outcome of Investigations

The difference in focus between the foreign subsidies regime and the EU State aid system is also reflected in the outcome of investigations. The default remedy under the latter is the recovery of unlawfully granted measures.[17] The Court of Justice (hereinafter, the 'Court' or the 'ECJ') has consistently held that the rationale underpinning this outcome is not to inflict a penalty on the EU Member State or the recipient, but to give effect to Article 108(2) TFEU, pursuant to which unlawfully granted aid that the Commission finds to be incompatible with the internal market is to be abolished.[18] The goal of intervention, in this sense, is restorative. It seeks, in other words, to revert to the market conditions that existed prior to the award.[19] Remedial intervention under EU State aid law is, moreover, relatively inflexible in relation to recovery: the Commission is under a duty to require it from the EU Member State unless it runs counter to a general principle of EU law.[20]

Since it places the focus on distortions in the internal market caused by foreign subsidies, rather than the latter as such, the Regulation allows for more flexibility in relation to the administration of remedies (that is, redressive measures within the meaning of Article 7). The repayment of the foreign subsidy is just one of the alternatives that the Commission has the discretion to impose, where deemed necessary. Put differently, abolishing the subsidy is neither an objective nor a requirement for the adequate operation of the regime. Other interventions are compatible with the award of the foreign subsidy, provided that they remedy its negative effects. Administrative action under the Regulation is, in this regard, closer in nature to competition law.[21] Remedies, under the foreign subsidies regime, are not restorative. They seek, instead, to preserve a level playing field and,

---

[17] ibid.

[18] Commission Notice on the recovery of unlawful and incompatible State aid [2019] OJ C247/1, para 36. National courts may order the recovery of unlawfully granted State aid without examining their compatibility (the latter being an exclusive prerogative of the Commission). See in this sense *CELF* (n 15) and Commission Notice on the enforcement of State aid rules by national courts [2021] OJ C305/1.

[19] Case C-75/97 *Belgium v Commission*, EU:C:1999:311, para 65.

[20] Article 16 of the Procedural Regulation (n 16).

[21] For a discussion, see Pablo Ibáñez Colomo, 'Remedies in EU Antitrust Law' (2025) 21 Journal of Competition Law & Economics 137.

in the same vein, ensure that the recipient of the foreign subsidy competes on the merits within the internal market.[22]

3. Substantive Features of the EU Foreign Subsidies Regulation

3.1. The Notion of Foreign Subsidy

3.1.1. *Financial Contribution and Attributability*

It has been mentioned above that the notion of foreign subsidy has a hybrid origin. From a formal standpoint, the concepts around which it revolves appear to be drawn, by and large, from the SCM Agreement. From a substantive standpoint, on the other hand, the influence of EU State aid law is present at every turn. It would be natural for the Commission to shape the notion in light of the relevant case law and administrative practice interpreting Article 107(1) TFEU. The Preamble is, in fact, explicit on this point. Recital 9 provides that the 'Regulation should be applied and interpreted in light of the relevant Union legislation, including that relating to State aid'. The fact that Article 3 refers to a benefit, as opposed to an advantage, or the fact that it avoids making an explicit reference to selectivity (and instead mentions that the measure must be 'limited' to one or more firms or industries), are not decisive.

Nothing, therefore, appears to preclude a consistent interpretation of the notion of foreign subsidy and that of State aid. One of the seeming differences between the two is the fact that the Regulation demands, pursuant to Article 3(1), that intervention take the form of a 'financial contribution'. The provision does not, however, refer to 'State resources', the presence of which must be established for Article 107(1) TFEU to come into play. As a result of this difference, it has been speculated that the notion of foreign subsidy could, at least in some respects, be broader than that of State aid.[23] It is true that the examples of financial contributions expressly mentioned in Article 3(2) all relate to instances that involve the use of third countries' resources. The provision mentions the 'transfer of funds or liabilities' (including not just grants but also, inter alia, loans, capital injections and guarantees), the 'foregoing of revenue that is otherwise due' (as in the case of a tax exemption but also where the third country awards special or exclusive rights

---

[22] Foreign Subsidies Regulation (n 6), Recitals 6 and 8.

[23] See in particular Morris Schonberg, 'The EU Foreign Subsidies Regulation' (2022) 21 European State Aid Law Quarterly 143; and Lena Hornkohl, 'Protecting the internal market from subsidisation with the EU state aid regime and the foreign subsidies regulation: two sides of the same coin?' (2023) 14 Journal of European Competition Law & Practice 137.

to a firm) and the 'provision of goods and services or the purchase of goods and services'.

It is equally clear from Article 3, however, that the foreign subsidies regime is based on a broad understanding of the concept of a financial contribution. Thus, the decisive consideration is not so much the origin of the resources (and, more precisely, whether they come from the budget of a public authority), but whether the third country (or sub-national entity within it) can rely on them to attain its aims. This conclusion is apparent from Article 3(2), insofar as it clarifies that 'financial contribution[s]' include not just resources coming from national or sub-national entities, but also those provided by a 'foreign public entity' and by 'a private entity'. From this perspective, therefore, there is no inconsistency between the concept of financial contribution and the expansive understanding of the 'State resources' condition endorsed in *Stardust Marine* in the context of Article 107(1) TFEU.[24] If anything, the scope of the former could be broader, at least if construed in light of WTO law.[25]

Where the case law interpreting Article 107(1) TFEU refers to the 'imputability' of a measure to the State, Article 3(2) speaks of attributability – which, incidentally, is not a concept borrowed from the SCM Agreement.[26] The provision identifies two factual scenarios considered by the Court in the case law that followed *Stardust Marine*. Pursuant to the Regulation, one of these scenarios arises where the measure is adopted by a 'foreign public entity', which is not defined but which presumably includes, among others, bodies such as publicly-owned banks and utilities (at issue in cases like *van der Kooy*[27]). The second scenario relates to instances where the financial contribution is formally provided by a private entity, with which the Court was confronted in, inter alia, *Pearle*[28] and *Banca Tercas*.[29] The criteria to establish attributability do not come across as fundamentally different from the set of indicators defined by the Court in *Stardust Marine*. In this sense, Article 3(2) identifies elements such as 'the characteristics of the entity and the legal and economic environment prevailing in the State in which the entity operates, including the government's role in the economy'.[30]

Because it was a relatively uncomplicated case, the Commission decision in *e&/ PPF Telecom Group* does not shed much light on the financial contribution element

---

[24] Case C-482/99 *France v Commission*, EU:C:2002:294 (hereinafter, '*Stardust Marine*').

[25] See in this sense Schonberg (n 23) and Hornkohl (n 23). For a more extensive analysis, see Luca Rubini, *The Definition of Subsidy and State Aid: WTO and EC Law in Comparative Perspective* (Oxford University Press 2009).

[26] See Agreement on Subsidies and Countervailing Measures [1994] UNTS 1869/14, Article 1(1.1)(a)(1)(iv), which refers to instances where the government 'entrusts or directs a private body to carry out one or more of the type of functions' identified in the preceding sub-paragraphs.

[27] Joined Cases C-67/85, C-68/85 and C-70/85 *Kwekerij Gebroeders van der Kooy BV and others v Commission*, EU:C:1988:38.

[28] Case C-345/02 *Pearle BV, Hans Prijs Optiek Franchise BV and Rinck Opticiëns BV v Hoofdbedrijfschap Ambachten*, EU:C:2004:448.

[29] Case C-425/19 P *Commission v Italy, Banca Popolare di Bari SCpA and Fondo interbancario di tutela dei depositi*, EU:C:2021:154.

[30] See in this sense the criteria identified in *Stardust Marine* (n 24), paras 55–56.

of the analysis. The case considered several interventions but ultimately focused on the award of an unlimited guarantee by the third country.[31] The legal regime to which the firm was subject, together with the fact that the said firm owned strategic assets, created the expectation that the government would intervene to ensure its continued viability. Against this background, establishing an actual (insofar as guarantees are typically granted against remuneration) and potential (in the event of insolvency) financial contribution was straightforward. In fact, loan guarantees are expressly referred to in Article 3.[32] Attributability was no less straightforward to establish in the case. On the one hand, the unlimited guarantee was found to originate in the insolvency rules of the third country in question. On the other, the choice by the firm not to revert to the ordinary insolvency proceedings was one made by the State via a government agency.

3.1.2. *Benefit*

Article 3(2) of the Regulation provides some examples of the sort of measures that may amount to a benefit, including the 'setting off of operating losses', 'debt forgiveness' and 'tax exemptions'. However, the provision is not particularly explicit about the meaning of the concept. The Preamble, on the other hand, suggests that, just like an advantage within the meaning of Article 107(1) TFEU, a benefit within the meaning of the Regulation is a measure that departs from normality. More precisely, Recital 13 provides that a 'financial contribution should be considered to confer a benefit on an undertaking if it could not have been obtained on normal market conditions'. This wording implies that financial contributions in the form of, inter alia, loans, guarantees and the sale and acquisition of assets will be assessed under the 'market economy operator' principle (or variation thereof).[33]

In fact, some of the approaches to the 'market economy operator' principle discussed in Chapter 3 are mentioned in Recital 13. For instance, it is clear from the Article 107(1) TFEU case law that there is no advantage where the public authority organises a genuine tender procedure. This same idea is codified in the Preamble, which states that a 'competitive, transparent and non-discriminatory tender procedure' is presumed not to involve the award of a benefit. In addition, it refers expressly to indirect methods for assessing whether the measure departs from normal market conditions. Recital 13 expressly mentions benchmarking as a method and identifies scenarios such as 'the investment practice of private investors, financing rates obtainable on the market, a comparable tax treatment, or the adequate remuneration for a given good or service'.

e&/PPF Telecom Group complements the Preamble in that it addresses the specific instance of an unlimited guarantee. As discussed in Chapter 3, such a measure can be presumed to provide an advantage within the meaning of

---

[31] *e&/PPF Telecom Group* (n 14).
[32] ibid, para 116. See also Article 3(2)(a) of the Foreign Subsidies Regulation (n 5).
[33] See in this sense Schonberg (n 23).

Article 107(1) TFEU, insofar as no 'market economy operator' would have the incentive to provide support that is not limited in time and/or amount. In its decision in *e&/PPF Telecom Group*, the Commission focuses on the impact that the financial support necessarily has on the credit status of the recipient and on its improved ability to receive loans and use debt.[34] In the specific circumstances of the case, the existence of a benefit was compounded by two factors: first, the fact that the undertaking did not pay a fee for the guarantee (and, moreover, that there were no circumstances in which a fee could be determined);[35] and, second, there were no limits as to the risks incurred by the third country.[36]

The Preamble is less explicit about financial contributions that do not arise in the context of market transactions. Article 3(2) identifies a number of scenarios where the 'market economy operator' principle would not be of relevance. To begin with, the provision mentions 'compensation for financial burdens imposed by public authorities'. These instances sometimes amount to an advantage under Article 107(1) TFEU, namely where the conditions laid down in *Altmark* are not met. It would not be unreasonable to assume that the same principles apply where a third country awards a financial contribution in the same context. This is so, in particular, where the compensation involves the organisation of a genuine tender procedure. Second, Article 3(2) suggests that a benefit within the meaning of the Regulation is awarded where special or exclusive rights are granted 'without adequate remuneration'. This reference evokes the scenario at issue in *Commission v Netherlands*,[37] where the EU Member State awarded emission allowances free of charge and which is expressly mentioned in the Commission Notice on the notion of aid.[38]

3.1.3. *Limited in Law or in Fact*

A financial contribution must be 'limited, in law or in fact, to one or more undertakings or industries' for it to qualify as a foreign subsidy within the meaning of Article 3. The Preamble clarifies that this condition is different from the question of whether a measure confers a benefit on the recipient.[39] In other respects, however, both the Preamble and the provision are far less specific about the scope of the provision. This said, it is valuable that the Regulation makes it explicit that this condition may be met as a matter of law or fact. Accordingly, instances of de facto selectivity such as those discussed in Chapter 4 (in particular in light of the *Gibraltar* case law[40]) could potentially qualify as foreign subsidies within the

---

[34] *e&/PPF Telecom Group* (n 14), para 123.

[35] ibid, para 126.

[36] ibid, para 128.

[37] Case C-279/08 P *Commission v Netherlands*, EU:C:2011:551.

[38] Commission Notice on the notion of State aid as referred to in Article 107(1) of the Treaty on the Functioning of the European Union [2016] OJ C262/1, para 53.

[39] Foreign Subsidies Regulation (n 6), Recital 11.

[40] Joined Cases C-106/09 P and C-107/09 P *Commission v Government of Gibraltar and United Kingdom*, EU:C:2011:732.

meaning of Article 3. One should note in this regard that the SCM Agreement also comprises instances of de facto selectivity.[41]

It remains to be seen how this condition will be interpreted in the case law and administrative practice. The analysis in *eɔ/PPF Telecom Group* was relatively straightforward on this point of law. The Commission noted that the unlimited guarantee was only available to a limited number of recipients, namely those that were wholly owned by the federal or local authorities in the relevant third country.[42] In such circumstances, the sort of complexities that were addressed in Chapter 4 did not arise. That said, it is reasonable to expect that the case law interpreting the concept (and in particular the three-step test around which the default approach revolves) will provide the basis for the assessment. This is so not just because the foreign subsidies regime is enforced by the Commission, but because it is arguably the most developed body of law from which to draw inspiration.[43]

3.2. Distortions in the Internal Market

3.2.1. *A Departure from* Philip Morris

The single most significant difference between the foreign subsidies regime and EU State aid law relates to the assessment of the distortion. This is true not simply because of the bifurcation of the analysis, discussed above, but because of the requisite threshold to trigger intervention. As explained in Chapter 1, the *Philip Morris* doctrine that applies in the context of Article 107(1) TFEU means that the jurisdictional conditions (namely the distortion of competition and the effect on trade between EU Member States) are deemed to be met once it is shown that a selective advantage involving the use of State resources and imputable to a public authority has been granted. The same is not true under the foreign subsidies regime. The Preamble makes clear, in Recital 17, that '[u]nlike State aid granted by a Member State, foreign subsidies are not generally prohibited'.

3.2.2. *Articles 4 and 5: A Spectrum of Scenarios*

The implication, as pointed out above, is that, as a rule, it will be necessary to conduct a case-by-case assessment to establish a distortion in the internal market. Setting a higher threshold of effects provides the Commission with an additional legal tool to manage the regime and focus on the most problematic cases. The Regulation is hardwired in this sense. Articles 4 and 5 provide, in effect, a hierarchy of scenarios that range from those that are presumed to have

---

[41] Article 2(2.1)(c) of the SCM Agreement (n 26).
[42] *eɔ/PPF Telecom Group* (n 14), para 132.
[43] This is a point made in Schonberg (n 23).

distortive effects to those that are assumed to fall outside the scope of the regime. Figure 8.1 seeks to capture the whole spectrum of scenarios. The default scenario, depicted in the middle of the spectrum, is the case-by-case assessment of the impact of practices in light of the factors identified in Article 4. The Regulation relies on a variety of techniques for the rest of the scenarios.

Figure 8.1 Distortions in the internal market – a spectrum of scenarios

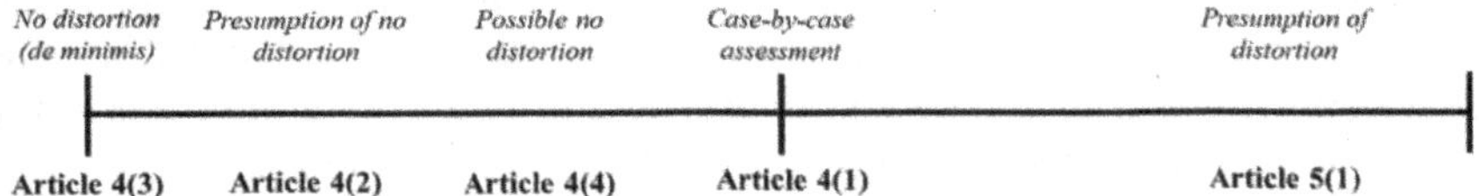

The least problematic foreign subsidies are those found towards the left end of the spectrum. First, Article 4(3) excludes outright from the scope of the regime so-called de minimis measures, which are defined by reference to the Regulation dealing with the matter in EU State aid law. Second, Article 4(2) introduces a presumption pursuant to which a foreign subsidy not exceeding EUR 4 million and granted over a period of three years is unlikely to distort the internal market. Finally, Article 4(4) provides that measures aimed at 'making good the damage caused by natural disasters or exceptional occurrences' may be 'considered not to distort the internal market'. This last scenario does not introduce a presumption strictly speaking, and this insofar as it gives the Commission some leeway in the assessment (and which it does not enjoy under Article 107(2) TFEU).

At the right end of the spectrum, one can identify measures that are presumed to distort the internal market, and which are set out in Article 5(1). The scenarios identified in the provision concern, generally speaking, instances where the very object of intervention is the distortion of competition and which, by the same token, are unlikely to advance a public interest objective. These include support to ailing undertakings, the award of unlimited guarantees (whether in time or amount), export financing measures departing from the OECD standards, as well as foreign subsidies specifically aimed at favouring a concentration or the submission of an 'unduly advantageous tender'). Since these measures are merely presumed (not assumed) to distort the internal market, the undertaking subject to an investigation can produce evidence showing that, in the specific circumstances of the case, the contentious award does not meet the requisite threshold.[44]

The rest of scenarios are subject to the default case-by-case analysis, which is undertaken in light of the (non-exhaustive) factors identified in Article 4(1). The overarching question around which the assessment revolves relates to whether – and, if so, to what extent – the foreign subsidy strengthens the position of the recipient within the internal market, thereby distorting competition therein. There is

---

[44] Article 5(2) of the Foreign Subsidies Regulation (n 6).

a two-step exercise that is implicit in the letter of the provision (and that was confirmed in a Staff Working Document issued by the Commission[45]). It appears, first, that it is necessary to establish a causal link between the measure and the (actual or potential[46]) improved position of the undertaking (that is, that the latter is attributable to the former). Second, intervention by the third country will need to be significant enough for it to affect competition within the internal market. The Regulation, however, is silent about the requisite threshold of effects. The two-step assessment is captured in Figure 8.2.

Figure 8.2 Distortions in the internal market – two-step assessment

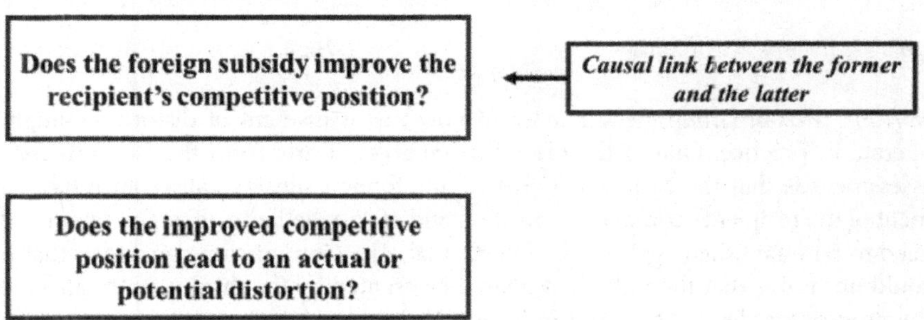

Instead of defining a threshold, Article 4(1) and the Preamble identify a number of contextual indicators that allow the Commission to calibrate the probability of a distortion of competition. The factors expressly mentioned in the Regulation include the amount involved (the larger the amount, in absolute or relative terms, the more likely the distortion), the nature of the subsidy (in particular, operating subsidies are known to be particularly harmful[47]), the position of the undertaking within the market or sectors concerned (the higher its degree of activity within the internal market, the more likely it is that the subsidy will cause distortions). The Preamble adds other factors, such as the structural features of the market. As the experience of enforcement under Article 107 TFEU shows,[48] distortions are more likely in industries characterised by overcapacity.[49] Figure 8.3 summarises these factors.

---

[45] Commission Staff Working Document: Initial clarifications on the application of Article 4(1), Article 6 and Article 27(1) of Regulation (EU) 2022/2560 on foreign subsidies distorting the internal market COM(2024) 201 final.

[46] Article 4(1) of the Foreign Subsidies Regulation (n 6) chooses the expression 'liable to improve'.

[47] Recital 19 of the Foreign Subsidies Regulation (n 6) ('If a foreign subsidy is granted for operating costs, it seems more likely to cause distortions than if it is granted for investment costs').

[48] Guidelines on State aid for rescuing and restructuring non-financial undertakings in difficulty [2014] OJ C249/1.

[49] Recital 19 of the Foreign Subsidies Regulation (n 6) ('Foreign subsidies in markets characterised by overcapacity or leading to overcapacity by sustaining uneconomic assets or by encouraging investment in capacity expansions that would otherwise not have been built are likely to cause distortions').

Figure 8.3 Distortions in the internal market – factors identified in Article 4(1)

Distortion less likely	**Distortion more likely**
–	+
Low amount	*High amount*
Investment	*Operating*
Horizontal	*Targeted*
No overcapacity	*Overcapacity*
Low activity or weak position	*High activity or strong position*

e&/PPF Telecom Group gives a sense of how the assessment of distortions might operate in practice. One of the ideas that emerges clearly from the Commission's assessment is that the two steps (whether the foreign subsidy causes an improvement of the recipient's competitive position and, if so, whether it affects competition) need to be established against a counterfactual. The Commission concluded that it could not prove that the unlimited guarantee granted by the third country affected the process that led to the acquisition of PPF Telecom by e&. It noted, against the relevant counterfactual, that the transaction could have occurred even in the absence of the unlimited guarantee. It emphasised two factors in support of its conclusion: first, the fact that the acquisition of the target firm could have occurred in the absence of the guarantee;[50] and, second, that there were no other potential acquirers that were outbid in the process.[51]

On the other hand, the Commission concluded that the transaction would lead to a distortion following its completion. Even though the foreign subsidy involved was, as mentioned above, an unlimited guarantee, which is presumptively a source of negative effects, the Commission conducted an extensive analysis on both how the measure would improve the position of the target and how it would alter the dynamics of competition within the internal market.[52] The assessment proceeded in three steps. First, it identified the activities (not necessarily markets in the competition law sense) that would be affected by the concentration.[53] Second, it explained the mechanisms by which the acquisition would improve the competitive position of the new entity. The improved position would be reflected, in particular, in the credit ratings obtained by the target.[54] Finally, it considered the impact on competition in the relevant industry

---

[50] *e&/PPF Telecom Group* (n 14), para 284.
[51] ibid, para 282.
[52] ibid, para 320.
[53] ibid, para 304.
[54] ibid, para 326.

(telecommunications), which is characterised by the substantial investments required.[55]

The assessment of the actual or potential distortions in the internal market is central to the foreign subsidies regime. Its shape and reach are likely to depend, by and large, on how it is construed. The Commission must strike a balance between effective enforcement and administrability. More importantly, it is imperative for it to articulate, in advance, how the balance struck will be applied on a case-by-case basis. This need is all the more pressing considering that the analytical framework is, in many respects, a novel one. In accordance with the terms of the Regulation, the Commission conducted a consultation with a view to adopting Guidelines aimed, inter alia, at shedding light on how it intends to assess the distortions caused by a foreign subsidy (both in general and in the specific context of public procurement procedures).[56]

3.2.3. *The Assessment of Distortions in the Guidelines*

The process that led to the adoption of a set of Guidelines was completed – in accordance with the terms of Article 46 of the Regulation – in January 2026. The document[57] gives a sense of the Commission's approach to the assessment of distortions moving forward. Some of the overarching ideas that were incipient or implicit in the Regulation are developed in the instrument. In particular, the Commission defines a spectrum of scenarios based on their likely impact on the competitive position of the recipient. At one end of the spectrum, the Guidelines identify subsidies that are not deemed liable to have such effects.[58] These include not just insignificant interventions (including de minimis subsidies sensu stricto and other measures that are minor in relative terms), but also subsidies aimed at addressing a market failure outside the EU as well as those having a social character and those seeking to remedy the consequences of natural disasters or exceptional occurrences within the meaning of Article 4(4) of the Regulation. As a result of this choice, the Guidelines bring the approach under the Regulation in line with that applying under Article 107(2) TFEU.

The Guidelines are valuable insofar as that they break down the analytical framework enshrined in the Regulation into a number of operational sub-steps, and also due to the fact that they show how the overarching principles are to be applied

---

[55] ibid, paras 344–350, where the Commission explains, in para 344, that 'the Parties expect to have to undertake large investments to support their activities in the internal market in the provision of telecommunications services' and that such a finding 'is consistent with the Commission's anticipations and industry expectations'.

[56] Commission, 'Commission launches consultations on guidelines under the Foreign Subsidies Regulation' IP/25/685 (Brussels, 5 March 2025).

[57] Guidelines on the application of certain provisions of Regulation (EU) 2022/2560 of the European Parliament and of the Council on foreign subsidies distorting the internal market C(2026) 42 final.

[58] ibid, para 33.

in several factual scenarios. The case-by-case assessment of whether the subsidy improves the recipient's competitive position is based on a divide between targeted and non-targeted measures. The first category – also the most likely to distort the internal market – encompasses two separate situations. One of these scenarios relates to instances where the recipient 'uses or intends to use the foreign subsidies for its economic activities in the internal market'.[59] Evidence in this sense is deemed conclusive by the Commission and does not require further assessment. This is so regardless of the nature, scope or purpose of the measure.[60]

A subsidy is also deemed to be a 'targeted' one where an analysis of its 'purpose, nature and scope' (or of 'other relevant elements') reveals that it supports, objectively speaking, the recipient's activities within the internal market.[61] The Guidelines identify a number of scenarios that give a sense of the boundaries of this category. In particular, a measure granted to support directly economic activity within the internal market (such as a measure subsidising the manufacturing or distribution activities of the recipient in an EU Member State[62]) is characterised as a targeted subsidy. Measures that support activities do not take place within the internal market but indirectly benefit economic activities that do (such as the subsidisation of research and development occurring in a third country, with the results indirectly benefitting the recipient's activities within the internal market) are also treated as such.[63]

Subsidies are deemed to be 'non-targeted' – and therefore less likely to improve the competitive position of the recipient in the internal market – where they are neither aimed at supporting economic activity in the said internal market or where there is no clear evidence suggesting how the recipient 'uses or intends' to use them. In these circumstances, the Commission commits to analysing, on the basis of a case-by-case assessment, whether the subsidy is liable to improve the firm's competitive position within the internal market by allowing it to engage in cross-subsidisation.[64] The Guidelines provide a non-exhaustive list of indicators which includes, among others, factors such as the 'design and conditions' for the award of the subsidy,[65] the 'shareholding structure',[66] whether there are 'agreements with third parties',[67] the legal and regulatory context[68] and the economic situation of the recipient.[69]

Once it is shown that the subsidy improves the recipient's competitive position in the internal market, it is necessary to ascertain, under Article 4(1),

[59] ibid, para 19.
[60] ibid.
[61] ibid.
[62] ibid.
[63] ibid.
[64] ibid, para 21.
[65] ibid, para 27.
[66] ibid, paras 23–24.
[67] ibid, paras 28–29.
[68] ibid, paras 30–31.
[69] ibid, para 32.

whether it negatively affects competition. The fundamental legal question is whether the measure influences competitive dynamics in such a way that other economic actors are affected by it.[70] The Guidelines lay down principles that guide this assessment. First, negative effects may be actual or potential.[71] In fact, a subsidy may affect competition even when the recipient has not yet entered the internal market but merely contemplates doing so.[72] In the same vein, the Commission cannot be required to show that the foreign subsidy has produced an actual effect on competition.[73] Second, a subsidy is unlikely to have negative effects where the impact on competitive dynamics within the internal market is not appreciable.[74] Third, the distortions may be manifested in the sector or activities where the recipient operates, but also in other sectors or activities indirectly affected by the award.[75]

The assessment of the distortive effects of the foreign subsidy considers two aspects. The first aspect revolves around the identification of the mechanisms by which the measure can influence the conduct of the recipient in the internal market. In this regard, the Commission explains that the subsidy can be expected to affect the undertaking's conduct where there is a 'link' between the former and the latter. This causal relationship will be reflected, inter alia, in the firm's decisions in terms of pricing, output, choice of commercial partners and business strategy.[76] The link will be easy to establish where the measure is a targeted one in law or fact.[77] It may be more challenging to prove where the subsidy does not have a 'specific purpose, or conditions'.[78] In such scenarios, the Commission commits to taking into account a number of indicators, including the nature of the subsidy, the features of the sectors where the recipient operates and the status of the latter in the internal market.[79]

The second aspect of the assessment relates to the impact of the foreign subsidy on other economic actors (and, more specifically, to their detriment). The Guidelines suggest that the Commission commits to conducting a counterfactual assessment, whereby it commits to comparing the competitive dynamics as they would unfold with the foreign subsidy and in its absence. Pursuant to the approach sketched in the Guidelines, the analysis of this second aspect takes into account a number of factors, including the 'scope, purpose and conditions' of the measure, the amount involved (inevitably, the higher the amount, the more likely the distortion), the type of subsidy (with subsidies falling within the scope of

---

[70] ibid, para 41.
[71] ibid.
[72] ibid, para 45.
[73] ibid, para 42.
[74] ibid, para 43.
[75] ibid, para 37.
[76] ibid, para 51.
[77] ibid, para 49.
[78] ibid, para 50.
[79] ibid. paras 51–54

Article 5 being deemed more likely to distort the internal market), the features of the relevant sector and the economic and legal context.[80]

3.3. Balancing Test and Remedies

3.3.1. Balancing Test

Pursuant to Article 6, the Commission may engage in a balancing exercise and thus weigh the distortion identified in its assessment under Articles 4 and 5 against the positive effects, whether equity- or efficiency-related, that one might expect from the award of the foreign subsidy. Even though the Regulation is relatively quiet on the issue, the experience acquired under EU State aid law is directly relevant in this context. Generally speaking, the larger and the more targeted the foreign subsidy, the more likely it is that it will, on balance, be negative. Where a financial contribution is, for instance, expressly aimed at completing a particular transaction, it would be difficult for the firm to argue that it contributes to a public interest objective. Conversely, the more general (or horizontal) the measure, the more credible such claims will be.

The letter of the Regulation is consistent with this idea. As already pointed out above, the scenarios identified in Article 5 all concern measures that are both targeted (such as a subsidy aimed at directly facilitating a concentration or one enabling a firm to submit a bid in a tender) and difficult to link to a public interest objective (for instance, it is at least safe to presume that a measure in support of an ailing firm only seeks to ensure that the recipient remains viable). In *e&/PPF Telecom Group*, the Commission assessed the potential positive effects of an unlimited guarantee (also listed in Article 5). Unsurprisingly, it found that the notifying party had not sought to articulate how the measure would advance a public interest objective and noted, in addition, that any such contribution must relate to the foreign subsidy, as opposed to the efficiency gains to which the concentration might give rise.[81]

The Guidelines shed light on the nature of the balancing assessment, both from a substantive and a procedural standpoint. As far as the substantive aspects are concerned, the Commission emphasises, to begin with, the need for the recipient to establish that any positive effects are specific to the foreign subsidy (that is, that the former flow from the latter).[82] In addition, the Commission confirms that the negative effects are likely to outweigh any positive contributions to a public interest objective where the foreign subsidy falls within the scope of Article 5(1) of the Regulation.[83] More generally, the balancing exercise will have to quantify both the negative and the positive effects on competition. Accordingly, the larger the foreign subsidy, the less likely that it will be, on balance, positive overall.[84] In the same vein, the Commission will take into account factors pertaining to the

---

[80] ibid, para 57.

[81] *e&/PPF Telecom Group* (n 14), para 375.

[82] Guidelines on the application of the Foreign Subsidies Regulation (n 57), paras 118–119.

[83] ibid, para 123.

[84] ibid.

alleged contribution to a public interest objective, including the nature of the positive effects and their intensity.[85]

3.3.2. Remedies

If it appears (as in *e&/PPF Telecom Group*) that the foreign subsidy is, on balance, a net source of negative effects, the Commission may impose redressive measures or, alternatively, accept commitments from the undertaking. In line with what has been briefly explained above, the point of remedial intervention under the foreign subsidies regime is to preserve a level playing field within the internal market.[86] The non-exhaustive list of measures expressly contemplated in the Regulation can be broadly grouped into four categories, depicted in Table 8.2. One can identify, first, access remedies, whereby the recipient may be required to share an infrastructure or intangible asset. There are, second, structural interventions, pursuant to which the firm may be required to sell certain assets or, similarly, dissolve a concentration. Third, some redressive measures focus on the strategic decisions of the firm, relating among other things to investment and capacity. There is, finally, the possibility for the Commission to order the repayment of the foreign subsidy.

Table 8.2 Remedies within the meaning of Article 7

Category	Measures
Access remedies	FRAND access to infrastructure FRAND licensing Share R&D results
Structural measures	Divestment of assets Dissolution of the concentration
Strategic decisions	Reduce capacity/market presence Refrain from investments Adapt governance structure
Repayment	Repayment of foreign subsidy

[85] ibid, para 124.

[86] See the discussion above in Section 2. The need to preserve a level playing field is prominent throughout the decision. See in particular *e&/PPF Telecom Group* (n 14), para 352, where the Commission explains that 'to maintain a level playing field in the provision of telecommunications services in the internal market where the Target currently – and in all likelihood the combined entity post-Transaction – is active, a crucial consideration is access to finance based on the merits of each undertaking'.

In *e&/PPF Telecom Group*, the Commission accepted commitments that can be characterised as a variation on the third category of remedies outlined above. On the one hand, the distortive effects of the unlimited guarantee were addressed by means of an amendment to the articles of association of the acquiring firm, following which it would be subject to the ordinary insolvency procedures of the third country.[87] On the other, the firm committed to introducing what could be aptly described as the functional separation of the EU division of the undertaking from the rest of its activities.[88] This is so at least in relation to the financing of the EU division. The point of this measure, as explained by the Commission, is that no foreign subsidy would flow into the activities of the EU division, thereby improving its competitive position within the internal market.[89] In line with Article 7(5),[90] the remedies were assorted with monitoring and reporting obligations.[91]

4. Procedural and Institutional Framework

4.1. General Framework

The framework for the assessment of foreign subsidies follows, in essence, the one that applies to the assessment of State aid.[92] The procedure is, accordingly, divided into two phases, a preliminary (or informal) review – set out in Article 10 – and an in-depth (or formal) investigation, which is outlined in Article 11. The latter is triggered when, based on the findings in the first phase, the Commission has 'sufficient indications' that the intervention by the third country amounts to the award of a foreign subsidy which is, moreover, liable to distort the internal market. The framework is common to all procedures. It applies both in the context of the default procedure (that is, the ex officio review of subsidies by the Commission) and where the undertaking concerned notifies a concentration within the meaning of Article 20 or a public procurement procedure as defined in Article 2(3).

---

[87] ibid, para 387.

[88] ibid, para 406. On the issue of functional separation in the telecommunications sector, see Directive (EU) 2018/1972 of the European Parliament and of the Council of 11 December 2018 establishing the European Electronic Communications Code (Recast) [2018] OJ L321/36.

[89] ibid, where the Commission explains that the final iteration of the commitment 'gives full effect to the undertaking not to allow any foreign subsidy to flow into the internal market (through paragraphs 7 and 10 of the Final Commitments) and therefore addresses the concerns'.

[90] Pursuant to Article 7(5) of the Foreign Subsidies Regulation (n 6), 'The Commission shall, where appropriate, impose reporting and transparency requirements, including periodic reporting regarding the implementation of the commitments and redressive measures listed in paragraph 4'.

[91] *e&/PPF Telecom Group* (n 14), paras 388 and 409. In particular, e& accepted the introduction of a monitoring trustee, subject to the Commission's approval, to oversee compliance with the obligations.

[92] Procedural Regulation (n 16).

Figure 8.4 The ex officio procedure – preliminary review

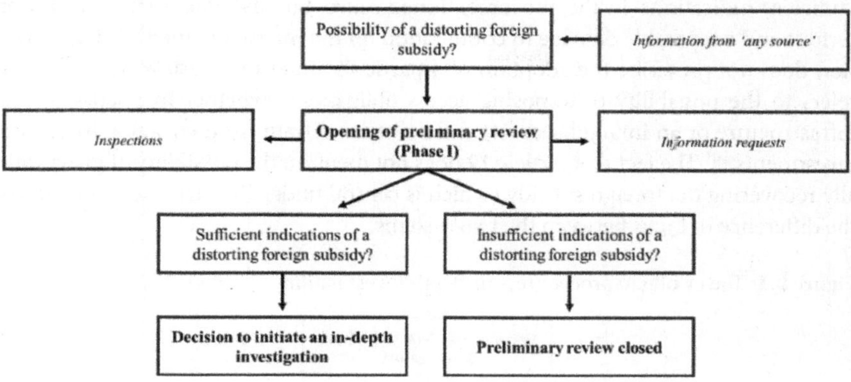

The default procedure, depicted in Figures 8.4 and 8.5, seems to be directly inspired by the one that applies to unlawful State aid under Regulation 2015/1589.[93] The Commission may, in both instances, initiate an investigation on its own motion, based on information from any source (including, in the case of the foreign subsidies regime, EU Member States, a natural or legal person or an association).[94] There is not, however, a formal complaint procedure under the foreign subsidies regime.[95] If the information gathered indicates the possibility that a foreign subsidy within the meaning of Article 3 may have been granted, the Commission may request information from the potential recipient[96] and, similarly, may conduct an inspection within the EU and (with the agreement of the third country) outside of it.[97] As is true of the examination of unlawful State aid, it is not bound by any time limits when evaluating evidence at the preliminary stage.[98]

If the Commission finds during the initial phase of the procedure that there are insufficient grounds to move to the formal stage, it need not issue a formal decision.[99] The preliminary review will result in the opening of an in-depth investigation (that is, the second phase) where the Commission 'has sufficient indications that an undertaking has been granted a foreign subsidy that distorts the internal market'. In such instances, it may, pursuant to Article 12, also order interim measures. The

---

[93] ibid, in particular Articles 4, 6 and 9.

[94] See in this sense Article 9 of the Foreign Subsidies Regulation (n 6) and Article 12 of the Procedural Regulation (n 16).

[95] The formal complaints procedure exists, by contrast, under the Procedural Regulation (n 16), which requires the Commission, pursuant to Article 12, to 'examine without undue delay any complaint submitted by any interested party'.

[96] Article 13 of the Foreign Subsidies Regulation (n 6).

[97] ibid, Articles 14 and 15.

[98] See, by analogy, Article 15(2) of the Procedural Regulation (n 16).

[99] Article 10(4) of the Foreign Subsidies Regulation (n 6). This provision merely imposes a duty to close the proceedings and inform the undertaking and, if necessary, the EU Member State having alerted the Commission, as well as the contracting body (the latter in the context of a public procurement procedure).

Commission will have to establish, by means of a decision, not only that there are 'sufficient indications' in the abovementioned sense, but also that 'there is a risk of serious and irreparable damage to competition on the internal market'.[100] The provision does not prescribe the adoption of a particular interim measure, but expressly refers to the possibility of imposing access obligations (whether in relation to an infrastructure or an intangible asset) and a duty to refrain from engaging in certain investments.[101] The fact that Article 12 does not mention the possibility of provisionally recovering the foreign subsidy (which is central under EU State aid law) reflects the difference in focus between the two systems.

Figure 8.5 The ex officio procedure – in-depth investigation

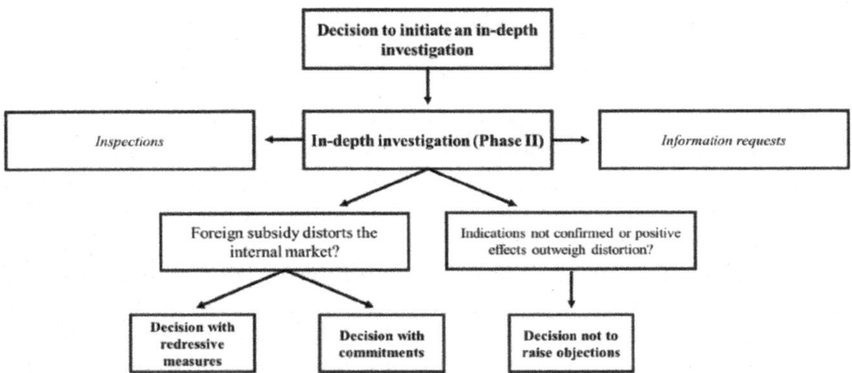

In the context of an in-depth investigation (Figure 8.5), the Commission may exercise the same information-gathering powers mentioned above (namely to request information and conduct inspections). The formal phase of the procedure may lead to three potential outcomes. First, the Commission may conclude that the 'sufficient indications' justifying the opening of the formal probe have not been confirmed or that any actual or potential distortions are outweighed by the positive effects resulting from the foreign subsidy. In these two instances, the Commission will issue a 'no objection decision' within the meaning of Article 11(4). Second, it may, pursuant to Article 11(2), adopt a 'decision with redressive measures' where it finds that the foreign subsidy entails a distortion of the internal market. Alternatively, third, it may seek a negotiated outcome with the undertaking leading to a 'decision with commitments' in accordance with Article 11(3). It may accept commitments where it considers that the measures proposed by the firm are 'appropriate and sufficient to fully and effectively remedy the distortion'.

Irrespective of the outcome of the investigation, Article 11(5) provides that, 'as far as possible', the Commission shall endeavour to adopt a decision within a period of 18 months following the opening of the in-depth investigation.

Decisions with commitments within the meaning of Article 11(3) are not a feature of EU State aid law. Regulation 2015/1589 does not provide for the closure of the formal investigation procedure by means of a negotiation between the Commission and the EU Member State. The introduction of the commitments feature in the Regulation betrays the difference between the two systems, and more precisely the focus of the foreign subsidies regime on the undertaking (as opposed to the third country awarding the financial contribution) and on the elimination of distortions of competition (as opposed to the restoration of the status quo ante by means of recovery). Decisions with commitments are a transplant from Article 9 of Regulation 1/2003, which implements Articles 101 and 102 TFEU.[102] This instrument has become a pre-eminent feature of EU antitrust law.[103] It would not be a surprise, therefore, if it emerged as an equally prominent tool in the foreign subsidies regime.

e&/PPF Telecom Group, which concerned a concentration and was closed with commitments, exemplifies another feature of the negotiated route: the so-called 'market test'. Unlike a 'decision with redressive measures' (or an infringement decision under Articles 101 and 102 TFEU), the commitments proposed by an undertaking will undergo a process of consultation with interested parties (typically, the firm's rivals), who will be given the chance to submit their observations about whether the proposed course of action fully remedies the potential distortion identified. The commitments may be refined following the market test. In *e&/PPF Telecom Group*, for instance, the final commitments that were made binding upon the firm were altered to, inter alia, delineate more clearly the boundaries of the EU business[104] and to clarify what amounts to financing for the purposes of the functional separation of the said business.[105]

At the time of writing, the Commission had not adopted a final decision following the ex officio opening of proceedings. However, it has indicated that it is conducting a number of investigations. In April 2024, Vice-President Vestager mentioned the opening of an inquiry into Chinese suppliers of wind turbines and, more precisely, the conditions for the development of wind farms in a number of EU Member States.[106] It has been reported that the case concerns the impact of the alleged foreign subsidies on the said suppliers' ability to offer lower prices

---

[102] Article 9 of Council Regulation (EC) No 1/2003 of 16 December 2002 on the implementation of the rules on competition laid down in Articles 81 and 82 of the Treaty [2003] OJ L1/1.

[103] See, on the prominence of commitment decisions in the EU antitrust landscape, Niamh Dunne, 'Commitment decisions in EU competition law' (2014) 10 Journal of Competition Law and Economics 399; and Ryan Stones, 'Commitment decisions in EU competition enforcement: Policy effectiveness v. the formal rule of law' (2019) 38 Yearbook of European Law 361.

[104] *e&/PPF Telecom Group* (n 14), para 406.

[105] ibid, para 407.

[106] Margrethe Vestager, 'A lecture on technology and politics' (Institute for Advanced Study, Brussels, 8 April 2024).

than their rivals.[107] In the same month, the Commission announced that it had exercised its powers under Article 14 of the Regulation to conduct an inspection at the premises of a firm operating in the 'production and sale of security equipment in the European Union'.[108] It has been reported in the press that the case relates to contracts awarded to governments within the EU.[109] Interim measures seeking to suspend the inspection were not granted by the President of the General Court[110] (and an appeal against this decision was dismissed by order[111]).

4.2. Concentrations

Chapter 3 of the Regulation introduces a mechanism aimed at assessing, ex ante, whether a foreign subsidy in a concentration leads to a distortion in the internal market.[112] The evaluation under the ad hoc procedure is limited to the operation in question and considers only the foreign subsidies granted in the three years preceding the transaction. Chapter 3 is largely inspired by Regulation 139/2004, pursuant to which the effects of concentrations on competition are considered.[113] All the fundamental elements of the latter instrument are transposed to the foreign subsidies regime. These features include not just the duty to notify the operation prior to its implementation,[114] but also the definition of the substantive scope of the regime (that is, what qualifies as a concentration), the use of turnover thresholds as a proxy for the significance of the transactions (as well as a trigger of the procedural obligations) and the introduction of strict time limits for the assessment.

The notion of concentration within the meaning of the foreign subsidies regime therefore comprises the three categories of transactions introduced in Regulation 139/2004, namely a merger (that is, the amalgamation of previously independent undertakings),[115] an acquisition of control of one or more undertakings[116]

---

[107] Gutermuth, Simphal and Routsi (n 10).

[108] Commission, 'Commission carries out unannounced foreign subsidies inspections in the security equipment sector' (Brussels, 23 April 2024).

[109] Foo Yun Chee, 'China's Nuctech raided in EU over foreign subsidies concerns' *Reuters* (23 April 2024), available at www.reuters.com.

[110] Case T-284/24 R *Nuctech Warsaw Company Limited sp. z o.o. and Nuctech Netherlands BV v Commission*, EU:T:2024:564.

[111] Case C-720/24 P(R) *Nuctech Warsaw Company Limited sp. z o.o. and InsTech Netherlands BV v Commission*, EU:C:2025:205.

[112] Article 19 of the Foreign Subsidies Regulation (n 6).

[113] Council Regulation (EC) No 139/2004 of 20 January 2004 on the control of concentrations between undertakings [2004] OJ L24/1.

[114] Article 21 of the Foreign Subsidies Regulation (n 6).

[115] ibid, Article 20(1)(a), which refers to 'the merger of two or more previously independent undertakings or parts of undertakings'.

[116] ibid, Article 20(1)(b), which refers to 'the acquisition, by one or more persons already controlling at least one undertaking, or by one or more undertakings, whether by purchase of securities or assets, by contract or by any other means, of direct or indirect control of the whole or parts of one or more other undertakings'.

and the creation of a so-called full-function joint venture.[117] The turnover thresholds vary between the two regimes. The overarching logic, however, is not fundamentally different. The proxy for the significance of the transaction is set at EUR 500 million in terms of turnover, whereas that for its impact on the internal market is defined by the requirement that the merging firms (or, in the case of an acquisition, the target) be established in the EU.[118] There is a proxy that is specific to the foreign subsidies regime. A concentration is notifiable under the Regulation where, in the three years preceding the operation, the aggregate financial contributions exceed EUR 50 million.[119] In addition, the foreign subsidies regime provides for a call-in mechanism for transactions falling below the thresholds where foreign subsidies may have been granted.[120]

There are a number of ways in which the two-phase assessment of foreign subsidies is adjusted to this ad hoc procedure. One of these adjustments relates to the outcome of the in-depth investigation. Article 25(3) contemplates three possibilities where concentrations are duly notified: a 'decision with commitments', a 'no objection decision' and a third option that is not referred to in Article 11, namely a decision prohibiting the concentration, if the Commission finds that the foreign subsidy distorts the internal market.[121] Where a concentration is implemented in breach of the notification obligation, it may order the dissolution of the concentration and adopt any associated remedy.[122] The second adjustment in Chapter 3 has to do with the introduction of strict time limits, in line with the philosophy underpinning EU merger control. Thus, the Commission may initiate the in-depth investigation no later than 25 days following the notification.[123] Decisions following the opening of the formal procedure, in turn, shall be adopted within 90 days (after which period, and in the absence of a decision, the undertakings are allowed to complete the transaction).[124]

---

[117] ibid, Article 20(2), which refers to 'The creation of a joint venture performing on a lasting basis all the functions of an autonomous economic entity shall constitute a concentration within the meaning of paragraph 1'.

[118] ibid, Article 20(3)(a): 'at least one of the merging undertakings, the acquired undertaking or the joint venture is established in the Union and generates an aggregate turnover in the Union of at least EUR 500 million'.

[119] ibid, Article 20(3)(b) of the Regulation: 'the following undertakings were granted combined aggregate financial contributions of more than EUR 50 million from third countries in the three years preceding the conclusion of the agreement, the announcement of the public bid, or the acquisition of a controlling interest:

(i)   in the case of an acquisition, the acquirer or acquirers and the acquired undertaking;
(ii) in the case of a merger, the merging undertakings;
(iii) in the case of a joint venture, the undertakings creating a joint venture and the joint venture'.

[120] ibid, Article 21(5).

[121] ibid, Article 25(3)(c), pursuant to which the Commission may adopt 'a decision prohibiting a concentration' where it 'finds that a foreign subsidy distorts the internal market pursuant to Articles 4 to 6'.

[122] ibid, Article 25(6)(a).

[123] ibid, Article 25(2).

[124] ibid, Article 25(4).

Even though the decision in *e&/PPF Telecom Group* is the only final one published so far (as mentioned above, the Commission is not required to issue a decision where it does not initiate an in-depth investigation), it is possible to draw some conclusions about the regime as implemented. From an institutional standpoint, the number of notifications appears to be relatively high – and higher than anticipated by the Commission itself.[125] From a substantive standpoint, *e&/PPF Telecom Group* has clarified some central aspects about the scope of the analysis. As pointed out above, the assessment of the distortions caused by a foreign subsidy in a concentration comprises not only the impact it may have on the transaction itself (which might arise, for instance, where the benefit allows the recipient to outbid other potential purchasers) but also in the post-merger scenario (that is, how intervention strengthens the recipient in the post-merger scenario and how such strengthening distorts the internal market). The Guidelines issued by the Commission elaborate further on this analytical approach.[126]

4.3. Public Procurement Procedures

Chapter 4 introduces the ad hoc procedure that applies to public procurement. It provides a framework to ascertain two substantive questions, namely whether a foreign subsidy allows the recipient to submit a bid that is 'unduly advantageous' (which is the first question), thereby resulting in an actual or potential distortion in the internal market (which is the second).[127] Despite the large number of notifications under Chapter 4,[128] the Commission was yet to adopt a formal decision at the time of writing. This said, it is arguably in the context of public procurement that the impact of the foreign subsidies regime has been most immediate. Following the announcement of an in-depth investigation into its participation in a public tender for the supply of trains in Bulgaria, the alleged recipient of the foreign subsidies – a publicly-owned Chinese manufacturer – withdrew from it.[129] The same outcome was observed in another tender for the construction of a solar farm in Romania.[130]

The principles for the assessment of foreign subsidies in public procurement procedures do not depart in fundamental ways from those that apply to the

---

[125] See Gutermuth, Simphal and Routsi (n 10) and the discussion in the introduction. See also Luis Moscoso and Iveta Stoyanova, 'The Foreign Subsidies Regulation – 100 days since the start of the notification obligation for concentrations (2024) Competition FSR Brief, available at https://competition-policy.ec.europa.eu/.

[126] Guidelines on the application of the Foreign Subsidies Regulation (n 57), paras 60–77.

[127] Article 27 of the Foreign Subsidies Regulation (n 6). The provision refers to foreign subsidies that 'cause or risk causing a distortion in a public procurement procedure shall be understood as foreign subsidies that enable an economic operator to submit a tender that is unduly advantageous in relation to the works, supplies or services concerned'.

[128] See the figures provided in Gutermuth, Simphal and Routsi (n 10).

[129] 'Chinese train maker withdraws from Bulgaria tender after EU probe' *Euractiv* (27 March 2024).

[130] 'Chinese firms exit Romania solar tender after EU probe' *France 24* (13 May 2024).

evaluation of concentrations. There is therefore a duty to notify to the Commission the participation in public tenders exceeding EUR 250 million in value,[131] where the firm taking part in it has received aggregate financial contributions exceeding EUR 4 million over a three-year period.[132] The procedure is complicated by the involvement of the authority organising the public tender. In this sense, Article 29 provides that the economic operator is to notify to the said public authority all the financial contributions received,[133] which is then transmitted to the Commission.[134] Similarly, the assessment is subject to strict time limits, which are not to exceed, in principle, 20 days[135] – as far as the preliminary phase is concerned – and 110 days, in principle, as far as the in-depth review is concerned.[136] In terms of outcome, the procedure may close with commitments,[137] with a 'decision prohibiting the award of the contract',[138] or with a 'no objection decision'.[139]

4.4. Market Investigations

Article 36 empowers the Commission to conduct market investigations into 'a particular sector, for a particular type of economic activity or based on a particular subsidy instrument'. In order to fulfil this function, it may, in the exercise of its powers under the Regulation, request information – whether from the firms themselves or from EU Member States and third countries concerned – and conduct any inspections deemed necessary. The evidence gathered during the investigation is to be published in the form of a report.[140] In and of itself, however, this procedure cannot lead to legally binding action. The information obtained may, however, feed into subsequent investigations.[141] Sector inquiries have long been a feature in EU antitrust law. Since the adoption of Regulation 1/2003, the Commission has made frequent use of the instrument.[142] Regulation 2015/1589 provides a legal basis to carry out such inquiries in the EU State aid law context.[143]

---

[131] Article 28(1)(a) of the Foreign Subsidies Regulation (n 6).
[132] Article 28(1)(b) of the Foreign Subsidies Regulation (n 6).
[133] ibid, Article 29(1).
[134] ibid, Article 29(2).
[135] ibid, Article 30(2), which clarifies that 'the Commission may extend this time limit by 10 working days once' in 'duly justified cases'.
[136] ibid, Article 30(5), which goes on to add that the 110-day period 'may be extended once by 20 working days, after consultation with the contracting authority or contracting entity, in duly justified exceptional cases' including in instances of non-cooperation and in the context of multi-stage procedures.
[137] ibid, Article 31(1).
[138] ibid, Article 31(2).
[139] ibid, Article 31(3).
[140] ibid, Article 36(2).
[141] ibid, Article 36(3).
[142] Article 17 of Regulation 1/2003 (n 102).
[143] Article 25 of the Procedural Regulation (n 16).

Market investigations may fulfil a valuable role under the foreign subsidies regime. The organisation of the economy and, similarly, the relationship between the public and the private sector (or even the relationship between governmental institutions and publicly-owned firms) may differ significantly from those prevailing within the EU. As a result, it may not always be obvious to understand the mechanism – if any – by which firms receive foreign subsidies and, similarly, how to detect and quantify them in practice. For instance, there may be multiple layers of government involved, thereby making the exercise particularly complex. The opacity of the system may be compounded by the intricate relationship between economic and governmental activities. A wide, sectoral approach, such as the one provided by a market investigation, may therefore be a useful preliminary step prior to enforcement.

5. Conclusions

The foreign subsidies regime is a testament to the rapid changes that trade relationships around the world are undergoing. The rules-based order that had as its ultimate aim the liberalisation of trade is being progressively replaced by one dominated by protectionism and industrial policy. In the new landscape, the adoption of an instrument that makes up for the deficiencies of a crumbling system and simultaneously responds to emerging challenges is to be expected. The interest and the peculiarity of the foreign subsidies regime is that it exports the essence of the EU model to measures adopted by third countries. Accordingly, the Commission is empowered to investigate awards by non-EU States, to balance their positive and negative effects and impose any remedial action. The overarching objective of the Regulation is consistent with the move towards the *repli sur soi*: preserve a level playing field within the internal market.

As a legal creature, the foreign subsidies regime is a composite of various systems. Because it cannot impose obligations on third countries in the same way as the EU State aid system does, it is for the recipients to notify the transactions that may involve the award of foreign subsidies and to address any concerns about the impact of the said subsidies on the internal market. As a result of this difference, the Regulation borrows from instruments such as Regulation 1/2003 (which provides for the possibility of closing proceedings with commitments) and Regulation 139/2004 (which lays down a framework for the notification of concentrations). There is another aspect where the foreign subsidies regime is closer to competition law than to EU State aid law. Under the Regulation, the distortive effects of measures cannot be presumed to be present when the substantive conditions are met. As a rule, they will have to be shown to be met on a case-by-case basis.

These differences between EU State aid law and the foreign subsidies regime raise the question of how the two will evolve over time. The latter amounts to the unilateral expansion of the EU model beyond its borders. At the internal level, it may also impact the interpretation and enforcement of Articles 107 and 108 TFEU. The substantive divergences between the internal and external variations of the EU model may progressively disappear over time and converge towards a uniform regime. From an institutional perspective, it remains to be seen how the balance in terms of enforcement is struck. As EU competitiveness rises in the agenda, the enforcement of EU State aid is likely to adjust to the new landscape. By the same token, intervention by means of the foreign subsidies control regime may emerge as the natural priority for the Commission and a necessary complement to a refocused EU State aid regime.

Conclusions

1. Anatomy of a Supernova

1.1. Expansion and Core

As the law of State aid and subsidies in the EU evolves, it moves simultaneously in two opposite directions. On the one hand, the case law interpreting the notion of State aid and the enforcement of Article 107(3) TFEU by the European Commission (hereinafter, the 'Commission') speak of a system that is becoming more deferential and accommodating to the demands of EU Member States. On the other hand, the external dimension of the discipline has undergone a remarkable process of expansion. The essence of the EU model has been exported to other jurisdictions by means of the twin mechanisms of legal convergence (which is reflected in the adoption of the Subsidy Control Act 2022 in the UK, discussed extensively in Chapter 7) and unilateral expansion (heralded by the entry into force of the Foreign Subsidies Regulation[1]). These two trends are a manifestation of the fundamental changes that the discipline is undergoing.

Like a supernova, the law of State aid and subsidies appears to be losing intensity at its core while widening its scope well beyond its original boundaries. It has become, somewhat paradoxically, both stronger and weaker. This analogy is appropriate in more than one sense. In the same way stars change their internal chemistry as they increase in size, the EU system of subsidy control that will eventually emerge from the transformations identified in this book is likely to bear little resemblance to the one that existed prior to the 2020s. The legal and economic assumptions underpinning the old model no longer hold true in a new context of deglobalisation where the rules-based order can no longer be taken for granted. As a result of this process (and its consequences), the objectives of intervention, the Commission's administrative priorities and enforcement techniques will all venture into different – and not necessarily predictable – directions.

1.2. The Core: EU State Aid Law

It is possible to distinguish three broad periods in the evolution of EU State aid law: a formative period, one of consolidation and one of (relative) retreat. An

---

[1] Regulation (EU) 2022/2560 of the European Parliament and of the Council of 14 December 2022 on foreign subsidies distorting the internal market [2022] OJ L330/1.

overview of the case law and administrative practice from the late 1990s to the early 2000s shows how long it took the system to come of age. As explained in Chapter 2, it was not even fully clear until the judgment in *PreussenElektra*[2] that State aid within the meaning of Article 107(1) TFEU necessarily involves the use of State resources – and it was not until the ruling in *Stardust Marine*,[3] delivered in 2002, that the boundaries of the concept were delineated. The default approach to ascertain the selective nature of an advantage was, in turn, defined on a piece-meal and incremental basis over the years. The three-step test did not emerge at once, but rather as the result of the contributions made during the 2000s onwards in landmark cases such as *Adria-Wien*[4] and *Paint Graphos*.[5]

The formative period was followed by one where the Commission tested the boundaries of its powers and, by extension, the notion of State aid. During this period, the EU courts proved receptive and created the conditions within which this process of expansion could take place. In a series of rulings – including *British Aggregates*,[6] *Commission v Netherlands*[7] and *World Duty Free*[8] – the Court of Justice (hereinafter, the 'Court' or the 'ECJ') repeated the formula – first intro-duced in *Italy v Commission*[9] – whereby Article 107(1) TFEU 'does not distinguish between the measures of State intervention concerned by reference to their causes or aims but defines them in relation to their effects'. It is on the basis of this formula that the Commission could embrace a wide understanding of the concept of selectivity. *Gibraltar*[10] is probably the defining and most emblematic case of the period, if only because it concerned a national regime that, on its face, did not favour specific firms or industries but which, in spite of this fact, was found to be in caught by Article 107(1) TFEU.

Inevitably, the process of expansion resulted in more frequent frictions with national legislation, in particular in the area of taxation. Over time, the *Italy v Commission* formula would give room to a different approach, characterised by deference to the design and operation of national regimes, with which EU State aid law can interfere where they are 'manifestly discriminatory' within the mean-ing of *Commission v Poland*[11] and *Commission v Hungary*.[12] The tax rulings saga, discussed in Chapter 5, exemplifies better than any other case the new

---

[2] Case C-379/98 *PreussenElektra AG v Schhleswag AG*, EU:C:2001:160.

[3] Case C-482/99 *France v Commission*, EU:C:2002:294.

[4] Case C-143/99 *Adria-Wien Pipeline GmbH and Wietersdorfer & Peggauer Zementwerke GmbH v Finanzlandesdirektion für Kärnten*, EU:C:2001:598.

[5] Joined Cases C-78/08 to C-80/08 *Ministero dell'Economia e delle Finanze and Agenzia delle Entrate v Paint Graphos Soc. coop. arl and others*, EU:C:2011:550.

[6] Case C-487/06 P *British Aggregates Association v Commission*, EU:C:2008:757.

[7] Case C-279/08 P *Commission v Netherlands*, EU:C:2011:551.

[8] Joined Cases C-51/19 P and C-64/19 P *World Duty Free Group SA and Spain v Commission*, EU:C:2021:793.

[9] Case C-173/73 *Italy v Commission*, EU:C:1974:71.

[10] Joined Cases C-106/09 P and C-107/09 P *Commission v Government of Gibraltar and United Kingdom*, EU:C:2011:732.

[11] C-562/19 P *Commission v Poland*, EU:C:2021:201.

[12] Case C-596/19 P *Commission v Hungary*, EU:C:2021:202.

equilibrium. *Fiat*[13] put an end to the idea that the award of a selective advantage can be established against an abstract benchmark that is external to the national regime, whereas *Engie*[14] emphasised that the Commission must defer to the interpretation of domestic legislation prevailing within the EU Member State.

Policy-making, in turn, has not been immune to the combined effects of a pandemic, the invasion of Ukraine and the crisis within the rules-based international order. In a context of uncertainty and rising protectionism, the enforcement of Article 107(3) TFEU appears to have taken a global turn. Just like *Fiat* and *Engie*, this global turn has led to limited interference with EU Member States' choices. The approach to the assessment of measures appears to have changed in line with the realities in which intervention occurs. Where the traditional balancing of the positive and negative effects of State aid sought essentially to manage distortions of competition and trade within the internal market, recent enforcement appears to pave the way for a different approach, that is, one that considers how measures benefit the EU as a whole vis-à-vis third countries (for instance by attracting investments that would otherwise have been undertaken elsewhere).

1.3. The Outer Limits: Convergence and Expansion

The UK Subsidy Control Act 2022 is a milestone in the expansion of the EU model of subsidy control across the continent. It reflects how economic realities influence the extent and reach of the legal relationship between trading partners. The UK's legitimate desire to carve its own path as an independent trading nation in the wake of Brexit could not ignore decades of integration and interdependence. In this sense, the UK subsidy control system is, above all, testament to the determinant role of economic gravity and its impact on law and policy-making. This factor explains the detailed nature of the subsidy control chapter in the otherwise unambitious EU-UK Trade and Cooperation Agreement.[15] The chapter imposes obligations on the parties (including the requirement to designate an 'independent authority' entrusted with an 'appropriate role') that go well beyond those encountered in comparable trade deals.

From a substantive perspective, the degree of convergence between both legal systems is remarkable. A specialist in the field will not fail to notice the extent to which the UK legislature codifies core aspects of the Court's case law and of the Commission's administrative practice. From *PreussenElektra* and *Stardust Marine* to *British Aggregates* and *Paint Graphos*, traces of the EU system can be found

---

[13] Joined Cases C-885/19 P and C-898/19 P *Fiat Chrysler Finance Europe, Ireland and Grand Duchy of Luxembourg v Commission*, EU:C:2022:859.

[14] Joined Cases C-451/21 P and C-454/21 P *Luxembourg and others v Commission*, EU:C:2023:948.

[15] Trade and Cooperation Agreement between the European Union and the European Atomic Energy Community, of the one part, and the United Kingdom of Great Britain and Northern Ireland, of the other part [2021] OJ L149/10.

across the definition of subsidy enshrined in the UK Act. From an institutional perspective, by contrast, the system introduces a number of innovations that break with the central role that the Commission plays in the EU legal order. In essence, the UK Act relies on the self-assessment of measures by public authorities. As a result (and as discussed in Chapter 7), it creates a set of incentives that differs from those prevailing in its EU counterpart. For the same reason, it may progressively move away from the latter.

If the Subsidy Control Act 2022 sought to expand, by means of convergence, the logic of the EU model to the UK legal order, the point of the Foreign Subsidies Regulation, instead, is to create a level playing field within the internal market. By limiting firms' ability to benefit from subsidies awarded by third countries, the Regulation seeks to reduce (if not eliminate) any competitive advantage from which they might benefit vis-à-vis their EU rivals. In this sense, the EU legislature appears to assume that the very constraints imposed on its Member States' ability to award State aid – and which are known to be indispensable for the appropriate operation of the internal market – may have unintended consequences in a global context where third countries pursue active industrial policies unfettered by similar rules (whether at the national or the supranational levels).

The Foreign Subsidies Regulation cannot operate in the same way that EU State aid law does. While the latter applies to EU Member States, the Regulation, by necessity, applies to undertakings exercising their economic activities within the internal market. As a result, it is in some respects similar to the EU competition law system. It imposes notification obligations in relation to concentrations and public procurement procedures and allows for the administration of redressive measures that are reminiscent of those applied in antitrust and merger control procedures. The experience since the implementation of the system suggests that enforcement in the area could well become as significant as that in the context of EU State aid law. It would be reasonable to expect such an outcome if the domestic system of control continues the trajectory described in this book and the international order continues to demand unilateral action from the EU to defend its interests.

1.4. Towards a Single Substantive Standard?

It may be the case that the impact of the Foreign Subsidies Regulation goes beyond the setting of administrative priorities within the Commission. While broadly aligned with the internal system, the Regulation departs from it in a key respect from a substantive standpoint. As mentioned in Chapter 1 (and again in Chapter 8), Article 107(1) TFEU nominally provides that a measure only amounts to State aid where it can be shown to distort competition and effect trade between EU Member States. Pursuant to the *Philip Morris*[16] doctrine, one can safely presume that the

---

[16] Case 730/79 *Philip Morris Holland BV v Commission*, EU:C:1980:209.

two conditions are met as soon as it is shown that a measure that is imputable to the State and that involves the use of State resources provides a selective advantage. The threshold is higher – and it is expressly said to be higher in the Preamble – under the Foreign Subsidies Regulation.

Considering the direction of travel of EU State aid law and the potential redefinition of enforcement priorities, the remaining question is whether the substantive standards enshrined in the Foreign Subsidies Regulation will influence the interpretation of the distortion of competition and effect on trade conditions within the meaning of Article 107(1) TFEU. Such an outcome would not be unreasonable. First and foremost, the disparity of substantive standards may not be sustainable, not least because it would apply stricter conditions to the award of advantages by EU Member States. Second, such a trend would be broadly consistent with the current trajectory of law and policy, which is marked by a deferential attitude to national regimes. In this sense, it would allow the Commission to justify the internal reallocation and rebalancing of resources to address emerging challenges.

2. From Internal Market to Global Competitiveness

The transformations observed in the preceding chapters raise the question of whether the objectives and the very *raison d'être* of the law of State aid and subsidies will change over time, perhaps incrementally and imperceptibly. From a system aimed at managing inter-State competition within the internal market, the system could turn into a legal device essentially aimed at improving the competitiveness of the European industry on a global scale. EU State aid law, described at length in Part I, remains a canonical one. It pursues, in this sense, the aims one expects from a control system worthy of the name. The system may have undergone various iterations, but it has invariably sought to ensure that only interventions that are on balance positive (in the sense that their contribution to a public policy objective outweighs any distortions of trade and competition) are implemented. The evolution observed so far is not inconsistent with these objectives. If anything, enforcement might have become less ambitious than in the past.

Coming back to the categories identified in Chapter 1, EU State aid law may be regressing to a less far-reaching incarnation of a subsidy control system. After *Fiat* and *Engie*, it may be difficult to argue that it can be seen as a mechanism for the approximation of the legislation of EU Member States. In fact, the Court expressly held that the errors of law underpinning the tax rulings saga amounted, in essence, to the circumvention of the legal bases expressly designed to harmonise national regimes. As a result, EU State aid law may have become less ambitious, to focus on the prevention of trade and competition distortions within the internal market. Given the shifts observed in the enforcement of Article 107(3) TFEU, the Commission may focus instead on the most harmful of measures (namely those that pursue no plausible rationale other than the restriction of trade and/or competition).

The evolution of the system (and the wider economic and geopolitical context) will determine whether its nature is altered to such an extent that it becomes a fundamentally different legal animal. The moment industrial policy considerations enter the picture (in the sense that they are allowed to be invoked as justifications for the award of advantages in their own right) and the balancing exercise considers the global impact of intervention, the law of State aid and subsidies may be radically transformed. The assessment would no longer revolve around whether the distortions of competition within the internal market are to be tolerated insofar as they advance a public policy objective, but rather whether the intervention, by improving the EU's position vis-à-vis third countries (in the sense that it allows it to, inter alia, attract or preserve investments and/or gain in competitiveness), is in the interest of the Union as a whole.

Such a transformation, if it ever occurs, would have important consequences. The system would no longer be in a position to prevent the undesirable consequences of the unfettered award of subsidies, namely the diversion of trade and investment decisions. The global turn of the discipline would inevitably favour the EU Member States with the deeper pockets and larger financial muscle, thereby giving rise to tensions within the internal market. It may, in the same vein, exacerbate the sort of subsidy races that the very EU State aid system was designed to bring down. One may wonder, however, whether, in such a scenario, the law of State aid and subsidies would be the symptom rather than the concern itself. If such trade distortions occur, they may well be nothing other than a sign of a clear mismatch between the power and capacity of the EU and the demands of contemporary geopolitical realities.

BIBLIOGRAPHY

Books (including edited collections and textbooks)

Auerbach AJ and Feldstein MS (eds), *Handbook of Public Economics*, Vol 2 (North-Holland 1987)

Bacon K (ed), *European Union Law of State Aid* (3rd edn, Oxford University Press 2017)

Baistrocchi E and Roxan I (eds), *Resolving Transfer Pricing Disputes: A Global Analysis* (Cambridge University Press 2012)

Baquero Cruz J, *Between Competition and Free Movement: The Economic Constitutional Law of the European Community* (Hart Publishing 2002)

Barnard C, *The Substantive Law of the EU: The Four Freedoms* (7th edn, Oxford University Press 2022)

—— and Leucht B (eds), *Cassis de Dijon: 40 Years On* (Hart Publishing 2021)

Bradford A, *The Brussels Effect: How the European Union Rules the World* (Oxford University Press 2020)

Brealey RA, Myers SC and Allen F, *Principles of Corporate Finance* (McGraw-Hill 2014)

Buccirossi P (ed), *Handbook of Antitrust Economics* (MIT Press 2008)

Buendía Sierra JL and Smulders B, 'The Limited Role of the "Refined Economic Approach" in Achieving the Objectives of State Aid Control: Time for Some Realism' in *EC State Aid Law: Liber Amicorum in Honour Francisco Santaolalla* (Kluwer 2008)

Buts C and Buendía Sierra JL (eds), *Milestones in State Aid Case Law* (2nd edn, Lexxion 2022)

Constantinesco V, *Competences et pouvoirs dans les communautes europeennes: contribution à l'etude de la nature juridique des communautes* (LGDJ 1974)

Craig P and de Búrca G (eds), *The Evolution of EU Law* (2nd edn, Oxford University Press 2011)

De Cecco F, *State Aid and the European Economic Constitution* (Hart Publishing 2012)

Decker C, *Modern Economic Regulation: An Introduction to Theory and Practice* (Cambridge University Press 2023)

Haley UCV and Haley GT, *Subsidies to Chinese Industry: State Capitalism, Business Strategy, and Trade Policy* (Oxford University Press 2013)

Hancher L, Ottervanger T and Slot PJ (eds), *EU State Aids* (4th edn, Sweet & Maxwell 2012)

—— and Piernas López JJ (eds), *Research Handbook on European State Aid Law* (Edward Elgar Publishing 2021)

—— and Herrera Anchustegui I (eds), *Research Handbook on EU Competition Law and the Energy Transition* (Edward Elgar 2024)

Helpman E and Krugman P, *Market Structure and Foreign Trade* (MIT Press 1985)

Herwig CH Hofmann HCH and Micheau C (eds), *State Aid Law of the European Union* (Oxford University Press 2016)

HJI Panayi C, *European Union Corporate Tax Law* (2nd edn, Cambridge University Press 2021)

——, Haslehner W and Traversa E (eds), *Research Handbook on European Union Taxation Law* (Elgar 2020)

Ibáñez Colomo P, *The New EU Competition Law* (Hart Publishing 2023)

Joliet R, *The Rule of Reason in Antitrust Law: American, German and Common Market Laws in Comparative Perspective* (Martinus Nijhoff 1967)

——, *Monopolization and Abuse of Dominant Position* (Martinus Nijhoff 1970)

Kanninen H, Korjus N and Rosas A (eds), *EU Competition Law in Context: Essays in Honour of Virpi Tiili* (Hart Publishing 2009)

Karpenschif M, *Manuel de droit européen des aides d'État* (4th edn, Bruylant 2021)

Kyriazis D, *Fiscal State Aid Law and Harmful Tax Competition in the European Union* (Oxford University Press 2023)

Larouche P, *Competition Law and Regulation in European Telecommunications* (Hart Publishing 2000)

—— and Cserne P (eds), *National Legal Systems and Globalization: New Role, Continuing Relevance* (Springer 2013)

Lovdahl Gormsen L, *European State Aid and Tax Rulings* (Edward Elgar Publishing 2019)

Mavroidis PC, *Industrial Policy, National Security, and the Perilous Plight of the WTO* (Oxford University Press 2025)

Micheau C, *Droit des aides d'État et des subventions en fiscalité directe* (Larcier 2013)

Pastor Merchante F, *The Role of Competitors in the Enforcement of State Aid Law* (Hart Publishing 2017)

Peiffert O and Thomas S, *Droit matériel des aides d'Etat* (Bruylant 2019)

Pescatore P, *Le droit de l'integration* (Bruylant 2005)

Piernas López JJ, *The Concept of State Aid Under EU Law: From internal market to competition and beyond* (Oxford University Press 2015)

——, Hancher L and Rubini L (eds), *The Future of EU State Aid Law: Consolidation and Expansion* (EU Law Live Press 2023)

Quigley C *European State Aid Law and Policy (and UK Subsidy Control)* (4th edn, Hart Publishing 2022)

Richelle I, Schön W and Traversa E (eds), *State Aid Law and Business Taxation* (Springer 2016)

Rubini L, *The Definition of Subsidy and State Aid: WTO and EC Law in Comparative Perspective* (Oxford University Press 2009)

Ruechardt C, *EU State Aid Control of Infrastructure Funding* (Kluwer Law International 2018)

Signes de Mesa JI and de Moncuit A, *Droit procédural des aides d'Etat* (Bruylant 2019)

Van den Bossche P and Zdouc W, *The Law and Policy of the World Trade Organization: Text, Cases, and Materials* (5th edn, Cambridge University Press 2021)

Vives X (ed), *Competition Policy in the EU Fifty Years on from the Treaty of Rome* (Oxford University Press 2009)

Werner P and Verouden V (eds), *EU State Aid Control: Law and Economics* (2nd edn, Kluwer 2025)

Articles (including working papers)

Ahlborn C and Piccinin D, 'The application of the principles of restructuring aid to banks during the financial crisis' (2010) 9 European State Aid Law Quarterly 47

Ambec S and Ehlers L, 'Regulation via the Polluter-pays Principle' (2016) 126 The Economic Journal 884

Anderson J and Van Wincoop E, 'Gravity with Gravitas: A Solution to the Border Puzzle' (2003) 93 American Economic Review 170

Avi-Yonah RS, 'The Rise and Fall of Arm's Length: A Study in the Evolution of US International Taxation' (1995) 15 Virginia Tax Review 89

——, 'Globalization, tax competition, and the fiscal crisis of the welfare state' (2000) 113 Harvard Law Review 1573

——, 'Globalization, tax competition and the fiscal crisis of the welfare state: a twentieth anniversary retrospective' University of Michigan Law & Econ Research Paper 19-002 (2019)

Baier S and Bergstrand J, 'The Growth of World Trade: Tariffs, Transport Costs, and Income Similarity' (2001) 53 Journal of International Economics 1

Bartosch A, 'Is there a need for a rule of reason in European State aid law? Or how to arrive at a coherent concept of material selectivity?' (2010) 47 Common Market Law Review 729

Besley T and Seabright P, 'The effects and policy implications of state aids to industry: an economic analysis' (1999) 14 Economic Policy 14

Biondi A, 'State aid is falling down, falling down: An analysis of the case law on the notion of aid' (2013) 50 Common Market Law Review 1719

Bown CP and Hillman JA, 'WTO'ing a Resolution to the China Subsidy Problem' (2019) 22 Journal of International Economic Law 557

Buendía Sierra JL, 'Finding Selectivity or the Art of Comparison: Annotation on the Judgment of the Court of Justice of the European Union (First Chamber) of 8 September 2011 in Joined Cases C-78 to 80/08, *Paint Graphos*' (2018) 17 European State Aid Law Quarterly 85

—— and Dovalo Martín A, 'State aid versus COVID-19: The Commission adopts a temporary framework' (2020) 19 European State Aid Law Quarterly 3

Cannas G and others, 'Looking back at the State aid COVID Temporary Framework: the take-up of measures in the EU' (2022) Competition State Aid Brief, available at https://competitionpolicy.ec.europa.eu/

Clausing KA, 'The effect of profit shifting on the corporate tax base in the United States and beyond' (2016) 69 National Tax Journal 905

Conrad K, 'Taxes and subsidies for pollution-intensive industries as trade policy' (1993) 25 Journal of Environmental Economics and Management 121

da Cruz Vilaça JL, 'Material and geographic selectivity in state aid – recent developments' (2009) 8 European State Aid Law Quarterly 443

Dadush U, 'Deglobalisation and Protectionism' (2022) Bruegel Working Paper 18

Daly S, 'The power to get it wrong' (2021) 137 Law Quarterly Review 280

——, '*Fiat v Commission*: a misconceived approach' (2023) 86 Modern Law Review 1489

——, 'United Kingdom and ITV Plc v Commission: comparing apples with apples?' (2024) British Tax Review 725

Deakin S, 'Regulatory Competition after Laval' (2008) 10 Cambridge Yearbook of European Legal Studies 581

Dekker C, 'Does a Tender Exclude an Article 107(1) Advantage? An Investigation into the Different Approaches by the Court Of Justice and the European Commission' (2018) 17 European State Aid Law Quarterly 387

Di Giulio M, 'Alitalia, or the inability to align regulation with industrial policies' (2018) 10 Contemporary Italian Politics 377

Dunne N, 'Commitment decisions in EU competition law' (2014) 10 Journal of Competition Law and Economics 399

European Commission, 'State aid modernisation – a major revamp of EU State aid control' (2014) Competition Policy Brief, available at https://competition-policy.ec.europa.eu/

Ferrari A and Ossa R, 'A quantitative analysis of subsidy competition in the U.S.' (2023) 224 Journal of Public Economics 104919

Ferraro S and Landa A, 'The use of crisis State aid measures in response to the Russian invasion of Ukraine' (2025) Competition State Aid Brief, available at https://competition-policy.ec.europa.eu/

Galanter, 'Why the "haves" come out ahead: Speculations on the limits of legal change' (1974) 9 Law & Society Review 95

García-Herrero A, Grabbe H and Kaellenius A, 'De-risking and decarbonising: a green tech partnership to reduce reliance on China' (2023) Bruegel Policy Brief 19/2023

Garicano L, 'Why tariffs won't save our car industry' (Silicon Continent, 9 October 2024), available at http://www.siliconcontinent.com

Gayger M, 'Infrastructure Funding at the Interface between the EU State Aid Rules and Member States' General Economic Policy' (2016) 15 European State Aid Law Quarterly 539

Grespan D, 'A Busy Year for State Aid Control in the Field of Public Service Broadcasting' (2010) 9 European State Aid Law Quarterly 79

Gutermuth A, Simphal C and Routsi S, 'The Foreign Subsidies Regulation: Where Do We Stand 18 Months Into Implementation of the Notification Obligations' (Arnold & Porter Advisories, 30 May 2025), available at www.arnoldporter.com

Hancher L and de Hauteclocque A, 'Strategic Autonomy, REPowerEU And The Internal Energy Market: Untying The Gordian Knot' (2024) 61 Common Market Law Review 55

Held A and Kliemann A, 'The 2009 Broadcasting Communication and the Commission's Decisional Practice Two Years after its Entry into Force' (2012) 11 European State Aid Law Quarterly 37

Hernández CE and Cantillo-Cleves S, 'A toolkit for setting and evaluating price floors' (2024) 232 Journal of Public Economics 105084

Hornkohl L, 'Protecting the internal market from subsidisation with the EU state aid regime and the foreign subsidies regulation: two sides of the same coin?' (2023) 14 Journal of European Competition Law & Practice 137

Ibáñez Colomo P, 'Law, Policy, Expertise: Hallmarks of Effective Judicial Review in EU Competition Law' (2022) 24 Cambridge Yearbook of European Legal Studies 143

——, 'Form and substance in EU competition law' (2023) 46 World Competition 401

——, 'Restrictions by object under Article 101 (1) TFEU: From dark art to administrable framework' (2024) 43 Yearbook of European Law 224

——, 'Remedies in EU Antitrust Law' (2025) 21 Journal of Competition Law & Economics 137

Joris T and De Cock W, 'Is Belgium and *Forum 187 v. Commission* a Suitable Legal Source for an EU "At Arm's Length Principle"?' (2017) 16 European State Aid Law Quarterly 607

Juhasz R, Lane R and Rodrik D, 'The new economics of industrial policy' (2023) 16 Annual Review of Economics 213

Kalintiri A, 'The Allocation of the Legal Burden of Proof in Article 101 TFEU Cases: A "Clear" Rule with Not-So-Clear Implications' (2015) 34 Yearbook of European Law 232

Kleiner T and Alexis A, 'Politique des aides d'Etat : une analyse économique plus fine au service de l'intérêt commun' (2005) 2 Concurrences 45

Klemperer P, 'Bidding Markets' (2007) 3 Journal of Competition Law & Economics 1

Kwon C-W and Hwang U, 'The Effect of Reshoring Policy on the Host and Home Countries' (2023) 37 International Economic Journal 555

Kyriazis D, 'Fiscal State Aid and Selectivity, or why we need a Keck Moment for Article 107 TFEU (*Case C-453/23, Prezydent Miasta Mielca*)' (EU Law Live, 26 May 2025)

Lamadrid de Pablo A and Buendía Sierra JL, 'A Moment of Truth for the EU: A Proposal for a State Aid Solidarity Fund' (2020) 11 Journal of European Competition Law & Practice 1

Lamp, 'What President Trump's "Reciprocal" Tariffs Mean for International (Trade) Law' (EJIL: Talk! Blog of the European Journal of International Law, 30 April 2025)

Lenaerts K, 'The Role of the Court of Justice in Enhancing Tax Fairness in the EU' (2025) 34 EC Tax Review 78

Leonelli GC and Clora F, 'Retooling the regulation of net-zero subsidies: lessons from the US Inflation Reduction Act' (2024) 27 Journal of International Economic Law 441

López H and Navarro A, 'EU State aid and the tax allocation of multinationals' profits' (2024) 61 Common Market Law Review 1255

Loughlin M and Tierney S, 'The shibboleth of sovereignty' (2018) 81 The Modern Law Review 989

Lyal R, 'Transfer Pricing Rules and State Aid' (2015) 38 Fordham International Law Journal 1017

Marenco G, 'Competition Between National Economies and Competition Between Businesses – A Response to Judge Pescatore' (1986) 10 Fordham International Law Journal 420

Mason R, 'Tax Rulings as State Aid – Part 4: Whose Arm's-Length Standard?' (2017) Tax Notes, 15 May 2017

——, 'Identifying illegal subsidies' (2019) 69 American University Law Review 479

——, 'The transformation of international tax' (2020) 114 American Journal of International Law 353.

——, 'Tax competition and state aid' (2023) 42 Yearbook of European Law 262

—— and Daly S, 'Rotten to the Core: The EU's Court of Justice Decision in Apple' (2024) 116 Tax Notes International 987

McMahon C, 'Selectivity as discrimination: lessons from the case law on fiscal measures for identifying State aid' (2024) 43 Yearbook of European Law 261

Melitz MJ, 'When and how should infant industries be protected?' (2005) 66 Journal of International Economics 177

Miró J, 'Responding to the global disorder: the EU's quest for open strategic autonomy' (2023) 37 Global Society 315

Moscoso L and Stoyanova I, 'The Foreign Subsidies Regulation – 100 days since the start of the notification obligation for concentrations (2024) Competition FSR Brief, available at https://competition-policy.ec.europa.eu/

Nicolaides P, 'State aid rules and Tax Rulings' (2016) 15 European State Aid Law Quarterly 416

——, 'A Test for Determining Whether State Aid Infringes Other Provisions of EU Law' (2025) 24 European State Aid Law Quarterly 43

Pearl FH, 'Too Big To Fail, Too Big To Bail: A Plan to Save the U.S. Auto Industry' (Brookings, 5 December 2008)

Peers S, 'So close, yet so far: the EU/UK trade and cooperation agreement' (2022) 59 Common Market Law Review 49

Petit N and Radic L, 'The Superiority of the Consumer Welfare Standard' (2024) EUI LAW Working Paper 2024/20

Piechucka J, Saurí-Romero L and Smulders B, 'Industrial Policies, Competition, and Efficiency: The Need for State Aid Control' (2023) 19 Journal of Competition Law & Economics 503

Piernas López JJ, 'When is a company not an undertaking under EU competition law? The contribution of the Dôvera judgment' (2021) 58 Common Market Law Review 529

Posner RA, 'Intellectual property: The law and economics approach' (2005) 19 Journal of Economic Perspectives 57

Quigley C, 'Direct taxation and State aid: recent developments concerning the notion of selectivity' (2012) 40 Intertax 112

Reich N, 'The "November Revolution" of the European Court of Justice: Keck, Meng and Audi Revisited' (1994) 31 Common Market Law Review 459

Rossi-Maccanico P, 'A new framework for State aid review of tax rulings' (2015) 14 European State Aid Law Quarterly 371

Sauter W, 'Case T-289/03, *British United Provident Association Ltd (BUPA), BUPA Insurance Ltd, BUPA Ireland Ltd v. Commission of the European Communities,* Judgment of the Court of First Instance of 12 February 2008, nyr' (2009) 46 Common Market Law Review 269

Schenk D, 'The Cuno Case: A Comparison of US Subsidies and European State Aid' (2006) 5 European State Aid Law Quarterly 3

Schonberg M, 'The EU Foreign Subsidies Regulation' (2022) 21 European State Aid Law Quarterly 143

Schütze R, 'On "Federal" Ground: The European Union as an (Inter)national Phenomenon' (2009) 46 Common Market Law Review 1069

Steinbach A, 'The EU's Turn to "Strategic Autonomy": Leeway for Policy Action and Points of Conflict' (2023) 34 European Journal of International Law 973

Stones R, 'Commitment decisions in EU competition enforcement: Policy effectiveness v. the formal rule of law' (2019) 38 Yearbook of European Law 361

Traversa E and Flamini A, 'Fighting Harmful Tax Competition through EU State Aid Law: Will the Hardening of Soft Law Suffice?' (2015) European State Aid law Quarterly 323

Van Cleynenbreugel P, 'Regulating tax competition in the internal market: is the European Commission changing course?' (2019) 4 European Papers 225

Weiler J, 'The Community System: the Dual Character of Supranationalism' (1981) 1 Yearbook of European Law 267

Westphal LE, 'Industrial policy in an export-propelled economy: lessons from South Korea's experience' (1990) 4 Journal of Economic Perspectives 41

Other Sources

EU Press Releases

European Commission, 'State aid: Ireland gave illegal tax benefits to Apple worth up to €13 Billion' IP/16/2923 (Brussels, 30 August 2016)
——, 'State aid: Sector Inquiry report gives guidance on capacity mechanisms' IP/16/4021 (Brussels, 30 November 2016)
——, 'State aid: Commission opens in-depth investigation into the Netherlands' tax treatment of Inter IKEA' IP/17/5343 (Brussels, 18 December 2017)
——, 'State aid: Commission opens in-depth investigation into tax treatment of Nike in the Netherlands' IP/19/322 (Brussels, 10 January 2019)
——, 'State aid: Luxembourg's tax treatment of Huhtamäki' IP/19/1591 (Brussels, 3 May 2019)
——, 'State aid: Commission prolongs and amends Temporary Crisis Framework' IP/22/6468 (Brussels, 27 October 2022)
——, 'The Green Deal Industrial Plan: Securing Europe's Net-Zero Industry Leadership' IP/23/510 (Brussels, 31 January 2023)
——, 'State aid: Commission adopts Temporary Crisis and Transition Framework to further support transition towards net-zero economy' IP/23/1563 (Brussels, 8 March 2023)
——, '€902 million German State aid measure to support Northvolt' IP/23/6823 (Brussels, 7 January 2024)
——, 'Commission carries out unannounced foreign subsidies inspections in the security equipment sector' (Brussels, 23 April 2024)
——, 'Extension of the application of state aid measures to manage the crisis for a limited period' IP/24/2332 (Brussels, 1 May 2024)
——, 'Commission approves €5 billion German State aid measure to support ESMC in setting up a new semiconductor manufacturing facility' IP/24/4287 (Brussels, 19 August 2024)
——, 'Commission launches consultations on guidelines under the Foreign Subsidies Regulation' IP/25/685 (Brussels, 5 March 2025)

Official reports and documents

CJEU, *Annual Report 2024: Statistics concerning the judicial activity of the Court of Justice*, available at http://curia.europa.eu
——, *Annual Report 2024: Statistics concerning the judicial activity of the General Court*, available at http://curia.europa.eu
Draghi Report, *The future of European competitiveness: Part A | A competitiveness strategy for Europe* (September 2024)
——, *The future of European competitiveness: Part B | In-depth analysis and recommendations* (September 2024)
European Commission, *Ex post assessment of the impact of state aid on competition* (November 2017)
——, Communication from the Commission: A Chips Act for Europe COM(2022) 45 final
——, Commission Staff Working Document: Initial clarifications on the application of Article 4(1), Article 6 and Article 27(1) of Regulation (EU) 2022/2560 on foreign subsidies distorting the internal market COM(2024) 201 final
——, Commission Staff Working Document accompanying the Report from the Commission to the European Parliament, the Council, the European Economic and Social Committee and the Committee of the Regions SWD(2025) 102 final
——, *State aid Scoreboard 2024* (April 2025)
Letta Report, *Much More than a Market* (April 2024), available at www.consilium.europa.eu/

OECD, *Action Plan on Base Erosion and Profit Shifting* (2013)

——, *Addressing Base Erosion and Profit Shifting* (2013)

——, *Model Tax Convention on Income and on Capital: Condensed Version* (2017)

——, *Two-Pillar Solution to Address the Tax Challenges Arising from the Digitalisation of the Economy* (2021)

——, *Transfer Pricing Guidelines for Multinational Enterprises and Tax Administrations* (2022)

Newspaper articles

BBC, 'Brexit: Trade talks "have reached critical stage"' *BBC News* (7 December 2020)

Beattie A, 'A crumbling system of trade rules awaits Trump's wrecking ball' *Financial Times* (14 November 2024)

Bond S, Chaffin J and Stacey K, 'Amazon reaps more than $3bn from New York, Virginia and Tennessee' *Financial Times* (London, 14 November 2018)

Euractiv, 'Chinese train maker withdraws from Bulgaria tender after EU probe' *Euractiv* (27 March 2024)

France 24, Chinese firms exit Romania solar tender after EU probe' *France 24* (13 May 2024)

Murray A and Kirby P, 'Denmark's postal service to stop delivering letters' *BBC News* (6 March 2025)

Sandbu M, 'European common debt is the way to topple the dollar' *Financial Times* (London, 19 June 2025)

Yun Chee F, 'China's Nuctech raided in EU over foreign subsidies concerns' *Reuters* (23 April 2024), available at www.reuters.com

Speeches

Kroes N, 'The State Aid Action Plan – Delivering Less and Better Targeted Aid' (UK Presidency Seminar on State Aid, London, 14th July 2005)

Vestager M, 'A lecture on technology and politics' (Institute for Advanced Study, Brussels, 8 April 2024)

INDEX